THE SLEEPING GIANT

HISTORIC TALES

OF

TALLADEGA

BY

E. Grace Jemison

First Printing Paragon Press, 1959
Second Printing The Strode Publishers, 1984
Third Printing The Gregath Publishing Company, 1993
Fourth Printing Talladega Press, 2010
ISBN: 978-0-578-05156-7

Dedicated
to the memory of my Father,
ROBERT MIMS JEMISON
Who was responsible for my interest in
Talladega County History.

FOREWARD TO 2010 EDITION

On Christmas morning, 1984, there was found, amongst my gifts and presents, a true prize: a copy of the second reprinting of the "Historic Tales of Talladega." As a youngster in Talladega County, I was already aware of this volume and had sat for many an hour enthralled in the tales of Indians and settlers and other ghosts long past. Here finally, though, in my hands, I held my very own copy of that great gateway to the past of Talladega County. Twenty-five years later, I still have that copy and consider it a treasure amongst many in my collection of the great works of history.

For the past two years, in anticipation of the 50th Anniversary of this book, it has been my great privilege, with the help of the Talladega County Historical Association to endeavor in the creation of this Fourth Edition of The Historic Tales of Talladega.

The intent of this edition is to prepare it for additional future revisions suggested by the previous editors including those in 1993 as well as Miss Grace Jemison herself. With this version, we started from scratch, a blank slate as it were, painstakingly re-formatting and re-editing the book with new technologies not available to previous editors. In addition, the Errata section and the Errata Index of the 1993 Edition was incorporated back into the pages of the book itself rather than as a separate component bringing together past and present efforts.

Robert Penn Warren said that "History cannot give us a program for the future, but it can give us a fuller understanding of ourselves, and of our common humanity, so that we can better face the future." With that thought in mind, on behalf of the Talladega Historical Association, I therefore humbly dedicate this 50th Anniversary Edition to the memory of Miss Grace Jemison and her passion for the history of Talladega County. This volume is also hereby dedicated to the citizens of Talladega County, both past and present, so that we too can have a "fuller understanding of ourselves and our common humanity."

Thomas D. Lavender Jr.

Alpine, Alabama
January 24, 2010

FOREWARD TO 1993 EDITION

We honor the memory of Miss E. Grace Jemison late author (1884-1980), for her forethought in giving to the Talladega County Historical Association rights to reprint her work.

Mrs. Joe (Frances Sweat) Upchurch, along with husband Joe, has given, without any remuneration, ten months of her time in preparing this book for its third printing. Many hours were spent in research and documentation, writing letters, and traveling to verify out of town sources. Special recognition goes to husband Joe for giving his time and for assuming duties as chauffeur and housekeeper to assist Frances in this endeavor.

We also express sincere appreciation to the following volunteers: William M. Kelly, Jr., CDR, President of the Talladega County Historical Association, for undertaking the third printing of this book "Historic Tales of Talladega";

Mrs. Richard F. Bliss for her guidance as Chairman of the Book Committee;

Vern Scott, Editor and Publisher of the "Talladega County Historical Newsletter" for his monthly reminders of this project and to the members who responded;

Mrs. Harry (Ruth Roberts) Embry, relative of the late author, for supplying the original book owned by "Miss Grace" with her handwritten notes, records of research, and suggestions for future reprintings. These notes inspired the need for the errata addition;

A special note of appreciation to the staff of the Talladega Public Library and the staff of the Probate Office in the Talladega County Courthouse for their cooperation and assistance.

FOREWORD

For thirty-five years I have collected historical data as an enjoyable hobby, with no idea what-so-ever of co-ordinating it for publication until recently. Hear-say is too commonly printed and quoted as fact. I have, therefore, endeavored to give the source of information contained in these sketches where possible.

Several of my friends have read the manuscript and, at my request, made constructive comments, which caused me to make some changes. One comment: "too much about Indians", I have disregarded, because school children are more interested in Indian lore than any other phase of county history. These chapters are dedicated to them. Another comment: "You've quoted too much", is true. But I'm at a loss to correct this.

I have had access to scores of scrap books and journals. People have been kind and helpful. I can't begin to mention them. But to Mr. E. A. Stewart, of Selma, I am especially indebted for the privilege of quoting at length from the journal of his great-grand-father, James Mallory. In my estimation this journal contains the most valuable historical material available in connection with Talladega County.

Some years before the death of Mr. Wm. H. Skaggs, and of Mr. J. E. Stone, they gave me in writing informative data regarding periods in which they were closely associated with the civic life of Talladega. For these courtesies I am deeply gratified. I am also grateful to Mr. J. A. Bingham, deceased, who willingly shared with me the contents of his wonderful scrap book.

To Mrs. Marie Bankhead Owen, deceased, then Director of the Dept. of Archives and History of Alabama, I am indebted for permission to quote at length from Dr. Owen's four volumes of "History of Alabama and Dictionary of Alabama Biography." Mrs. Owen, Mr. Peter Brannon and Miss Frances Hails gave me invaluable assistance during my visits to the Department for research.

Mrs. E. A. Stephens left to Talladega an interesting article regarding Civil War experiences, and Dr. B. W. Toole left a history of the Presbyterian Church. From these I have taken the liberty of quoting freely.

Nannie Bowie Golden has been my most valuable collaborator. Her constructive recommendations and her enthusiastic interest have been of great help to me.

Ruth Hamner has been my tireless and inspirational companion on most of my trips in search of material. Her encouragement has boosted my morale on countless occasions.

Willie Welch, librarian, has manifested an interest in my historical collection at all times, and has been instrumental in placing priceless material in my hand.

To these friend and dozens of others who have encouraged and aided me in my efforts, I give thanks.

I have neglected to give the manufacturing and mercantile establishments their just places in the civic advancement of Talladega in the Nineteenth Century. There are wells of material from which to draw. I have only touched the surface, but hope some future historians will avail themselves of this hidden material, and will also include, in a more thorough history of the county, sketches of Sylacauga, Childersburg, Lincoln, Eastaboga, Munford, and other towns which justly deserve more prominence in the history of Talladega County.

No doubt many distinguished persons have been inadvertently overlooked, and discrepancies will be found, which are natural to this type of book, due to a limited supply of source material, but I assure the readers that this is not intentional. I, therefore, hope that it will be borne in mind that this is not intended as a complete history. It is simply a collection of data accumulated over the years. Though it is almost entirely of people and incidents of the Nineteenth Century, I have stepped over into the Twentieth Century in several instances.

It is with keen appreciation of Talladega's past, her present and belief in her future that this volume is presented.

E. Grace Jemison.

Talladega, Alabama.
June 15th, 1959.

Contents

The Sleeping Giant
An Indian Legend[1]

Many years before the white man penetrated the forests of Alabama, there dwelt a happy, thrifty tribe of Indians in the central portion of the present county of Talladega. The chief of this tribe was the great Choccolocco; a man of vast possessions. He had only one daughter, the Princess Talladega, whom he treasured above all he possessed.

Talladega, as every princess should be, was the most beautiful maiden in all the realm. Choccolocco, realizing that he could not continuously keep Talladega within the walls of his selfish heart and domain, began to cast about for a suitable mate for his treasured daughter.

Now, in those days, as well as in these, one had only to think a thing, and the world anticipated the unspoken thought, and ran away with it. It so happened that great chiefs, mighty and rich, old and young, from far and near, began to make offers of handsome gifts to the stern old Choccolocco for the hand of his daughter. Some found favor in the sight of Choccolocco, but Talladega said:

"Nay. Give me time. The right companion will come along some day, who loves the things that I love, and we can be happy wandering through life together."

Time passed on, until one dawn of an April day, Talladega wandered down a winding path to the sparkling spring at the foot of the hill. The world seemed lovely in spite of the scheming father. Suddenly she heard a song in the distance. It was beautiful. The song grew nearer and nearer, and more beautiful, until the singer burst into view, as Talladega dipped her earthen pot into the water. She met the dark eyes of a comely young warrior, and at that moment she knew that in some way their future would be linked together. Thus began, in the spring of that year, an affair which clandestinely grew beyond the imagination of Choccolocco. Each morning a song was answered, a friendship ripened, and a love was strengthened. The wooing progressed, until one day Talladega, approaching her cabin, heard voices. Her name was mentioned. To her dismay she realized that Cheaha, an ugly old chief from an adjoining province, was

---

[1] First read from the pen of Frank Willis Barnett, about 40 years ago, in the Birmingham News; included in a "Sketch of Talladega county". Copy in my scrap book, but without date. The father of Frank Willis Barnett was one of the first newspaper publishers of Talladega, and from him he heard the Legend. Early records speak of the mountain also as "The Giant at Rest" and the "Resting Giant."

bargaining with Choccolocco. As she caught the glowering eyes of Cheaha, she immediately knew that she would not submit to wedlock with this eagle-eyed suitor. After Cheaha left, Choccolocco informed Talladega that he was the favored chief, and that she would probably soon follow him to his province. Talladega slept none that night, and soon after dawn she was out awaiting the song of her young lover, Coosa.

It was indeed a sad morning they spent together. Coosa possessed no property, and he was so overcome with the helplessness and pathos of their situation, that he plunged into the woodland, where he wandered up and down the banks of his favorite stream for days. His thoughts were only of Talladega. He could see her reflection in the still waters; hear her voice in the rapids; and to this day the stream that bears her name still echoes the voice, and reflects the beauty of Talladega.

After Coosa had wandered for days, he decided that he could stand it no longer, and he went back to speak to Choccolocco. Coosa found him alone and he immediately stated his business. He told him that he was not a man of property, yet he was young, and taller, swifter and stronger than any warrior of the province; aside from this, he knew where valuable minerals were stored in lands unpossessed, and he would direct Choccolocco to them, whereby he could enrich himself more plentifully than any chief in all the land. In fact, he pled so appealingly, and painted a picture so enticing, that Choccolocco listened with growing interest.

"If you can bring me samples of valuable ores, and assure me of the possibility of ownership," said Choccolocco "I shall consider your proposition more fully."

There was never a happier being since the world began than was Coosa at this hopeful remark. Turning he found that someone else had joined them, and from the scowl on his face, he discerned that this was the erstwhile acceptable suitor, who had overheard the latter part of Choccolocco's remarks.

Cheaha turned without a word. An idea was brewing. He hastened to put it into action. He had brought with him two young warriors, whom he immediately dispatched, one for a famous medicine man of his tribe, and the other to follow Coosa. The medicine man had discovered an herb that would put the strongest of men immediately to sleep, and he could not be aroused until the antidote was administered; that antidote being known to none but the medicine man himself.

Along about nightfall the young warrior who followed Coosa returned with the information that he had pitched camp at the west end of the valley. When Cheaha and the medicine man arrived they found Coosa peacefully sleeping, with arms folded on his breast and his face turned to the heavens. The medicine man stealthily crept to the sleeping Coosa and quickly administered the drug. When he assured Cheaha that the drug had taken the desired effect, Cheaha cruelly turned on the medicine man and killed him on the spot.

In the meantime Choccolocco, becoming disgusted at the delay of Coosa, ordered wedding preparations for Talladega and Cheaha.

Talladega had discovered her sleeping lover, and made many secret visits to him whenever chance permitted. She became so depressed and unhappy as the wedding day approached, that Cheaha decided that it would be wise to tell Talladega that Coosa could never be awakened. Talladega said nothing. She only sat motionless and gazed into space.

When the wedding day arrived, no bride was to be found. The woodland was searched, the hills and valleys scanned, but no bride was to be found. In the midst of the turmoil an Indian lad burst into the group with the exciting news that Talladega had been discovered, lying dead on the breast of her sleeping lover.

Although the drug was so powerful as to keep Coosa always sleeping, it also carried the power to make him grow, and while lying there sleeping, he has grown through the centuries until the mighty figure has become a great giant, now forming a mountain many miles long, where he can be seen from many roadsides. Mother Nature has lovingly covered him with earth, to protect him from the cold. She has planted trees and shrubs to shield him from the hot summer sun, and she has scattered flowers here and there, and each year birds flock to the Sleeping Giant to herald the coming of Spring. And there he lies, still dreaming of his beloved Talladega, "The Bride of the Mountain."

DeSoto's Visit
1540

July 16th, 1540 was an exciting day for the Coosas when Hernando De Soto, with an army of approximately 1,000 men, came marching into the capital of their Province.[1] Some arrived in canoes on the Coosa River, some on horses, and others marching. They had with them 500 captive Indians carrying equipment and driving herds of swine and cattle. The Spaniards were gaily arrayed; some in armor, and all bearing swords and guns.

De Soto was endowed with an adventurous spirit, and with this endowment he became distinguished. He made quite a reputation under Pizarro in Peru, and the King of Spain made him Governor of Cuba and Adelantado of Florida, the newly acquired country. De Soto no sooner received these appointments than he advertised the fact that, with his own funds, he would search the new country for gold, because there were fabulous stories regarding this precious metal in great quantities, to be found not too far from the coast. With this announcement, young men of royal blood and from the best families of Spain begged permission to join him. Some sold all their possessions to enter into the expedition. It took practically a year to make the necessary preparations for the great adventure.

He left his wife, Dona Isabella Bobadilla, and a Lieutenant Governor in charge of Cuba, and set out with a fleet of nine vessels for the coast of Florida. Upon his arrival in Tampa Bay on May 30th, 1539, he was fortunate in capturing 500 Indians to carry his equipment into the Indian country. Among these was one Jean Ortiz, a Spaniard, who had been taken in slavery by the Indians 12 years before. Albert James Pickett, in his History of Alabama, published 1851, gives the following description:

"Gratified at the appearance of Jean Ortiz, who became his interpreter, De Soto gave him clothes and arms, and placed him upon a charger. The Adelantado was now ready to penetrate the interior. His troops were provided with helmets, breastplates, shields, and coats of steel to repel the arrows of the Indians; and with swords, Biscayan lances, crude guns, called aquebuses, cross-bows and one piece artillery. His cavaliers, mounted upon 213 horses, were the most gallant and graceful men of all Spain. Greyhounds, of almost the fleetness of the winds, were ready to be turned loose upon the retreating savages; and bloodhounds, of prodigious size and noted ferocity, were at hand to devour them, if the bloody Spaniards deemed it necessary. To secure the unhappy Indians, handcuffs, chains and neck collars abounded in the camp. Workmen of

---

[1] Owen's His. Of Ala. & Dictionary of Ala. Biography, Vol. 1, Page 490

every trade, with their various tools, and men of science, with their philosophical instruments and crucibles for refining gold, were in attendance. Tons of iron and steel, and much other metal, various merchandise and provisions to last two years, were provided by the munificence of the commander and his followers. A large drove of hogs, which strangely multiplied upon the route, together with cattle and mules, was also attached to the expedition. The establishment of the Catholic religion appears to have been one of their objects; for, associated with the army were twelve priests, eight clergymen of inferior rank, and four monks, with their robes, holy relics, and sacramental bread and wine."[2]

De Soto was indeed a systematic and thorough adventurer, for he also had journalists and artists attached to his party. It was from records kept by this group that Albert Pickett derived his information. The journalists followed the expedition every step of the way with thrilling stories of adventure among the Indians throughout Georgia and Alabama. The army passed through fertile fields, over barren stretches, down beautiful and swift streams, until it reached the much publicized Province of Coosa, a portion of which was located in the present County of Talladega.

Again I quote from the History of Alabama by Albert J. Pickett, 1851: "The expedition now began to enter the far famed Province of Coosa, the beauty and fertility of which were known to all the Indians, even upon the seaside. Garcellasso asserts that it extended 300 miles, and other authors agree that it reached over the territory now embraced in the counties of Cherokee, Benton (Calhoun), Talladega and Coosa. Continuing through the rich lands of Benton, the expedition passed many towns subject to the Chief of Coosa. Every day they met ambassadors, one going and another coming, by which De Soto was assured of a hearty welcome at the capital. With joyful faces the Indians rushed to his lines every mile upon the route, furnishing supplies and assisting the troops from one town to another. The same generous reception attended him upon entering the soil of the county of Talladega. The hospitality of the Coosas surpassed that of any people whom he had yet discovered. The trail was lined with towns, villages and hamlets, and many sown fields which reached from one to the other. With a delightful climate, and abounding in fine meadows and beautiful rivers, this region was charming to De Soto and his followers. The numerous barns were full of corn, while acres of that which was growing bent to the warm rays of the sun and rustled in the breeze. In the plains were plum trees peculiar to the country, and others resembling those of Spain.

---

[2] Pickett's His. Of Ala., Vol. 1, Page 3

Wild fruit clambered to the tops of the loftiest trees, and lower branches were laden with delicious Isabella grapes."[3]

De Soto's journey through Talladega County is not very clear. Some modern students of his journey believe that he came through the interior of the county, rather than having followed the Coosa River. However, his record shows that the expedition came to a town, Tali, where they spent the night. This is believed to have been on the west bank of the Coosa in St. Clair County. They left there on Sunday or Monday, and crossed to the east bank of the river. "Monday they crossed a river and slept in the open country. Tuesday they crossed another river, and Wednesday another large river, and slept at Tasqui."[4] Dr. Owen seemed to think that the two large rivers mentioned were Cane and Blue Eye Creeks. This, I believe is not true. There is a hairpin curve in the Choccolocco Creek at this point, and it is possible that the army crossed this same stream twice. The village of Tasqui is easily recognized as the "Dickinson Mill Site", Sec. 14, T. 17, R. 4,. E., of the Huntsville Meridian.[5] This site was granted to Shadrach Dickinson March 16, 1844, and is still in possession of his descendants. Many valuable Indian relics have been, and still are, found at this point. This site is located in this bend of the creek. Since none of the records mention the route from Tasqui to Coosa, it is possible that De Soto followed the Indian trail from this point into Coosa, which would, no doubt, have taken them through the interior of the western portion of the county.

"On the 16th of July, 1540, the army came in sight of the town of Coosa. Far in the outskirts, De Soto was met by the Chief, seated upon a cushion, and riding in a chair supported upon the shoulders of four of his chief men. One thousand warriors, tall, active, sprightly and admirably proportioned, with large plumes of various colors on their heads, followed him, marching in regular order. His dress consisted of a splendid mantle of martin skins, thrown gracefully over his shoulder, while his head was adorned with a diadem of brilliant feathers. Around him many Indians raised their voices in song, and others made music upon flutes. The steel-clad warriors of Spain, with their glittering armor, scarcely equaled the magnificent display made by these natives of Alabama."[6]

The Coosa Micco, or Cacique, was only 26 years of age, but was gifted with unusual intelligence, which was displayed in the speech he made when he greeted De Soto, which his journalists recorded: "Mighty Chief: Above all

---

[3] Ibid, Vol.1, Page 16
[4] Owen's Vol. 1, Page 490
[5] Ibid
[6] Pickett's Vol. 1, Page 17 – Pickett states July 26th, Dr. Owen, July 16th

others of the earth! Although I come now to receive you, yet I received you many days ago deep in my heart. If I had the whole world, it would not give me as much pleasure as I now enjoy at the presence of yourself and your incomparable warriors. My person, lands and subjects are at your service. I will now march you to your quarters with playing and singing."[7]

De Soto responded in his best style, after which they proceeded to Coosa, where the Chief of Micco had set aside his royal house for the accommodation of De Soto. His army occupied over half of the other 500 houses of the town.

This town of Coosa was situated on the east bank of the Coosa River between the mouths of the Tallassahatchie and the Talladega Creeks. The river derived its name from the Coosa Province, since it bordered the province on the north and the west. The name "Coosa" means "Canebrake".[8] The town was designated as a "City of Refuge" for many generations, and was still in existence as such in 1796 when Benjamin Hawkins, Indian Agent, made a visit to this district.

De Soto was offered territory in which to establish a colony, and considered the matter, but being in search of gold, he moved on, leaving a desperately sick Christian Negro, and a number of swine as a gift to the chief. Furada, a Spaniard, also remained, and became the first white settler in the state of Alabama.

Ranjel recorded: "On Friday, August 20th (1540), the Governor and his people left Coosa."[9] They stopped at Talimachusy Saturday night. The town was "located at the mouth of Emauhee Creek as it enters Tallassahatchie Creek, just east of the highway from Talladega and about four miles north of Sylacauga."[10]

A swollen stream detained De Soto, and he lingered in a village by the name of "Itua" for six days. He then continued his march to a village by the name of "Ullebahale", situated on Hatchett Creek. He states that this last village was surrounded by a wall; that posts were driven in the ground; poles were laid horizontally and were stuccoed with clay and straw; and that port holes were placed at intervals.

Thus ended the first recorded visit of the white man to Talladega County, and it is with shame that we record that De Soto was unkind in taking the Coosa Micco as hostage when he left the district, after having been treated so kindly during his visit.

---

[7] Ibid, Vol. 1, Page 18
[8] Place Names in Ala., by Wm. A. Reed, Page 24
[9] Owen's, Vol. 1, Page 491
[10] Ibid

There are many traditional stories of De Soto's visits over the interior of the county, and there are some evidences of such visits, but we have no proof that these are true. It does seem plausible that during a stay of several weeks at Coosa, many expeditions for food must have taken place, which would involve the trading of articles brought here by De Soto. Since he was in search of gold, some search may have also been made for this precious metal. It is quite certain that 1,000 soldiers would not have calmly sat in an Indian village this length of time.

The course of events might have changed completely had the veins of gold, which later created such a sensation, been discovered in 1540.

Indian Agent's Visit
1796

Benjamin Hawkins, "Agent of the United States among the Creeks, and General Superintendent of all the tribes South of the Ohio River,"[1] visited the Upper Creek country in 1796. While traveling through the district he acquired accurate information concerning the Creeks. He wrote a "Sketch of the Creek Country in 1798 and 1799", and the Historical Society of Georgia published, some years ago, "Letters of Benjamin Hawkins 1796-1806." From these publications I have derived information contained in this chapter.

About Thanksgiving of 1796 Benjamin Hawkins set out for his good will tour of the Creek country. His pack horses carried beads, ornaments, farming and cooking implements, blankets, garden seeds and many other articles to be given as presents to the Creeks, or to be traded along the way for food.

He passed through the Cherokee country where he found that most of the men were on their annual hunt, but the women treated him courteously, and he found them to be industrious. They were making baskets and sifters out of split canes which had been dyed, in workmanship, superior to that of white people. These friendly Cherokees furnished him interpreters and guides from village to village, which system he continued to use throughout the Indian country. News of his visits always preceded him, and he was greeted with kindness. They recognized him as a representative of the United States who was there for the purpose of helping them.

At the time of Hawkins' visit to Alabama, the state was occupied almost entirely by what was known as the "Four Civilized Indian Tribes". The Cherokees occupied the north-east corner of Alabama; the Chickasaws the north-west corner. The Choctaws the central west. The Creeks were in fact Muscogees and occupied the greater part of east Alabama. The British began calling them "Creeks", because they were found living almost entirely in villages along creek and river banks. They frequently traveled by water in canoes. An act passed in the legislature of Alabama, January 13, 1833 "That Talladega Creek, from its mouth to the mouth of Jumpers' Spring Branch, and Chocklocko Creek from its mouth to David Conner's, are hereby declared public highways" is evidence that this was true as late as 1833. Hawkins followed the English custom of calling them "Creeks", and they are still known as such.

---

[1] Vol. IX, Collection of the Historical Society of Ga., Page 9

This Creek country was divided into two confederacies, the Upper Creek Country and the Lower Creek Country. Talladega County lies within the Upper Creek country. While the country was dominated by the Creeks, there were many other tribes than Muscogees within the confederacy. There were colonies of Uchees, Coosaus, Alabimos, Natchez, Choctaws, Chickasaws, Aubicoos, Hillabees, Shawnees, and many other tribes of Indians, some having come to this country for protection.

Hawkins arrived on Friday, Dec. 9th, 1796, in the Hillibee country, a portion of which was originally in Talladega County. This portion of the county was included within the bounds of Clay County in 1866, when Clay County was established. However, to get an insight into conditions among the most prosperous white settlers, I quote from Hawkins journal regarding his visit to a white settler:

"Robert Grierson, a native of Scotland, who was intelligent, had lived many years as a trader, and had an Indian family. He spoke the language well, and had large possessions, negroes, cattle and horses.—Mr. Grierson received me with a sociable and hospitable frankness. He had his family around him ginning and picking cotton—He was sending it to Tennessee, where he expected 34c for pound—He had planted the last season two acres of cotton in drills four feet asunder. The land apparently not very good, high, dry and gravelly, but the cotton grew well, many of the stalks 8 feet high.—He informed me he finds no difficulty in hiring the Indian women to pick out cotton, he hired them to pick by the basket of about a bushel; he gave half a pint of salt, or 3 strands of mock wampum beads a basket, or half a pint of taffra for two baskets."[2]

Mr. Grierson owned 40 negroes, 300 head of cattle and 30 horses. He further records: "There were 30 acres on the farm, the product of corn, cotton, rice, peas, beans, squashes, pumpkins, watermelons and colewarts. Peaches grow well, but he has but few trees, and not any other fruit trees."[3]

Mr. Grierson accompanied Mr. Hawkins further into the country, where he visited Coosau, having arrived on Dec. 13, 1796, and which he placed on the Coosa River between the mouths of the Eufaula-hatchie (or Kiamulgee) and the Nauche. He describes it as a pretty spot on a hill. This is the same Coosa visited by De Soto in 1540. He speaks of the country as being well watered, with beautiful springs and pretty valleys, with cane on the creeks and reeds on the branches. "Throughout the whole of this country there is but little fruit of any kind; in some of the rich flats there are fox grapes and muscadines;

---

[2] Ibid, Pages 29 and 30
[3] The Creek Country – Hawkins, Page 24

the small cluster grapes of the hills are destroyed by fire, and the persimmon, haw and chestnut by the hatchet. There are few blackberries in the old fields, red haws on the poor sand hills, and strawberries thinly scattered, but not a gooseberry, raspberry or currant in the land.—The traveler, in passing through a country as extensive and wild as this, and so much in a state of nature, expects to see game in abundance. The whole of the Creek claims, the Seminoles inclusive, cover three hundred miles square; and it is difficult for a hunter, in passing through it, in any direction, to obtain enough for his support."[4] I rather resent Hawkins remarks regarding Talladega County, because when we take into consideration that his visit was in middle December, and that his journal shows that he followed only the Tallasseehatchie and Talladega Creeks for about 15 miles, and was here only two days, he really had little opportunity actually to see the country. This part of the country was then classed in the "District of the Aubacoos", and Mr. Hawkins found that these people manifested quite a friendly attitude toward the United States government, which pleased him very much. He asked Mr. Grierson and several others "What would most likely the soonest disturb this friendly disposition of the Indians?" The answer was that many whites had moved into the nation who were more depraved than the savages, that they had all the vices without one of their virtues. This group had reduced the stealing of horses to a system, having connections in several states; that the evil had become so deeply rooted that it would require drastic measures to put an end to it. This class of whites had Indian families, but took no care of them whatsoever, either to feed or educate them. The fathers resorted to making money by any and every means in their power, however roguish, and were using their children as aids. If this custom was not abolished, the Indians would assuredly discontinue their friendly attitude toward the government.[5]

Benjamin Hawkins did everything in his power to ameliorate such a condition. He was employed for more than 30 years by the Government in its activities among the Indians, who called him "The Beloved Man of the Four Nations." He was intimately associated with the leaders of the nations, and with their co-operation, was instrumental in bringing about vast improvements.

During these years, the benevolent societies of the thirteen states supplemented the Government supply with needful clothing, garden implements, seeds, etc. Especially was this true of the Quakers of Pennsylvania and Maryland. They were in constant touch with Mr. Hawkins and sent supplies regularly. In fact many young Indian boys were taken into the Quaker homes to educate them.

---

[4] Collection of the Historical Society of Ga., Vol. IX, Page 35
[5] Collection of the Historical Society of Ga., Vol. IX, Page 35

While Benjamin Hawkins never lived in the Upper Creek Country, he kept in touch with it and encouraged every progressive movement through traders and chiefs. He, therefore, played an important role in the early history of this county. He impressed the tribes with the fact that he had "come to correct abuses, and to fix the management of Indian affairs in those who will zealously and steadily execute the orders of the Government." This he did to the satisfaction of both the Indians and the Government.

Creek Indian Customs

The Muscogees, or Creeks, followed the custom of living in crudely constructed houses. There was no mention by early historians of wigwams or tepees being evident. These houses were made of split timber standing upright, or slanting against a wooden frame of logs. There was neither floor nor window. The roof was made of boughs, barks, and corn stalks. Houses were used only for protection. Beds were no problem, because every Indian possessed his own blanket, or skin, and he simply rolled himself into it for the night.

The Creeks also had the habit of building in groups, or small villages, and on streams. There were many well traveled paths throughout the country, but the recognized highway was the water. A self-respecting Indian owned his own canoe. A study of the Indians reminds one of the old Scottish Highlanders. Each Highland Clan had a Chief, and the clan was recognized by its tartan. Smaller clans took refuge among the larger clans. This was true of the Creeks. Each tribe of Indians had a chief, and its insignia, and the smaller took refuge among the larger tribes. The habits of the Creeks must have varied some as different tribes were admitted to the district, and different customs were introduced, but there seems to have been little noticeable change in their mode of living as described by De Soto in 1540, and by Benj. Hawkins in 1796.

Flourishing corn fields are mentioned during both periods. Corn, as we know it, was discovered by the American pioneers, as a basic food of the Indians, and was known for years as maize or "Indian Corn." Corn, meat and fish were their principal foods.

In 1564 a French artist, Jacob le Moyne, visited the Creek country and painted a number of pictures from life. These pictures give us a clearer understanding of their mode of dress and customs at that time. One of these pictures, entitled "Indians Employed in Planting Corn",[1] shows two men, wearing loin cloths (Buck-She-Ah-Ma-Flap), tied in the back. Skins, open at the top, are stretched over their heads, with long hair sticking out of the opening. These men are digging holes with an axelike hoe, with handles about three feet long. There are three women. Two have on short skirts (Hoo-Nau) made of either leather strips, beads or grass, hanging about half way to their knees. They carry reed-woven trays or baskets, from which they drop corn. The third

---

[1] Frontispiece, Pickett's History, 1851, Vol. I

woman, similarly dressed, covers the corn with a long pole. These three women have hair parted in the middle, loosely flowing almost to their waists.

Frequently during their hunting season, every man of the village embarked on an expedition, which lasted for several months, according to the distance necessary to procure their winter kill. At such times women were left in complete charge of children and property. Meat was cured by smoking and, where obtainable, with salt. The word "salary" was derived from salt, because centuries ago wages were paid in salt. This method of exchange was followed by the Indians. Furs were sold to the traders for so much salt.

Another one of Jacob le Moyne's pictures gives us an insight into their method of curing meat. His "Indians Preparing Meats to be Deposited in their Winter Hunt Houses"[2] shows logs placed across the top of a wooden frame about three feet high, and on these logs are a fish, a deer, a fox or dog, and a small alligator. Underneath is a fire, being fanned with palmetto leaves by two men, from which pours smoke which cures the meat.

Mr. Wm. L. Lewis, who lived among the Creeks in Talladega County several years before their removal, gives an enlightening description of the Creeks' method of storing corn, hunting, fishing, cooking and eating—"Their little corn cribs (which were raised on posts 5 or 6 feet long, the sills, or first timber, laid on the top of the posts) were 4 or 5 feet by 6 feet in length, the corners neatly finished off and the crib well covered. They would lay a row of the ears very carefully all around, and another on top of that, and so on, until all was put in, with the regularity of brick work. This corn was beaten in mortars with a pestle, until reduced to coarse grits, then boiled in water, not thick, but thin like gruel. If they had fresh beef or game, it was cut into small pieces nearly an inch square and boiled with the corn, making a broth. This they called 'sofka'. They would pour it into a round bowl or tray, 15 inches in diameter and five inches deep, and eat with a spoon that would hold more than a gill, and a handle 15 inches long. The first one would take the spoon by the end of the handle and raise it up with the spoon lengthwise, directly in front of him, turn his head back and drop the contents of the spoon into his mouth opened wide enough to receive it; then, with a peculiar sling, he would throw the handle of the spoon 'round to the next person, who would go through the same motions as the first, and so on, until finished, all using the same spoon."[3]

"The Indians were nimble, active to walk or run, and generally expert with the bow and arrow, trained to its use from infancy, also in swimming. Men, women and children took to the water like ducks. I have seen children six or

---

[2] Pickett's History, 1851, Vol. I, Page 68
[3] Wm. L. Lewis' "Chapters of Unwritten History," Our Mountain Home, 1884, Page 42, as copied. Tall. Public Library

seven years old dive under water a distance of 30 feet. I have seen a company of children 8 to 15 years of age, shoot with bows and arrows at the edge of a dime fixed on a split stick 3 feet high from the ground, and soon some one would knock it out, shooting at a distance of 10 paces, and the one who knocked it out always obtained the prize. They would also enter Cheaha Creek, at Jemison's ford, and when they would get up to Chinnabee, would have a string of fish 2 feet long, killed with their bows and arrows. They also used blow guns for shooting birds and squirrels on land. The blow guns were made from canes six or eight feet long, the joints being smoothly bored out so as to permit the arrow to pass out easily. The arrow was generally made of lightwood 8 or 10 inches long, and very sharp at one end, the large end of the arrow spirally grooved like an auger, and wrapped with something like elastic, so as to fit the inside of the gun or cane. The Indian would get as nearly under the bird or squirrel as he could and shoot the arrow by blowing it out with his mouth. I have seen them bring down birds that were 20 or 30 feet high. I never saw a squirrel shot with one of the blow guns."[4]

Micco's, or kings, lived in the larger towns, and had jurisdiction over a group of smaller towns with chiefs at the head. These larger towns were also distinctive in that they had a "Choo-Co-Thluc-Co," or Big House, and a "Choo-Co-Fau-Thluc-Co", or Assembly Room.

"The Choo-co-thluc-co or Big House,"[5] was in reality a public square, consisting of four buildings of one story each, forming an open court, and each side, or building, was about 40 X 16 feet, with an 8 foot pitch. The entrances were at the four corners of the square. Each crude building was wooden, supported on posts set in the ground, open across the front, which faced the court. Each side was divided into three parts, or compartments. These were divided lengthwise into two levels, the front filled in two feet from the ground, on which Indians sat or laid. Half-way back, the rooms were raised two more feet, thereby making two platforms, or wide steps for sitting or lying on.

The building fronting north was called "Is-te-cha-guc-ul-gee In-too-pau", or the Cabin of the Beloved Men. Here sat men of importance who had distinguished themselves in some way and members of the Micco's family.

The building fronting east was called the "Mic-ul-gee Intoo-pau," or "The Micco's Cabin", where he presided in the middle compartment with his counselors, or chiefs, about him.

The building fronting south was called "Tus-tun-nug-ul-gee In-too-pau," or "The Warrior's Cabin." The Great Warrior, or general, was appointed

---

[4] Ibid, Page 35
[5] History of the Creeks, by Benj. Hawkins, Page 65-67

by the Micco and his counselors. The warriors were chosen according to their conduct and achievements in war; in the art of scalping, in bravery, etc.

The building fronting west was called "Hut-to-mau-hug-gee," or "The Cabin of the Young People and Their Associates."

The Micco and his counselors and warriors met daily, smoked pipes, received complaints, and dispensed with all business matters pertaining to their tribe. Perhaps they indulged in games and talked over the news.

"The Choo-co-fau-thluc-co, or Rotunda and Assembly Room,"[6] was a large crude building, where a fire, without a flue, was kept burning in the center. Old and young assembled here at their pleasure to sing, dance, or gossip. In cold weather those who cared to do so, could sleep in the building. In this assembly hall the "Boo-Ske-Tau," or Green Corn Dance was annually celebrated. It lasted eight days, and was celebrated at different times, according to the ripening of the corn, which usually occurred around August. In reality this was a Feast of the Harvest.

Both Benjamin Hawkins and Albert Pickett give detailed descriptions of the daily celebrations. On certain days they had the "Pin-e-bun-gau" or Turkey Dance; another the "Toc-co-yula-gau," or Tadpole Dance; the "Its-ho-bun-gau," or Gun Dance; the "Obun-gau-chap-co," or Long Dance; and many other tribal dances.

This Boo-Ske-Tau was celebrated almost entirely in later years in the old towns, but other towns had the privilege of entering into the activities.[7] Hillaube, Wewocau, Coosuh, Aubecoochee, Nauche, Eufaulauhatchie were mentioned by Benj. Hawkins in 1796 among 26 "Mother Towns" of the Upper Creeks. Boo-Ske-Tau was celebrated at Eufaulauhatchie for this district as late as 1835. The initiating ceremony of youths, 15 to 17 years of age, took place during this celebration. At this time the youth would emerge into adulthood. The youth spent a year in preparation for this event. He must eat bitter herbs, during this period, drink brews from their leaves; abstain from eating meat, peas and salt, and he must associate only with young persons taking the same treatment. Through self denial and endurance tests he became a man. The youth carried the name of his mother until he distinguished himself by bringing home a scalp, or in some way proving his fearlessness; nor could he marry until he had attained a name for himself. After he had proved himself worthy, the counselors assembled at the Grand Cabin to give him a name, one suitable to his capabilities and attainments. Then, and then only, could he establish a home of his own.

---

[6] Ibid
[7] Pickett's History, 1851, Vol. I, Pages 107-111

The Indian boy's marriage was planned by the women of his family, with the men of the bride's family. When an agreement between the families was made, the girl immediately became his property, but the marriage ceremony lasted frequently for months, sometimes for a year. The groom must first build a house, plant his crop and gather it, and go on a hunt and stock his larder. Then the ceremony was completed and he could lead his wife to his home. Jacob le Moyne gave us an insight into one celebration of this kind in his picture entitled "Indians Bearing in a Chair a Young Girl who has been selected as one of the Future Wives of the King."[8] Two young men, with head coverings of skins, wearing loin cloths, and playing flutes made of reeds, or canes, with small animal tips hanging at intervals from the long flutes, lead the procession. Back of these musicians, the bride rides in a cushioned sedan chair fastened to two long poles which are carried on the shoulders of four men. On each side of the bride is a man carrying a peacock-like fan at the end of a long pole. Four women follow, with flowing hair parted in the middle, and adorned with beads, ear-rings, armlets, bracelets, and wearing short skirts. These four women are carrying baskets of various sizes, some with handles; another woman carries an earthen bowl. All are filled with fruit. Following these are warriors with javelins. The bride is covered with painted or tattooed figures. She wears three strands of beads, ear ornaments, bracelets and armlets.

Either the wife or the husband had the right to divorce, on small provocation. The wife fell heir to the property and children in case of divorce. For infidelity a woman's hair was cut, and she became an object of disgrace. For the same offense, a man was punished severely by his superiors.

When a war chief appointed a day for taking up arms, he sent out a club painted red to the chief nearest him, and this chief, in turn, passed it on. Each was given pieces of red wood equal to the number of days until an assembly was to be held. From this custom came the title of "Red Sticks." Each chief would have a drum beaten before his cabin announcing the assembly to his warriors. At the assembly, the required warriors were selected and they remained in the public square for three days and partook of the medicine of war. At the end of the period, squaws brought packets containing a blanket, material to mend moccasins, and a small sack of parched corn meal as a war ration. The fighters' food consisted of an ounce of corn meal, put in a pint of water, where it stayed until it became as thick as soup. This would sustain him for 12 hours and was indispensable; for during war the party had no time to kill game. This corn meal drink was called "Wis-soe-taw" by the Cherokees; "sofka"

---

[8] Ibid, Page 73

by the Creeks. The Great Warrior (Tus-tunn-up-gee-thluc-co) had the right to declare war, but the Micco had the right to veto it. The Micco and his counselors declared peace.

The Creeks believed in a Supreme Being, or Master of Breath, called E-sau-ge-tub E-mis-see. They believed in a future existence, in a Happy Hunting Ground, and they believed that the good would be rewarded and the evil punished.

It is remarkable how a savage people arrived at so many true conclusions and that just laws prevailed among them. Certainly a civilization must have existed many years prior to the white man's invasion of this period of savagery. One wonders whether the word "Savage" should be applied to the Indian or to the White Man who violently destroyed the peace of the Red Man.

Indian Villages

Information contained in this chapter is derived almost entirely from "A Sketch of the Creek Country," by Benjamin Hawkins, and from Dr. Thomas Owens' "History of Alabama and Dictionary of Alabama Biography," 1921, Vols. I and II.

Benjamin Hawkins records that he arrived at Coosa on December 13th, 1796, and made explorations up the Eufaula-hatchie (Talladega Creek) and the Nauche (Tallasehatchie Creek) for about 15 miles. Since he was in the district, which he called the "Aubbecooche District," for only parts of two days, he evidently went up the Talladega Creek, crossed over by land to the Natchez village on Tallasehatchie Creek and back to Coosa. He mentions in his report to the government only villages located on those two creeks. He mentions in his report in the spring of 1797 twenty-six towns in the Upper Creek Country as "Mother Towns". Among these were "Wewocau, Coosuh, Nauche, Eufaula-hatchie and Hillaube." Four of these were in what is now Talladega County. Hillaube was included in Clay County when established in 1866.

These Mother Towns were towns where the Micco transacted official business of his tribes. They were very much like our county seats, as outlined in the chapter on Indian Customs. In such towns were located the public houses where the tribal affairs were administered; and where the recreation buildings were located, in which the annual celebrations took place.

A group of minor towns were mentioned by Hawkins as belonging to, or subject to, the Mother towns.

George Stiggins stated in his "History of the Creeks" that the inhabited part of the nation was laid out in town districts designated from some creek, ridge or some point well known, and the boundary of one town extended to that of another.

There were certainly many towns in other parts of the county, of which we know little. There was one near Chandlers' Springs. Others have been mentioned at Rushings Springs, Blue Eye, Silver Run and Ironaton. There was certainly one at Chinnabee, and no doubt there were many located on the banks of Choccolocco Creek and in its fertile valley. But the following have been located:

A-BIH-KA – "Near the Coosa River, and just South of Tallasehatchie Creek on the S ½ of the S ½ of Sec. 17, T. 20, R. 5 E. of the Huntsville

Meridian."[1] Found on a map of Delishe's of 1704. This was probably the same as AU-BE-COO-CHEE of Benj. Hawkins' 1796 report.

A-BIK-UD-SHI – On map of Crenay's of 1733, "At a council held at Savannah, Ga., July 3, 1761, to regulate Indian trade, this town with its 50 hunters was assigned to the Indian Trader, J. McGillivray. It was the same as the NAUCHE of Benj. Hawkins' 1796 report.[2]

AU-BE-COO-CHEE – "Is on Nauche (Tallasehatchie) Creek, five miles from the river, on the right bank of the creek, on a flat one mile wide. The growth is hard-shelled hickory. The town spreads itself out and is scattered on both sides of the creek, in the neighborhood of very high hills, which descend back into waving, rich land, fine for wheat and corn; the bottoms all rich; the neighborhood abounds in limestone, and large limestone springs; they have one above and one below the town; the timber on the rich lands is oak, hickory, walnut, poplar and mulberry.

There is a very large cave north of the town, the entrance of which is small, on the side of a hill. It is much divided, and some of the rooms appear as works of art; the doors regular; in several parts of the cave saltpeter is to be seen in crystals. On We-Wo-Cau Creek, there is a fine mill seat; the water is contracted by two hills, the fall twenty-feet; and the land in the neighborhood very rich; cane can be found on the creeks, and reed on the branches. From one or two experiments, tobacco grows well on these lands.

The town is one of the oldest in the nation; and sometimes among the oldest chiefs it gives the name to the nation, Au-be-cuh. Here some of the oldest customs had their origin. The law against adultery was passed here, and one to regulate marriage. To constitute legal marriage, a man must build a house, make his crop and gather it in, then make his hunt and bring home the meat; putting all this in possession of his wife, ends the ceremony, and not till then. This information is obtained from Co-tau-lau, (Tus-se-ki-ah Micco), an old and respectable chief, descended from Nauche. He lives near We-o-Coof-ke, has accumulated a handsome property, owns a fine stock, is a man of much information, and of great influence among the Indians of the towns in the neighborhood of this.

They have no fences, and but few hogs, horses and cattle; they are attentive to white people who live among them, and particularly to white women."[3]

---

[1] Owen's History of Ala. Vol. 1, Page 1

[2] Ibid Vol. 1, Page 2

[3] Ibid Vol. 1, Page 406, Hawkins Sketch of the Creek Country, Page 39

CHICK-A-SAW TOWN – "A Chickasaw settlement or village, noted on Mitchell's map of 1755, and spelled "CHIC-A-CHAS, and located near and on the south side of the head waters of Talladega Creek, Talladega County. It is to be identified as the "TCHI-A-CHAS' village noted in the French census of 1760, with 40 warriors, from which a total population of 200 would be estimated."[4]

CHE-AR-HAW – The land grants of Robert Jemison, signed by Andrew Jackson in 1834, for 2,880 acres of land "In Che-ar-haw Town of Indians," place this town in Townships 17 and 18, and would be the 'Willow Glen" and "Sunnyside" plantations on both sides of Cheaha Creek. The property was purchased from O-Chub-Pipa-Hadjo, Hi-Bilt-Henne-Har; Ar-sin-But-Hadjo, O-Se-Yo-Ho-Lo, Talladig-Hadjo, Hil-Li-Che, and Se-Lit-Ca.[5]

CHOCK-O-LOCK – The same as Choccolocco. Judge J. W. Vandiver, in Chapter XII of his History of Talladega, states "Robert Jemison bought the entire section from four Indians in Choccolocco Town,—the aggregate price paid being $2,650.00."[6] This property is in the forks of Choccolocco and Cheaha Creeks, and is now known as the "Turner Mill" property. Old letters of Robert Jemison are headed "Chock-o-lock."

CHAK-IH-LA-KO – Probably the same as Choccolocco, and is so erroneously placed by Dr. Owens "near Dam 5, Coosa River, within a mile of the influx of Choccolocco Creek."[7] However, this could have been what we now know as "Rushing Springs."

CHAL-A-KA-GAY – "An Indian town established in 1748 by a band of Shawnees from Ohio." It was located near the present site of Sylacauga, and means "Buzzard Roost."[8]

COSA – One and one-half miles from Childersburg, between the Tallasehatchie and Talladega Creeks, and visited by De Soto in 1540.

"Tristan de Luna's expedition visited Coosa in June or July, 1560 and remained three months. De Pardo, in 1566, found the district populous and fertile."

"Friendly Indians declared that there were 6,000 or 7,000 warriors in the party from the several towns on the Coosa River, who had assembled against De Pardo." It was a refuge for "Those who killed undesignedly" in 1775.

In 1796 the authorized trader was John O'Kelly, a half-breed, and his father was also a trader at Coosa, as well as at the town of Tuc-pauf-cau.

---

[4] Owen's History of Ala. Vol. 1, Page 240
[5] Indian Deeds to Robert Jemison, owned by Grace Jemison
[6] History on file at Public Library
[7] Owen's History of Ala., Vol. 1, Page 221
[8] Hawkins Sketch of the Creek Country, Page 39

"The town (Coosa) gives name to the river."[9]

EU-FAU-LAU-HAT-CHE – see Yu-FA-LA.

HILL-A-BI – Once in Talladega County, and situated on the left bank of Little Hillabee Creek. When Clay County was formed in 1866, the village was located on the border of the counties. This was made widely known because of the Hillabee massacre which took place Nov. 18, 1813 under Gen. James White. It also was the home of Robert Grierson, a prosperous and influential white man.[10]

IS-TA-PO-GA – Located near the mouth of Eastaboga Creek, and possibly the site of the old town of Eastaboga, which still bears that name. It means "Where people reside."[11]

KAN-CHA-TI – Possibly near the site of Conchardee, S.W. of the town of Talladega. Means "Red Dirt" or "Little Earth."[12]

KAY-O-MUL-GI – A town recorded on old maps on the south side of Talladega Creek, about where Kymulga now is located–or perhaps nearer the river. The lower part of Talladega Creek was known, in the early history of Talladega County as the Kymulga, the upper as Eufaula-hatchie.[13]

LAN-UD-SHI A-PA-LA – Listed in early Talladega County, on Hillabee Creek. Now in Clay County.[14]

NAU-CHE – "On Nauchee Creek, (Tallasehatchie) five miles above Au-be-coo-che, below fork of the creek, on a rich flat of land, of a mile in width, between two small mountains. This flat extends from the town three-quarters of a mile above the town house. The settlements are scattered on both sides of the creek for two miles: they have no worm fences, and but little stock. One chief, a brother of Chin-a-be, has a large stock of hogs, and had ninety fit for market in 1798.

This town is the remains of the Natchez who lived on the Mississippi. They estimate their gun men at one hundred, but they are, probably, not more than fifty. The land, off from the mountains is rich; the flats on the streams are large and very rich; the high waving country is very healthy and well watered; cane grows on the creeks, reed on the branches, and pea-vine in the flats and hill sides. The Indians get the root they call Tal-e-wau in this neighborhood;

---

9 Owen's History of Ala., Vol. 1, Page 406
10 Ibid Vol. 1, Page 693
11 Ibid Vol. II, Page 797
12 Ibid Vol.. II, Page 822
13 Ibid Vol. II, Page 825
14 Ibid Vol. II, Page 851

which the women mix with bears' oil to redden their hair." James Quarles was listed as trader and Thomas Wilson as saddler of the village in 1796.[15]

OAK-CHIN-A-WA – On both sides of Salt Creek near its influx with Big Shoal Creek.[16]

SAW-WA-NOOS – A Shawnee Indian Village recorded on Mitchell's map of 1755; located on Tallasse-hatchie Creek.[17]

TAL-A-Ti-Gi – Meaning "Border Town". The French census of 1760 spelled it KA-LA-LE-KIS, and stated that is contained 130 warriors. "It was originally settled from A-BIH-KA",[18] and was no doubt the town in which was fought the Battle of Talladega on November 9th, 1813. The town probably covered a district which bordered on that of the Natchez; hence the name "Border Town".

TALIMACHUSY – "NEW Town", where De Soto spent the night of August 21st, 1540. Situated south-east of Talladega Town at the mouth of Emauhee Creek as it entered Tallasehatchie creek, four miles north of Sylacauga near the Talladega-Sylacauga Highway.[19]

TAS-QUI – 9 miles from Coosa River, north, near the mouth of Choccolocco Creek. De Soto spent one night here on his journey to Coosa.[20] It lies in Sec. 14, T. 17, S., R. 4 E, and was deeded to Shadrach Dickinson in 1844. It is still owned by his descendants. A great number of Indian relics have been found here.

WE-O-WO-KA or WE-WO-CAU. Described by Benjamin Hawkins: "from We-cau, water, and wo-cau, barking or roaring, as the sound of water at high falls. It lies on a creek of the same name, which joins Gis-cun-tal-lau-has-see, on its left bank, sixteen miles below that town. We-Wo-Cau is fifteen miles above O-Che-Au-Po-Fau, and four miles from Coosau, on the left side. The land is broken – with coarse gravel. The settlements are spread out on several small streams for the advantage of the rich flats bordering on them, and for their stock. They have cattle, horses and hogs. Here commences the moss, in the beds of the creeks, which the cattle are very fond of; horses and cattle fatten very soon on it with a little salt. It is of quick growth, found only in the rocky beds of creeks and rivers north of this."[21]

---

[15] Ibid Vol. II, Page 1070
[16] Ibid Vol. II Page 1087
[17] Ibid Vol. II, Page 1241
[18] Ibid Vol. II, Page 1288
[19] Ibid Vol. 1, Page 491 DeSoto's route
[20] Ibid Vol. 1, Page 487 DeSoto's route
[21] Hawkins Sketch of the Creek Country, Page 39

Weowoka was an important community in pioneer days. It was one of the early voting precincts. It was well known over the entire county as the Baptist Camp Meeting Ground. The Riser plantation is located on a portion of the scattered village. "Walnut Hill", the Riser ancestral home, was one of the county's most imposing dwellings.

WE-O-COOF-KE – Mentioned by Hawkins as the home of Co-Tau-Lau, was no doubt located where the present Wee-Guf-Kee is located.

YU-FAU-LA – or EU-FAU-LAU-HATCHIE–Is of special interest to the citizens of Talladega, since it was the "Mother Town" of this district. Hawkins described it as being 15 miles up the Eufaulauhatchie, on the left side of the creek, and bordering on a branch. It was well watered and the residents had a fine stock of cattle, horses and hogs. James Leslie was trader at the time. He mentions him as "a decent, respectable man,"[22] and that he died in 1799. This village was still in existence when the Treaty was signed in 1832, and is described by various early historians as a town where the annual celebrations took place. It was located near what is known as the Weisinger Place, on Talladega Creek, between Bemiston and Allison's Mill.

---

[22] Ibid, Page 41

Influential Indians of the Upper Creeks

The portion of Alabama, located in Talladega County, was first under the Spanish flag as a part of Florida; then the British flag as a portion of the Georgia Colony. Under the United States flag it was a part of the State of Georgia, the Territory South of the Ohio, Mississippi Territory, Alabama Territory, and finally on December 14th, 1819, the State of Alabama.

Prior to 1819 some white men had taken up residence in the Creek country as traders or blacksmiths. It was considered advisable for any white man anticipating settling in the Indian country to take a wife among the Indians. This was the first step toward amity with the Indians and was almost invariably followed. Since many of the half-breed children born to these parents became notable leaders among the Creeks, it is well to become acquainted with a few of those traders and leaders who were probably intimately associated, or at least familiar, with the Talladega community.

We are inclined to agree with Mr. Albert J. Pickett in most of his findings recorded in his History of Alabama (1851). However, General Thomas S. Woodward, who was part Creek Indian, and who lived among the Creeks for years, disagreed with Mr. Pickett on a number of statements. General Woodward wrote a series of articles for the Montgomery, Ala., "Mail" soon after the publication of Mr. Pickett's history, under the title of "Reminiscences of the Creeks, or Muscogees."[1] Gen. Woodward fought in the Creek wars, knew the leading Creeks intimately during the early part of the Nineteenth Century, and was qualified to give accurate information. He stated that the Tallassee Indians occupied a village by that name on a creek by the same name, Tallassehatchie, in Talladega County, for a number of years. He stated further that they were moved by James McQueen about the year 1756; that "The Tallassees quit their old Settlement in the Talladega country and it was immediately occupied by a band of Natchez Indians under the control of a Chief called Chinnubby (Chinnabee) and a Hollander by the name of Moniac – The Chief Chinnubby lived to be a very old man, and I knew him as well as I did any Indian in the nation. He was with General Jackson in the Creek War. He was with me in Florida in 1818. I have often, by a camp fire, sat and listened to him tell over his troubles among the French on the Mississippi, and how the French had drove them from their old houses, and he had helped to drive the

---

[1] These articles were published in a book by the Ala. Book Store, Tuscaloosa, and Birmingham Book Exchange some years later.

French from their trading houses at the forks of the Coosa and Tallapoosa."[2] This was the point where the Tallassees moved and established the village of "Little Tallassee."

General Woodward stated that James McQueen was a Scotchman, and was the first white man ever heard of among the Creeks. That he came to this country in 1716 and settled among the Tallassees, who were then residing in Talladega County, and that he married a Tallassee woman. Therefore, it will be noted that the first known white man to settle in the Creek country, settled in Talladega County. He moved with the Tallassee Indians to the forks of the Tallapoosa and Coosa Rivers in 1756, and died there at the age of 128 years in 1811. As long as James McQueen lived he was instrumental in keeping the Tallassees and Natchez Indians neutral. Hence, this portion of the Creek country experienced peace for years, while surrounding neighbors were constantly at war. James McQueen no doubt had many children, but one born in his old age, by the name of Peter McQueen, became quite prominent. Peter married Betsy Durant, a daughter of Benjamin and Sophia McGillivray Durant. Sophia was a daughter of Lachlan Lia McGillivray, and a sister of Alexander. This united two of the wealthiest and most influential Indian families among the Creeks, and is perhaps the reason Peter McQueen became at one time Chief of the Tallassees. He was one of the leaders in the Creek War.

Another white man who came to the Creek country was Lachlan Lia McGillivray, who arrived in Charleston, S. C., about 1738. He evidently pushed his way into the frontier of the Creek country sometime about 1740. He arrived in the early days at Fort Toulouse of the French, soon after it fell. A Captain Marchand, one of the French officers, had married a Creek maiden, Sehoy(I), Princess of the Running Wind Clan and their daughter Sehoy(II), a woman of charm, became the wife of Lachlan Lia McGillivray. The birth of their son, Alexander is placed variously from 1740 to 1759. Lachlan soon settled at Little Tallassee, and this portion of the Creek country from that time on became the most important section of the entire Creek confederacy. It became the home of the most important and influential leaders. Because of his association with, and the esteem with which he was held by the Creeks, Lachlan Lia McGillivray became a sort of Superintendent of Indian Affairs for England until his return to Scotland.

Lachlan Lia McGillivray recognized in his son, Alexander, the capacity for an education, and sent him to school in Charleston, where he received a well-rounded education. The mantle of Lachlan fell upon this gifted son as

---

[2] Thomas S. Woodward's "Reminiscences of the Creeks, or Muscogees" Page 77

leader of the Indians, and he became a sort of Emporer of the Creeks, as well as Advisor to the Cherokees, Chickasaws and Choctaws. Mr. Pickett pictures Alexander not only as a scholar and prodigious writer, but as the greatest leader among the Creeks. Other historians agree with him. However, General Woodward disputes the fact that he was a "scholar and prodigious writer." He states that "if there is any one living that can or could identify the hand of writing of a Scotchman by the name of Alexander F. Leslie, he could easily tell who wrote those letters (of McGillivray's). This man Leslie did McGillivray's writing, and was worthy of (so far as intellect is concerned) the notice of his distinguished relative of our own country, General Alexander Hamilton."[3]

Because the son of Alexander F. Leslie resided in Talladega, around whose home a fortification was built, it seems in order to include this interesting fact.

Since the writings of Mr. Pickett and Gen. Woodward over 100 years ago, much has been disclosed about Alexander McGillivray, which was not available earlier. While doing research, some years ago, among the documents in the Archives of Seville, Spain, Dr. John Walton Caughey, then professor of History in the University of California, ran across the correspondence of Alexander McGillivray and other allies of the Spanish Government of East and West Florida. This wonderful collection of valuable material was edited and published in 1938 by Dr. Caughey and the University of Okla. Press, of Norman, Oklahoma, under the title of "McGillivray of the Creeks."

These letters reveal that McGillivray constantly appealed to the Spanish government for protection from the Georgians. In a letter dated July 10th, 1785, he pleaded with the Governor of Florida to urge his King to help them in asserting their just rights. He reminds him that the "Treaty of Peace between the King of Great Britain and the States of America" claimed their land, and adds "declaring that as we determined to pay no attention to the manner in which British navigators has drawn out the lines of the lands in question ceded to the States of America – it being a notorious fact to the Americans – known to every person who is in any way conversant in, or acquainted with American affairs, that his Britannic Majesty was never possessed with, by session, purchase, or by right of conquest to our territories, and which the said Treaty gives away. We have repeatedly warned the states of Carolina and Georgia to desist from their encroachments, and to confine themselves within the lands (granted) to Britain in the year 1773. To these remonstrances we have received friendly talks and replys it is true; but while they are addressing us by

---

[3] Ibid, Page 61

appellations of FRIENDS and BROTHERS, they are stripping us of our natural rights by depriving us of that inheritance which belonged to our ancestors and hath descended from them to us since the beginning of time."[4]

At one time he speaks of one Moniac as his interpreter, but never referred to Alexander F. Leslie as writer, although that proves nothing, since if Leslie did write the letters he would probably not have referred to himself.

McGillivray was not a military man, though he was instrumental at times in inciting the nation to war. He was a man of affairs and was possessed with unsurpassed executive and diplomatic abilities. He was shrewd and cunning. At one and the same time he held the titles of Lt. Col. In the French Army; Colonel in the Spanish Army; and Brig. General of the American Army, with salaries from each country. He was of the Tribe of the Wind, and was accorded certain privileges not permitted to other tribes, and a statesman who was recognized by America, England, Spain and France as the Emperor of his people. He simply signed himself as "a native of and Chief of the Creek Nation." His cousin, William McGillivray, was one of the signers of the Creek Treaty of 1833.

Spain controlled the large trading posts at St. Augustine, Pensacola, Mobile and Savannah. These posts, of necessity, must be seaport towns where ships could bring into the country merchandise to be exchanged for furs of the natives. Hence, it was only natural that the Creeks should look to the Spanish for protection.

McGillivray died on Feb. 17th, 1793 while on a trip to Pensacola to see his partner, Panton, and was buried in the garden of his friend. There was never another such leader of the Creeks who could hold the nation together, and they drifted back to war.

The largest trading posts were operated by Panton, Leslie & Co., which we should pause to consider, because they were the authorized traders and agents of the Creek country, and operated until the early part of the Nineteenth Century. The Company was composed of William Panton, John Leslie, Forbes and several other Leslies, all originally from Great Britain. The "Company" perhaps also included McGillivray, since his letters indicate that he was in partnership with them. Panton, Leslie and Forbes were conservative, peaceable men, peculiarly fitted for the parts they played in the affairs of the nation. These traders had charge of the posts at St. Augustine in East Florida and Pensacola in West Florida; and later in Mobile and Savannah.

---

[4] McGillivray of the Creeks, by John Walton Coughey, Pages 90, 91, 92

There was little money handled. Salt and trinkets were the important mode of exchange. These seaboard posts were exchanges or clearing houses for the small traders of the interior. In return for the privilege of operating, the traders acted as agents or envoys for the nation granting the privilege. They reported regularly to the governors of East and West Florida. As well as to the acting emperor of the Indian country. Every small trader was known, as well as all the leading Indians. Gossip was common at the posts, and traders were in position to know the pulse of the nations.

William Panton was the principal and dominating figure of the firm; a born diplomat and intellectual gentleman, who was instrumental on many occasions in calming troubled waters. He held the respect of the English, Spanish and Indians throughout his life. However, it is not of Panton that we are so deeply interested, though he had a wonderful influence over the entire Creek country; but the Leslie family was directly connected with Talladega County.

There was at Eufaulahatchie, on Talladega Creek, one James Leslie, a trader of this district. He was mentioned several times by Benjamin Hawkins, Indian Agent, in his reports to Washington. At Talladega Town, there was Alexander Leslie, about whose home a fortification was built, so that when danger was evident, the people of the community might repair to his home. To this home about 120 people did go when trouble was brewing in 1813. The building of this fortification would indicate that the home of Alexander Leslie was the most spacious in the community and at a strategic place. As previously stated, he was the son of Alexander F. Leslie, who supposedly wrote McGillivray's letters. Certainly the Leslies played a prominent part in framing the background of Talladega.

William McIntosh, of Scotch-Indian extraction, and quite a prominent man was associated with Talladega only as a trader. His father, William McIntosh, belonged to the English Army. He married a Creek Indian woman, and their son, William, Jr., born about 1775, became a great Indian chief. While his home was at Indian Springs, Ga., near where he was killed by his own people for illegally signing away their land in a Treaty of 1825, he was widely known throughout the Creek country as a trader. A branch of his trace, or trail, came up through the Sylacauga district, directly through the town of Talladega, east on Battle Street, cutting diagonally across to North St. from Johnson Ave. & Battle Sts., to about 150 feet west of the intersection with Morgan Ave. It continued out North Street and turned north at the intersection of the Socapatoy Road, turning east about 1000 feet west of Curry Station. Many old deeds carry the description of property as bordering on the McIntosh Trail.

William McIntosh was made a General in the United States Army during the Creek War, and fought in the Battles of Otossee and Horse Shoe Bend. He was one of the signers of the Treaty of Fort Jackson in 1814.

General Woodward stated that Sam Dale, the famous hero of the Canoe Fight, was a trader of the Upper Creek Towns, and that Hillabee, Nauche, and Talladega were included in his itinerary. His partner was Col. Harrison Young.[5] They were probably well known by the Talladega Indians.

George Stiggins was mentioned by both Pickett and Woodward[6] as having lived in Talladega County. He was of special interest because he had written an 81 page history of the Creeks. He was born at Nauche in 1788, the son of Joseph Stiggins, an Englishman and trader. Joseph married a Natchez Indian woman, called Nancy Grey, the widow of a white man, and a niece of Chinnabee. George Stiggins married a white woman, Miss Elizabeth Adcock. He left this county and went to Baldwin Co. where he resided for some years, but returned to Talladega after the Treaty of 1832 to receive his allotment, and must have been here for some time, since Mr. Pickett visited him while residing here. George's sister, Mrs. Susan Stiggins Hathaway was in Fort Mims during the massacre, but was one of the very few who escaped. She was befriended by Efa Tus-ta-nug-gee. George Stiggins died in 1845, and is buried in Macon Co. in a Baptist Cemetery.[7]

Chinnabee was an influential Indian of pure blood, of the Natchez Tribe of Indians which came to Talladega County in 1756 under his leadership. We feel closer to Chinnabee, (spelt Chennuby, Chennube, Chenaby, by Woodward, Jackson, and others) because of his close association with the early white settlers of the county; and particularly with the McElderry family, who purchased his reservation, and who perpetuated his memory by placing a monument over the grave of his son Selocta Chinnabee at McElderry Station. Chinnabee was friendly toward the Americans, and beloved by his own followers. He was made a Brig. General of Indian troops during the Creek War. Perhaps his hatred for the French, who had routed his people from the Mississippi, caused him to lean heavily on the Americans for protection of his people. General Woodward states that "it was his son, young Chennuby, or Selotta Fixico, who left Fort Leslie and went to General Jackson's Camp."[8] The son is better known now as Selocta. Chinnabee was a man of property and

---

[5] Thomas S. Woodward's "Reminisces", Page 83
[6] Ibid, Page 129 and Pickett's His. Of Ala., Vol. 1, Page 31
[7] From "A Historical Narrative of the genealogy, traditions and downfalls of the Ispocoga, or Creek Tribe of Indians" by Geo. Stiggins, a copy of which is in the files of the Dept. of Archives and History in Montgomery, Ala.
[8] Thomas S. Woodward's "Reminiscences", Page 77

acted as messenger for American officials on many occasions. Benjamin Hawkins speaks of him as bringing messages to Savannah. Hawkins also speaks of Chinnabee's brother, who lived at Nauche in 1796, as being quite well-to-do, having at that time 90 hogs for market.[9] While in an intoxicated condition, and racing his horse too close to a tree, Chinnabee was killed instantly soon after Talladega was settled by the whites.

Jim Fife (or Fyfe) resided on Choccolocco Creek about two miles northeast of Eastaboga. This place was one of the prominent trading points of the county in its early history. David Conner, of St. Clair County purchased a portion of his reservation and erected one of the first, if not the first, brick store houses in the county. Fife Post Office. was one of the first four post offices established in the county. It was later known as Conner's Brick Store, and still later as Simmons' Mill. Jim Fife was mentioned by Andrew Jackson as having been of great assistance to him during hostilities in 1813. Wm. L. Lewis stated in his "Reminiscences" that Jim Fife told him that he led Andrew Jackson's troops into Talladega. His great-grand-son claimed that Jim Fife was the one who donned the pig skin and saved Fort Leslie. Because of this claim, this grand-son, Jim Fife, who lived at Renfroe in 1913, was asked to represent him on a float at the hundredth anniversary of the Battle of Talladega celebration staged by Andrew Jackson Chapter of the D. A. R.

Some records state that Jim Fife was forced to leave this country with other Creeks for Oklahoma in 1836. Others claim that he is buried at the old brick store. I have never been able to prove either.

There were certainly many other influential Indians who were deserving of mention, about whom we know nothing. One Scott was mentioned as aiding Jackson's troops during the Battle of Talladega, and there was Forse-Hatchie-Fixico, Chief of Talladega, whose life is briefly reviewed in the chapter on "Mardisville."

---

[9] "The Creek Country" by Benjamin Hawkins, Page 41

The Battle of Talladega

The Battle of Talladega took place on November 9th, 1813, at 8:00 A.M., and lasted one and one-half hours. The battle was commonly believed to have been fought between William Weatherford, or "Red Eagle" as he was called as leader of the hostile Creeks, and Major General Andrew Jackson, leader of the Tennessee Volunteers and friendly Creeks.

There seems to be no proof that Weatherford was leader of the hostile Creeks, though tradition claims that he did lead them. Gen. Thomas S. Woodward, part Creek Indian, was intimately acquainted with Weatherford and he denies emphatically that he took any part what-so-ever in the conflict. However, there are intimations of Weatherford's hostile attitude toward the whites as revealed in various letters written by Alex McGillivray some years before the Creek War and we know of his leadership against Fort Mims. Certainly he was in accord with the movement to crush the friendly Indians in the upper Creek country.

William Weatherford was a son of Charles Weatherford, a white man who came to the Creek nation shortly after the American Revolution, in company with Sam Mims and George Galpin, who were traders. His mother was Sehoy(III)[1], a half-sister of Alexander McGillivray whose father was a Scotchman. He had more white blood than Indian. He was born in Baldwin County in 1765, later moved to Lowndes County where he had a large plantation; but died in the county of his birth on March 4th, 1824, and is buried there. Because of his bravery in surrendering himself after the Battle of Horse Shoe Bend, and pleading with Andrew Jackson for protection of the Indian women and children, he endeared himself to the General, and they later became great friends.

Andrew Jackson was of Irish descent, and he was everything that the name "Irish" implied. He was red-headed and hot headed, and would fight at the drop of a hat. He was born in America in 1767, two years after his parents arrived from Ireland. He took part in the Revolutionary War at the early age of 13 or 14. Both his father and mother died while he was quite young. He was left a small estate by his parents and his grand-father, which he quickly squandered. Therefore, he was delighted at the opportunity to go to the frontier and start anew. He had studied law and soon established himself in the new country. In

---

[1] Family genealogical chart submitted by H. M. Carter, III, of Montgomery, Alabama. (The book committee used I, II, III to identify the three Indian maidens named "Sehoy.")

1791 Andrew Jackson was married to Rachel Donelson Robards. She was the divorced wife of Lewis Robards, who had purposely placed some flaw in the divorce proceedings, and who publicly announced that Rachel and Andrew Jackson were not legally married two years later when Jackson was running for public office. Both Andrew and Rachel refused to consider another ceremony until 1794, when public opinion forced them to do so. This flaw in the divorce proceedings was destined to follow them all their lives. Because Andrew Jackson was a lawyer himself, the public refused to believe that he was ignorant of this discrepancy. He fought many times over the disparaging use of Rachel's name, and when he received his commission to proceed to the Mississippi Territory, he was too ill to leave for eight days, because of a fight of this kind.[2] He sent General Coffee ahead with 1500 volunteers, and he soon joined them at Ditto's Landing, near Huntsville. He carried his arm in a sling for some weeks later, and was really in no physical condition to have taken part in the Battle of Talladega at all. There were 3500 volunteers with him, including those who had gone ahead with General Coffee. Davy Crockett and Sam Houston were among the volunteers. Crockett gives a personal touch to his activities in connection with the army, outlined in his autobiography.

General Coffee was sent from Ditto's Landing to enter into battle at Tallassehatchie, an Indian village near Jacksonville, Alabama. Andrew Jackson proceeded to Fort Strother.

Few battles are fought spontaneously. Something in the past prompts the war of the present. The Revolutionary War ended about 30 years prior to 1813, and the frontier was still suffering the enmity of the British. The British were hard losers, and the Spanish felt that they justly had claims on America. They secretly conspired to get possession of certain portions of the country. With this end in view, the Spanish and English did everything they could to stir up strife among the Indians, making them feel that the Americans were mistreating them. In this way the Americans were kept busy handling the Indian population, while the Spanish and English were planning their strategy. James Madison stated in an address to the Senate in the winter of 1813 regarding their influence over the Indians that "wherever they could be turned against us, no exertions to effect it have been spared. On our south-western border, the Creek tribes, who yielding to our persevering endeavors, were gradually acquiring more civilized habits, became the victims of seduction – it was necessary to crush such a war before it would spread among contiguous tribes, and before it could favor enterprises of the enemy in that vicinity."

---

[2] The Life of Andrew Jackson by Marquis James

The British are given credit for having sent Tecumseh as an emissary to this territory to stir up strife, where his father and mother had been reared. He was instrumental in making the Creeks feel it imperative that they rid the country of the white man from the Lakes to the Gulf of Mexico.

In the late summer of 1813 the horrible massacre of Fort Mims took place. There were 553 people, including soldiers who had been sent from New Orleans to protect them, in the fort. All of these people except 36 were unmercifully murdered. It was the most horrible Indian massacre the country had known, and what wonder that it stirred the nation to immediate action. The news of this horror was the urgent reason for having brought Andrew Jackson and his volunteers to this section. They were on their way to avenge this massacre when they were notified of the endangered position of the people in Leslie's Fort in the Indian Town of Talladega.

Andrew Jackson was camping at Fort Strother, which was located at Ten Islands on the west side of Coosa River in St. Clair County, and about 30 miles from Talladega. In one of his letters, Andrew Jackson spoke of one Strother as his "Topographer", having preceded him. We, therefore, assume that the fort was named for him.

When the volunteers arrived at Fort Strother they were tired and sick and hungry. They expected food along the way, but there was none. Days passed and none arrived as promised. They had only what they could find for themselves in the mountains and streams, and because of this suffering for food, there was mutiny in the camp. In the meantime the community around Talladega had received information that hostile Indians were so angered over the destruction of Tallasehatchie on November 3rd by General Coffee, that they planned to destroy every friendly Indian village if they refused to enter into battle with them. The villagers and surrounding friends repaired to Fort Leslie immediately for safety. Andrew Jackson stated that there were 160 within the fort, but later figures were fixed at 17 whites and 120 friendly Creeks. A fortification had been built around the home of Alexander Leslie, a half breed Indian. His home was on a hill on the east side of the Talladega-Sylacauga Highway, about one mile from Court Square, Andrew Jackson speaks of the fort as "Fort Lashley", and Albert J. Pickett so called it. Thomas Woodward took issue with Pickett for having called it "Lashley". He stated that it was built around the home of Alexander L. Leslie, the half-breed son of Alexander F. Leslie, a Scotch-man, who was a highly educated gentleman, and who wrote the letters of Alex. McGillivray. The family was also connected closely with the Leslie who was a member of the firm of Panton, Leslie & Co., authorized traders of the entire Indian country.

It has been suggested that because Leslie was pronounced by the foreigner "Lashley", that it was spelled phonetically by Jackson. However, Jackson was a notoriously poor speller.

People within the fort found themselves in a perilous position, with most of their leaders absent. They had hurried to the fort with only a small supply of provisions and water, so it behooved them to take a desperate chance. Tradition says that an Indian conceived the idea of donning a hog's skin, with legs dangling; that he slipped out of the fort, rooted and grunted about the sleeping Indians, and when out of reach mounted a horse and rode with all speed to Fort Strother. Jim Fife claimed that he was the young warrior, and John T. Morgan in an address to Congress, asking for an appropriation for a monument, stated that Jim Fife was the hero. However, other Indians claimed the honor. Selocta, the son of Chinnabee, has also been given credit for the feat, and perhaps justly so. General Woodward stated that "it was young Chennuby, or Selotta Fixico, who left Fort Leslie and went to Jackson's camp. The story of the hog skin over the Indian is a hoax."

Andrew Jackson simply states that a courier arrived at Fort Strother just about dark on the 7th of November, 1813, wearing a deer's tail in his hair; which had been agreed on as a sign of a friendly Indian. Either that or a white "plume" was the customary signal. Mr. Pickett states that it was a warrior from Hickory Ground Town who donned the hog skin and saved the fort. The story has thrilled children throughout the years. How such a story could have been fabricated without some foundation seems incredible, and most people are inclined to believe it.

By midnight the Volunteers were crossing the river. The cavalry and mounted riflemen crossed and recrossed the river with men on the backs of their horses until the entire army had crossed. That day, the 8th of November, they marched 24 miles and camped within 6 miles of Talladega.

As Jackson was leaving Fort Strother, Chinnabee and Leslie, two of his loyal Indian couriers, arrived with a message from General White stating that he would not join him at Fort Strother as Jackson had requested. Jackson had depended on him to take care of the sick and wounded, and to defend the fort during his absence. In another direction had come the news that the supply house in Huntsville would be unable to furnish the food they had promised, due to the fact that food was neither available nor would the cost justify it.

At 4:00 on the morning of the 9th Jackson, worried, hungry and tired, could stand the suspense no longer. He aroused the army and in a short while they were within a mile of the enemy, where they breakfasted. This spot was identified later by Mr. Isaac Estill, the grand-father of Mr. George Cruikshank, as east of the spring that feeds a stream on property once known as the Judge Henderson place, The Lake, and later the Hicks property. This is north of what is now the Country Club golf course. Mr. Estill, a young soldier in Jackson's army, later purchased this property, and built a home, but it was burned years ago.

At 8:00 A. M. of the 9th of November, 1813, Andrew Jackson was within 80 yards of the enemy. He had instructed his men to arrange themselves in crescent shape, giving the hostile Indians a chance to come into the crescent, at which time they were to close in, encircling them. Lt. Bradley failed to follow directions, leaving a gap, through which a number of Indians escaped. There were picked up dead on the battle field 299 Indians and 15 whites. Jackson felt that every Indian was injured, while only 87 of his men were wounded, 2 of whom died later, bringing the total white dead to 17. Lt. Barton was one of the two who died later. Years later dozens of skeletons of Indians were found on the hill known as Oak Hill, where our local cemetery is located. General Coffee was not with Andrew Jackson at the Battle of Talladega, but later on, when his army passed through, they camped one night in Talladega, and he pitched camp on what is now called Coffee Street, thereby giving occasion for the name.

It seems in order to record the actual findings of persons who visited the scene of battle 20 years later, and who conferred with participants in the Battle of Talladega.

Mr. Wm. L. Lewis came to Talladega in 1833 or 1834. He was an educator, and at one time Superintendent of Education of Talladega County. He knew Jim Fife and many other Indians intimately, and acquired quite a lot of Indian history. He also learned the Muscogee language, and was considered the best versed man in Talladega on local Indian history. The following description is taken from an article appearing in Our Mountain Home of Feb. 13, 1884, entitled "Early Settlement in Talladega County. Chapters of unwritten History. Some early memories of an old pioneer" by Wm. L. Lewis:[3]

"I visited the battlefield first on the 7th day of October, 1834, being one of four young men traveling together – Humphrey Jemison, Edwin Jordan, Alfred Sanders and Wm. L. Lewis. We arrived at the battle ground about eleven o'clock A. M. Thomas Rowland kept the only house of entertainment in the place, a double cabin about 50 yards west of the spring. After an early dinner he piloted his guests over the battle ground, which at that time was covered with Indian bones of those that had perished in the fight. He conducted us east from the spring to the ridge where the D. D. & B. Institute (Ala. School for Deaf) now stands, and along the southwest through the lots owned by Mr. McAlpine and Thomas Plowman and down the hollow in the rear of the cemetery. We

---

[3] Copy of the Reminiscences at the Tall. Public Library

saw an immense number of bones. Some entire skeletons lying with not a bone missing from skull to toes, the ligaments having decayed so as to let the bones fall apart and lie in regular order – I counted 14 such skulls twenty-one years after the battle was fought in 1813. A strong party of hostile Indians had realized a party who were in a fort near Talladega, on a hill known for many years as the Givan place, and afterwards as the Stone place. The hostile party were encamped from the Hogan Spring (Isbell Spring) up towards the south part of the cemetery; and had given the other party till sunrise on a certain morning to surrender, or they would storm the fort. Eluding the sentinels, Jim Fyfe, Sam (Alex) Leslie and another noted Indian, crept from the fort and hastened to Jackson's camp and informed him of the condition of the fort. Jackson without delay crossed the river by daylight, and under the guidance of Jim Fyfe, marched directly for Talladega. His army crossed Choccolocco at Fyfe's place[4] afterwards Conner's, and crossing Cheaha at the ford where S. M. Jemison now lives,[5] encamped for the night. At 3:00 o'clock next morning the army marched for the Indian encampment, in three divisions – four hundred yards apart by a trail way leading in a direct course from the camp to Talladega, six miles distant. The trail led by the McClellan Place,[6] intersecting the Macintosh Trace near Col. Storey's place, and by the trace to P. D. Simmons place, and were halted; one division was ordered to a position on the hill on which Talladega College (for Negroes) now stands; a second to the hill where the Exchange Hotel[7] stands; a third to remain. The Cavalry were sent in the direction of Southwood, to be between the Indian encampment and their Town House, on the Terry Mill farm;[8] a company was detailed to march to the encampment to deliver a fire upon the Indians and retreat. Their fire was to signal for the divisions to close up in the direction of the firing, which, being done, brought on the fighting on the ground above mentioned. After 20 minutes of obstinate fighting, the Indians were completely routed, being met and pursued by the Cavalry, they were cut down and slain in great numbers before they could cross Talladega Creek. Fifteen whites were killed on the field and 3 died from their wounds before they crossed Choccolocco on the return, and they sent back and buried them in the same pit with the 15, on the west side of the spring branch, opposite Mr. Thomas Isbell's residence.

The Indians never remove their dead or wounded unless they can take them off with them at the time. The army returned to Fort Strother by the

---

[4] Conner's Brick Store, about 2miles above Eastaboga
[5] "Sunny Side" Farm
[6] "Idlewild" now owned by T.J. Jones
[7] Hill on which the Post office is now located, but which has been cut down ten to twelve feet.
[8] Allison's Mill

Jackson Trace, it being blazed out by pioneers for that purpose." The following description of the battle is copied from Pickett's History of Alabama, 1851.[9]

"In Lashley's fort in Talladega town, many friendly Creeks had taken refuge. The war party, in strong force, had surrounded them so effectually, that not a solitary warrior could escape from the fort unseen, to convey to the American camp intelligence of their critical condition. One night, a prominent Indian, who belonged to the Hickory Ground town, resolved to escape the lines of Jackson, by Indian stratagem. He threw over him the skin of a large hog, with the head and legs attached, and placing himself in a stooping position, went out of the fort and crawled about the camps of the hostiles, grunting and apparently rooting, until he slowly got beyond the reach of their arrows. Then, discarding his swinish mantle, he fled with the speed of lightning to Jackson, who resolved immediately to relieve these people. The commander-in-chief, leaving a small guard to protect his camp and sick, put his troops in motion at the hour of midnight, and forded the Coosa, here six hundred yards wide with a rocky, uneven bottom. Each horseman carried behind him a footman, until the whole army was over. Late that evening he encamped within six miles of Talladega. At four o'clock the next morning, Jackson surrounded the enemy, making a wide circuit, with twelve hundred infantry and eight hundred cavalry. The hostiles, to the number of one thousand and eighty, were concealed in a thick shrubbery that covered the margin of a small rivulet, and at eight o'clock they received a heavy fire from the advance guard under Colonel Carroll. Screaming and yelling most horribly, the enemy rushed forth in the direction of General Robert's brigade, a few companies of which gave way at the first fire. Jackson directed Colonel Bradley to fill the chasm with his regiment, which had not advanced in a line with the others; but that officer failing to obey the order, Colonel Dyer's reserve dismounted, and met the approaching enemy with great firmness. The retreating militia, mortified at seeing their places so promptly filled, recovered their former position, and displayed much bravery. The action now became general along the whole line, while the Indians, who had at first fought courageously, were now see flying in all directions.

But, owing to the halt of Bradley's regiment, and the cavalry under Alcorn having taken too wide a circuit, many escaped to the mountains. A general charge was made, and the wood for miles was covered with dead savages. Their loss was very great, and could not be ascertained. However, two hundred and ninety-nine bodies were counted on the main field. Fifteen Americans were killed, and eighty-five wounded. The latter were conveyed to

---

[9] Albert J. Pickett's His. of Ala., Vol. II, Pages 295-7

Fort Strother on litters made of raw hides. The fort contained one hundred and sixty friendly warriors, with their wives and children who were all to have been butchered the very morning that Jackson attacked their assailants. Never was a party of poor devils more rejoiced at being relieved. General Pillow of the infantry, Colonel Lauderdale of the cavalry, Major Boyd of the mounted riflemen, and Lieutenant Barton were wounded – the last named mortally. Colonel Bradley was arrested for disobedience of orders, but was released without trial. Jackson buried his dead, and marched back to Fort Strother as rapidly as possible, for he was out of provisions. Arriving there, he was mortified to find none at that point for him."

The dead were buried on property later purchased by The Alabama Iron Smelting Company, Ltd., and now owned by private citizens. When the Company purchased the property, the bodies were moved in 1900 by the Andrew Jackson Chapter of the D. A. R. to Oak Hill Cemetery. With the aid of the Government and the citizens of Talladega, a suitable monument in the shape of a pyramid was placed over the bodies.

On the south side of the monument it states:

Erected by The Andrew Jackson Chapter of the D. A. R. to
The immortal Jackson and his gallant soldiers
The heroes of the Battle of Talladega
Nov. 9, 1813

On the east side –
    Officers killed Nov. 9, 1813
        Lt. Larkin Bradford
        Lt. Robert Moore
        Lt. Samuel Barton
On the north side –
    Privates killed Nov. 9, 1813
        Nathan Harris
        David Gold
        Adam Matts
    Wounded, afterwards died –
        Jeremiah Gurley
        William Arnold
        John Hopkins
        James Patton
        Absalom Russell
On the west side –
    Privates killed Nov. 9. 1813

William McCall

Asa Hardin

Thomas Taylor

Henry Barnes

James Gwin

James McClish

William Fletcher

Thomas Saunders

Note that there are 19 listed as having died, whereas most reports stated 17. There is also a bronze memorial plaque in the U. S. Post office building, placed there by the Andrew Jackson Chapter of the D. A. R. during a celebration commemorating the hundredth anniversary of the Battle of Talladega in 1913, in memory of those who gave their lives to save Talladega. The plaque has been moved to the Big Spring monument on west Battle Street.

A letter from Andrew Jackson to Willie Blount, Governor of Tennessee, follows:

"Camp Strother, November 15,1813

Sir:

In my letter of the 11th I gave you a hasty account of the battle of Talladega; and of the causes which compelled me to return to this place. I now do myself the honor of transmitting you, a more detailed account of the action; together with the report of the Adjutant Genl. of the killed and wounded.

About thirty miles below here, at a place known by the name of Talladega, a hundred and sixty men of the friendly party of creeks with their women and children were forted in; more effectually to resist the efforts of the 'Red Sticks' or hostile party. Late in the evening of the 7th: one of the principal men of the fort arrived here with the information that the enemy had arrived there in great numbers that morning and would certainly destroy the fort and all within it, unless speedy relief could be obtained from this army. Urged by this representation I immediately gave orders for taking up the line of march with 1200 Infantry and 800 cavalry and mounted riflemen; leaving behind me the sick, the wounded and all the baggage, with what I considered a sufficient force to protect them, until the arrival of Genl. White who was hourly expected. At 12 o'clock at night the army was in motion and I commenced crossing the river at Ten Islands opposite our late encampment which in a few hours was effected. On the night of the 8th I encamped within six miles of the enemy and about 11 o'clock two of the friendly Indians with George Mayfield whom I had sent forward to reconnoitre the enemy returned with intelligence that they were encamped, within a quarter of a mile of the Fort, on the North side; but were unable to approach near enough to give me any accurate information of their numbers or precise situation. Within an hour afterwards old Chinnubby arrived from Turkey Town with a letter from General White, advising me of his retrograde movement occasioned by an order of Majr. Genl. Cocke. Finding that the utmost dispatch had become necessary for the protection of my rear, I immediately ordered the Adj. Genl. to prepare the line of march and at 4 o'clock we were in motion. The infantry in three columns, the Cavalry and mounted riflemen in the rear with flankers on each wing. The right wing of the Infantry was led on by Col. Bradley. The centre by Col. Pillow and the left by Col. McCrowry: the right wing of the Cavalry by Col. Alcorn I left by Colo. Cannon. The advance consisting of Capt. Deaderick's company of Artillery with muskets, Capt. Bledsoe's and Capt. Caperton's companies of Riflemen and Capt. Gordon's company of Spies, were marched 400 yards in front under the command of Col. Carrol the Inspector Genl., to bring on the engagement. At 7 o'clock having arrived within a mile of the enemy, I ordered the cavalry and mounted Riflemen to advance on the right and left of the Infantry, and enclose the enemy in a circle. Two hundred and fifty of the cavalry and mounted riflemen commanded by Lt. Colo. Dyer were placed in the rear of the centre, as a corps de reserve. Genl. Hall's Brigade occupied the right; Genl. Robert's the left; and were ordered to advance by heads of companies.

The Cavalry were ordered after having encircled the enemy by uniting the fronts of their columns and keeping their rear connected with the Infantry; to face and press inwards towards the centre, so as to leave the enemy no possibility of escape. In the execution of this order it unfortunately happened that too great a space was left between the rear of the right wing of the cavalry and Genl. Hall's Brigade through which a part of the enemy ultimately effected their retreat. At 8 o'clock the advance having arrived within 80 yards of the enemy, who were concealed in the thick shrubbery which covered the margin of a branch, received from them a heavy fire, which they returned with great intrepidity, charged and dislodged them from their position; and turned them upon the right wing of Genl. Robert's Brigade. The advance then fell back as they had been previously ordered, to the center. At the approach of the enemy three companies of the militia, having given one fire, commenced a retreat notwithstanding the exertions of Colo. McCrowry and Majr. Sevier, who are entitled to great praise for their bravery on the occasion. To fill the vacancy occasioned by this retreat, I immediately ordered up Colo. Bradley's Regt. of Volunteers, but finding the advance of the enemy, too rapid to admit of their arrival in time, I was compelled to order the reserve to dismount and meet them. This order was executed with great promptitude and gallantry and the enemy in that Quarter were speedily repulsed. The Militia who had retreated seeing the spirited stand, which was making by the Reserve, immediately rallied and recovering the position which the enemy had just driven them from, poured upon them a most destructive fire. The engagement now became general; and within 15 minutes the enemy were seen flying in every direction. On the left they were met and repulsed by the mounted riflemen. On the right a part of them escaped through the opening of the right wing of the cavalry and the Infantry; and were pursued with great slaughter to the mountains, a distance of three miles. In this pursuit the brave Colos. Pillow of the Infantry and Lauderdale of the Cavalry, Majr. Boyd of the mounted Infantry, and Lieut. Barton, were wounded; the latter of whom since died. You will perceive from a draft I shall send you that had there been no departure from the original order of battle; not an Indian could have escaped; and even as the battle did terminate, I believe that no impartial man can say that a more splendid result had in any instance attended our Arms, on land, since the commencement of the war. The force of the enemy is represented by themselves, to have been one thousand and eighty and it does not appear from their fires and the space of ground which they occupied that their number can have been less. Two hundred and ninety-nine were left dead on the ground; and no doubt many more were killed who were not found. It is believed that very few escaped without a wound. In a very few weeks if I had a sufficiency of supplies, I am thoroughly convinced, I should be able to put an end to Creek hostility.

The friendly Creeks from Talladega tell me that the enemy consider themselves already completely beaten, and state as a proof of their sense of the magnitude of the defeat they have sustained, and of their returning disposition for peace that they have since the battle, liberated several of the friendly party whom they had previously taken as prisoners.

Too much praise cannot be bestowed upon the advance, led on by Colo. Carrol for the spirited manner in which they commenced and sustained the attack, not upon the Reserve commanded by Lt. Colo. Dyer and composed of Captns. Smith's Molton's Acum's, Edward's and Hammond's companies for the gallantry with which they met and repulsed the enemy. In a word the officers of every grade, as well as the privates realized the high expectations I had formed of them and merit the gratitude of their country.

I should do injustice to my staff composed of Majrs. Read and Searcy my aids, Col Sitler and Majr. Anthony Adjt. and Asst. Adjt. Col. Carroll, Inspector Genl. Majr. Strother topographer, Mr. Cunningham my secy. and Col. Stockley D. Hays Quarter Master Genl., not to mention that they were everywhere in the midst of danger, circulating my orders – they deserve and receive my thanks.

I have the honor to be etc. . . ."[10]

The Battle of Talladega was the decisive battle of the Creek War, as stated in a letter to Major Gen. John Cocke, written by Andrew Jackson November 18th, 1813, at Camp Chennubee, I quote:

"Previous to my setting out, a flag arrived from the Hillabee's accompanied by a letter from Robert Grayson (Grierson), soliciting peace for the Indians of those towns, and offering to receive it upon any terms I might think proper to propose. They admit that the late engagement at Talladega had proved fatal to their hopes, and they believed it had brought the greater part of the nation to a proper sense of their duty."[11]

Andrew Jackson readily wrote his terms, but in the meantime Genl. White, not knowing that the Creeks had sued for peace, brought battle against them, and the war continued.

---

[10] Letter recorded in "John Hardie of Thornill" by Mr. B. Palmer Lewis

[11] Ibid

PLAN

OF THE

BATTLE OF

TALLADEGA.

Order of March.

Cavalry & Mounted Riflemen

Col. Alcorn

Col. Wm.

Infantry

Col. Bradley

Col. Pillow

Col. McCrowNey

Flankers.   *Flankers*

REFERENCES.

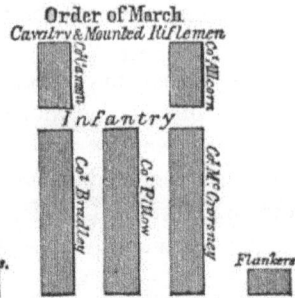

1 Jackson's position.
2 Friendly Indians.
3 Hostile Indians en-
  camped around the
  Spring.
4 Advance under Col.
  Carroll, sent forward
  to bring on the en-
  gagement.
5 Gap between the Ca-
  valry and Infantry,
  through which many
  Indians escaped.

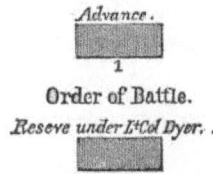

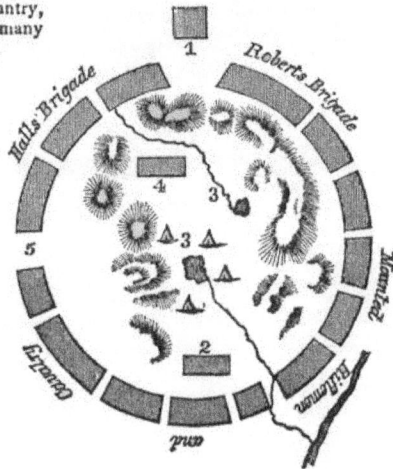

Advance.

1

Order of Battle.

Reserve under L.t Col. Dyer.

1

Tales of the Creek War

The Battle of Talladega was evidently publicized far and wide, because other parts of the country were apparently well informed regarding the particulars. While people in this part of the country were inclined to view the battle from one angle only, those in other parts of the country were more concerned about the Creeks who were defeated. There appeared in The North American Quarterly Magazine of April, 1836, a poem entitled "Aldana of Talladega." This was written by the editor, Sumner Lincoln Fairfield, of Philadelphia. It is a stirring story of Aldana, a Creek maiden, who stood upon a hillside and watched her lover, Roldan, all through the Battle of Talladega. He stood his ground for a long time, towering above a group of American soldiers; but seven swords were eventually passed through his body and he fell dead. Aldana rushed to his side and fell on Roldan's breast, weeping over her lover. There she died of a broken heart.

> A Christian soldier stood over them with heavy heart—
> "The victor turned—he could not speak;
> He wept—and there the Creeks reposed."

One wonders if this poem was not founded on the Legend of the Sleeping Giant.

There is still another poem, more beautiful and more stirring, written in 1826 by Henry Rowe Colcroft (Schoolcraft) of Pennsylvania, an eminent writer, and published in book form in 1843 by Wiley & Putnam. It is dedicated to William Cullen Bryant. The title is "Alhalla, or Lord of Talladega, a Tale of the Creek War." The scene is laid on a small island in Lake Superior. A missionary, a trader and several travelers embarked on the island at sunset one evening and found Alhalla, Lord of Talladega and King of the Hillabees, his sister and daughter, living in a cave.

About a camp fire conversation is continued throughout the night.

Alhalla drifts into reminiscences of his old home in Talladega, a small portion of which follows:

> "Hear my words : - Thrice twenty snows
> Have bleach'd and chill'd these frontless brows,
> And sun and frost, and wind and rain
> Prevail'd alternate o'er the plain,
> As moons revolved – since erst with joy

I roved a careless hunter boy,
Full free from sorrow, care and pain,
On Talladega's sunny plain,
And every year with fresh delight
Gleamed on my fond enraptured sight,
And youth fled fast, and manhood came,
But manhood found me still the same.
I swept the woods with bended bow;
I sail'd the streams with net and line
And captive schools were often mine;
I marched against the Western foe,
I sung my war-song, danced my round,
Spurning with manly tread the ground;
I met my peers in wood and glen,
And knew no want, and fear'd no men,
But look'd, and spoke, and felt, and thought,
As one that lack'd and dreaded naught;
And all was glorious - all was gay,
A happy, bright, transcendent day."

He reviews the Battles of Tallasehatchie, Talladega and others, and
adds:

"But I had oft seen danger near,
And knew not that base feeling - fear!
I roused my warriors from the rest
That with short, fitful dreams they prest
And armed for fight, and strife and pain,
Stood firm in Talladega's plain,
Oh, Talladega! Thou art still
My native wood, my native hill!
There knew I first my father's voice,
And felt my infant mind rejoice,
And all those sweet endearments start,
That nature winds about the heart,
And home, and love, and bliss and fame,
That cluster round a parent's name.
And there I hoped to live and die,
In nature's sweet simplicity;
Unmov'd with arts, or cares, or strife,
That mingle in the white man's life;

Nor knew I whence th' intruder came;
Nor car'd, nor wish'd, nor sought to be
Else than I was – a Hillabee.
And still I hoped, when nature threw
Around my brows the silver hue,
And fainting limbs proclaimed the close
Of earthly cares and earthly woes,
To lay me down with sober care,
And slumber with my fathers there.
Ah! Land of all my heart holds dear,
Thy graves are desolate and sear –
The echoes of thy winding shore
Shall charm my listening ears no more –
The winds that whistle o'er thy plain
Repeat a sad and hollow strain,
And all thy haunts are fill'd with moans
And whitened by my nation's bones."

He again reviews the horrors of the battle, and continues:

"And when the night closed on that plain,
To veil the dying and the slain,
Few, out of all my gallant band,
Had 'scaped the mark of ball or brand;
And death, of brave Muscogee men,
Had numbered fourteen score and ten."

"The sun went down that fatal night
Not as it wont, in glory bright,
But veil'd in clouds of sombre trace,
Prophetic of my falling race.
I stood upon the rising ground,
As darkness flung her mantle round,
And head the last, departing din,
Of horse and footmen, gathering in,
With clank of steel, and sharp hallo,
As from the onset they withdrew,
Far winding down the distant hill,
Faint, and more faint, then all was still,
Save crackling tread, or groan severe,
Of hapless comrade, weltering near;

For all that wide, extended wood,
Was strewed with carnage, death and blood. –
I stood as petrified, with thought
Of all one fleeting day had wrought –
Of friend and foe – the brave and dead –
And those who fought, and those who fled;
And bitter were the pangs that came
That hour within my inmost frame;
For I had seen a father slain;
A father old in years and pain;
Two brothers stricken at my side
And a fond parent's dearest pride,
The child hope shone most brightly on,
My loved, my first-born, only son!
In grief absorbed and musing high,
And yet no tear escaped my eye –
No sigh my bosom heaved – no moan
Bespoke my heart's forsaken tone;
But sealed in woe, within that word,
Unmoved as storm-beat rock I stood."

He states that throughout his years of wanderings and in his cave, he has had many visions of the past, and continues:

"But why repeat the bitter tale?
I saw each manly effort fail;
We fought as if against a spell,
And failed when Tuscaloosa fell.
The poor Muscogee race may say,
They yet may see a happier day;
That happier day I ne'er shall see,
I deem none happy if not free;
And with the war – so fates conspire –
Went out the brave Muscogee fire –
I, scorning on that soil to be
No longer honor'd, lov'd or free!
Resolved to leave those sunny strands,
For distant woods and strangers' lands,
And bending far, still onward hied,
By vale and torrent, rock and tide,
With purpose high, and aim severe,

To close a life of suff'ring here.
Here in my house, which nature made
Without the white man's skill or aid.
A few short years shall close my eyes,
And leave my bones in Northern skies,
And not a trace be left to show
Alhalla's fate – Alhalla's woe."

As he finished his soliloquy, unconscious of the others present, he looked up to see approaching the lover of his daughter, who, too, had been wandering, in search of the group, ever since the Creek War. Alhalla sought him for days after the battle, but decided that he was dead, since he had heard nothing about him. The reunion brought about happier reflections, and the scene ended.

The Creeks Surrender
1814

After the Battle of Talladega General Jackson returned to Fort Strother, where he remained a week. He then went up to Fort Chinnabee; He returned to Fort Strother and remained there for some days, after which time he resumed his trip south, blazing the trail throughout Talladega County. A road still follows this trail and is called the "Jackson Trace" road. Some years ago the Sylacauga and Talladega chapters of the Daughters of the American Revolution marked this Trace down to Fort Williams. Jackson continued further south in the state, and on his return was attacked at Enitachopco. The enemy was repelled and Jackson moved in the southern part of the county where he built Fort Williams. The fort was located below Fayetteville, and near Talladega Springs, at the mouth of Cedar Creek where it enters Coosa River. The exact spot was inundated some years ago by back waters of the river, caused by the erection of Mitchell Dam. From that point Jackson entered into preparations to attack the fortifications at Horseshoe Bend on the Tallapoosa River, which the Creeks considered impregnable.

The Battle of Horseshoe Bend took place on March 27th, 1814. 557 Indian bodies were counted on the battle field after the battle, and it was believed that at least 250 Indians were killed in the river. Jackson lost 54 soldiers and friendly Indians fighting with him. There were around 156 of Jackson's men wounded, most of whom were taken to Fort Williams for treatment. A number of them died and were buried there. Some were left to recuperate after Jackson moved the army. An imposing monument was erected near old Fort Williams some years ago by the Fort Williams Memorial Association bearing the following inscription:

To the Memory of General Jackson and his

Tennessee Volunteers

While camped here, 1814, fought the Battle of Horse Shoe Bend

and discharged his Volunteers

Sometime later the Government placed marble markers in memory of each of the 80 soldiers who were buried there:—

Joseph Kathcart	Jacob Crumley, Sr.	Isom O'Neal
Able Rice	Joseph Marshall	Joseph Beeler
William Moiers	Peter Masoner	Riley Panky
John French	Caleb Horton	Allen Duncan
Joseph Homes	Richard Hill	John Austin
David Fields	Samuel McConka	Joshua Laton
Nicholas Alstadt	Spencer Rogers	Jacob Sharper
Moses Thompson	Wm. Payne	George Watson
David Rankin	Moses Freeman	Samuel Abbott
John Leeper	Robert Yates	Robert Miller
Able Dockrey	Thomas Ford	Paris Tracy
George Hellums	Stephen Pankey	Henry Sawry
Jacob Yount	Jeffry Reffew	John Jones
James Boaz	Alfred Sims	James Ellis
William Miltonberger	Briant Smith	Elijah Bright
Nicholas Gibbs	Edward King	William Pursell
Robert Glasco	Elias Waddle	David M. Cants
Reuben Hutchinson	William P. Harden	Thomas Dawson
Sawyer Smiley	Archibald Nail	James McCoy
Joseph Robertson	Enoch Rector	James Hamilton
Andrew Cahoon	Thomas Ritchey	Thomas Hamblen
Gale Cox	John Usher	Phillips Bell
Jacob Bruner	William Cloud	Solomon Bray
George Gross	Rowling Rice	Johnston Summers
Thomas J. Johnson	Spencer Hill	William Magill
William Bunch	Willis Pickets	Everett Stubbs
John Huffman	George Brooks	

The Battle of Horse Shoe Bend between the volunteers under the leadership of Andrew Jackson, and the Creeks under the leadership of the powerful Menawa, was the finishing stroke of the Creek War. The outcome was a surrender of the Creeks, concluded with the Treaty of Fort Jackson on August 9th, 1814, at Fort Jackson, located on the site of Fort Toulouse, in Elmore County.

This treaty of the Muscogees ceded that portion of their country lying west of the Coosa River. The Treaty was signed by "Tus-te-nug-gee Thluc-co" (Big Warrior), as Speaker of the Upper Creeks, and by 31 miccos and chiefs over the nation. Among them were six, who were of this district. Esho-Loc-Tee from Nauche (perhaps Selocta); Stin-Thel-Lis-Haujo, Abecoochee; John O'Kelly (trader), Coosa; Es-Po-Ko-Ke Haujo, Wewoka, Alexander Grayson (white man) Hillabee; Che-Ha-Haw Tus-Tus-Nug-Gee, Chehahaw.

The land ceded included not only all lands owned by the Creeks west of the Coosa River, but also a small portion of land on the east side of the river, including two miles in the vicinity of Fort Williams. The territory east of the river was described in part as follows:

"Beginning at a point on the eastern bank of Coosa River where the south boundary line of the Cherokee nation crosses the same; running from thence down the said Coosa River with its eastern bank according to its various meanders to a point one mile above the mouth of Cedar Creek, at Fort Williams, thence east two miles, thence south two miles, thence west to the eastern bank of the Coosa River, thence down the eastern bank thereof according to its various meanders to a point opposite the upper end of the great falls (called by the natives Weotumka), thence east from a true meridian line to a point due north of Okfuske."[1]

Thus a small area in the lower part of Talladega County was ceded 18 years before that of the remainder of the county.

Many of the Indians from this territory west of the Coosa moved into the country east of the river, which was still in possession of the Creeks.

The newly acquired territory became a part of Monroe County, which was established in 1815, and that lower two miles in the present Talladega County was included in it. The very next year Montgomery County was established, and this ceded Talladega Territory became a part of that county. On February 7th, 1818 Shelby County was created, and this was included in that county. That same year, on November 20th, 1818, St. Clair County was created out of a part of Shelby, and this two mile area was divided between the two counties. The first deeds recorded in Talladega County seem to have been transferred from St. Clair County. Shelby and St. Clair Counties became quickly settled with white men, many of whom came over into Talladega County when it was created in 1832.

The signing of the Treaty of 1814 crushed the power of the Creeks forever, and they found themselves bottled in a country without outlet, surrounded by foreigners. Americans were on the north, east and west, and the Spanish on the south.

---

[1] Footnote on page 34 of Brewer's "Alabama, Her History, Resources," etc. 1872

Early Trails and Roads

De Soto and other explorers found the Creek country, "not a pathless wilderness", but a country engaged in agricultural pursuits; with people living in villages in crude houses; and with well-traveled trails. "That Indian America was, in fact, a vast network of such trails, connecting not only village with village of the same tribe, but extending far off to other tribes, so that it was feasible by means of these trails to traverse the entire continent."[1]

Dr. Thomas McAdory Owen's "Roads and Highways, Historic",[2] concisely described the early trails leading through Alabama. From this article I quote his descriptions of trails through Talladega County.

"THE GREAT CHARLESTON-CHICKASAW TRAIL crossed Savannah River at Augusta, whence the trail ran to Okfuskee in the Upper Creek country. From this town it ran to Coosa, thence to Squaw Shoals on the Black Warrior," etc.[3] This trail was in use as early as 1698, and was later used by English traders.

"COOSA-FORT TOMBECHE TRAIL from Coosa Town in Talladega County, to Tuscaloosa, thence direct to Fort Tombeche."[4]

"BROKEN ARROW-COOSA RIVER PATH, from Broken Arrow – LIIKATSKA – 12 miles below Fort Mitchell on Chattahooche River, through the present Oswichee community via Fort Mitchell to Tukabatchi, thence to Coosa River, northwest and above Fort Jackson – Fort Mitchell Path up to Coosa Town."[5]

"CHICKASAHAY-LITTLE OKFUSKEE TRAIL from Chickasahay town to Natchez village in Talladega County, thence southeast to Little Okfuskee, thence to the Chattahoochee River settlement."[6]

"HIGHTOWN PATH from High Shoals on the Apalache River to High Town in the fork of the Oostenolla and Etowa Rivers, the site of the modern Rome, Ga., thence to Turkey Town in Cherokee County, to Coosa, thence to Flat Rock in the northwestern part of the State, thence to Copper Town of the Chickasaw Nation."[7] This was one of the two great trails leading into the East.

---

[1] Thomas M. Owen's History of Alabama, Vol. ii, Page 1203
[2] Ibid
[3] Ibid, Vol. II, Page 1204
[4] Ibid, Vol. II, Page 1206
[5] Ibid, Vol. II, Page 1207
[6] Ibid
[7] Ibid

"CREEK PATH – COOSA TO CUMBERLAND RIVER TRAIL. This trail, noted in history as the CREEK PATH, led from Coosa Town, but may be considered as starting from the Hickory Ground. It ran northward to the present Red Hill in Marshall County, which was founded about 1790 Brown's Village, a well known Cherokee Town. At this place the trail divided, one branch crossing the Tennessee River at Ditto's Landing, the other crossing it about two miles below Guntersville, and another crossing two or three miles above it. The Creek Path was the noted trail used by the Creeks living at Coosa and the Hickory Ground in their inroads into the Cumberland settlements in Tennessee."[8]

These well traveled paths crossed streams at strategic points. Therefore, the development of the pioneer road was an easy and natural process, with these trails as basis for the white man's early roads. It was along these paths that the pioneer built. Thus we can visualize Indians traveling single file over the hills and streams, and through the forests and valleys to his hunting ground, or to war with his enemy. We can also see him in his small canoe upon the great streams of his beloved Creek country.

Then came the white man, passing through the country, seated on the most envied of all possessions, the pony. More Indians were punished for stealing horses than for any other offense.

As the white population increased, a more commodious mode was advisable, and the Hogshead appeared with a pole through the center, to which the pony was in some way hitched. The hogshead, filled with possessions of the traveler, rolled along the trails to his destination. One can well imagine the condition upon arrival, of belongings carried in this manner.

Then came the gig, or sulky, which was a two-wheeled contraption, to which, also, was hitched a horse, and which jogged along over the mountains and streams with the pioneer's possessions.

Later came the one horse springless wagon, when the traveler had to blaze the trail wider as he traveled. Thus most of the pioneers arrived in Talladega County, and it behooved them to bestir themselves in the matter of road building, that larger wagons and carriages might bring their families and furniture to the new country.

The most important modern trail was a branch of the McIntosh Trail. This passed from Wetumpka through Talladega going east across Georgia to Augusta. The earliest shipping and trading of the pioneer was done at Wetumpka and Augusta. After the railroad was built, Selma was a trading point.

---

[8] Ibid

One of the earliest planned roadways in Talladega Co. about which we have record is that applied for in 1823, but not approved until Jan. 3, 1832. "To turnpike a road" from Fort Williams, east. The road to be 20 feet, and cleared of "stumps, grub, roots, etc." for 12 feet. Application was made for this road by Daniel Welch and others.[9]

Another road was authorized to "turnpike a road, to commence on the east bank of the Coosa River, at the mouth of Tallashatchy Creek, thence through the Creek nation to intersect the Georgia Road at or near Littleberry Clark's place." This road was to be 20 feet wide, with "14 ft. cleared of stumps, grub, roots, etc." Two gates were authorized, first to be at least five miles from Coosa River. The rates were:[10]

> A Four Wheeled Carriage.................50¢
> Two Wheeled Vehicle .... 25¢
> Man and Horse ....12½¢
> Loose, or led horse ....6¢
> Head of Neat Cattle...................... 3¢ each
> Sheep, Goats and Dogs.................1½¢

Application was made by Thomas and Samuel Smith for a ferry to be established "at the place known as Kymulgy" in 1829. The charges for a four horse team was to be $1.00 and "double in high water." Evidently Talladega Creek was much deeper in that day than now. However, it is possible that the Ferry was to be on the Coosa River near the present village of Kymulga.[11]

These roads under construction, leading from the Coosa River; the McIntosh Trail, leading from Wetumpka to Augusta; the Jackson Trace into North Alabama, which was blazed by Andrew Jackson's soldiers in 1814; the Socapatoy Trail, joining the McIntosh Trail west of Curry Station; were the best known roads within the bounds of Talladega County when the Commissioners Court turned its attention to road building in 1833.

"Be it remembered that on the second day of September, A. D., 1833, the Commissioners Court of Reviews and Roads held for the County of Talladega" etc., was an important meeting with Judge McAfee presiding, John Lawler, Jesse Hill and James Drennon, commissioners being present. They had a full day ahead. "Juries of Review', to review and mark out roads "the nearest and best way" to certain points were appointed.[12]

---

9 Alabama Acts, 1831-37, Page 80
10 Alabama Acts, 1831-37, Pages 79-80
11 Commissioners Court Record Book A, Page 20, in Dept. of Archives and History, Montgomery
12 Ibid, Page 3 through Page 9

I record these first routes with names of "Jurors," that we may place early settlers along routes where they first located.

Road 1 Reviewers: John Driskell, William Nance, Henry Creswell, J. W. Bishop and G. B. Tankersley to review a road "From Talladega Springs (Talladega) to the county line where the Old Jackson Trace crosses the same, leading to Old Ft. Strother."

This was ordered established Dec. 2, 1833 as a "Second Class Road."

Road 2 Reviewers: John Ellis, John Scott, Charles Murch, Isaac Runyan, Elijah Sparks, David Mitchell and Wm. E. Sawyer to review a road "From McAdams Ferry on by Jumpers Springs to Kelly's Springs."

This ordered established Dec. 2, 1833 as a Second Class Road.

Road 3 Reviewers: William Maherg, Patterson McRhea, John Hill, Benj. Hubbart, J. S. Calvert, E. W. Thomas and David Griffin. To review a road "From Frederick Lee's Ferry on Coosa River to Court House in said County."

This establishment deferred.

Road 4 Reviewers: Jacob Hoyt, Reece Howell, Joseph Hill, Samuel Cunningham, Thomas Rowland, Wm. Wills and M. T. Cotton. "From Robinson Ferry on Coosa River to Talladega Springs (Talladega), so as to cross Choccolocco at Hoyt's."

A new committee was appointed later and establishment deferred.

Road 5 Reviewers: Rowlin Box, James Hill, Solomon Bynum, Willis Bass, Thomas Goodwin, Benj. Smith and Benj. Easley. "From Isaac Alred's to Riddle & Walker's Store (Curry Station), thence to the Court House in Talladega County."

Road 6 Reviewers: J. B, Cleveland, Wm. McGahey, Philip Archer, John Slaton, Ansel Sawyer, Wiley Madison and Cunningham Wilson. "From the Court House in said county to intersect the Turnpike Road at or near Cleaveland's/Cleveland's Store in Talladega County." Because this became our most important highway, it is interesting to make further record regarding the "Apportioners" who were appointed to build roads over a certain portion of the road.

James Malone, Pharo Hill, and Berry Madison were appointed Apportioners to see that "the road leading from Cyllagoggee to the Court House be established and that said road be of the first grade."

Ordered by the Court that Joseph Terry be overseer of the first precinct in said road, from Talladega Battle Ground to Jumpers Spring; Walker Reynolds overseer of the second precinct from Jumpers Spring to Weoky; Robert Taylor overseer of the thud precinct from Weoky to Tallasehatchie, and James Lindsay overseer of the fourth precinct from Tallasehatchy to Cleaveland's Store, to intersect the turnpike."

Road 7 Reviewers: Jacob Freeze, Joseph Tumlo, James R. Bagwell, James Hancock, James A. Givens, John W. Moore and Andrew C. Bain. "From Barnett Clouch's Ferry on Coosa River to the seat of Justice in said County." Road ordered established Dec. 2, 1833. Third Grade.

Road 8 Reviewers: Nathan Bagley, Thomas Little, John Wills, James Prather, Harry Goodwin, John Greenwood and Andrew Criswell. "From Talladega Court House to meet the recently reviewed road from Coffeeville in Benton County to the Talladega Co. line." Ordered established Dec. 2, 1833 via Proctor's and Harmon's and of Second Grade.

Road 9 Reviewers: William Mullady, A. Price, A. C. Caldwell, J. W. Carter, Gideon Riddle, Arthur Harris and Wm. C. Walker. "From Talladega Springs (Talladega) to Judge Hearn's." Ordered established First Class Road Dec. 2,1833.

A "First Class Road", as I understand it, was to be cleared of "stumps, grub and roots, etc." for 14 feet; the Second Class, 12 ft., and perhaps the Third Class, 10 ft.

These proposed roads are outlined on Mitchell's Map of 1834, and connected with important roads in every direction. There were only a few villages listed on this early map within the bounds of the present Talladega County. On Choccolocco Creek, almost in the corner of Talladega, Benton (Calhoun) and Randolph Counties was "Hickory Level, P. O.", which was one of the earliest post offices in the county.

When Cleburne County was established in 1866, this portion of the county was embraced within the bounds of Cleburne.

"Fife P. O." was also listed on Choccolocco Creek, now known as the "Old Brick Store", near Eastaboga. Fife for years was the Post office of that end of the County.

"Kelly's Springs P. O." was also listed, which is now Curry's Station.

Other towns listed on this 1834 map, but without the P. O. Added, were Talladega, Mardisville, Suellacauga, Franklin Sulphur Springs (Talladega Springs), and Ft. Williams.

Work immediately began on these roads, but it was 1834 before they could be opened to the public, whereby carriage and wagon travel was convenient.

There were no Stage Coach routes outlined on maps as late as 1836, though Coach passage must have been possible as early as 1835. Certainly the stage coach was running as late as 1867, tri-weekly, and the ticket to Montgomery amounted to $10.00, as advertised by J. H. Sargent, Agent, in a local Talladega paper.

There was a toll bridge across Choccolocco Creek, near David Conner's house, built by Eli Rogers in 1836, with gates on each end, allowed by the Commissioner's Court, with fees of 12½c for man and horse; 5c for two wheeled vehicle; 37½c for a 2 horse wagon; 75c for a 4 horse wagon and 6½c for footman. This was a convenience for those who traveled east, and to Hickory Level Post office.[13]

On January 12, 1833, the Legislature passed an Act as follows: "That Talladega Creek, from its mouth to the mouth of Jumper's Spring Branch, and Chocklocka Creek, from its mouth to David Conner's are hereby declared public highways.

If any person or persons shall obstruct the navigation of said creeks by building mill dams, fish traps, or in any other way, such person or persons shall forfeit and pay the sum of $1,000.00."[14] Half was to go to the State and half to the person suing. However, we find that, within a year, acts were passed allowing several dams to be constructed on these creeks. In the meantime, roads had been opened and the water "highway" was no longer a necessary source of arrival at certain places of residence.

---

[13] Local Alabama Acts, Act. 108, Page 131
[14] J. W. Vandiver's History of Talladega, Chapter XII

White Settlers Prior to the Creek Treaty of 1832

It is absurd, at this late date, to attempt to locate names of those persons who settled in Talladega County while the Indians still ruled this territory. However, since a number of people have been named in various records, it is interesting to call attention to some of those who did venture into the savage wilderness.

We are told that a Spaniard by the name of Furada remained at Coosa when De Soto left – and that he was the first white man to take up residence in Alabama. Thomas Woodward stated that the first white man who ever penetrated the Creek country was James McQueen, a Scotchman, who married an Indian maiden, and settled on Tallasehatchie Creek in 1716, at what was later known as Nauche. He lived there until 1756 when a group of Natchez Indians, under the leadership of Chinnabee and a Hollander by the name of Moniac came into this country. The Tallassees then moved to the Tallapoosa River.[1]

Benjamin Hawkins mentioned in 1796 James Leslie as a trader at Eufau-lau-Hatchie, who married an Indian girl. He also stated that Indians were especially kind to white women, which would indicate that some did live in the Creek country, though I have found no other mention of white women in the country,

In 1805 a treaty was made with the Creeks granting a horse path through their country. The Creeks agreed to establish ferries, bridges and accommodation houses for the convenience of travelers, and the United States agreed to furnish them blacksmiths and strikers, which must have been white men. This treaty undoubtedly was responsible for having brought some white settlers into the Creek country, who no doubt had white wives.

In 1813 there were 17 whites who repaired to Fort Leslie when the Battle of Talladega took place. These were probably traders, blacksmiths, strikers, their wives and children, from Talladega and surrounding country. Traders almost without exception married Indian women, both for protection, and because it was considered unsafe for a white woman to live within the Indian country.

After the Creek War of 1813-14, the resulting treaty provided in Article 4 that "the United States demands an acknowledgement of the right to establish military posts and trading houses, and to open roads within the territory

---

[1] Reminiscences of the Creeks, By Thomas Woodward, appearing in a series of articles in the Montgomery Mail soon after the publishing of Albert Pickett's History of Ala. In 1851

guaranteed to the Creek Nation by the Second Article, and a right to free navigation of all waters."[2]

Fear and unrest followed the Creek War for some years, and but few white men ventured to settle in the country until the uprisings were quelled. Those who did venture to purchase land, recorded deeds in Shelby and St. Clair Counties, since these counties established in 1817 and 1818 had jurisdiction over this part of the state. Some early deed records reveal that such deeds were transferred from these counties to Talladega County. Those families about whom we have record settled on or near the Coosa River, prior to 1832.

Daniel Welch, whose wife was Mary George, was stationed at Fort Williams in 1814 after having fought in the battles of Talladega and Horseshoe Bend. He returned to the County later with his family and in 1823 settled near old Fort Williams. He stated that his wife was the first white woman who ever stood upon the soil of the county. His place of settlement was called "Welch Spring", and he lived there the remainder of his life. He had a large family, among whom were Missouri, Alabama, Louisiana and Virginia. Missouri was born in 1827, and is the first white child born on the soil of Talladega County of whom we have record. She married William Wallis, and many descendants still live in and around Fayetteville, as well as other parts of the county.[3]

In Vol. 11, page 1652 of Dr. Owen's History of Alabama and Dictionary of Biography, the biography of Thomas Jones Taylor is given, in which it states that he was born July 2, 1829, at Talladega. He was the son of Mai and Ann Johnson (McCortney) Taylor. He later moved to Madison Co. where he eventually became Probate Judge.

Mai Taylor was one of Talladega's first merchants. So Judge Taylor must have been one of the county's first-born children, and Mai Taylor must have resided here prior to the signing of the Treaty.

Benjamin C. Heaslett and wife Ellenor K. McCullough, settled in a log cabin near the Coosa River in 1830, close to the Welches. He was also one of the volunteers who fought with Andrew Jackson in the Creek War.[4] Joseph Ray, another Tennessee soldier, helped to cut the Jackson trail through Talladega County, and later settled here. He was listed among the first members of the Talladega Baptist Church before Talladega County was created.

An Act was passed by the Legislature of Alabama in 1836 "to pay claims of $10.00 to Henry S. Harrison, a Corporal; and Elijah R. Chism, Henry Warren, Wm. Farmer, Moses Hendrix, Langdon C. Pool, John Michaels and Anthony Pistole, privates in Capt. Boston's Company, who were left sick at

---

[2] U.S. Statutes at Large, Vol. 7, Art. 4, Page 121
[3] Memorial Records of Ala., Vol. II, Page 965
[4] Ibid, Vol. II, Page 962

Talladega on their return from the Creek Nation. One Hundred and Twelve Dollars and 50 Cents shall be paid Cornelius Carmack for their use." Whether all of these remained in Talladega County permanently is conjecture.[5]

The first minutes of the Talladega Baptist Church, organized six months before the county was created, lists the names of John Lawler, Drennon, Millender, Hubbart, Cross, Barny, Ray, Foster, McDaniel, Hinkle, Sawyer, Eldridge and Hudgins.

An appeal was made to the legislature before the county was established in 1832 for a "Turn-pike Road on the east side of the Coosa River", and signed by John A. Chapman, Simeon Chapman and Daniel Welch. Commissioners to examine were George Hill, Wm. Condon, Thompson Coker, Henry Gooch and Abner Hughs. We, therefore, assume that they were living at that time in that portion of the county, then a part of Shelby Co.

Another application was made for a ferry to be established "at the place known as Kymulgy", signed by Thomas and Samuel Smith, about the same time.

Thomas Rowland was undoubtedly well settled in Talladega Town in 1832, with a double log tavern on the McIntosh Trail. His hostelry seems to have been the meeting place for all the early settlers, and records show that official business affairs were first transacted at the tavern. Rowland had a daughter who married a Rathbone. She died December 25th, 1831, and her grave was one of the early graves in Oak Hill Cemetery, and is probably the reason for having permanently located the cemetery. However, Mr. Wm. L. Lewis, in his reminiscences, states that Mrs. Hugh Barclay was the first white person buried in Oak Hill Cemetery on June 1st, 1833. That part of the cemetery was the garden of Thomas Rowland, and back of the tavern which was located on the south-west corner of the present West and Battle Streets. Mr. Rathbone was one of Talladega's first merchants, if not the first, though Judge Green T. McAfee claimed to be the first merchant. The earliest death date is that of Charlotte Henderson, b. 6-15-1831, d. 9-29-1831.

Another daughter of Thomas Rowland married Dr. William Edwards, who was the first doctor to locate in the county. Dr. William Summers followed him and settled at Pond Springs (Elliott Lake).

This known group of white citizens, and certainly others of whom we have no record, were within the limits of Talladega County when it was created December 18th, 1832.

A careful study of journals, diaries and articles regarding pioneer families, indicates that the earliest homes were of log construction, with two

---

[5] Acts of Alabama, 1831-37, Page 67

large front rooms divided by an open hall-way, called "Dog-Trot" with chimneys made of sticks and mud. The more imposing houses added "lean-tos" or "shed rooms" back of the two front rooms with kitchens in the back yard. Saw mills made their appearance in 1835 and more comfortable homes were erected. Many of the farmers made their own bricks for dwellings and chimneys.

Interesting adventures and exciting experiences with the Indians are recorded in biographies of these pioneers who settled in the Creek country prior to 1832.

Creek Land Sessions

The Mississippi Territory was created out of the Georgia Colony on April 7th, 1798, and comprised the present states of Alabama and Mississippi, with the exception of a strip in the lower portion of each state, which was not ceded by the French until 1812, nor fully surrendered until 1814.

Alabama was made a Territory March 3rd, 1817, and Mississippi a State Dec. 10, 1817. Alabama was made the Twenty-second State on Dec. 14th, 1819.

While this state was created by the United States, most of it was still in rightful possession of the Indians, from whom the land was yet to be purchased. Therefore, it is well to note some of the many treaties made before the property was actually fully possessed by the United States, and the State of Alabama.

July 23, 1805 — The Chickasaws ceded territory in the bend of the Tennessee River.

Oct. 7, 1805 — The Cherokees granted a mail route from Knoxville to New Orleans.

Nov. 14, 1805 — The Creek chiefs granted a horse path through their country, and agreed to establish ferries, bridges and accommodation houses.

Nov. 16, 1805 — The Choctaws ceded 5,000,000 acres and agreed to open for settlement their country in the lower part of Mississippi and south-west Alabama.

Aug. 9, 1814 — The Creek session at Fort Jackson covering territory west of the Coosa River, including what is now Shelby and St. Clair Counties.

Sept. 14, 1816 — A Cherokee Treaty was signed, conveying an additional amount of land.

Mar. 24, 1832 — Creek Treaty at Cusseta.

Dec. 20, 1835 — Balance of the Cherokee lands.

Talladega County was created Dec. 18th, 1832, from land purchased from the Creeks at Cussetta on March 24th, 1832. Therefore, it is interesting to read the Treaty in full; and it is distressing to note that the United States Government did not meet her full obligation to the Creeks, resulting in a sad aftermath for the Creeks.

A copy of the Treaty follows:

TREATY
between
The United States of America
and the
Creek Tribe of Indians
Concluded March 24, 1832 — Ratified April 4, 1832
ANDREW JACKSON, PRESIDENT OF THE UNITED STATES OF AMERICA, To all and singular to whom these presents shall come, Greetings:

Whereas, a treaty, between the United States of America and the Creek Tribe of Indians, was made and concluded at the City of Washington, on the twenty-fourth day of March, in the year of our Lord one thousand eight hundred and thirty-two, by Lewis Cass, Commissioner on the part of the United States, and certain Chiefs of the Tribe aforesaid, on the part of said Tribe; which Treaty is in words following, to-wit:

ARTICLES OF A TREATY,

Made at the City of Washington, between Lewis Cass, thereto specially authorized by the President of the United States and the Creek tribe of Indians.

Art. 1 — The Creek tribe of Indians cede to the United States all their land, East of the Mississippi River.

Art. 2 — The United States engage to survey the said land, as soon as the same can be conveniently done, after the ratification of this treaty, and when the same is surveyed to allow ninety principal Chiefs of the Creek tribe to select one section each, and every other head of a Creek family to select one half section each, which tracts shall be reserved from sale for their use for the term of five years, unless sooner disposed of by them. A census of these persons shall be taken under the direction of the President, and the selections shall be made so as to include the improvements of each person within his selection, if the same can be so made; and if not, then all the persons belonging to the same town, entitled to selections, and who cannot make the same, so as to include their improvements, shall take them in one body in a proper form. And twenty sections shall be selected, under the direction of the President, for the orphan children of the Creeks, and divided and retained or sold for their benefit, as the President may direct. Provided however that no selections or locations under this treaty shall be made as to include the agency reserve.

Art. 3 — These tracts may be conveyed by the persons selecting the same, to any other persons for a fair consideration, in such a manner as the President may direct. The contract shall be certified by some person appointed for that purpose by the President, but shall not be valid till the President approves the same. A title shall be given by the United States on completion of the payment.

Art. 4 — At the end of five years, all the Creeks entitled to these selections, and desirous of remaining, shall receive patents therefor in fee simple, from the United States.

Art. 5 — All intruders upon the country hereby ceded shall be removed therefrom in the same manner as intruders may be removed by law from other public land until the country is surveyed, and the selections made; excepting however from this provision, those white persons who have made their own improvements, and not expelled the Creeks from theirs. Such persons may remain 'till their crops are gathered. After the country is surveyed and the selections made, this article shall not operate upon that part of it not included in such selections. But intruders shall, in the manner before described, be removed from these selections for the term of five years from the ratification of this treaty, or until the same are conveyed to white persons.

Art. 6 — Twenty-nine sections in addition to the foregoing may be located, and patents for the same shall then issue to those persons, being Creeks, to whom the same may be assigned by the Creek tribe. But whenever the grantees of these tracts possess improvements, such tracts shall be so located as to include the improvements, and as near as may be in the centre. And there shall also be granted by patent to Benjamin Marshall one section of land, to include his improvements on the Chattahoochee river, to be bounded for one mile in a direct line along the said river, and to run back for quantity. There shall also be granted to Joseph Bruner, a colored man, one half section of land, for his services as an interpreter.

Art. 7 — All the locations authorized by this treaty, with the exception of that of Benjamin Marshall shall be made in conformity with the lines of the surveys; and the Creeks relinquish all claim for improvements.

Art. 8 — An additional annuity of twelve thousand dollars shall be paid to the Creeks for the term of five years, and thereafter the said annuity shall be reduced to ten thousand dollars, and shall be paid for the term of fifteen years. All the annuities due to the Creeks shall be paid in such manner as the tribe may direct.

Art. 9 — For the purpose of paying certain debts due by the Creeks, and to relieve them in their present distressed condition, the sum of one hundred thousand dollars, shall be paid to the Creek tribe, as soon as may be after the ratification hereof, to be applied to the payment of their just debts, and then to their own relief, and to be distributed as they may direct, and which shall be in full consideration of all improvements.

Art. 10 — The sum of sixteen thousand dollars shall be allowed as a compensation to the delegation sent to this place, and for the payment of their expenses, and of the claims against them.

Art. 11 — The following claims shall be paid by the United States.

For ferries, bridges and causeways, three thousand dollars, provided that the same shall become the property of the United States.

For the payment of certain judgments obtained against the chiefs eight thousand five hundred and seventy dollars. For losses for which they suppose the United States responsible, seven thousand, seven hundred and ten dollars. For the payment of improvements under the treaty of 1826 one thousand dollars.

The three following annuities shall be paid for life:

To Tuske-hew-haw-Cusetaw two hundred dollars.

To the Blind Uche King one hundred dollars.

To Neah Micco one hundred dollars.

There shall be paid the sum of fifteen dollars, for each person who has emigrated without expense to the United States, but the whole sum allowed under this provision shall not exceed fourteen hundred dollars.

There shall be divided among the persons, who suffered in consequence of being prevented from emigrating, three thousand dollars.

The land hereby ceded shall remain as a fund from which all the foregoing payments, except those in the ninth and tenth articles, shall be paid.

Art. 12 — The United States are desirous that the Creeks should remove to the country west of the Mississippi, and join their country-men there, and for this purpose it is agreed, that as fast as the Creeks are prepared to emigrate, they shall be removed at the expense of the United States, and shall receive subsistence while upon the journey, and for one year after their arrival at their new homes. Provided, however, that this article shall not be construed so as to compel any Creek Indian to emigrate, but they shall be free to go or stay, as they please.

Art. 13 — There shall also be given to each emigrating warrior a rifle, moulds, wiper and ammunition, and to each family one blanket. Three thousand dollars, to be expended as the President may direct, shall be allowed for the term of twenty years for teaching their children. As soon as half their people emigrate, one blacksmith shall be allowed them, and another when two-thirds emigrate, together with one ton of iron and two hundred weight of steel annually for each blacksmith. These blacksmiths shall be supported for twenty years.

Art. 14 — The Creek country west of the Mississippi shall be solemnly guaranteed to the Creek Indians, nor shall any State or Territory ever have a right to pass laws for the government of such Indians, but they shall be allowed to govern themselves, so far as may be compatible with the general jurisdiction which Congress may think proper to exercise over them. And the United States will also defend them from the unjust hostilities of other Indians, and will also, as soon as the boundaries of the Creek country West of the Mississippi are ascertained, cause a patent or grant to be executed to the Creek tribe, agreeably to the third section of the act of Congress of May 2nd, 1830, entitled, "An act to provide for an exchange of lands with the Indians residing in any of the States or Territories, and for their removal West of the Mississippi."

Art. 15 — This treaty shall be obligatory on the contracting parties, as soon as the same shall be ratified by the United States.

In testimony whereof the said Lewis Cass, and the undersigned Chiefs of the said tribe, have hereunto set their hands at the City of Washington, this 24th day of March, A. D. 1832.

LEWIS. CASS	
Opothleholo	his X Mark
Tuchebatcheehadgo	his X Mark
Efiematla	his X Mark
Tuchebatchie Micco	his X Mark
Tomack Micco	his X Mark
William McGillivray	his X Mark
Benjamin Marshall	

In the presence of Samuel Bell, William R. King, John Tipton, William Wilkins, C. C. Clay, J. Speight, Samuel W. Mardis, J. C. Isacks, John Crowell, I. A.

Interpreters
Benjamin Marshall
Thomas Carr
John H. Brodnax

Now, THEREFORE, BE IT KNOWN, that I, ANDREW JACKSON, President of the United States of America, having seen and considered said Treaty, do, in pursuance of the advice and consent of the Senate, as expressed to their Resolution of the second of April, one thousand eight hundred and thirty-two, accept, ratify, and confirm the same, and every clause and article thereof.

IN TESTIMONY WHEREOF, I have caused the seal of the United States to be hereto affixed, having signed the same with my hand.

DONE at the City of Washington, this fourth day of April, in the year of our Lord one thousand eight hundred and thirty two, and of the Independence of the United States the fifty-sixth.

ANDREW JACKSON
By the President:
    EDW. LIVINGSTON,
    Secretary of State.

A census of Indians was taken immediately after the signing of the Treaty of 1832. Talladega Town included 92 families:

    181   Males
    180   Females
     11   Slaves
    372   Total

Talladega Town, as designated by the Government, was a community, or district, and not a village. Forse-hatch-ie-fixico headed the census list, although he lived more than two miles from the battle field, at Mardisville. Mrs. L. M. Taylor was perhaps correct in stating that he was the Chief of Talladega, since he does head the list, although his name does not carry the title of "Micco".

Other names are identified by Indian Deeds as having lived as far as Turner's Mill on the north, and others some miles out in different directions. As previously stated, Indians divided their districts very much as we do our counties, with a micco in the mother town, who ruled over the smaller ones in the district. We know that there was a Coosa District and an Abecooche District, and no doubt there was a Talladega District.

The census was taken by Enoch Parsons and Thomas J. Abbott in 1832, compiled pursuant to the provisions of the second article of the treaty concluded March 24, 1832.

Mardisville
First White Village

After the Creek Treaty of 1832 was ratified, and a census of Indians was taken, the first step was the selection of a certifying agent, agreeable to both the Indians and whites. The Indians were given the opportunity to express their preference and the outcome was the appointment of Leonard Tarrant by Andrew Jackson. He was at the time Judge of the Courts of Shelby Co.

Judge Tarrant's duties as agent were responsible and delicate. Standing between purchasers with their cunning, and the ignorant Indians, was a true test of his character. He was unswerving, and firmly stood for justice in this difficult task of protecting the Indian on the one side, and resisting temptations, bribes and threats on the other. It was said that in conversing with a gentleman on the subject of sales of Creek lands, and the allegations of corruption and collusion between agents and purchasers, President Jackson remarked that every agent he had commissioned had disappointed him except one, and he was a Methodist preacher. That preacher was Judge Tarrant.[1]

The next step was to survey the country. General John Coffee, who had served with Andrew Jackson during the War of 1813-14, and who married the sister of Andrew Jackson's wife, was in 1832 Alabama Surveyor of Public Lands, and it became his duty to survey the newly acquired territory. In a letter to the Government in Washington, dated Nov. 8, 1832, General Coffee stated, "The survey of the Creek land is in process, and will be completed, in all probability, in the course of this year. The precise contents are not yet known, but it may be estimated that the survey will amount to $70,000.00."[2] An appropriation had already been made, but General Coffee asked for an additional one in this letter.

A rough survey must have been completed within ten days after this letter was written, because another letter dated Nov. 29th, 1832, stated that the territory was estimated to contain 277 and fractional Townships; 165 in the Tallapoosa District, and 112 in the Coosa Land District.[3] A Township comprises 6 miles square, divided into 36 Sections of one square mile each.

Immediately after the survey of the country had been completed, the Alabama Legislature in session at Tuscaloosa, established nine counties: Barbour, Benton (Calhoun), Chambers, Coosa, Macon, Randolph, Russell, Talladega and Tallapoosa. In 1866 portions of these counties were placed into

---

[1] Garrett's Reminiscences of Public Men in Ala., Page 532
[2] American State Papers, Vol. V, Public Lands, Page 638
[3] Ibid, Page 698

new counties: Clay, Cleburne, Elmore, Bullock and Lee. Therefore, the Creek country now lies within fourteen counties.

The establishment of these first nine counties on December 18th, 1832, wiped out forever the rule of the Muscogees.

The third step to be taken was the location of land offices within the ceded territory, and Jumper's Springs was chosen in the Coosa District. Leonard Tarrant transacted all Government business in Shelby County for several months prior to moving into the newly ceded territory. Why Jumper's Springs was selected is not known. It was perhaps because the McIntosh Trail and the Creek Path traversed it, and that the Socopatoy Trail connected with the McIntosh Trail within a few miles.

Jumper's Springs was purchased from Forse-hatchie-Fixico, which being interpreted means "a heartless jumping stream (or water) bird". He was commonly known by the whites as "Jumper". At the time of locating the land office, there were five springs rising from the hillside north of the village. These flowed through the lovely woodland surrounding Jumper's Springs to Talladega Creek half a mile to the west. A one room log office was erected on a knoll above the largest spring; streets were laid off, and the axe and hammer echoed through-out the forest. The crude log room housed the records of the Coosa Land District, where Leonard Tarrant, as Certifying Agent; Joab Lawler, as Keeper of Public Funds; and Jacob Tipton Bradford, as Register, carried on the affairs of the government.

Forse-Hatchie-Fixico was said to be the Chief of Talladega. His name heads the list of residents of Talladega Town in the census of Indians taken in 1832. He was an interesting character who held the respect of the white citizens. It is recorded in the court house that he acknowledged a power of attorney to his friend Ansel Sawyer to transact all business for him, giving Mr. Sawyer full authority. He stated in this Acknowledgement that he was ignorant of the laws of the white man, and that he had often been swindled. Other Indians followed his example, and gave legal authority to certain white men to transact their business for them.

Not long after Forse-Hatchie-Fixico signed this Power of Attorney, he sickened and died. The ladies of the town made a long white shroud, and the gentlemen made a black coffin, and he was given a civil burial. No sooner were the proceedings over than a group of Indians appeared, exhumed the body, destroyed the coffin, removed the shroud, and buried him Indian fashion in the corner of his cabin in a sitting position. One of the Indians dressed in the ghostly shroud, strutted about as proud as a king in his coronation robe, to the horror of the women and the amusement of the men and boys, until it was in rags and tatters.[4]

Within a few months after the location of a land office, the name of the village was changed to that of Mardisville, in honor of Samuel W. Mardis, who was Congressman from Shelby County at the time the treaty was signed, and who was one of the witnesses to the signatures of Indians to the treaty. After he left Congress he moved to Talladega where he died in a short time and is buried in Oak Hill Cemetery.

Thousands of emigrants immediately began pouring into this country before allotments could be made to the Indians. Miccos and chiefs wrote John Gale, Governor, imploring him to protect them, but he replied that he was powerless to prevent tricks of dishonest men. However, he appealed to the United States, and Francis Scott Key, author of the "Star Spangled Banner", was sent to the capital at Tuscaloosa as pacifying agent, but little was done to stop the speculators. They were ordered out but orders were disregarded and for some months there was so much disorder and confusion that it was almost impossible to transact legitimate business.

Further information contained in this chapter regarding the town of Mardisville came from many sources, but more particularly from Mr. Sam Hancock, a native of Mardisville, and a grandson of Leonard Tarrant; and from "Aunt" Nancy Taul, a Negress, who was a slave in the home of Dr. James Hogan, who married the daughter of Leonard Tarrant. She lived to be 116 years old. Although she was blind and bedridden when I visited her on several occasions when she was 108 years old, her mind was perfectly clear about old Mardisville and her early life, which Mr. Hancock verified.

There were never any imposing homes or buildings in Mardisville. Leonard Tarrant built a very modest log house with two large rooms, and a "dog trot" between, to which he later added two "shed rooms" and a kitchen in the back yard. This home was burned some time later by white men because Judge Tarrant refused to certify their fraudulent transactions. On the same spot was built the present house which is owned by Negroes of the Harmon family. The home is on the highest knoll west of Mardisville where the Sleeping Giant can be seen towering majestically in the distance, at the foot of which Talladega Creek flows through a small valley reaching to the hill on which the home was built.

There was a tavern containing 16 rooms on the main street in Mardisville, which street was none other than the old McIntosh Trail from

---

[4] This story was told by Mrs. L.M. Taylor in her History of Talladega, and was verified by Miss Mittie McElderry, who added that the Indian who donned the shroud was Chinnabee

Wetumpka, and which was the main road through Talladega, until it was changed in the early part of the 20th century.

This road entering Mardisville from the south had a row of beautiful oak trees along the border, many of which still stand. Four of the 16 rooms of the tavern were on the second story. There were two staircases leading to the second floor; one staircase and two rooms were reserved for lady guests, and the other two rooms and staircase were reserved for gentlemen guests. Transients frequently spent the night when the stage coach, drawn by four horses, with driver and footman, found its way into the wilderness once a week, beginning about 1835. There was no such thing as a private room. Frequently ten or twelve people occupied the same room.

The sound of the bugle of the stage coach many miles away, was a signal for residents to assemble at the tavern to see the new arrivals, and to get the weekly mail. The tavern was first kept by Mrs. Lovedy Campbell Cruikshank-Estill. First husband, George Cruikshank died 1830; second husband, Isaac Estill, married 1838.

Mrs. Cruikshank-Estill is ancestress of Winford Hugh Sims (1898-1980) of Renfroe, Alabama. There were hoards of transients during the first years, which the tavern could not accommodate, and it was customary for travelers to bring their tents and to camp about the village. Frequently 65 or more were guests at the table of Mrs. Cruikshank-Estill.

Allen Killough was one of the earliest settlers. His widow married James C. Burt, and she followed Mrs. Cruikshank-Estill as keeper of the tavern. She had a beautiful garden across the street from her home, which was invariably mentioned when the subject of Mardisville was brought up. On the opposite corner from the tavern was a general merchandise store owned and operated by John Hardie and Ansel Sawyer, where for many years the post office was kept.,

There was a cake shop, or baker's shop; a wood shop, containing hoes, plows, buckets, troughs, etc.; a tailor shop, and a dry goods store located south of the tavern, owned by a Mr. Schuesbach.

Back of the tavern was the harness and repair shop of David Waugh, who also kept the post office at one time in front of his shop. This small building was still standing several years ago, as well as the home of David Waugh across the street, which was at one time occupied by a Mr. Caddy. Two large log rooms with an open hallway were still standing. Back of the house could be seen the remains of a formal garden with partially buried brick walks, bordered with Irises, varieties of Cacti, Crepe Myrtles, Cherokee Roses, Locust and Chestnut trees. Surely box woods and other shrubs must have been there many years ago. David Waugh is spoken of as late as 1868 as still a resident of Mardisville.

There were two churches – Presbyterian and Methodist. The present Negro church is on the site of the Methodist. The Presbyterian was a block west in the valley. 'Tis interesting that the bell from this old Presbyterian church was brought to the First Presbyterian Church in Talladega when Mardisville church was abandoned.

There was a boys' academy taught by Mr. Finn, and later by Mr. Jack King. There was also a girls' academy.

The Micah Taul (Sr.) home was the most imposing dwelling. It was a two story log house that was later weather boarded. It was located northeast of the Land Office, below the hill on the east of the spring, which is now the only spring flowing. According to a diary owned by the McAlpines, the old Taul home must have been the social center of the elite of the village.

The Ansel Sawyer home on the east of Mardisville still stands. It was once owned by Benjamin Smoot, and later by H. M. Burt.

The Dr. Augustine J. McAlpine home on the south-west of Mardisville still stands.

John Hardie built his home, "Thornhill" a short distance north of Mardisville, and others who transacted business in the village followed his example, of building on plantations.

In 1836 Drs. Wheeler, Osborn L. Echols, Joel W. Watkins and John Watkins were listed as resident physicians of Mardisville. Dr. Augustine J. McAlpine moved from Coosa County to Mardisville several years later, as well as Dr. J. V. Huff.[5] It would appear, therefore, that Mardisville was well supplied with doctors. This was also true of the early lawyers. W. P. Chilton, and many other prominent lawyers, first settled at Mardisville before coming to Talladega. They were no doubt awaiting the survey of the town and sale of lots, which did not occur until 1834. After the county seat was chosen, surveyed, and lots offered for sale, a majority of the residents of Mardisville built homes in Talladega and moved to this point.

There are three cemeteries at Mardisville. The family cemetery of Leonard Tarrant is west of Mardisville and is now a Negro cemetery. The graves of Judge Tarrant and his wife were unmarked until 1956, when the Andrew Jackson Chapter of the D.A.R., through the kindness of Albert Jones, placed a stone over the graves. The Taul family Cemetery is on the hill north of Mardisville. There are several monuments, among them, that to Micah Taul (Sr.), who served as a Colonel of the Wayne County Volunteers, Kentucky, in the War of 1812. His grave was marked in 1930 by his great-granddaughter,

---

[5] From an article by Dr. J. L. Stockdale, appearing in Our Mountain Home, found without date in the scrap book of Mr. J. A. Bingham

Marianne McClellan, with the official grave marker of the National Society of the United Daughters of 1812.

On the hill to the south-east is the public cemetery, which is still occasionally used by some of the pioneer families. This cemetery has many beautiful monuments and quaint epitaphs, where the wife, or husband, is spoken of as the "Consort", and virtues are lauded in rhyme.

The tavern was almost demolished in a windstorm many years ago. The stores fell into decay, or were moved away. The Taul, Hogan, and Hancock homes were burned. The land office was well preserved 65 years ago, when Mr. Abner Williams appealed to the public, through Our Mountain Home, to erect a brick building over it to protect the historic old structure; but nothing came of his plea, and it burned several years later.

The streets have long since been closed, the schools and churches abandoned and destroyed. The mineral rights on the property have been sold. Four of the five original springs have been filled from erosion, and only one is now visible.

Once the seat of justice of the entire Coosa Land District, the once thriving town of Mardisville has buried her past, and one is reminded of the Biblical admonition "let the dead bury their dead." Most Abstracts of Titles for property at, or adjoining Mardisville revert back to three Indians – Forse-hatchie-Fixico, Tree-ko-chu-ka, and Hor-tor-se.

(1) Jumper's springs
2 Old Residence of Chief Fosse-Hatche-Fixico
3 Tawl Home Formerly Fosse-Hatche-Fixico Property
4 Tawl Cemetery
5 Judge Leonard Tarrant Home
6 Tarrant Cemetery
7 McAlpine Home
8 Negro Church Formerly a Boys School
9 Smoot Home
10 Store
11 Methodist Church
12 Judge Tarrant's Land Office
13 Waugh's Store
14 Store
15 Hancock's Store
16 Capt. J.C. Burt's Home
17 J.A. Hoag's Home
18 Capt. Hancock's Home
19 J.M. Hancock's Home
20 W.P. Eddin's Home
21 Eddin's Carpenter Shop
22 Waugh Home
23 Burt's Home Formerly Smoot
24 Presbyterian School
25 Mardisville Cemetery

MARDISVILLE, ALA   BEFORE CIVIL WAR
NOT TO SCALE
ACCURACY NOT GUARANTEED BUT CLOSE
DRAWN BY: SAM L. HODGE SR. 1971

A County Is Born

As stated, Talladega County, with other counties, was created December 18, 1832. The Act creating the counties was not approved by the Legislature until Jan. 12, 1833.

This same act, which related to the entire Creek country, named Henry Carter, Hugh Barclay, James Calvert, James Drennon, John Lawler, Andrew Crawford and Jesse Upton, Commissioners of Talladega County.

Section 2 of the Act states "Commissioners shall have power to contract for and receive in behalf; and for their respective counties, by good and sufficient title, a lot of land not exceeding one hundred and sixty acres, so fixed on respectively for the seats of justice for the purpose of erecting thereon public buildings for the use of said counties respectively."

The Commissioners were given "power to erect, or superintend the erection of court houses and jails," and to sell lots of "convenient size, and sold on a credit of six and twelve months." Also, power to levy a tax on all county citizens for funds to erect court houses and jails, "not to exceed 50 percent of the State Tax." It also provided that "There shall be elections held in the aforesaid counties on the first Monday in March, (1833), at the different precincts for the election of a Clerk of the Circuit Court, Clerk of the County Court, a Sheriff, a Tax Collector and Assessor." Also "Commissioners shall locate seats of justice near the centre of the counties – not exceeding six miles of the center."[1]

Green Taliaferro McAfee, a lawyer and Representative from St. Clair County in 1832, drew up the bill establishing Talladega County,[2] and immediately moved to the new county. He was appointed Judge of the County Court of Talladega. Precincts were established at William Moore's, Joseph B. Cleveland's, David Conner's, Daniel Welch's and Thomas Rowland's.[3]

An election was called, according to Law, the first Monday in March, which was on the 4th, 1833. 300 votes were cast.[4] Granting that there were some women and children among the citizens, and a few men, who did not vote, there must have been around 1,000 white inhabitants in Talladega County in March of 1833.

The result of the election was –

---

[1] Public & General Laws of Ala. 1832-33, Page 49 – Act 69
[2] Thomas M. Owen's History of Alabama and Dictionary of Ala. Biography, Vol. IV, Page 1085
[3] Ibid, Vol. II, Page 1291
[4] History of Talladega, by Mrs. L.M. Taylor – Talladega Pub. Library

Circuit Clerk.....................J. D. Shelley
County Clerk....................Hugh G. Barclay
County Sheriff.................James H. Beavers
Tax Assessor and Collector.....Wm. Easley

Commissioners were appointed to select suitable sites to be voted on for a county seat, within 6 miles of the center of the county. H. G. Barclay, Henry McKenzie, James Lawson and James A. Givens were appointed. Three suitable sites were presented to the Legislature, and on Dec. 18th, 1833, exactly one year after the creation of Talladega County, an Act was passed providing "That the Talladega Battleground, the Ford of Talladega Creek, (or Widow Anson's place), and Mardisville, be and they are hereby designated as eligible sites to be voted for as the Seat of Justice for the County of Talladega."[5] The election took place, as ordered, on the second Monday in January, 1834. This date may be designated as the birthday of the town of Talladega.

The seat chosen was "Talladega Battleground." Early records speak of it as "Talladega Springs", "Big Spring," "Talladega Big Spring" equally as much as "Talladega Battleground" before it was later shortened to that of Talladega.

As well as I can make out of the various records in Deed Book "A" with regard to the site chosen, there were many deeds exchanged before the land could be finally legally acquired.

The Creek Treaty granted to "Joseph Bruner, a colored man", his choice of half a section, or 320 acres, of land, for having acted as interpreter. He chose that portion of the Talladega Battleground which included the Talladega Big Spring. In the meantime, speculators had purchased the property, anticipating that Talladega Battleground would be chosen county seat. Therefore, a deed is recorded made by Wm. H. Moore, Thompson Lane (or Lovin), Devereaux Q. Lane (or Lovin), David Conner, Issie Dunkin, William Walker and Henry McKenzie to the Commissioners appointed to make such transactions.

The Commissioners then deeded it to Joseph Bruner, who immediately sold it back to individuals, and to whom a deed was finally issued, which in part reads: "Whereas, by a certain deed conveyance dated the 31st day of March, 1834, the said Joseph Bruner sold and conveyed to Jesse Dulin (Duran), of the County of Talladega; William Walker, of the County of Macon; Thompson Lane, of Smithton (?); Devereaux Q. Lane, of Morgan; William H. Moore, of Madison; and David Conner, of Talladega, the South half of Section 27, in

---

[5] Local Acts of Alabama, 1833-34 No. 21, Pages 64-67

Township 18, of Range 5, E., containing 318-38/100 of an acre in the Coosa Land District of the State of Alabama, as being the section which, and the said deed of conveyance for the tract above mentioned having been approved by the President of the United States on the 24th day of April, 1834." Signed by "Andrew Jackson."

These men, and their wives, then signed individual deeds to the Commissioners. Some of them stipulated that it was a gift, others that they must receive one-sixth of the returns from the sale of their portion.

During this period of legal transactions, Judge McAfee had called sessions of the County Court to more fully set in motion legislation to carry out the stipulations of the creating Act. The first Circuit Court was held in the third Monday in March, it being the 18th, in 1833, and, as stipulated in the Act, "At the Talladega Battle Ground." The court was held in a room in Rowland's Tavern.

The first County Commissioners Court was held May 6th, 1833, "at the Talladega Battle Ground," in the same place as that of the Circuit Court. Court, however, was held in various places before the Court House was completed. For instance, on Page 39, of the County Court Minutes, there appears "To Charles Miller for the use and occupation of the Building now the Presbyterian Church, in the Town of Talladega, but at the time his property, for the holding of the April, (1835) term of Circuit Court of said County $25.00." On Page 88, "Ordered by the Court that the sum of $25.00 allowed the Trustees of the M. E. Church for the use of the same in holding Circuit Court for Spring, 1835."

Again "Ordered by the Court that the sum of $50.00 be, and is hereby allowed, James Lawson for the use of his house for holding one term of Circuit and two terms of County Court in 1836." At the first Court meeting, an appropriation of $110.25 was made to purchase record books, paper, a sand box 50c, 500 Quills @1.50 per 100; 1 doz. Ink $2.50 and Sealing Wax $1.00.

At almost every session of the Commissioners Court "Commissioners" and "Juries" were appointed to transact responsible commissions. Therefore, the records are confusing, as evidently Commissioners served without compensation, were constantly resigning and new ones appointed. It is therefore, unwise to attempt to record certain groups who were responsible for important and progressive movements.

At the meeting of the Commissioners Court on May 6, 1833,[6] the following appointments were made –

---

[6] Commissioners Court Record Book A, Dept. of Archives & History, Montgomery

Ansel Sawyer......................County Surveyor
W. M. Morriss....................County Treasurer
John Box..........................County Coroner
William Easley.................. County Census Taker

There was also approved one important Commission: that of James A. Givens, H. H. Wyche, James M. McCann and Wm. D. Lovell, Commissioners, to transact business for establishing the Town of Talladega. After appointing the necessary officers and commissioners to start the county business moving, the Commissioners turned their attention to opening roads throughout the county. In the meantime, hundreds of settlers had moved into the county, and trading with the Indians for the land allotted them by the Government was constantly in evidence. Therefore, the Court was better prepared to know now in what direction roads were most needful.

The First Financial Report

On the first Monday in March, 1834, reports were made of the first year's transactions. William W. Morriss who had been appointed County Treasurer in May of 1833, was ordered from time to time to pay for rent, supplies, etc. One wonders from whence came funds with which these items were paid. The desirable land over the county had been apportioned to-the Indians, in accordance with the Treaty, and emigrants purchased land from them. Some lands were available later at $1.25 per acre, but there were no public lands offered for sale in 1833. The Court admitted at this annual meeting that the disbursements were more than receipts.

Mr. Morriss reported the following receipts:

1833

Oct. 14	To Fine received from Clk. Circuit Court, the case State vs. J. W. Moore, Oct. Term, 1833	$10.00
Oct. 18	To Fine received from Clk. Circuit Court, the case State vs. James Yates, Oct. Term, 1833	5.00
Oct. 18	To Fine received from Clk. Circuit Court, the case state vs. John Watkins, Oct Term 1833	1.00
Dec. 19	To Cash received from Wm. Easley, Tax Collector for County Tax 1833	195.35
	Total	$ 211.35[1]

The Treasurer received a commission of 5%, $10.55, for having collected this amount.

Reports at previous meetings showed that the Treasurer had paid the following amounts:

Books, Stationery, Quills, Sand, etc..	181.00
Transportation, Board and Keep in Montgomery for Ruffin Curtis	124.62½
Thomas Rowland, Rent for court meetings.............................	10.00
W. W. Morriss for Record book...	4.50
W. W. Morriss, 5% of amount collected................................	10.55
Hugh Barclay, Clerk, Book Case, Desk and Paper Box................	13.00
To Sheriff for chains and handcuffs for Ruffin Curtis...............	5.62 ½
Already paid out	$349.30

---

[1] Commissioners Court Minutes, Book A, Page 11

At this meeting the Treasurer was ordered to pay the following salaries and expenses incurred during 1833:

To Jacob D. Shelley, Clerk of the Circuit Court......................	50.00
To James H. Beavers, County Sheriff.................................	50.00
To Hugh G. Barclay, Clerk of the County Court......................	25.00
To John F. Jones, "for furnishing a house to hold the last Circuit Court in"..	20.00
To Willis Smith "For guarding Wm. T. Porter, who was convicted for an assault with an intent to murder Giles Driver.".................	4.00
To William Blythe, for the same purpose.............................	4.00
Total	$153.00

The Sheriff's report of expenditures for guarding prisoners, and for transportation to Montgomery for board and keep, must have prompted the following recommendation: "It being suggested to this Court by the Sheriff of said county that a certain Log house, situated at the Battleground is suitable as a temporary jail, (16 feet square), that the public good as well as sound policy calls for such building. It is ordered by the Court that said house be secured as a temporary jail until further provision be made for a permanent jail."[2]

The County was one year old, and organization progressing rapidly. Lots in the county seat were soon to be offered for sale at public auction, so James Beavers was made auctioneer. Roads were under construction, and during the year two permits had been given for the erection of dams. Porter R. Vardeman and Thomas Robertson were given permission to "raise a head of water ten feet for a saw mill and grist mill on the west half of the northwest quarter of Section 14, fractional Township 22." Robert Jemison was also granted permission to "raise a head of water 9 feet on Che-Ha-Ha Creek", for a grist and saw mill, where one "Smith" already had a saw mill. Judge Vandiver thinks these were the first grist and saw mills in the county. Mr. Wm. L. Lewis says the first saw mill was located at Smith's Mill, now Turner's Mill, and some distance from town. Mrs. Taylor said that John. F. Henderson, who came to Talladega in 1835, erected the first saw mill. This latter was probably the first from which local residents could obtain lumber to build town houses, because it was located on the edge of town.

---

[2] Ibid, Book A, Page 15

Roads, saw mills, grist mills, and other necessary plants having been established, the dense forest resounded with saw and axe. As great trees were felled along the routes, log houses were built. Many planters had brought slaves with them, and they were put to work clearing roadways and building temporary houses until the saw mills could furnish lumber appropriate to building the handsome homes which later came into existence.

While these pioneers were bending every effort toward getting permanently established, the County Court turned its attention back to the Seat of Justice.

Talladega Is Born

The location of a Seat of Justice having been selected on the first Monday in January, 1834, the purchase of 160 acres having been made, to which the commissioners appointed for the purpose, had received a clear title; the site was now ready to be surveyed.

Ansel Sawyer, Surveyor, assisted by Bennett Ware, immediately went to work and in several months was prepared to submit a map to the authorized commissioners. James A. Givens, H. H. Wyche, James M. McCann and William D. Lovell were duly authorized commissioners to transact all business, and were to receive 5% on all sales as compensation. As ordered by the Legislature, an auction sale of lots was held July 12th, 1834. Many planters had already permanently settled over the county, but business and professional men had temporarily settled at Mardisville awaiting a choice of county seat and a sale of lots. The sale of city property was a great event, and brought around $30,000.00.[1] Considering the price lots bought, this was a large amount.

As an example of prices paid for lots offered for sale, Lot No. 26, sold to Peter Ragsdale, brought $144.00.[2]

Lots Nos. 144, 165 and 133 were sold to Oliver K. Freeman for a total of $380.50.[3]

Lot on the N. W. corner of Battle and Court Sts., sold to John R. Walden for $167.00.[4]

Lot No. 113, facing South St., extending back to Coffee St. between Court and Spring Sts., was sold to the Methodist Church for $100.00.[5]

Lots were set aside for a male academy and a female academy. Trustees of churches—Baptist, Methodist and Presbyterian—selected lots for buildings.

Deeds were not issued until some months later on account of the pressure of business.

The town being properly surveyed, lots marked off and sold around the Square, it became the duty of the Court of Commissioners to arrange for street construction. Not until their meeting on the first Monday in September, 1834, was it "ordered by the Court: That the streets in the bounds of the Town of

---

[1] Early History of Talladega, by Mrs. Taylor, copy on record at The Talladega Public Library.
[2] Deed Book "A", Page 25
[3] Ibid, Page 107
[4] Copy of original deed owned by the family of J. A. Bingham
[5] History of Methodism, Dr. Anson West, Page 466

Talladega as designated in the plan of said town be established as Public Roads, and that they be cut out the same width as roads of the First Grade."[6]

It was further "ordered by the Court: that Overseers be appointed" as follows:

Henry A. Rathbone.. Overseer of Battle Street
John A. Rooker..Overseer of South Street
Jacob D. Shelley... Overseer of North Street
William Driver.. Overseer of Coffee Street
Charles Miller... Overseer of East Street
James W. Talmadge... Overseer of Court Street
Abner Howard.. Overseer of Spring Street
William McLane...Overseer of West Street

Thus the eight main streets of Talladega were permanently fixed, and these eight streets are still the only cross town streets in the town of Talladega. Dozens of streets have been opened but none traverse the full length of the boundaries.

There was evidently some controversy over the name of Battle Street. In the same court proceedings of the 1st Monday in September, 1834, it was "ordered by the Court: That John Bass, Wm. Easly, Wm. Hogan, James M. McCann, Jess Tifton, Green B. Tankersly and James A. Givens be, and they are hereby appointed a jury to review and view or mark out a road from the upper corner of Moor's field the natural and best way to Talladega to intersect BROAD Street, alias BATTLE Street."[7] The names Broad and Main Street were used by many early merchants instead of that of Battle St., in the newspaper advertisements. The street was, and is, the broadest in Talladega.

It should be observed that the town of Talladega was built with the spring as center, and not the Public Square; also note that property facing North Street was the northern boundary; property facing East Street was the eastern boundary; property facing South Street was the southern boundary; and property facing West Street was the western boundary of the original town of 160 acres allotted them by the Government. Hence, the names were applied accordingly and are of historic significance.

It was the law, and custom, in 1834, for property owners along public roads to oversee and keep them in order through their property. Since the streets of Talladega were treated as public roads at the time, it must have kept

---

[6] Commissioners Court Record Book "A", Page 19
[7] Ibid

the early settlers busy building houses, getting established in business, and overseeing the building of streets.

Talladega was incorporated on January 9th, 1835.[8] An election of five councilmen was to be held, conducted by James M. McCann, James R. Bracken, Charles Miller, Francis Mitchell and James W. Talmadge. Those elected were to be known as "The Town Council of Talladega." The act incorporating the town with streets as "public roads" was revised on Dec. 8th, 1837, changing that clause with the statement "All persons residing within the corporate limits of the said town shall not be liable to work on any street or square within the limits of the town."[9]

In February of 1836 a special tax was levied on citizens for the purpose of erecting a Court House. Among the items taxed were: "a race horse 50c; Race track kept for use $10.00; every pack of playing cards sold, loaned, given away or otherwise disposed of $1.00"

Before the business lots were sold a few buildings on the McIntosh Trail, west of the Square, were clustered around the spring, about which we would be ignorant if Mrs. L. M. Taylor, daughter of Dr. Henry McKenzie, had not written her History of Talladega. She was born on Sept. 22, 1836, and claimed to be the first white child born in the Town of Talladega. She married Richard Nixon Taylor, father of Hannis Taylor, renowned writer. From her own childhood memories, and from hearsay from her father, Mrs. Taylor wrote our first "Early History of Talladega," which was published serially in Our Mountain Home around 1885.[10]

From Mrs. Taylor's sketches, information was derived regarding the locations of dwellings and business houses of the earliest settlers. Before they could build dwellings, most of the first comers pitched tents about the spring, which became the center of the new settlement. As time passed and the group enlarged they branched out along the McIntosh Trail until the town could be surveyed.

The first houses were, of necessity, of log construction, since there were no saw mills for several years after the territory was ceded.

Mrs. Taylor described the spring as "a thing of beauty with a thick grove of beautiful cedar trees surrounding it, and huge white rocks clustered in wild profusion, from which the pure clear water gushed and rushed into a broad stream filled with long moss."

Rowland's Tavern was the oldest known building, and where earliest county business transactions took place. The second tavern was erected by

---

[8] Local Acts of Ala., 1835-36, Page 99
[9] Ibid, 1837, Page 4
[10] Early His. of Talladega, by Mrs. L. M. Taylor

Larndy and Lovel on the N. E. corner of Battle and West Streets, diagonally across from Thomas Rowland's. A third tavern was built on the south side of the McIntosh Trail (Battle St.), on the corner of Spring and Battle Sts., by Abel and Upton in the spring of 1833. This was the most imposing structure in the village for several years. In 1834 it was improved with a piazza running the full length of the building, and with the first brick chimney ever built in Talladega. This building stood for half a century and was called "The Simmons House" the latter part of its existence. All three of these structures were of logs.

Taverns played quite a part in the early history of Talladega. Andrew Lawson's Tavern on the south side of Battle Street was the accepted place of meeting for years, because the post office was located there for some time, and the Lawson family became prominently associated with religious and civic affairs of the county.

Another hotel on the south side of the Square, where the store of Douglas & Hiett was burned (Goldberg & Lewis corner), a large and commodious hotel was erected by Robert Douglas, which he called the "Indian Queen Hotel," and which became quite a social center. Mrs. Taylor records in her sketches an invitation signed by 15 "managers":

The Pleasure of your Company is Respectfully Solicited
At a Ball
To be Given
At the Indian Queen Hotel
on Thursday
December 27th, 1837
Dancing to Commence at 2 o'clock P. M.

In a local newspaper, "The Patriot" dated May 6, 1840, the following interesting advertisement appeared:

Indian Queen Hotel,
R. Douglas, Prop.
Rates:
Single Meals...................... .25
Horse Feed .... .25
Man and Horse per night...... 1.00
Man and Horse per day 1.20
Board per month 9.00
Lodging per month 2.00
Horse per month 9.00

John F. Henderson, later turned his home on the N. W. corner of North and Court Sts., into a hotel, which he called "The Globe."

While Mr. Rathbone, son-in-law of Thomas Rowland, had some sort of trading post before Talladega was chosen county seat, credit is given Judge G. T. McAfee for having opened the first store house on the N. W. corner of Spring and Battle Sts. His first dwelling was erected north of his storehouse on Spring Street.

Mrs. Taylor places the first dwellings on the north of the spring as follows:

Mai Taylor on the S. E. Corner of West and North Sts. John Townsend diagonally across from Mr. Taylor, and Frank Mitchell opposite John Townsend.

Dr. Henry McKenzie, Mrs. Taylor's father, built on the N. E. corner of North and Spring Sts., and J. R. Bracken built a log cabin on the S. E. corner of North and Spring Sts. Col. Eve built a cabin east of the McKenzie home. This was probably what is now the two front rooms of the present home of Misses Louise and Minnie Belle Jacob, which are of log construction, weather-boarded. Home razed in 1965.

They apparently liked corner lots in those days, or it is possible that the streets were constructed after the erection of the cabins.

West of the spring, homes were erected by the Caruthers, McLeans, Weathers, Adams and George Plowman.

Col. Hogan and Samuel Mardis built on the south side of the spring branch some distance west.

Mr. Jordan Williams located about where Mr. T. L. Isbell later erected his home, on what is now known as the dairy farm house of the School for the Deaf.

Mr. Given purchased the Alexander Leslie place, where the settlers were forted in during the Battle of Talladega.

Mrs. Taylor does not mention cabins on either East, South or Coffee Streets, though some must have located on these streets. However, streets were not surveyed until the latter part of 1834, and most of the first settlers on these streets were residing in Mardisville until the county seat was properly mapped. Mrs. Taylor states that houses extended some distance on the McIntosh Trail, but mentions only that Dr. Knox built his home about 1835.

Pioneers, of necessity, had to settle first about the spring because of the water situation. There were no wells among the Indians.

Mrs. Taylor places the following as first merchants about the Square:

On the north side - Talmadge & Casey on the N. E. corner of Court and North Sts. W. T. Lundie and J. T. Eve about the center of the north side, and Copeland and Howard on the N. W. corner of North and East Sts.

On the East side - Rathbone & Lovel on the S. E. corner of North and East Sts. Barclay & Stennett south of them; and beyond them, Hill & Scales. At the N. E. corner of East and Battle Sts. William Hogan and Jesse Duran operated a store.

The south side of the Square was occupied by Andrew Lawson's Tavern, Thomas Cox, Rumage & Cast and Ramsey and on the S. E. Corner of Battle and Court Sts., Douglas & Hiett, which was burned in a short while, and was the first fire hazard of the town. As stated previously, "The Indian Queen Hotel" was then erected.

The west side of the Square was apparently left entirely to bar-rooms. These locations are awkwardly expressed, and some may be in error, for memory is deceiving and these locations were placed by Mrs. Taylor after she became an old woman.

The scene shifted, for in the next decade new and larger merchants replaced this first group, and handsome dwellings were erected by more permanent settlers.

While Mrs. Taylor did not mention in this group of first settlers, cabins on East and Coffee Sts., she later stated that Mr. George Miller, one of the first settlers, lived on East St. in a two room log house. His son, Judge G. K. Miller was born on Dec. 30th , 1836 in this cabin, and was the first male child born in Talladega. This is one of two cabins which were rolled together years ago, and are now a part of the Whitson home, "Whitwood", on South St.[11]

There are two other known houses of log construction still in constant use in Talladega. The two front rooms of the Jacob home; and the front rooms of Mrs. Lera J. Graham's home on Coffee St., which was built by Felix G. McConnell.

---

[11] Information from the daughter of Judge Miller – Mrs. Rosa Miller Greene

Early Marriage Records

Date Issued	To Whom	Executed
1-6-1833	Lorenzo D. Stover – Ann Drennon	1-7-1834
3-16-1833	John French – Caroline Tarrant	3-20-1836
6-24-1833	Claiborne Hill – Elizabeth H. Starling	6-24-1833
6-15-1833	Thomas Summers – Winny Adams	6-16-1833
7-22-1833	Charles D. Archer – Lucinda Ball	7-23-1833
9-3-1833	Henry Mallory – Sarah Criswell	9-3-1833
10-20-1833	Overton Hutton – Jane Irvin	10-20-1833
10-28-1833	Hensley Thomison – Narcissa Criswell	10-28-1833
4-8-1833	Elisha Dodson – Sarah Council	4-8-1833
4-8-1833	William Febrick – Mary Council	4-9-1833
6-11-1833	Robt. G. Ferguson – Harriet Forman	6-11-1833
9-6-1833	James Forman – Sarah Row	9-6-1833
9-28-1833	James H. Smith – Letty Hughes	10-3-1833
10-9-1833	Charles Williams – Nancy Watkins	10-9-1833
11-14-1833	Stervil Box – Eunice Halmark	11-14-1833
9-16-1833	Edward Frost – Elizabeth Rogers	9-16-1833
11-16-1833	Benj. B. Clary – Malissa McClellan	11-20-1833
11-20-1833	John Shealy – Betsy Wethorford	11-20-1833
11-27-1833	Eli Bynum – Maranda Pace	11-27-1833
11-29-1833	Elias Davis – Mary Rhinehart	11-29-1833
12-7-1833	Toliver Hughs – Rody Dobbins	12-15-1833
12-10-1833	Robt. Little – Sinthy Greenwood	12-11-1833
12-21-1833	Wm. Caruthers – Mary McCullough	12-27-1833
12-21-1833	Wm. Mathis, Jr. – Drucella Brown	12-21-1833
12-23-1833	Hezekiah Jackson – P. Greenwood	12-23-1833
1-11-1834	Green Holland – Mariah Louisa Bishop	1-14-1834
1-22-1834	John I. Penick – Nancy Casey	1-22-1834
2-3-1834	James F. Johns – Nancy Jones	3-6-1836
2-4-1834	David M. Hearn – Rachael Trussell	2-9-1834
2-1-1834	William Hughs – Elizabeth Dulaney	2-1-1834
2-18-1834	Thomas Pain – Esther McInness	2-18-1834
2-22-1834	James Lawson – Mary Elliott	2-23-1834
4-2-1834	Daniel C. Connor – Ann Pinkard	4-3-1834
5-3-1834	Wm. C. Crawford – Rhody Watkins	5-3-1834
11-9-1834	Peter Hare – Nancy Murry	11-9-1834

12-20-1834	Benjamin Lewis – Manerva Ward	12-23-1834
12-20-1834	Jas. MacDaniel – Grizzellar Drennon	12-23-1834
12-20-1834	Israel Barnett – Charity Lewis	12-23-1834
12-23-1834	Jery H. Hall – Elizabeth Carter	12-23-1834
12-29-1834	Dennie S. Dodd – Lidia Hill	12-29-1834
8-9-1834	Jas. A. Hogan – Virginia C. Tarrant	8-17-1834
1-9-1835	Geo. W. Jones – Mary Ann Downing	1-12-1835
1-24-1835	W. H. Malone – Parmelay McCartney	1-24-1835
2-14-1835	Henry McKenzie – Amanda Talmadge	2-19-1835
2-19-1835	Geo. Bright – Nancy McClurkin	2-27-1835
3-7-1835	Jas. A. Fowler – Mary Hays	3-8-1835
3-21-1835	John Mitchell – Asa Mitchell	3-22-1835
3-26-1835	Benj. Clarkson – Elizabeth Easley	3-26-1835
4-1-1835	James Kelly – Rebecca Smith	4-1-1835
4-3-1835	John Connor – Helen Walker	4-6-1835
4-7-1835	Realy Eustiss – Frances M. Embry	4-8-1835
5-5-1835	James Smith – Elizabeth Stephens	5-5-1835
6-3-1835	Hardy Benton – Polly Bearden	
6-5-1835	Pleasant Ray – Mary Ann Black	6-7-1835
7-9-1835	Wm. Thompson – Sarah U. F. Brown	7-9-1835
7-23-1835	Alex. W. McAlister – Sarah J. Jones	7-23-1835
7-27-1835	Jas. Hawthorne – Rachel Johnson	7-30-1835
7-31-1835	Cornelius Connor – Sally Ray	
8-8-1835	R. Garner – Betsy Call	
8-11-1835	Geo. P. Plowman – Agatha T. Scales	8-11-1835
8-31-1835	John S. Randle – Eliz. A. Gibson	9-3-1835
9-7-1835	Samuel Killough – Narcissa Harris	
9-7-1835	B. C. Heaslett, Jr. – Eleanor K. Rogers	9-10-1835
9-25-1835	Matthew Sparks – Virginia Christian	10-1-1835
9-28-1835	Joseph McClung – Janie Wilson	9-28-1835
9-29-1835	Thos. Robertson –Epson Vardiman	10-2-1835
10-5-1835	Wm. R. Moon – Elizabeth Casey	10-7-1835
10-7-1835	Butler Harrell – Eliza Burk	10-8-1835
12-12-1835	James Hoyle – Sally Norman	
10-14-1835	H. W. Harper – Juliann Pearce	10-14-1835
10-5-1835	Wm. D. Hughs – Martha Kelly	10-5-1835
10-22-1835	John J. Stephenson – I. Abercrombie	
10-22-1835	Felix McConnell – Eliz. J. Hogan	
10-30-1835	Alex. P. Kerr – Margaret Hubbard	10-31-1835
11-2-1835	A.W. Floyd – Lindey C. Whitenburg	11-3-1835

11-5-1835	C. R. Cross – Edna J. Armbrester	11-5-1835
11-11-1835	John F. Jones – Eliza Forman	11-15-1835
11-12-1835	Josiah B. Pinson – E. E. Carter	11-12-1835
11-24-1835	James M. Butler – Nancy Roberson	11-28-1835
12-13-1835	Thomas Terry – Elminer Forman	12-14-1835
12-21-1835	Wm. Hughs – Sephronia C. Golden	12-21-1835
12-21-1835	Wm. N. Wallis – Martha Cornelius	12-23-1835
12-26-1835	Wm. O'Neill – Lucinda Obanion	12-28-1835
12-31-1835	Wm. G. Ryan – Malinda Edwards	12-31-1835
1-4-1836	Richard N. Brazier – Mahala C. Stewart	1-7-1836
1-5-1836	Richard Baines – Susan Trussell	1-7-1836
1-20-1836	F. M. Thomason – Elvira Hall	1-21-1836
1-20-1836	Wm. Little John – Malissa Kendrick	1-21-1836
1-23-1836	Lewis Neighbours – Jane A. Black	1-28-1836
2-8-1836	Obediah Cocran – Charlotte Ford	2-10-1836
3-5-1836	Wm. Sims – Frances Chile	
3-4-1836	Will Kidd – H. Eliza Tarrant	3-9-1836
3-4-1836	M. K. Ryan – Nancy Cottingham	3-4-1836
3-7-1836	Joel F. Cash – Sarah Rogers	3-7-1836
2-18-1836	Reuben Carpenter – Ellen Kendrick	
3-9-1836	Alexander Hill – Sintha Bush	
3-15-1836	Moses A. Lee – Eliz. Ann Russell	3-17-1836
3-25-1836	Wm. N. Kennedy – Margaret Irvin	3-27-1836
3-29-1836	Christopher McClure – Nancy Scales	3-29-1836
3-30-1836	Joel Jones – Ellen Mahan	3-31-1836
3-31-1836	Samuel F. Swan – Harriet Eason	3-31-1836
4-7-1836	Moses Toliver – Charity Roads	
4-9-1836	George Thomas – Rebecca Orr	4-16-1836
4-11-1836	Sylvanus Walker – Luvicy Vardiman	4-14-1836
5-25-1836	Wm. L. Wallis – Lucinda L. Ward	5-27-1836
6-7-1836	John H. Townsend – Elizabeth Shelley	6-7-1836
6-16-1836	James Trussell – Nancy Barnes	7-6-1836
7-8-1836	James M. McGough – Nancy Childress	7-8-1836
7-12-1836	R. R. Rogers – Susan Watters	
7-27-1836	Carol Lea – Elizabeth Scisson	
8-5-1836	James Yates – Sally Moore	8-7-1836
8-10-1836	Chas. Clabaugh – Eliz. J. Lawler	8-10-1836
8-13-1836	Jeremiah Skelton – Anny Asby	8-14-1836
8-13-1836	Madison Fuller – Mary Forman	8-14-1836
8-17-1836	John Henderson – Essie Thomason	

8-23-1836	John Roberson – Permelia Allison	8-23-1836
8-26-1836	Wm. Easley – Emily Ellington	9-7-1836
8-24-1836	John Scisson – Susan Mitchell	8-24-1836
9-2-1836	James Forman – Priscilla Fuller	9-3-1836
9-7-1836	A.L. Hanna – Sarah N. Nichols	9-9-1836
9-14-1836	Geo. W. Kennedy – Mariah Thompson	9-14-1836
9-15-1836	L. M. Hall – Lucinda Gaskill	
9-28-1836	John W. Hill – Martha Gooden	
9-28-1836	Elisha Autry – Elizabeth Connor	10-2-1836
10-5-1836	Seth L. Randall – Mary L. Watkins	10-5-1836
10-5-1836	John V. Compton – Janes Johnson	10-5-1836
10-11-1836	Robert M. Lawler – Nancy Bosian	10-12-1836
10-12-1836	Timothy W. Foster – Mary Rogers	10-13-1836
11-2-1836	A.B. Criswell – Nancy Wright	
11-2-1836	John E. Deshazo – Rachel Johnson	11-10-1836
11-15-1836	Henry B. Carbow – Troupe Bulridge	11-16-1836
11-10-1836	Benj. L. West – Rebecca Jones	11-30-1836
11-10-1836	Shadrick D. Drennon – Manerva Hill	11-10-1836
11-23-1836	John P. Shaw – Nancy Bullard	
11-25-1836	David Conner – Thersa Brannon	11-27-1836
12-17-1836	J. W. Stovall – Angeline Earnest	12-18-1836
12-20-1836	Bailes Brasher – Nancy Brasher	
12-20-1836	Lewis S. Burton – Margaret Tailor	
12-24-1836	John Hinkle – Louisa Sawyer	12-25-1836
1-2-1837	Joseph D. Wilson – Judah Knight	1-3-1837
1-10-1837	William Scott – Nancy Townsend	1-10-1837
1-13-1837	Barnett Ragsdale – Margaret Smith	1-14-1837
1-18-1837	John H. Morrison – Elizabeth Savery	1-18-1837
1-19-1837	Elijah Bynum – Elizabeth Martin	1-26-1837
1-23-1837	Martin H. McHenry – Marg. M. Moore	1-25-1837
1-19-1837	William Payner – Elizabeth Mahan	1-19-1837
1-2-1837	Floyd Goodgame – Hulda Fulton	1-3-1837
2-4-1837	Samuel Clark – Jane Metcalf	2-5-1837
3-25-1837	Edward A. Givens – Sarah Sanders	3-25-1837
2-14-1837	Lewis Harrison – Sarah Thomason	2-16-1837
5-1-1837	Robert Hampson – Catherine Rutland	5-2-1837
4-8-1837	J. L. Higgins – Louisa Reynolds	4-13-1837
5-16-1837	Cornelius Price – Mary Noris	5-18-1837
6-20-1837	Reece Martin – Malinda Hammon	6-22-1837

The Trail of Tears

The Creek Treaty of 1832 clearly stated in Art. 12 "the United States are desirous that the Creeks should remove to the country west of the Mississippi. . . . This article shall not be construed so as to compel any Creek Indian to emigrate, but they shall be free to go or stay, as they please."

This treaty was no doubt made with a majority of the Creek chiefs; however, many of the Creek Indians were not in accord with the agreement. Wm. McIntosh had signed a treaty at Indian Springs, Ga., Feb 12th, 1825, ceding Upper Creek territory illegally, with fatal results. He was ruthlessly murdered by the Creek Indians. Therefore, there was still discord among the Indians themselves on the one side, and trouble between the whites and Indians on the other.

The Treaty stated in Art. 5, "all intruders upon the country hereby ceded shall be removed therefrom in the same manner as intruders may be removed by law." Many whites had rushed into the country without authority, and fraudulent trading began. The State made appeals to them, without avail, and referred the problem to the U. S. Government, but their appeal to these whites also failed and the fraudulent trading continued. Money meant to the Indian only one thing—the coveted articles of the white man; so the money came back to the white man. Land, stream and woodland was the natural possession of the Indian, and hunting for game was his free privilege. Little did he dream that when he sold his reservation, all his hunting and fishing rights were relinquished, and he was homeless. Being dispossessed of his money and property, hunger, want and suffering took place and they became wanderers. Therefore, of necessity, begging and pilfering followed. They began to realize their helpless situation, and were a menace to the whites.

The Indians had been friendly at first, but now they were remorseful and revengeful, and the whites were fearful. Because of this growing animosity, the Government found it advisable, in 1836, to remove the Indians by force to the Indian Territory west of the Mississippi. O-poth-le-ho-lo was at the time principal chief, or speaker of the councils, and proved a great friend to the Government. An Upper Creek town had revolted and the painted warriors began waylaying and murdering white travelers along the highways. Without delay Opothleholo assembled the friendly warriors and they marched against the insurgent town, captured it and delivered the prisoners into the hands of the military authorities. He next, at the request of the Governor, took his 1500 friendly warriors to Talladega and offered their services to General Jessup, who was stationed in Talladega at the time with regular troops. The united regulars and friendly Indians, all under the command of General Jessup, without delay marched to other hostile villages. Opothleholo was made a Colonel, and proved invaluable during the period of removal. The hostile Indians were so over-awed by such an imposing force that they surrendered. The trouble was quelled, and plans for their removal went forward. Starvation was facing the Creeks and they realized that a transfer to the Indian Territory was their only salvation. Their spirits were broken. They could no longer cope with the white man.[1]

The United States contracted with the Alabama Emigrating Company to remove the Indians, with an agreement that the company was to follow stipulations as outlined in the Treaty of 1832. Army officers also accompanied each group to its destination, to see that the emigrating company carried out Government regulations. However, there was constant friction between the representatives and the company. There was no stipulation as to the number of miles traveled per day, nor any provision for travel during inclement weather. Therefore, the emigrating company, which was fully responsible for transportation, food and medical care, moved as rapidly as possible in rain, sleet or snow, which proved disastrous to the extremely young, aged and sick. They averaged 12 miles per day, and one day traveled 20 miles.

One group of Indians was assembled in Talladega County under Lieut. Edward Deas to await orders to move on to the territory. This group consisted of 3490 Indians collected from Randolph, Benton (Calhoun) and Talladega Counties, including 400 or more who had been captured in Tennessee.

They were assembled in camp between McGowan's Ferry and Howell's Cove, and most of them remained a month. "Aunt" Nancy Taul, the Negress about whom I have previously spoken, and who lived to be 116 years of age, told me some years ago that "the scaredest she ever was" was when, at the age of 14, she was milking the cow and looking to the south saw in the distance a lot of dust, which always heralded travelers; then she saw a long line of dark objects which "looked just like ants" moving toward her. It didn't take her long to realize that the dark objects were Indians. She was so excited she let the cows out and ran to the house to give the alarm. The Hogan family, with whom she was living, hastily barricaded the doors and shutters and prepared for the worst. But the army of Indians passed by. She later learned that they were Creeks being assembled for removal to the Territory.

There is another interesting story, told by J. M. Douglas, which appeared in a local newspaper, about the stay of Indians in Talladega County, portions of which follow:

---

[1] Owen's History of Ala. Vol. II, Page 759

"My father moved from South Carolina in the latter part of the year 1835. I was then 6 years old. We camped the first night on the commons between the spring and Mynatt & Hillsman's tan yard. . We moved out four miles north of town in 'Howell's Cove', named for Reese Howell . . .

"An occurrence happened near the Cove in 1835 (should be 1836), that indelibly impressed my mind. Capt. Jacob Shelley raised a company to guard the Indians that were being gathered up to be sent to the territory west of the Mississippi. The camp was in the pine hills about a mile from the Cove. The Indians outnumbered Capt. Shelley and company three or four to one. There was great fear that the Indians would revolt, overpower the soldiers, and take their guns and kill and wound the people. My father belonged to Capt. Shelley's company, and mother was left without protection. Bob Scales was plowing in a field near our house. One morning when the guards were relieved, they emptied their guns, the vollies were much like a battle was on. Scales thought the Indians had taken the soldiers' guns and were murdering them. He at once loosened his pony from the plow, but left the gear on, jumped on his pony and posted to town at full speed, whipping his steed at every jump; the trace chains flying in the air; and gave the alarm. The news spread. Some of the men prepared to defend the town, others, and the women and children, gathered into the old brick building on the S. E. corner of the Square and went to barricading. The report was soon dispelled."[2]

On August 6th, 1836, 1170 of the Creeks were removed to Gunter's Landing to join other tribes, and there remained some weeks before crossing the Tennessee River. Lt Deas returned to Talladega for the remaining 2320 in September, and they continued on their journey. That fall was cold and wet. They traveled more than three months on foot, through rain and sleet and snow.

The emigrating company expected to purchase food on the way, and agents were sent ahead for the purpose of obtaining it; but the country was sparsely populated and food was not sufficiently available to feed such a vast number of people. The Government had allotted the Indians only one blanket per family. The nights were cold and damp, bon-fires were few, and the destitute and impoverished Indians suffered dreadfully.

They traveled approximately 1,000 miles over rocky mountains, muddy valleys and swamps, and turbulent streams. They were almost naked and starved, poor and sick. A pitiable lot of human beings to begin a completely new existence in a cheerless country. Many deaths occurred along the way, but the remnant arrived at Fort Gibson on December 20th, 1836, with bleeding feet

---

[2] Clipping from J. A. Bingham's Scrap Book, without date.

and broken spirits. Their troubles were not at an end. They had to experience another long period of waiting before getting their land assignments, and thus ended their journey, and a disgraceful chapter in the history of the United States. Their feelings were expressed by a group of Indians who addressed a letter to one of the Government escorts:

"You have been with us many moons — you have heard the cries of our women and children — our road has been a long one — and in it we have laid the bones of our men, women and children. When we left our homes the great General Jesup told us that we could get to our country as we wanted to. We wanted to gather our crops, and we wanted to go in peace and friendship. Did we? No! We were drove off like wolves — lost our crops — and our peoples' feet were bleeding with long marches. Tell General Jackson if the white man will let us, we will live in peace and friendship — but tell him these agents came not to treat us well, but make money and tell our people behind not to be drove off like dogs. We are men — we have women and children, and why should we come like wild horses?"[3]

---

[3] Letter found in Indian Removal, 1932, by Grant Foreman, and used by written permission of Mr. Foreman.

First Postal Service

In the present period of hurriedly written notes, and daily mail delivery at our very door, we can scarcely conceive of the inconveniences of postal delivery experienced by our forefathers.

Mail in pioneer days frequently passed from messenger to messenger, and was sometimes weeks, or even months, in transit, before reaching its destination along the frontier.

In 1753 Benjamin Franklin was made Postmaster General for the North British colonies, and served until 1774, when he was dismissed on account of his sympathy with the American colonists. During that period mail was dispensed once a week in summer, twice a month in winter, and monthly between England and America. Mail was then carried by Pony Express, through private enterprise, over the colonies. When the Revolutionary War began in 1776, there were only 28 post offices in operation in the American colonies, and 14, or half, of those were located in the state of Massachusetts.

Under the Continental Congress Benjamin Franklin was again placed at the head of the American Postal system, which operated under the Treasury Department until 1820.

In 1789 Samuel Osgood was appointed the first Postmaster General under the United States Constitution, at which time only 75 post offices were listed in the United States.

Mail was rare as late as 1812. The City of New York at that time had only four clerks in the post office, and they were so poorly paid, that a part of their compensation was lodging with the Postmaster. These conditions existed only twenty years prior to the opening of the Creek country.[1]

Mail service was not rendered to the Pacific Coast for some years after the "Gold Rush" of 1849.

While Talladega was not in such a remote location as California, it was situated in a new country without roads, and many inconveniences were suffered by the early settlers, because of the tardiness of mail. In fact, most of the earliest mail was brought into the county by private messengers, though post offices existed as early as 1833.

Postage stamps were not placed on sale in the United States until 1847. Therefore, postage was charged at the point of sending, according to number of sheets mailed, and the distance it was to travel, which, no doubt, accounted for

---

[1] Information derived from a Pamphlet entitled "A Brief History of the United States Postal Service" furnished me by the Post office Department, Information Service,

the closely written pages of the old letters. A single sheet, less than one ounce was charged at the rate of 6c, not exceeding 30 miles. The charge increased according to sheets of paper, weight and distance. The same one ounce sheet traveling over 400 miles cost 25c. These rates were in use at the time Talladega was created.

Letters were highly valued. Many were literary gems, and were passed from one member of the family to another, and eventually from generation to generation. Copy books were a part of a pupil's school equipment, and a great deal of attention was given to writing and phrasing. There were no manufactured envelopes in pioneer days. The proper folding of a letter, so that the outside would carry the address only, was taught in the school room. The letter was then sealed with heated wax, frequently stamped with a signet ring, which sometimes bore the Coat of Arms of a family.

Five post offices were in existence the first year after the county was created.[2] Others followed within a few years.

TALLADEGA POSTOFFICE "(Formerly in St. Clair County)" was established on Jan. 19th, 1833, two months before it was chosen county seat, with Hugh G. Barclay postmaster. He served until May 8, 1840. J. G. L. Huey followed Mr. Barclay, and Felix G. McConnell followed Mr. Huey.

MARDISVILLE POSTOFFICE was established as "Jumper's Springs" some time during the first part of 1833. The date is not recorded. Wm. Morriss was first postmaster, and served until Jan. 26, 1838. The name of the post office was changed to that of MARDISVILLE POSTOFFICE May 21st, 1833.

KELLY'S SPRINGS POSTOFFICE was established on August 26th, 1833, with Elijah C. Walker as postmaster. He served until March 9, 1835, when Zemri Madden succeeded him, and served until Dec. 7, 1837. This post office existed for some years after the Civil War.

HICKORY LEVEL POSTOFFICE, located in the extreme north-east corner of Talladega County, was established on October 17, 1833, with John Patterson as postmaster. He served until May 23, 1834, when John M. Neal was made postmaster. He served until August 4, 1838. In 1866 this portion of Talladega County was incorporated in Cleburne County.

FIFE POSTOFFICE, located near Eastaboga on Choccolocco Creek, was established on April 26, 1834, with David Conner as postmaster. This post office existed for many years and served the upper part of the county.

Note that early towns where there were located post offices carried the name "Postoffice", which was sometimes abbreviated to "P. O.". Such places were noted on the maps also in this manner.

---

[2] List of post offices from National Archives & Records Service Washington, D.C.

Post offices were established at –

Sylacauga............................... March 8, 1837
Fayetteville............................. March 8, 1837
Lincoln................................... Jan. 29, 1850
Eastaboga............................... Jan. 31, 1854
Childersburg............................ Feb. 2, 1855
Alpine..................................... July 22, 1858
Munford................................. Jan. 14, 1867

A post office existed in the village of Talladega before it was chosen county seat. The first record we have of Talladega postal receipts is "the amount of postage accrued for the year 1835 was $248.57." It is generally understood that the first Talladega post office was located in Lawson's Tavern, but since this was not erected until after the town was surveyed in 1834, one naturally infers that the office was either in Hugh G. Barclay's home, or in the Thomas Rowland Tavern, which was the first known building in town. ,

Pony Post mail was replaced by stage coach delivery about 1835, and was probably brought into Talladega County once a week for a short period; or until the stage coach expanded transportation service to twice a week, and eventually to three times a week.

Mail was brought in from Alpine after the railroad reached that point; and in 1859, when the railroad reached Talladega, mail came daily for six days a week. Trains were not operated on Sundays.

There was no United States post office building in Talladega until the present one was erected in 1911 and 1912. The post office was moved from location to location at the discretion of the acting postmaster. At one time is was located on the south side of the Square in Lawson's Tavern; at another time on the west side of the Square. When Cleveland was elected President, Mr. John Donahoo was made postmaster, and he moved it to the Donahoo Building, which is located on the north-east corner of North and Court Sts. and is now known as the Browne Building.

Mr. J. A. Bingham followed Mr. Donahoo as postmaster, and the office was moved to his building on the east side of East Street, N., back of Belk-Hudson's Department Store. Mr. Bingham was postmaster when the present United States Post office building was erected, and was the first postmaster to occupy the building.

In looking back over the century and considering the inconveniences of communication our ancestors experienced, we are gratified that we are privileged to live in this generation of tremendous progress in postal service. However, there are drawbacks even to progress. We no longer consider the penning and phrasing of letters an art, nor do we value them. To keep up with the speed of the era we hurriedly scribble disconnected letters our children no longer value as literary gems to be treasured for future generations to enjoy.

"Flush Times"
Depression and Recovery

Dr. Owen states that "Flush Times" is a phrase descriptive of a period of the State history, covering approximately the five years ending with 1837. The period was featured in humorous anecdotes related by Joseph G. Baldwin in "The Flush Times of Alabama and Mississippi."[1]

Joseph G. Baldwin was a prominent lawyer of Alabama. He married Miss Sidney White, daughter of Judge John White, and sister of Alexander White, pioneers of Talladega County.

The beginning of "Flush Times" was simultaneous with that of the purchase of the Creek country, when thousands of people began migrating into the state. Many of the emigrants were speculators and promoters. The governing, or land dispensing point, of the Coosa Land District being located at Mardisville, Talladega County experienced more fully than some other portions of the state, the consequential influence prompted by the usual circumstances incident to such periods of inflation.

The Flush period in Talladega County lasted several years later than 1837. Mr. Baldwin states that during this "golden Era" bank bills were as thick "as autumn leaves in Valambrosa."[2] Money was plentiful, and slaves were numerous, though expensive. A good house servant or farm laborer cost around $1,000 to $1,500, and healthy youths were worth $500 to $750. A skilled blacksmith or miller was easily worth $3,000. Large planters owned from 50 to 200 slaves at the time. Some were known to have owned more than three hundred.

During this period of prosperity home sites were selected, and handsome dwellings were begun. Many were not finished when depression followed, and a great number of the pioneer families moved into unfinished homes, which were not completed until some years later.

Eight streets were opened in Talladega, trees planted to add beauty and comfort, and by 1835 Talladega was getting into shape for a permanent existence. During the years of 1840 to 1845, the speculative merchants were moving out and the permanent merchants were moving in, who were destined to be instrumental in establishing Talladega as the trading center of several counties. Such names as Hardie, Henderson, Isbell, Huey, McMillan, Cunningham, Adams, Storey, Vandiver, Stringer, Wood, Woodward, and

---

[1] Dr. Owen's History of Alabama, Vol. I, Page 602
[2] Joseph G. Baldwin's Flush Times in Ala. & Miss., Page 1

dozens of other moneyed business men of unquestionable integrity, entered the mercantile business in Talladega during this time. Land was bringing the fabulous price of $39.00 as late as 1837,[3] but money was no consideration of the early settler. It was plentiful. The land was fertile and desirable. There were plenty of slaves to till it; and it soon paid for itself. General Woodward stated "No State that has come into the Union since the old thirteen, (which) at its early settlement equaled Alabama as to intellect or large planting interests."[4] Transients poured into Talladega on every stage coach, and by private vehicle. To take care of these people, Talladega had almost as many hotels as she did mercantile establishments. There were six within the City of Talladega, besides boarding houses: Rowland's Tavern. Lovell & Larned's Tavern. Lawson's Tavern, The Indian Queen Hotel, The Simmons Hotel and The Globe. The Globe was operated by John F. Henderson at his residence on the N. W. corner of the Square. He advertised that he was "prepared to accommodate Travellers and Drovers."[5] Drovers frequently passed through with droves of hogs, cows or horses, and it was necessary to find a corral for the animals at night. Certain laws were passed regarding drovers with regulations as to the condition of their animals.

There were other hotels dotted about over the county. One could travel only a limited number of miles per day, and country villages nearly all had a hotel in operation. Notable among these were —

The Burns Tavern, located at Old Eastaboga (and which building, still stands, apparently well preserved) was noted for the delectable food and the hospitality afforded. Over the door of the Tavern hung a sign "Rest for the Wary," and many a wary and weary stage coach passenger found comfort at the hostelry.[6]

Another one was located on the old Sylacauga road just north of the intersecting road which leads into Sycamore. It was called the "Red House." On both sides of the entrance large eagles were painted. Under one was printed "If Unmolested, PEACE", and under the other "But if Molested, WAR."[7] The proprietor was noted for his eccentricities. His tavern was well patronized, and it was one of the resting places of the stage coach travelers.

The period of prosperity brought about revelry and intemperance unbecoming to citizens of a cultured group, and must have been the cause which prompted the more serious minded to call the "Sons of Temperance" to

---

[3] J. L. M. Curry's Reminiscences of Talladega
[4] Gen. T. S. Woodward's Reminiscences, Page 81
[5] Southern Register, Sept. 1, 1838, Dept. Archives & His., Montgomery
[6] Letter from Mrs. Bettie Boswell to me, dated Nov. 29, 1927
[7] D. B. Oden's Recollections, in J. A. Bingham's Scrap Book

a public meeting "at early candle lighting at the Baptist Church on July 29th, 1840," for the purpose of organizing a "Talladega County Temperance Society."[8] The meeting was well attended and organized with prominent men over the county as members. The organization functioned for many years.

While the women turned their attention to the social life of the community, the male intelligentsia of the town turned their attention to the weightier subjects for entertainment and amusement. "The Talladega Literary Society was organized in 1838 for the purpose of discussing subjects in "Law, Theology, Morals, Medicine, Mechanics and What Not." Witty, intelligent and eloquent essays and speeches were delivered and discussed by members, among whom were: Eli Shortridge, Thomas Chilton, W. P. Chilton, H. H. Wyche, Frank L. Bowden, O. M. Roberts, Felix G. McConnell, Wm. H. Campbell, R. B. Cater, and Samuel F. Rice.[9] This was indeed a distinguished group, a great number of whom became widely known throughout the State of Alabama.

Talladega County began to sense that her prosperity was slipping in 1840. The Court House and Jail had not been completed at that time. The special tax assessed in 1835 was not sufficient to take care of expenditures, and another special tax was proposed, which brought forth public clamor, and much adverse criticism. The Democratic Watchtower of July 29th, 1840, reprimanded the public, and reminded them that the Commissioners appointed for superintending the erection of the buildings were, Robert H. Chapman, Simeon Douglas, James Lawson, James A, Given, and Felix G. McConnell, and were unquestionably above reproach. The article further stated that "it is known to the community that Jacob D. Shelley and Robert K. Hampson were the undertakers for the building of the Court House at the price of Ten Thousand Dollars, the greater part of which sum had to be raised by taxing the people. It is also known that the: Court House is nearly finished." But the Watchtower reminded the public further that the special tax amounted to only $5,872.90; that the amount had already been expended, and that further work could, of necessity, not be done until funds were available. The building was not completed until sometime in 1843 or 1844. However, the contract and bond for the building of the courthouse, Book A, pp. 417-420, required: "to make the house complete in all its parts to be finished within two years from the date hereof." Signed, "26th day of February, 1836."[10]

---

[8] Watchtower of July 27th, 1840
[9] Our Mountain Home, June 14, 1876. Article by "Memorabilia"
[10] Records in the Talladega Co. Probate Office.

In the latter part of 1842, the State deemed it advisable to close all State Banks, which had flourished in the large towns during "Flush Times". Money had been "easy", and politicians had been too eager to over borrow. The result was seriously felt when the entire state was thrown into hopeless confusion and depression. Currency exchange jumped from 20% to 30%. Cotton went as low as 4c to 7c.[11]

There was a serious reaction in Talladega County where people had been enjoying the luxuries of a land of plenty. Practically all building activities ceased. By this time Talladega had fortunately taken firm roots as an agricultural county; it was established with good roads and well traveled stage routes. Weekly newspapers were being regularly published, and Talladega was enjoying a complaisant and satisfactory existence, when this confusion and depression exploded all feeling of security. Cotton was the planters monied crop. With prices now below production, farmers, business and professional men became restless. Many turned their attention to mining industries. Some to manufacturing, and others immigrated to Mississippi, Louisiana, Texas and later to California.

Mr. Walker Reynolds, one of Talladega County's largest and most prosperous planters entered into a daring adventure, in an effort to evade the high cost of transporting cotton to Wetumpka, by floating it to the Coosa River. Mr. James Mallory records this experiment in his Journal, under date of Jan. 19, 1844. He states that Mr. Reynolds "lashed 56 bales of cotton together on Tallassehatchie. Some 30 or 40 took passage to the mouth of the creek, some 4 miles, where we got off, giving the pilot and his men a parting cheer, feeling hopeful that the enterprising experiment would succeed."[12] There had been much rain for days prior to this experiment, and the creek had a larger volume of water than usual. Even though this was true, we cannot now visualize 56 bales of cotton being floated on the Tallasehatchie Creek. Mr. Mallory records under date of Jan. 30, 1844. "Have heard from the cotton rafted by Mr. Reynolds, and it is much injured and likely to prove a failure."[13]

Cotton was selling around 5½c at the time. Not only were there crop failures on account of droughts, low prices and hard times generally, and disturbing elements, but politics was seething all over the country. Whigs and Democrats were about equally divided in Talladega County. The Whigs were bitterly opposed to secession, and the Democrats were demanding it. 1844 marked one of the greatest political upheavals in the history of the country. Henry Clay was candidate for President of the United States on the Whig ticket,

---

[11] Journal of James Mallory, Jan. 1, 1843. Journal owned by Mr. E. A. Stewart, Selma, Ala.
[12] Ibid
[13] Ibid

and James K. Polk was candidate on the Democratic ticket Issues of the day were abolition of slavery, the annexation of Texas, and the Great Oregon controversy. The Republican Party had not yet been organized.

Politics is brought into the picture because Talladega County played a prominent part in the election of 1844. At the time, Felix G. McConnell was a leading Democrat, and was serving as United States Representative in Washington. Other leading Democrats were Samuel F. Rice, Wm. McPherson, John J. Woodward, Thomas A. Walker, J. L. M. Curry, Wm. Curry, J. G. L. Huey, and Frank L. Bowden.

Felix G. McConnell had won his seat in Congress over Wm. P. Chilton, who ran on the Whig ticket. Other notable Whigs were, L. E. Parsons, James Mallory, Alexander White, M. H. Cruikshank, and Walker Reynolds.

In October of 1844 a great Henry Clay rally took place in Montgomery and citizens from all parts of the State went to Montgomery to take part in the gala festivities. An unusual feature of this event, was that the women of the State took quite a part in the celebration. They accompanied their husbands to Montgomery to honor the distinguished candidate. The Talladega County group left on October 20th, spent the first night near Sylacauga, the second near Rockford, and the third near Wetumpka.[14] They were a congenial group, and made an enjoyable holiday of the journey. During the evenings they pitched camp, and indulged in song, music and anecdotes, about a cheerful camp fire. Although it was a pleasant trip, they must have been worn travelers by the time they arrived in Montgomery on October 23rd, 1844. Some of them had traveled in carriages with servants in attendance, but others traveled by horseback or in wagons, but all of them traveled over rough roads about 25 miles per day for four days.

There were about 20,000 visitors present from all parts of Alabama. The crowd was feasted, and a banner was presented to the county having the largest number present, and with the best display. One county had a few more people present, but the Talladega County delegation won the pennant, because they "had a large cannon in the parade, cast by Mr. Moore, from Talladega, a good Whig." The pennant donated to the Talladega delegation "presented a portrait of Mr. Clay seated on a rock in the midst of the ocean, calmly holding up the Constitution in his hand, with other suitable devices on and around it."[15]

The delegation returned to Talladega on the 29th of October, highly elated over the success of the important event.

_____

[14] Ibid
[15] Ibid

In the meantime, the Democrats supporting James K. Polk, staged a County rally near Eastaboga. Dixon H. Lewis, one time Governor of Alabama, United States Senator, and a great advocate of the annexation of Texas, was orator of the occasion. Pokeberry stalks were in evidence in every direction as decorations. Mr. Lewis, an enormous man, arrived in a specially built cart, driving horses in tandem.[16]

The Democrats of Alabama did not stage so great a demonstration as the Whigs, but their candidate was elected, and James K. Polk became President of the United States.

In 1845 and 1846 the County was grieved to have many of her young men march off to the Mexican War, which was the national problem at the time.

During these years of depression, many attempts were made to supplement revenue. Some turned their attention to Wool and Cotton Carding Mills. Prior to this, most of the carding was done by slaves on individual plantations, using their own product. Among such carding mills which began operations was one at Cragdale on Talladega Creek, owned by John K. Taylor, another was operated by Arthur Bingham on Choccolocco Creek, at old McKibbon's Mill, which is now known as Priebe's Mill, in the upper part of the county. There was also such a mill operated by Messrs. Robert A. McMillan and Richie on Choccolocco, which was burned.

Messrs. Walker Reynolds, Darby and James Mallory, and also William Curry, Jr., opened up tanneries and shoe manufacturing plants. Prior to this, many large planters tanned their own leather and had shoes made on their individual plantations. The matter of shoes for 100 slaves was a major problem for the large slave holder.

1845 marked some change in trading posts for Talladega products. The first steamboat was launched above Ten Islands at Greensport, to ply from that point to Rome, Ga. A free barbecue was prepared and thousands assembled to witness the novel spectacle of launching the boat. "With flags flying and drums beating, the fastenings were cut away."[17] From that day until the railroad was built, profitable commerce was enjoyed through Coosa River transportation at that point. Greensport was for many years an important river port for Talladega County commerce, and for travelers going East. The road which intersects the present Anniston Highway, a few hundred feet beyond, or east of, Curry

---

[16] Ibid; Also Democratic Watchtower Jan. 5, 1848

[17] J. L. M. Curry's Reminiscences of Talladega

Station, and which passes Sunny Side and Willow Glen and running north, is still known as "the Greensport Road" by old residents.

An effort toward cheaper marketing of farm products was made in 1847 when the planters of Talladega County, feeling the need of co-operation, made a progressive step in organizing "The Agricultural Society" with the following charter members:[18]

Gen. Wm. McClellan, President; Col. Micah Taul, (Sr.), First Vice President. S. S. Riddle, Second Vice President

W. S. Carpenter	Rev. James Stockdale	Thomas L. Pope
J. A. Brown	Walker Reynolds	James Welch
Hon. A. Bowie	Tames Donley	John W. Rice
L. E. Parsons	John Mallory	James Mallory
Dr. Heacock	Robert Jemison	

In 1848 Mr. James Isbell launched into the banking business in connection with his mercantile establishment, and by 1850 it was separated as a profitable venture, and has operated throughout the years.

The year 1848 marked another restless period in the history of the County. Mr. Mallory records "The entire country is in a state of great excitement from the discovery of gold in California. It is said a hand can get from $20.00 to $50.00 per day."[19] Hard times continued, and this discovery brought about another "spirit of immigration", and Talladega experienced the loss of still more citizens. As late as 1852 there was still a perfect mania on the subject of immigration. Some land in the county sold as low as $8.50 per acre.

1853 brought more prosperous conditions, and full recovery was experienced by 1854. Mr. Mallory records on July 13, 1854:[20] "The country seems to be in a great state of prosperity. All the products of the earth (but sugar) are bringing fair prices. Population is increasing. New territories are opening (Kansas and Nebraska), and great efforts are being made to secure the most convenient and profitable locations. Should wise council prevail, and the people remain virtuous, a great nation we must become." On Dec. 24, 1855, he records "Never was there so much plenty in the nation before."[21] Full recovery at last.

---

[18] Data in copies of Democratic Watchtower, and Mr. Reynold's diary
[19] Journal of Mr. James Mallory
[20] Ibid
[21] Ibid

While prosperity to individuals appeared fully restored, a report of the Mayor and Aldermen of the City of Talladega, certainly did not indicate that the financial affairs of the City were in a profitable monetary condition.[22] A report published in the April 3rd, 1856 issue of the Alabama Reporter, indicates that there was little money for use in City operation or improvement. The report covered receipts from October, 1854 to October, 1855:

To Amt. of Taxes, 1854.................................	$358.36
To Amt. of Taxes, 1855.................................	$2083.28
To Amt. of Fines.......................................	$127.00
To Amt. Collected of Circus............................	$25.00
To Amt. Collected of Street Magicians.................	$2.00
	$2595.64
Amt. Received of P. A. Stamps, Former Treasurer....	$74.86
	$2670.50

The Mayor and Aldermen received no salaries, but policemen had to be paid, and there were a few gas lights scattered about the Square. With minor expenses incurred, there was no fund left for upkeep of streets and other city property. Therefore, the town experienced many dormant years, while individual farmers and business men experienced prosperity.

Prosperity was an enjoyable innovation to those who had suffered through the great depression, but a cloud soon shadowed this exultation. Silver tongued orators were disturbing the peace by demanding secession, because Congress was gaining support for the abolition of slaves. Heated discussions took place on every street corner, farmers would stop their vehicles as they passed on the public roads, to discuss the subject. Neighbors, brothers and friends had heated arguments; each with his own view on the subject which threatened their prosperity and peace. Unrest prevailed everywhere, until secession was evident. Then every man, woman and child withheld their energy.

---

[22] Issue of paper in Talladega Public Library

Early Newspapers([1])

It is a fascinating pastime to scan the newspapers of our forefathers. These newspapers are frequently well preserved because the paper used a hundred years ago was superior to that which is used today. Newspapers were essential in those days to the economical and political life of a community. Certainly more so than at this period of telephone, telegraph, radio and television. At that time newspapers were the only mode of transmitting news, with the exception of the "grape vine", which was surprisingly rapid. This whispered "grape vine" news was sometimes shockingly accurate, and often came through the kitchen door.

The first newspapers of Talladega were printed on patented or syndicated sheets. National and international news was already printed before delivery to the local publisher, and the sheets were delivered in time for small town editors to add local news and advertisements before distribution weekly to subscribers.

It was customary, and ethical, for professional men to purchase space annually for their respective professional cards. Doctors, dentists and lawyers are easily traced because of this custom. Most of them patronized the papers regularly, listing their professions and addresses.

Early newspapers usually stated, after the price of subscription, "No paper discontinued (except at the option of the proprietors) until arrearages are paid." They, no doubt, found this unprofitable, for the custom was dropped before the middle of the Nineteenth Century.

Editors were more concerned with national political questions than with local ones. After all, national political matters of that period were subjects which were framing the life of the pioneers, and it behooved them to be deeply concerned in them. Speeches and articles written by the leading politicians of the day were published in full; frequently filling many columns of each issue. Editorials were usually on political issues of the day.

Features of each issue of weekly papers were obituaries. They were sometimes more than a column in length, and a full genealogy and history of the deceased, who was lauded and sainted, and carried to Heaven on "flowery

---

[1] Information contained in this article was found in various newspapers located in the Talladega Public Library; The Dept. of Archives and History, Montgomery; J. A. Bingham's collection; "Reminiscences of J. L. M Curry" and in "Memorial Records of Alabama", Vol. II, Pages 198 through 207.

beds of ease". Genealogies are easily traced through these old obituaries, but accurate characteristics are not so easily established because of this custom of praising the departed. Notices of marriages and deaths were published free of charge, but "Obituaries and Tributes of Respect" were charged "as other Advertisements."

Other features of old papers, especially those published during the latter part of the Nineteenth Century, were news items from communities scattered over the county. Apparently they vied with each other in descriptive headings. News items appeared in length under such names as: Cass Beat News, Cove Cullings, Coleta Chips, Cyprian Items, Eureka Bubbles, Echoes from Chandlers Springs, Hatchett Creek Gossips, Lincoln Locals, Ragan Ripples, Renfroe Puckerings, Silver Run Notes, Sycamore Sayings, Sylacauga Incidents, Sunny Side Dots, and many other descriptive headings of community news appeared from every part of the county.

The first newspaper published in Talladega County was "The Southern Register and Talladega Advertiser." This was established on August 7th, 1834, before the Town of Talladega had been incorporated. However, the first issue was not published until July 17th, 1835. The subscription price was "$2.00 in advance. $3.00 if not paid within three month."

John F. Henderson, whose home and office was located on the N. W. Corner of Court and North Streets, was publisher. His son, Samuel, a Baptist minister, was printer's "Devil", and Robert H. Chapman, a lawyer and Presbyterian minister, was editor. Mr. Chapman later became a Confederate General. The name of this first newspaper was soon shortened to "The Southern Register."

In 1837 Thomas L. Barnett, father of Frank Willis Barnett, who was connected with the Birmingham News for some years, was editor. On August 4th, 1838, Samuel Henderson, "in a neatly written Salutatory, assumed editorship." He retained it but one week, as on August 11th, 1838, Samuel F. Rice, bought the establishment and became editor. He was "'brimfull of Democracy and States Rights.'"[2] While Mr. Rice was editor, he was elected to the State Legislature, and was enabled to secure the contract for the State printing for his paper. Mr. Rice eventually became Chief Justice of the Supreme Court of Alabama.

In 1839 the Southern Register went back in the hands of John F. Henderson, and the name was changed to that of "The Patriot", edited by Samuel Henderson.

---

[2] From "Reminiscences of J. L. M. Curry" found in the collection of J. A. Bingham, and at the Talladega Public Library

In 1842 the name was changed to "The Southerner", and was edited for a short period by Lewis E. Parsons, who later became Provisional Governor of Ala. On Mr. Parsons' retirement, B. H. Spyker became editor, and in January, 1843, the paper was discontinued.

In the meantime, a rival paper had appeared. In February of 1840, The Democratic Watchtower was founded by a company consisting of G. T. McAfee, Wm. Curry, D. A. Griffin, J. G. L. Huey, and Samuel F. Rice. Mr. Rice was editor. In 1842 John J. Woodward became editor. He was followed by J. G. L. Huey in 1844. The paper was established as a democratic Journal with a slogan "Principles - Not Men." Sometime later the name was changed to that of "Talladega Watchtower."

In the latter part of 1844 the paper was purchased by James H. Joiner & Company, and in 1846 Mr. Joiner became sole editor until May, 1852, when Gen. R. W. Higgins appeared as co-editor.

Robert H. Chapman, who was previously connected with the Southern Register purchased an interest in the Watchtower in 1854, at which time he became co-editor and manager. His brother, William S. Chapman succeeded him in 1856, but soon resigned and Mr. Joiner again had full control of the paper until after the War Between the States, when in 1869 his son, G. A. Joiner, became a partner. The Joiners were owners and editors until 1873, with the exception of a few years, when Dr. Wm. Taylor was on the editorial staff, and Col. J. A. Woodward was part owner. The Joiners were prolific writers and journalists, as well as beloved citizens.

The Alabama Reporter was established May 6th, 1843, preparatory to the great presidential contest of 1844. The type, press and other equipment of the Southern Register were purchased, and the Alabama Reporter made its appearance under the editorial supervision of B. H. Spyker and Daniel Sayre. In 1850 the paper passed into the hands of M. G. Shelley, who was succeeded by his cousin N. W. Shelley. In 1855 it was sold to Marcus H. Cruikshank, "A gentleman of much personal worth and popularity." With Mr. Crukshank, Thomas J. Cross was associated.

In 1873 it consolidated with the Watchtower under the proprietorship of T. J. Cross and M. H. Cruikshank as the "Reporter and Watchtower." Mr. Cruikshank died in 1883, and Thomas J. Cross became sole owner Feb. 11, 1883. His son was connected with the paper, and the name was changed to "The Talladega Reporter." In March of 1890 the paper was sold to W. E. Henkel. One of the presses originally used by the old Southern Register, and on which the State Laws of Alabama were printed when Samuel F. Rice was editor, was still in use. Mr. Henkel some years later sold his interest to E. L. C. Ward, who edited and managed the paper until ill health forced him to dispose of the equipment.

"The Sun" came into existence soon after the War Between the States, but lived only a short while. It was the official organ of the Board of Education, the Board of Regents and of the State of Alabama, as well as of Talladega, Randolph and Coosa Counties.[3]

The "Talladega News" began publication about Dec. 1, 1871, with Moseley Brothers, owners. This publication was an adventure as a Tri-weekly, issued Tuesdays, Thursdays and Saturdays, at the price of $4.00. The paper was smaller in size than was usual, and a neat looking magazine-like paper. It lived only a few months when it was absorbed by "Our Mountain Home", but was continued as the "Talladega News" for several months. On July 2, 1873 the announcement appeared that we have this day sold 'The Talladega News' and 'Our Mountain Home' to Mr. Edward Bailey, late of Greenville, S. C. He will carry out the contracts for advertising and subscription." R. A. Moseley, Jr. was retained as managing editor. The Talladega News was then discontinued.

"The Advance" was established June, 1886, and speaks for itself: "Born Prosperous, Lives Progressive." "Skaggs & Bowie, Proprietors; R. E. Skaggs, Business Manager, Published weekly on Tuesdays at the rate of $1.50 per year, cash in advance."[4]

This paper came into existence during "Boom Days", and died with them. "Our Mountain Home" was born two years after the surrender of Lee, during depressing days of discouragement and sorrow, but it existed longer than any other publication of Talladega County, under the same name. It still bears practically the same name under that of "The Talladega Daily Home." "Our Mountain Home" was established in 1867 by Moseley Brothers and B. H. Shanklin, and in 1872 was sold to Edward Bailey, of S. C., who also purchased the "Talladega News", and combined the two papers. Mr. Bailey published the paper only about two years, when it went back into the hands of the Moseleys, who sold it in 1876 to John E. Ware, a son of Horace Ware, the iron and steel magnate of Shelby, Jefferson and Talladega Counties. Mr. Ware conducted the paper ably and with dignity. His daughter, Mrs. Graham Perdue, of Birmingham, treasured a scrap book of editorials written by Mr. Ware during this period of ownership, from 1876 to 1881. These editorials convey interesting facts regarding Talladega during this interval. The scrap book contains a "Valedictory" of John E. Ware, and a "Salutatory" of G. K. Miller from the issue of May 25th, 1881, when John C. Williams, a young man who had worked in the Mountain Home office for twelve years, published his first issue, as publisher and proprietor", with G. K. Miller and John C. Williams as editors.

---

[3] From collection of J. A. Bingham
[4] From copy of papers found at Tall. Public Library, and in J. A. Bingham's collection

Mr. Williams remained owner and editor as long as he lived, and Talladega is indebted to him for having collected and published valuable historical data during his period of management. For years he urged pioneer citizens and children of pioneers to write recollections for publication. Mrs. L. M. Taylor, Judge J. W. Vandiver, Mr. Wm. L. Lewis, D. B. Oden, Otis Nickles, J. L. M. Curry, and Dr. Stockdale, were among those who contributed written articles of historical value, during Mr. Williams ownership of the paper.

Mr. Williams was recognized as an outstanding editor, and was at one time made president of the Editors' and Publishers' Association of Alabama. Mr. William's son, Tom R. Williams, became co-editor, the latter part of the century, and also became well known throughout the State as an outstanding editorial writer.

"Our Mountain Home", in 1909, began the publication of "The Talladega Daily Home", but continued the weekly for some time.

There must have been other papers published over the county prior to 1900, about which I have no information. There were small publications issued at the Presbyterian Home for Children, and at the School for the Deaf, but they were not issued for the general public, and did not appear until the 20th century. Sylacauga papers were not established until the Twentieth Century. The Sylacauga Advance, was established in 1907, and the Sylacauga News in 1917. There may have been papers published in Sylacauga prior to this century, but I have no available material about them.

The Central Plank Road

Paved roads at this period are accepted as a matter of course, without any thought of the evolution of the mode of travel, and it is hard for us to visualize the inconveniences our forefathers experienced in traveling. The first arrivals to Talladega County probably came on horseback with their belongings in saddle-bags via some Indian trail. When the Creek country was opened to the white man it became necessary to widen these trails that vehicles might bring food and furnishings. One of the most important of these was the McIntosh Trail from Wetumpka through Talladega, and this road became the main artery of travel. The stage coach found its way over this widened trail about 1835, but it was still not properly graded, and travel was uncomfortable, when the announcement was made in 1850 that a plank road, connecting Montgomery with Talladega County, was being promoted over this route. One can well imagine the excitement over the project. At the time most of our purchases were made through commission merchants at Wetumpka. Goods came via water from Mobile and New Orleans to that point. The sale of products— cotton, corn, meal, flour, etc., was sold at the same place through these merchants.

The road was surveyed in 1850 with the idea of connecting the Alabama River at Montgomery with the Tennessee River at Guntersville, but only about 60 miles between Wetumpka and Winterboro were ever completed. Talladega business men, already interested in building a railroad from Selma, refused to take stock in the plank road. Mr. Levi W. Lawler seems to have been the only stockholder from Talladega County.[1] This being true, the promoters of the road decided not to bring the road through Talladega, but surveyed around the town. John G. Winter, then of Montgomery, was the largest stock-holder and President of the Company. The first lap of the road was to have a terminus in Talladega County. Because citizens of Talladega stubbornly refused to take part in the project, land was purchased twelve miles south of Talladega, and a village was laid off. Lots were sold and the town was called "Winterboro", in honor of Mr. Winter. It was his hope that Winterboro would develop into a metropolis and that the county seat would eventually be changed to that town. A number of homes were erected, and Simon Glazner's Tavern, below Winterboro, became a popular stopping place.

---

[1] Letter from Mr. W. A. Cook, Alpine, 2-23-1928

One old resident of the county, in speaking of the Plank Road, recalled that, the day the road was opened to Winterboro, Wm. L. Yancey made the trip from Montgomery, having changed "rigs" every ten miles. He had breakfast in Montgomery, dinner in Winterboro, where he made a speech at a barbecue in celebration of the occasion, and was back in Montgomery for supper.[2] This was considered a great feat of that period. Certainly Mr. Yancey must have suffered for weeks after riding over the corduroy road at such speed.

The planks were split logs placed parallel across the road, round side up, which made riding very uncomfortable. Portions of the road were kept in repair for some years, especially in low places. But as a whole it proved an unfortunate venture. Some say that the principal reason the road was not a success, was because planters refused to observe regulations regarding weight, and continuously hauled loads too heavy for the road construction.[3]

A preliminary survey for the route was made early in 1850 by A. A. Dexter, and "engineers estimated that plank road construction would cost $1200.00 to $1500.00 per mile, but by the first of January the cost was known to be from $2,000.00 to $4,000.00. While some of the route of the Central was along the Indian trails, even so, there was grading and bridging and the cost and upkeep far outdistanced the income."[4] Rates were very much like those of other Toll roads, and were collected at intervals, but there were added stipulations regarding weight. "Empty wagons could claim 25% reduction, but if a vehicle was loaded beyond 2,000 pounds to the animal, then 33% must be added to the toll."[5]

Stage coaches and regular paying patrons had the right of way and casual users were required to get off the planks on the approach of these favored vehicles. The road was not wide enough for vehicles to pass on the planks.

The maintenance was too costly to be practicable, and the construction of railroads soon killed the plank road enthusiasm entirely.

The road was opened in Winterboro in the fall of 1852, and the company was bankrupt in 1854.

A much more concise history of the road is found by culling from the Journal of James Mallory his recordings regarding the old Plank Road:[6]

---

[2] Ibid
[3] Ibid
[4] From an article in the Montgomery Advertiser by My. Peter Brannon dated June 2, 1935.
[5] Ibid
[6] Journal of James Mallory, owned by Mr. E. A. Stewart, Selma, Ala.

June 3, 1850 "Attended a plank road meeting at Talladega Town. Mostly attended by the Wetumpka Plains. I doubt its success."

Nov. 3, 1852 "Commenced hauling my cotton to the Plank Road to be hauled off at two bits per hundred by the road train."

Aug. 15, 1853 "Took the Plank Road to Montgomery. Found it a great improvement over the old road. Made several miles from sun rise to sunset."

Feb 6, 1854 "Attended the sale of the Plank Road and appertenances in Talladega Town. It sold for less than $3,000.00" This no doubt referred to that portion of the road located in Talladega County. Thus the Old Plank Road was salvaged, and the scene shifted to the various railroad terminals as it progressed along the route.

Winterboro played an important part in the early history of Talladega County. It was the focal point of trading for several years. Heavily loaded wagons of cotton and other commodities could be seen on the way to this shipping center at all times of the year. Especially so during the fall when cotton was being shipped. A large warehouse had been erected for the convenience of storing these commodities until the plank road train could conveniently transport it to Wetumpka for southern ports, and all incoming freight was stored in the warehouse until the purchaser could remove it. Both buyer and seller were on hand at all seasons of the year, and Winterboro was the common meeting ground where issues of the day—social, business, religious and political—were discussed among the waiting groups.

This must have been true at other points along the route: Equality, Santuck Central Institute (which gave the road its name) Nixburg, Goodwater. "Sylacauga was some miles west and the route is not exactly through the present Millerville."[7]

---

[7] From Mr. Brannon's article dated June 2, 1935

The First Railroad

An important incident in the early history of Talladega County was the advent of a railroad. Prior to this, marketing of cotton and other products had been a great problem. It took seven days to make the trip to and from Wetumpka, the early shipping point. It was possible then to carry only a few bales of cotton behind four mules, over the rough roads. The arrival of the Plank Road to Winterboro shortened the time by one day, and enabled the producer to increase the load by one bale of cotton. Therefore, a railroad meant a saving of still more time and money.

A train was put into operation in the United States, as early as 1809 pulled by horses. Not until 1830 was steam used as train power. Soon after, in 1831, a short railroad of two miles was built by David Hubbard out from Tuscumbia. In several years it was extended to Decatur, 44 miles. The cars were at first drawn by horses. The road never ceased to be a novelty, and was the envy of citizens all over the state. The excitement and interest over the success of this first railroad in Alabama, brought about 25 requests to the Legislature for charters between the years of 1830 and 1839. However, the panic, which followed "Flush Days", caused nearly all of the undertakings to fail. The aim of these first railroads was to connect one navigable stream with another. Freight was hauled at a distance entirely by water during that period.

Among the first chartered railroads granted by the Legislature was one on January 20th, 1832, which empowered the promoters to build several sections of railroad. One section was from Selma to Ten Islands, on the Coosa River. Another section of road was to begin at Ten Islands and run to Gunter's Landing where it would connect with the Tennessee River. Nothing came immediately of this charter. It was renewed, and in 1836 grading began for some miles out from Selma. Financial reverses caused this to fall through.

A map of 1838 shows this route from Selma, in Dallas Co.; through Centerville, in Bibb Co.; through Montevallo, in Shelby Co.; through Asheville, in St. Clair Co.; to Gunter's Landing, in Marshall Co., thus avoiding the crossing of the Coosa River.

This enterprise was again revived when Talladega and Benton (Calhoun) Counties came into the picture. A group of men met in convention at Shelby Springs on August 27, 1849,[1] for the purpose of fixing a new route to connect the Alabama and Tennessee Rivers, either from Montgomery or from

---

[1] Owen's History of Ala. Vol. 1, Page 506

Selma. Montgomery failed to send representatives to the meeting, so Selma was chosen; not, of course, for that reason alone, but because of the grading already made some years prior to 1849.

Commissioners for this renewed charter were James E. Saunders, Joseph W. Sesesne of Mobile Co.; John W. Lapsley, Thornton B. Goldsby, of Dallas Co.; Daniel E. Watrous, of Shelby Co.; Richard Nickles, of Marshall Co.; James Neal and William Horton of St. Clair Co.[2] These people were really in earnest this time. The route had not then been mapped by Talladega, and there were no Talladega people on the Board of Commissioners, but they must have done some genuine pulling at that meeting, because a meeting of the next convention was called to meet in Talladega on Sept. 24, 1849.

James Mallory records this meeting on Sept 26, 1849, and he was probably one of the local committee: "Have been in convention for three days in Talladega Town for the purpose of fixing our _____ (?) route for the construction of railroad connecting the waters of the Tennessee with the Mobile. It was ably and largely attended. The routes were fixed to begin at Selma and run to Gunter's Landing."[3] Mr. Mallory also states that at a meeting at Wewokaville on March 13, 1850, that $40,000.00 in stock was subscribed, and that engineers were in the neighborhood running different routes for the road.

The year 1850 was a memorable one. Real Estate prices picked up. The panic was over. The town of "Leoti" "on the east side of the Coosa River in Benton Co." was booming; being the lower terminus of the navigation for steamboats. Lots sold with the assurance of the "reasonable prospect of the Alabama & Tennessee Rivers Railroad crossing the river there".[4]

An election took place on October 26, 1850, for choice of directors for the Alabama & Tennessee Rivers Railroad. Managers in Talladega County were: Wewokaville _____ T. L. Pope, Isaac Hudson and J. D. Griffin Talladega James Isbell, A. R. Barclay, J. G. L. Huey, A. W. Bowie Kelly's Spring _____ J. L. M. Curry, W. B. McClellan, W. W. Mattison, John W. Lapsley of Selma, was chosen president.

Walker Reynolds, W. B. McClellan and William Curry, of Talladega Co.; Hudson Allen and T. A. Walker, of Benton Co.; Edmund King, Shelby Co.; Phillip J. Weaver, Thornton B. Goldsby, John F. Conoly and Wesley Plattenburg, of Dallas Co., were elected Directors.

In the same paper[5] announcing the result of this election sealed bids were requested for "graduation, masonry and bridging of 56 miles of the

---

[2] Ibid, Page 505
[3] James Mallory's Diary in possession of Mr. E. A. Stewart, Selma.
[4] Ala. Reporter, October 1, 1850
[5] Ala. Reporter, October 1, 1850

southern division of railroad, extending northwardly from Selma." The notice stated that 26 miles of the division were graded in 1839, and only needed repairs. Lewis Troost, Chief Engineer, was to inspect iron rails to be made of Alabama iron 18 feet in length, and "weighing 63 lbs. per line of yard." They were to be delivered at a landing to be hereafter designated between Kymulgee and Fort Williams, commencing their delivery first of November, 1851, and continuing it at the rate of from 80 to 100 tons per week until the quantity required (16,500 tons) was delivered. It is reasonable to believe that most of these rails, if not all of them, came from Talladega County iron, since a number of forges were in operation at the time, and the deliveries were to be from Talladega County landings on the Coosa River.

Work had already proceeded rapidly at the Selma end of the line, and a 30 ton locomotive bearing the name of "Alabama", was put into operation on May 10th, 1851, when a group of Selma people crowded a flat car and tender for a four mile test of the finished roadbed. A second engine called "Tennessee" was purchased in 1852, and in 1856 the "Walker Reynolds" and "Shelby" were put on the tracks.[6] Until recent years all locomotives carried names instead of numbers.

The road reached Montevallo in the summer of 1853. Here track laying ceased for fifteen months, when it was continued and reached the Coosa River in 1855. Cotton and other produce of Talladega County was hauled to the river, ferried across and shipped to Selma for some time before the road crossed the river. Selma from that time became the trading center for Talladega people. From Selma, commodities were shipped down the river, as from Wetumpka.

Soon after the bridge was built across the river, it was burned. This retarded progress, because a new one was not completed until January, 1857.

Again we are indebted to Mr. James Mallory for his brief and dependable record of events in his Journal:[7]

Dec. 12, 1855 "Finished picking cotton; nearly done ginning, baleing and hauling to the railroad. Making a trip every three days. Five and six bales to the load. It often took seven days to make a trip to Wetumpka with four bales."

Jan 17, 1857 "The railroad cars crossed Coosa River. Great rejoicing at the event. For 20 years have the people suffered for a conveyance to market. The neighborhood is making preparations for celebrating the occasion."

Feb. 10, 1857 "Planters are now making a trip a day to the Railroad Station." Over a year later the railroad was completed to the "100 Mile Station," at or near Alpine. Citizens met as early as April to make plans for a

[6] Owen's History of Ala. Vol. 1, Page 509
[7] James Mallory's Journal

celebration when a train should arrive. Mr. Mallory records the great event for us:[8]

June 12, 18588—"The cars reached the 100 mile station today. A barbecue is appointed on the 15th July as a day of rejoicing for the result. It will be a source of great convenience to the planters."

July 8, 1858—"Met at the Station to make arrangements for a Railroad barbecue."

July 13, 1858 —""The neighbors all met to dig pits, put up tables, etc., for the celebration at the 100 Mile Station on the 15th."

July 15, 1858—"The morning was clear and fair. People began pouring in from every road in one living stream until acres were covered with the crowd. The cars arrived, adding between one and two thousand to the vast crowd, from eight to ten thousand being present. Addresses were made. Two silver pitchers presented, one to Thomas Walker, President of the road, the other to our County man, Walker Reynolds, one of the directors, for their great efforts in forwarding the work. The dinner was ample. The very best order prevailed. Not a single accident occurred. Efforts are being made to extend the road."[9]

The population of Talladega Co. at the time was around 23,000. People from all the surrounding counties must have been present. Certainly only a few people in this part of the country had ever laid eyes on a railroad train. Mr. Walker Reynolds had cake pans made for the purpose of baking a layer cake several feet wide for this great occasion.

"Walker Reynolds not only helped by buying $100,000.00 of bonds for the railway, but in securing the right-of-way. His slaves were pressed into service by cutting cross ties and grading the road, for which the railway owed him and gave him a mortgage on lands they had gotten from the State."[10] The pitcher presented to Mr. Reynolds bore the following inscription:

To Walker Reynolds:
The energetic, liberal and
enterprising Director
of the Ala. & Tenn. Rivers R. R. from
His Talladega friends
1858

---

[8] Ibid
[9] Ibid
[10] From "Mt. Ida, Story of a Talladega County Home", by Mrs. Margaret Reynolds Smith, a grand-daughter of Walker Reynolds.

July 15

President Thomas A. Walker reported on June 18, 1859, that "the entire road will be finished to the town of Talladega in the month of September if no unavoidable occurrence prevents, a distance from Selma of 109.77 miles. Completed and equipped at a cost, exclusive of interest, of about $1,832,856, or $16,706 per mile. This distance from Talladega to Gadsden, the terminus fixed by the Company's charter is 57.65 miles. Of this distance 32.58 miles are graded, 8.83 miles partly graded, and 16.24 miles commenced. If the Company had the iron to clothe the road, the track-laying might progress to Gadsden without interruption."[11] The train reached Talladega as predicted in the fall of 1859. Mr. Mallory records: Oct. 13, 1859 "There was a large barbecue given in Talladega in joy for the arrival of the cars at that place."

Thus it will be seen that for over a year the citizens of Talladega boarded "the cars" at Alpine for traveling and shipping.

A tax of 2½% was imposed upon the real estate of Talladega to aid in the building of this road,[12] but it can be considered the greatest event toward progress in the history of the county.

Mr. Mallory stated that in February of 1861 he made a trip to Selma, purchased his groceries and attended to other business matters, and was gone only two days.

During the Civil War the Alabama & Tennessee Rivers Railroad was one of the greatest assets of the Confederacy. It not only transported soldiers, but coal, iron, ammunition and other important supplies. The road had been completed to Blue Mountain only in 1861, where construction ceased on account of the War. The Confederate Congress, realizing the importance of this road as a military necessity, passed a bill changing the route, and providing for the construction of an extension from Blue Mountain to Rome, Ga. an important post.

When the railroad first started operations the Government granted the Company 642,000 acres of public lands. During the War, in 1863, it became necessary to dispose of 300,000 acres, and it was announced that soldiers' families were eligible to purchase such lands at the price of $1.25 per acre. The proceeds went toward extending the road. The loss sustained by the stockholders during the War amounted to more than $1,000,000.00. Shops were destroyed, bridges burned and depots demolished, which bankrupted the road.

---

[11] Owen's History of Ala., Vol. 1, Page 507
[12] Democratic Watchtower, July 4, 1860

The Alabama & Tennessee Rivers R. R. Co. was merged into the Selma, Rome and Dalton Railroad in 1867, with eastern capital, and the road was extended to Dalton, Ga., in October, 1870. This road was facetiously called the "Sorry Road and Damn Rough Riding" until it was sold in 1881. Mr. Mallory records:

May 13, 1869—"Attended the Selma, Dalton & Rome R. R. convention held in Selma. It passed from the hands of the original Stockholders, into New York Capitalists. It will now be built to Rome and a connection made with the chain of roads running north. It is hard to yield to necessity, to give up the prospects (?) of it, to lose stock and all, to have such men as Walker Reynolds, Stone and others turned out, and names and faces new to friends of the road to manage it."

On June 14th 1881, the Selma. Rome and Dalton Railroad was sold to the East Tenn.. Va. & Ga. Railroad Co. for $2,200,000.00

The Southern Railway Company purchased the road in July, 1891 and has continued to own and operate it.

Several other railroads have come and gone, but none ever caused the thrilling elation evidenced in this first great enterprise.

Other Railroads

At one time in the history of Talladega County, there were six railroads within her bounds, and Talladega Town had four separate stations with sixteen passenger trains per day. All of these trains made connections with main lines, making Talladega one of the most conveniently accessible places within the State of Alabama.

The Alabama & Tennessee Rivers Railroad was the only road until after the Civil War.

Another railroad had its beginning when the Opelika & Talladega Railroad Company was incorporated Dec. 9, 1859, with the idea of intersecting the Alabama & Tenn. Rivers Railroads at Talladega. The charter was amended in 1861 to extend the railroad to Tuscumbia. War stopped all activities. Interest was revived in 1866 and the route changed, so that it should start at Columbus, Ga., and construction was to be made "On the Ala. & Tenn. Rivers R. R. between the east bank of the Coosa River and the Town of Talladega."[1] This became more certain in 1870.

In 1870 a large delegation went to Opelika to a meeting of the "Savannah & Memphis R. R." Mr. Arthur Bingham was made a director, and articles of approval appeared in the papers; engineers were on hand, surveying the route through Talladega, and the whole town was cheered and enlivened over the prospect of the railroad coming through Talladega. Talladega was doomed to disappointment, for in 1873 only 40 miles had been finished, and not until years later, after the road had changed hands. name and routes changed several times, did the road finally reach Sylacauga instead of Talladega, as expected. This was a great loss to Talladega. Old newspapers indicated that citizens fought valiantly to have the road pass through Talladega.

This road was finally merged into the present ownership of the Central of Georgia Railway Company.

THE CLIFTON RAILROAD, a narrow gauge road, was built 9 miles between Jenifer and Ironaton by Sam Noble and others, for the purpose of hauling iron ore to the furnaces at those points. The road was extended from Jenifer to Anniston and from Ironaton to Talladega in 1884, covering 30 miles. The charter was dated May 24, 1883, and under the name of Anniston & Atlantic R. R. CO.[2]

---

[1] Thomas M. Owen's History of Ala., Vol. 1, Page 219
[2] Ibid Vol. II, Page 907

The narrow gauge road entered Talladega Town from the southeast, via the eastern border of the Presbyterian Home for Children. When all narrow gauge railroads changed to standard gauge in 1886, a new entrance was opened into Talladega, shortening the route to the present one. At or about the same time extending the road to Sylacauga.

The Alabama Mineral Railroad Co. purchased the road in 1890. However, they sold to the L. & N. Railway the same year, and it has since been known as the Ala. Mineral Division of the L. & N. Ry. Co. Mileage has been added from time to time since the L. & N. acquired the property.

TALLADEGA & COOSA VALLEY RAILROAD COMPANY was chartered Dec. 19, 1883. The road was first built from the Coosa River to a station called "Murphy", on the A. & A. R. R. (L. & N.), a distance of 15 miles, from which point, two miles from Talladega, transportation rights were leased from the A. & A. into the town of Talladega.[3] It was opened in 1886. Certificates of the Talladega & Coosa Valley R. R. Co. were "first Mortgage Loan" of $48,000.00, with right to issue in addition thereto $6,000.00 per mile for each and every mile in excess of the eight miles of road first constructed or acquired." The value of each share was $250.00, with coupons attached from June 1, 1885 through Dec. 1, 1904.[4] The coupons read "Will pay to the bearer at the office of Robert H. Isbell, Trustee, Talladega, Ala., or its agency in the city of Talladega, Ala. Seven Dollars and Fifty Cents in Gold coin, being six months interest on Bond." Signed by F. A. Franks, Treas.

The road was first prospected for the purpose of removing the lumber for several large lumber mills near Renfroe.

In 1887 it was extended to Pell City, making the length 26.9 miles. The first 8 miles of road were built by Rogers and Franks, lumber dealers, and it was managed by D. M. Rogers for years.

On Oct. 1, 1890 it was merged into the Birmingham & Atlantic Railroad Co. Between 1886 and 1899 many short branches were built to ore beds throughout the county. The short road was built primarily for the hauling of lumber, but when the Talladega Furnace was erected, it became the road most used for hauling iron ore.

The B. & A. station at Talladega was located on the west side of East St. S., between Coffee Street and the L. & N. Railroad.

The railroad crossed the Coosa River at Stemley on a wooden bridge, which at one time collapsed under a loaded train, and would have proved a horrible tragedy if the bravery and presence of mind of a colored porter, Jordan

---

[3] Ibid, Vol. I, Page 143
[4] Certificates in my possession, presented by Jno. I. Tubbs, Pres. Isbell National Bank, Talladega.

Cranford, and the conductor Mr. Harry Fleetwood had not saved the lives of passengers. Jordan Cranford was lauded far and wide for having dived under the water and pulled out every passenger, handing them to Mr. Fleetwood and his brother Julian who stood on the top of the car, which was not submerged.

The bridge was repaired, but not considered safe for some time. Therefore, for months the engineer, Henry Sims, put on only enough steam to transport the train across the bridge; he and the passengers would walk across the bridge, and the fireman would start the engine, jump off, and the engineer would catch it as it reached the other side. On one occasion the engineer failed to catch the engine and it proceeded for some miles on its own. A new bridge was built and transportation became safe again.

The present Stemley bridge used by the County on the Talladega—Cropwell road, is the "new" railroad bridge.

After the lumber mills at Renfroe and the furnaces in Talladega ceased operations, the road was no longer needed, and the right of way was sold to individuals.

This little road was the most convenient mode of travel from Talladega to Birmingham and Atlanta, since it made connection with the A. G. S. at Pell City.

General John B. Gordon was made President of a prospective railroad which was to extend from Atlanta, Georgia, to Texarkanna, Ark., in 1881. It was finally built from Atlanta, crossing Alabama through the mineral district, with a terminus at Greenville, Miss. It crossed Talladega County, with several county stops, one at McFall and one at Lincoln. Some years later, because of the urgent request of citizens, the name of the station at McFall was changed to Eastaboga. The old town of Eastaboga was only about a mile distant and eventually business houses moved nearer the post office and railroad station.

The road was thrown into bankruptcy and was purchased August 18, 1894, at foreclosure, by the Southern Railway Company.

THE EASTERN RAILWAY OF ALABAMA, with Mr. Percy H. Smith as its young President, contracted with the L. & N. Railroad Company for the use of their track to Stockdale, and from that point built a road 19.8 miles through the mountains to Pyriton. This road was built for the purpose of hauling pyrites and graphite from the mines located in Clay County. It was later sold to the Atlanta, Birmingham & Atlantic Railroad Co., which completed their own entrance into Talladega in Oct., 1907, and extended the road to Pelham the next year, leasing "passenger and freight terminal rights from the L. & N. R. R. Co. between Pelham and Birmingham."[5] Many changes have taken place since

---

[5] Thomas M. Owen's History of Ala., Vol. I, Page 70

the acquirement of the road by the Atlantic Coast Line in the Twentieth century.

Slavery

There was always some opposition to slavery in the United States. Most churches prohibited their ministers from owning slaves. However, the Constitution of the United States permitted it, and since there appeared no other labor solution, it became more and more commonly practiced.

An active movement was launched against it when the Anti-Slavery Society, organized in the early part of the Nineteenth Century in the northern states, sent representatives south to distribute antagonistic literature, and to organize the Negro slaves into secret societies. Regarding this organization, the Mobile Register of October, 1835, stated that a resolution was adopted by a group of farmers in Wilcox County, in which they said "our right of property in slaves is fixed and guaranteed by the Federal Constitution, and we regard the Acts of the Anti-Slavery Society at the North as a fearful crime and a treason against the Union."[1]

On September 19, 1835, a meeting of religious people was held at Owens Spring Camp Ground, in Talladega County, at which a resolution was passed denouncing this organization. They stated "Certain Fanatics to the North are publishing numerous incendiary papers on the subject of Abolition, calculated to stir up the Slaves to insurrection and rebellion, and thus endangering the peace and civil order of society and also the civil and religious institutions of the County." Etc.[2]

For many years this contending element was indoctrinated into the South, and there was a constant flow of controversy at public meetings and in newspaper articles. Many of the slave owners disapproved of slavery themselves, and a great many of them would have freed the slaves, but felt that the propitious time was not at hand. It was the custom, and legally right, and there was no other method of acquiring labor to open the ever moving frontier. Slaves were valuable property, and were usually well provided for and some states would not permit residence to freed slaves. It was an exceptional practice for an owner to mistreat his slaves. The abuser was not respected by his neighbors.

In our generation, we wonder how any slave drover could have been so depraved as to enter into the business of trapping human beings, though savages, chaining them, and bringing them across the sea to slavery. The slave trader was held in contempt by the public, though he was patronized. No

---

[1] Life & Times of Wm. L. Yancey by DuBose, Page 179
[2] History of Methodism in Alabama, by Dr. Anson West, Page 477

doubt, the purchaser of slaves eased his conscience to some extent in believing that a slave was much better cared for, and much happier in his hands than in that of the dealer. It was soon discovered that the African, having arrived from a tropical climate, could not survive so well in the north. Therefore, the volume of slave trading gradually shifted south, where work was in the open and the climate warmer.

As slaves arrived in ports, auctions were held and the unsold slaves were divided into droves, and the journey south began by foot. An advance agent was sent from town to town to announce the sale, and the heavy hearted, rebellious, foot-sore slaves were driven forward to fields unknown. No race perhaps is comparable to that of the Negro race, when it comes to adaptability. Although worn and tired and heart sick, the buoyant spirit of the Negro would burst forth in song about the camp fire in the evenings, where many of the beautiful chants and spirituals were born, which have long outlasted slavery. The ever recurring hope that some kind person would purchase them next day, and their tiresome journey end, would lull them to sleep, and make the journey endurable.

Arriving in a town, the slave was placed on the block. He was examined fully – legs, arms, skin and teeth, and was required to run a race. He was then put through any other tests the prospective purchaser requested.

The slave market fluctuated through-out the years. Small children were valued from $100.00 up; youths $500.00 up; adults from $1,000.00 up; based, of course, on qualification and need. For instance a good blacksmith was valued at $3,000.00 or more.

The planter who owned slaves was vitally interested in laws that governed them. During the years that abolition was discussed, he thought very seriously about the matter, and many large holders were willing to free their slaves, but there were no laws to protect them. No one was better prepared to decide this question than those who lived daily with the Negro; those who understood him, and who were genuinely fond of him. Fortunes were invested in slaves. They were a man's property, his personal property, and human property. There was a moral, as well as a financial responsibility involved.

The Constitution of the United States gave the separate states the right to make laws governing their property, and the Southern States felt very keenly that this right must be protected.

At the first Republican Convention in 1860, Abraham Lincoln was nominated for president on a platform to abolish, or prevent, slavery in the United States.

The Democratic National Convention met in Charleston, S.C., in April, 1860. Wm. L. Yancey, one of the nation's most talented orators, was leader of the Alabama delegation to this convention.

At the convention, he made a speech that so inflamed and influenced the members that they adopted the "Alabama Platform" to secede in case Abraham Lincoln was elected.

Abraham Lincoln was elected.

South Carolina was first to secede on Dec. 20, 1860, and in quick succession others followed. Alabama was the fourth to secede by a vote of 54 to 46, on Jan. 11, 1861. The conservative men of Alabama disapproved heartily of secession, and the vote at this convention indicated that there was no unanimity of opinion regarding secession.

Jeremiah Clemens, of Madison County, expressed the opinion of those who opposed secession when he said, among other things "Acting upon the convictions of a life-time, calmly and deliberately I walk with you into revolution. Be its perils, be its privations, be its sufferings what they may, I share them with you, though as a member of this convention, I oppose your ordinance."[3]

Representatives from Talladega County to this Secession Convention were N. D. Johnson, merchant; A. R. Barclay, farmer; and M. G. Slaughter, doctor, all of whom voted against secession.

The Democratic Watchtower of Talladega, dated Jan. 16, 1861, gave a detailed description of the celebration in Talladega following the news that Alabama had seceded. All homes and business houses were brilliantly lighted, and people went from home to home carrying and discussing the news. Bonfires burned in the streets. "The Talladega Artillery under Capt. Morgan, and the Alabama Rifles under Capt. Johnson, paraded in full dress uniform around the square. Fifteen guns were fired by the Artillery in honor of the South, after which the companies, with many citizens, repaired to the Court House, where patriotic and appropriate speeches were made by Maj. J. G. L. Huey, Capt. Johnson, Hon. Joseph Woodward and J. J. Woodward." This was done in good order.[4] It was held to be the Constitutional right of a state to withdraw from the Union, and it was quite commonly felt that the movement would not be followed by war. The States were "independent, sovereign states", and united under one constitutional agreement only. The Southern States had simply dissolved their connection with the other states of the Union in defense of their rights.

On Feb. 18, 1861, Jefferson Davis took oath of office as President of the Confederacy, standing on the portico of the Capitol at Montgomery. A new government was set in motion.

---

[3] History of Alabama, by Brown, Page 233
[4] Paper on file at the Talladega Public Library

At the Secession Convention, seven delegates were chosen to represent Alabama at the Provisional Congress, which met on Feb. 4th, 1861, with representatives from other states, to formulate plans for the confederate States. Among the seven were two from Talladega County, J. L. M. Curry, and W. P. Chilton, who was at the time living in Montgomery. This was quite an honor for Talladega County, because at this Secession Convention, after great deliberation, it was unanimously decided that "the ablest men of Alabama" must be chosen for this purpose.

Abraham Lincoln went into office on March 4, 1861, and announced that he would enforce the laws of the United States in the seceded States.

The Confederate States proceeded to ask for an evacuation of Federal Forts within their bounds, and Abraham Lincoln declared War by Proclamation April 15, 1861.

Talladega During the Civil War

The Citizens of Talladega County were perhaps equally divided in opinions regarding secession. Many opposed it bitterly. Some felt that abolition was eventually inevitable, but that the Southern States could come to a satisfactory agreement with the Federal Government, whereby the slave owner would receive ample remuneration for his property; and that the slaves, for whom he felt a deep responsibility, could be adequately provided for by the Government. They must have food. They must work to get food. The planter must have labor. Surely they could arrive at some amicable conclusion.

Others felt that the Constitution gave the States the right to regulate laws governing their property; that slaves were property; that abolition of slaves was an affair of the independent states; and that they intended upholding their sovereign rights, and were not inclined to argue further with the Federal Government.

Some feared war would follow. Others scorned the idea. War was declared. The declaration united those of differences of opinion into one solid mass of people, who joined forces to save their beloved southland. Preparations for defense were put into motion rapidly, and it astounded the people to know that so much could be accomplished in so short a while. Volumes have been written regarding conditions among the people, and laws governing them during the War. We shall concern ourselves only with those local happenings as depicted through the newspaper and journals of that period. Mr. Marcus H. Cruikshank was Mayor during the secession period and the early part of the War.[1] He issued a warning in December of 1860 to the public:

"As a measure of precaution and prudence on the part of our citizens, in view of the excitement and apprehension, I would respectfully suggest that each citizen keep a strict patrol over his own premises and servants, and that Negro gatherings be strictly prohibited during the approaching holidays. Patrol companies have been appointed, and persons who give their Negroes holidays should provide them with proper passes."[2]

Thus was voiced the unrest which continued, and increased, as the War proceeded.

As soon as war was declared, men and boys poured into town from all parts of the county to volunteer for service. Tents were pitched on vacant lots, and drilling was the order of the day. Tailors worked day and night cutting,

---

[1] Alabama Reporter of Dec. 18, 1860. On file at Talladega Public Library
[2] Ibid

fitting and making uniforms. Silver tongued orators inspired men, women and children to activities of every needful kind. Ministers called for prayers. Each church had candle-light services on separate nights, that people might attend them all. Business and schools practically ceased operations.

It was generally agreed that the large planter should not volunteer for military service, but should bend his every effort toward agricultural production. The Army must be fed. Therefore, a large percentage of production of beef, pork, flour, meal, potatoes, cotton, etc., was required of the farmer. He played an important part during the war. Many of them sheltered and fed needy families, and took care of refugees fleeing from occupied territories.

The Alabama & Tennessee Rivers Railroad having reached Talladega some time before war was declared was immediately extended to a focal point for transporting troops and army supplies. At Selma an arsenal was established. Privately owned forges and foundries were pressed into use. Samuel Clabaugh and James A. Curry, experienced operators, built the Salt Creek Iron Works at what is now called Jenifer, which was completed in 1863, and iron was manufactured to be used in making guns and cannons.

Nitre works were erected, under the management of J. G. Chadraun, on 10 acres of land located on the north side of the southern railroad, beginning about 300 yards east of the depot, and extending over land now known as Brignoli Street.

A Camp of Instruction, or Conscript Camp, was situated between East and West Streets, traversed by the present Sloan Ave., including the Edward R. Wren Memorial Hall property. Tents were placed all through the grove of oak trees.

A "Soldiers' Aid and Relief Association" was founded. 27 Companies of Volunteers were soon in action. Many slaves were impressed into service as cooks and blacksmiths. Excitement stimulated those left at home only a short time. Privations undreamed of materialized from every direction. There was hunger and need. In 1863 there were 976 families of soldiers, comprising 3,513 persons, listed as in want in the county.[3]

Talladega was asked to provide a hospital for the wounded who would be sent by rail, and the Exchange Hotel, located on the N. W. Corner of North and Court Streets, where the United States Post office now stands, was immediately prepared for that purpose. Advertisements appeared for clean rags at 6c per pound. Women and children went to work rolling bandages, making dressings, preparing food for the hospital, knitting socks and other garments for soldiers.

---

[3] History of Talladega, by J.W. Vandiver, Chapter 28

The Baptist High School was used as a prison for Federal soldiers, now Swayne Hall at Talladega College.

Some of the stores on the North side of the Square were pressed into use for Army supplies.

Concerts were frequently staged to acquire money for the wounded. On one occasion "Capt. O'Neal's Brass Band" gave a concert which brought receipts of $417.50 for the sick and wounded of the First Alabama Regiment.[4]

Still more relief was needed as the war raged, and the "Battle Field Relief Association" was organized for the purpose of sending relief to hungering and suffering soldiers on the battle field. In August, 1864, 3,200 lbs. of food was donated in Talladega County. M. H. Cruikshank, Dr. Jo. H. Johnson, Wm. McLane, Robert W. Huston and one servant took the trip to Columbus, Ga., to deliver the nine boxes of supplies, including meat, flour, bandages, vegetables and delicacies.

Passes to Selma were donated by the railroad with the understanding that individuals would accompany the supplies, and handle the boxes themselves. The boxes were carted to the warehouse of L. W. Pettibone, in Selma, who stored them free until a boat should arrive. When the boat arrived, the group loaded them and carted them to the "Duke", and they went by water up to Montgomery— "not entirely free." The committee later recommended that future committees take rations and blankets and take "Deck Passage", and recommended that smaller boxes be used. They experienced many difficulties unforeseen. In Montgomery they had to unload the goods onto a dray and carry them to the depot, where they were sent by rail to Columbus for distribution.

In one collection in 1865 for the wounded and needy, supplies valued at $14,573.00, were contributed. The people at home shared everything they had with those who needed help.

Mrs. E. A. Stephens read an article before the John T. Morgan Chapter of the U. D. C. in 1910.[5] which has been published several times throughout the years in local papers. Mrs. Stephens was the daughter of Judge of Probate Wm. Thornton, who was perhaps more closely in touch with all local conditions than any other one man. Therefore, Mrs. Stephens was qualified to give a clear and vivid picture of conditions in Talladega during the War. Portions of her article follow:

"Truly, desolation was apparent everywhere. The principal inhabitants were women, children and servants, a few non-combatants; the county officers, preachers and doctors and a few old men not able for field duty.

---

[4] Alabama Reporter, Sept. 24, 1863, at Talladega Public Library.
[5] Published in Our Mountain Home, summer of 1910

The manufacturing establishments embraced two tanneries, with shoe shops in connection.

The old carriage shop was turned into a workshop for making looms, reels, winding blades and other implements for making cloth. There was one furniture shop on the southwest corner of the Square, owned by Mr. A. Bingham, and there were also two or three blacksmith shops. Talladega supported three hotels before the war, the Renfro and Douglas, situated on the south side of the Square, and the Exchange. The Exchange was used during the War as a hospital. It was filled with patients, doctors, surgeons and their assistants.

The conscript, or camp of instruction, was situated in the oak grove between the two roads leading out of town, now known as East and West Streets, in the neighborhood of Wallis' saw mills and Mrs. Dean's place (Country Club). The camp was established by the War Department to catch all the poor fellows who shirked out of the war on the principle that it was a "rich man's war and a poor man's fight." We had two weekly newspapers, the Watchtower, editor and proprietor, Mr. Harvey Joiner, and the Reporter, which was owned and edited by Mr. Marcus Cruikshank. Our local papers often came out in single sheets and sometimes printed on brown paper. Paper was a very scarce commodity, letters often being written on brown paper, wall paper and scraps from old ledgers, or from anywhere it could be had. We often made our envelopes from like paper.

The news from the front was hard to obtain in the sixties, and at times the papers published private letters....There were no telegraph lines into Talladega until November, 1864. All the telegraphic news contained in the newspapers came to us through the Selma Times. Selma was the only town connected with us by railroad publishing a daily paper. My father went down to Montgomery in September, 1864, and while there bought 10 yards of black lawn at $35.00 per yard and one black veil for which he paid $100.00. At this time Confederate money was much depreciated. My father being Probate Judge, had charge of the distribution of money for the soldiers' families at this time, 1864. On his last visit to Montgomery, he brought back a salt sack of money. The night he was on the boat coming up to Selma, he put the money under his berth. Two passengers coming in later, one struck his foot against the sack and said "The fellow has a sack of tobacco."

It was certainly a pathetic sight we often witnessed – poor women coming to town 20 to 30 miles, to draw a few dollars, three or four bushels of corn and a little salt, sometimes driving a one-ox cart or a skeleton of a horse or mule. Sometimes they walked all the way. . .

Many times were our spare rooms and hall floors covered with pallets, and two meals, supper and breakfast shared with the best we had – corn bread, bacon and sorghum molasses, butter and milk, or coffee made of sweet potatoes, wheat and rye, sweetened with sorghum. My father was noted for his hospitality.

The best substitute we found for coffee was okra seed. My father rented some acres of ground from a nearby farmer and sowed it in okra the last year of the War...

During the summer of 1864 and the spring of 1865, the monotony of our lives was relieved by the unwelcome visits of Yankees. Quite a number of prisoners were brought here and domiciled for a few days in the male college, now known as the Negro College. I remember how exasperated the citizens were when they heard one of the officers saying, "Well boys, we are monarchs of all that we survey." Some of them had fine voices and they sat on the balcony at night and sang "My Country, Tis of Thee", "Home, Sweet Home," etc. The villages were entertained though the music was rendered by enemies. Some ladies were so appreciative that they were driven up in their carriages and presented them with beautiful bouquets."

On Friday, July 17th, 1864, Talladega had her first experience in a direct contact with the enemy. General Rosseau passed through the county moving south. An article appearing in the Alabama Reporter of July 28, 1864,[6] describes the visit:

"The Yankees under General Rosseau paid our Town a visit on Friday, the 17th inst. As might be expected their arrival created much excitement and confusion and occasioned some loss. . . .

Various estimates have been made as to their number. It is pretty certain however that there were about 2,000 of them. Though the number may have reached 2,400...They delayed in town but an hour or two and burned the Railroad Depot, the only building destroyed by them in the County. An order was issued to burn the Commissary building, but through the efforts of Dr. Smith, of the Hospital, who represented to them that the burning of the Commissary stores would necessarily involve the destruction of a large portion of the town, and seriously endanger the Hospital. The order was revoked, and an effort made to destroy such portions of the stores as they were unable to carry with them. They offered to give them away to any citizens or Negroes, or anyone who would take them away so they would be lost to the Government...

They did not either burn the Conscript Camp or the Nitre Sheds, we believe for the reason that they were afraid of being ambushed or bushwhacked, there being thick woods near the camp and the sheds.

---

[6] Ala. Reporter, July 27, 1864, on file Talladega Public Library

Almost every private residence in town was entered and the bacon from most of the smoke houses taken off. The corn and oats were also taken. They rode into yards, fed their horses under shade trees and along the streets throughout the town.

They took with them a few horses from our town and some two or three Negroes.

On leaving town they took the Sylacauga road, burning, as they passed, the Gin House of the Hon. Alex. White, with a large quantity of cotton, estimated at near 100 bales.

They fed their horses at Mrs. Hardie's and consumed a large quantity of her oats, corn, bacon, etc.

Maj. Walker Reynolds and his son, Thomas Reynolds, we understand, lost all their horses and mules—about 50 head.

Judge Cook, we understand, lost a number of horses and mules and some Negroes."

They moved at the rate of 40 to 50 miles per day, the paper stated, and they bemoaned the fact that Talladega citizens were helpless to defend themselves; that they needed some military leaders to take over should another occasion like this take place.

The estimated loss to the Confederate Government was 8,000 lbs. of bacon; 200 sacks of flour; 40 bags of meal; 9½ hogsheads of sugar; 2 tierces of rice; 100 lbs. of candles; several barrels of soap and 1800 sacks.

Mrs. Stephens adds a personal touch to this raid in the article previously referred to:

"We had heard some days before that they were coming. Every one was busy getting up and hiding their valuables. I had a few hundred dollars and I hid it in several places. Each time I would think they would be sure to find it. Finally, I turned it over to an old Negro man, and he hid it in the fodder loft at the barn. My father was running two two-mule wagons. The evening of the 20th (?), after partly loading them with things from home, such as bedding and so forth, they were driven up to the county courthouse and finished loading with county records. They left town that evening. The next morning about four o'clock my father mounted his horse and followed them. When he overtook them they were 30 miles from Talladega. These Negro men were true and faithful servants and they were determined the Yankees would not get those things.

We were agreeably surprised that the raiders did not commit any serious depredations. The greatest damage was the burning of the depot. Of course they helped themselves to the commissary stores. They passed down Battle Street for Sylacauga, the next town, and by two o'clock, there was not a Yankee in town."

During the interval between Lee's surrender on April 9th, 1865, and that of other generals, Talladega experienced another raid, which was described in the Alabama Reporter of April 27th, 1865:[7]

"Our town has been visited by another group of Yankee raiders. On Friday night last it was ascertained that the Yankees were crossing the Coosa River at Collins and Truss Ferries, and it was believed would reach Talladega that night. They were delayed in crossing the river and did not enter the town until Saturday evening (afternoon). Colonel Hughes, with about 100 men met them near town and after a short skirmish fell back through town, the enemy pursuing at a pretty rapid rate.

The raiding party consisted of a brigade of Cavalry under General Croxton, numbering about 2,100. Our county jail, the railroad depot, government depot, conscript camp, and the Nitre sheds were burned. The stores were broken open and robbed. Many of our citizens suffered severely in the loss of mules, horses and other valuables. Some Negroes went off with them, but not a very large number. Most of the private residences in the town were entered and searched for valuables. All the watches, silverware, plate, etc., that had not been previously removed, was taken and carried off. Colonel Hugh Caperton, formerly of DeKalb County, a most estimable and exemplary citizen, residing about 5 miles from town, was shot through the window of his own home by one of a squad of Yankees and died almost instantly. No cause can be assigned for this cold-blooded and wanton act. Major G. P. Plowman, mayor of the town, was knocked down with a gun barrel, and was severely injured by a crowd who were endeavoring to extort from him money which a Negro had told them he had concealed. They subsequently returned for the purpose of hanging Mr. Plowman, but he succeeded in effecting his escape. Mrs. X. Willman, a worthy lady, was choked down and compelled to bring and deliver a little jug of gold and silver, the savings from hard earnings of years.

At Mrs. Curry's, 6 miles from town, they burned some cotton, the old store house, and crib containing about 1,000 bushels of corn. The iron establishment of Clabaugh and Curry (at Jenifer) was destroyed, as were the other iron establishments of Oxford, Calhoun Co., Ala.

The Yankees left our town on Sunday morning and moved in the direction of Oxford."

Mrs. E. A. Stephens adds interesting facts regarding this raid:

"The next raid was in the spring of 1865, commanded by General Croxton.

---

[7] Ala. Reporter, Aug. 27, 1865, on file Talladega Public Library.

My father, Judge John Henderson, Andrew Lawson and other prominent men went out to meet them with a flag of truce, and stationed themselves on the hill beyond Mr. Henry Lawson's place.

They sent a young man, Mr. Jule Chaudron, on to meet them with the flag. A company of Confederates were camping near Munford, I think it was, and came down and met them in a skirmish and were run into town. In a little while the town was swarming with Yankees, chasing and shooting at the Confederates. I was so anxious about my father that I remained on the sidewalk until I saw a horse of a Confederate fall near the big spring. I then ran into the house where I found my mother, two little sisters and my sister-in-law, all kneeling in the middle of the floor praying.

My father and the men on hearing the firing came in and took refuge at the hospital. The conscript officers, doctors and their assistants skedaddled to the woods. My father walked out on the sidewalk and a Yankee Captain rode up and asked for Judge Thornton and my father said, "I am he." The Captain said "Judge I want to tell you the young man you sent to meet us with the flag of truce is all right." My father then asked the captain to introduce him to General Croxton, saying "I want to ask of him protection for our defenseless women." The Captain replied, "It will be useless. He never gives protection when we have to fight our way into a town; but," he continued, "Judge, you shall have a guard if I have to come myself."

When my father came home, he found a Yankee in the house opening all the drawers and trunks, scattering things around generally. Father said to him, "What are you doing here?" He said "I am hunting for gold, silver, and your valuable things." Father said, "You had better get out of here; Captain will be here soon."

When he heard the captain was coming he skedaddled on double-quick time.

About seven o'clock the captain and guard came. They sat at supper with us—our usual menu of corn bread, bacon, sorghum molasses and cereal coffee. We always had plenty of milk and butter, and occasionally we could get home raised wheat flour and sometimes we could get bolted corn meal.

When supper was over we went into the family sitting room. The Captain asked permission to smoke. He said to my father, "Judge, I suppose it has been some time since you have had any fine-cut tobacco. Let me fill your pipe and let's take a social smoke and bury the tomahawk." My father spoke of going to Mr. Chaudron's[8] to let him know that his son was safe – he was kept a

---

[8] About 6 Miles East on Old McIntosh Road

prisoner that night – but the captain advised him not to go out of the house, saying it would be dangerous to do so.

The next morning we heard of several of the citizens having been beaten and badly treated. We found the Captain to be an intelligent and entertaining gentleman. When he left he told the guard to remain until he came to relieve him. The next morning when he came, he told of Lee's surrender and said the war was over and that they were on their way home. He showed us photographs of his family, the first photographs we had ever seen. He said to my father, "Judge, I am afraid the General is going to leave your town in ashes, he gave orders to have fire set to the Commissaries."

My father asked him if he would conduct him to the General. The General's headquarters were in the house on West Street, after the War owned by Mr. John Adams. During the War it was a one-story building with the porch the full length of the house. The General was promenading the porch - the house was some distance from the gate. When my father entered the gate he gave a Masonic sign, the general recognized it and met my father half way between the house and the gate. He extended his hand saying, "What is your request?"

My father told him he had heard of his order to burn the town, and asked him to countermand the order, which he did by sending an orderly in great haste to have the fire extinguished.

He then rode up town with my father and turned over all the commissary stores to him, to be distributed to the indigent families of soldiers.

Two or three prisoners of the jail were released and the jail burned. This, with the burning of the depot, was the only real damage to property in Talladega."

Many thrilling stories are told of the raid on the plantations, where union troops felt free to pillage and plunder without interference. Women, children and slaves were helpless, since by 1865, the large planter had been called into service. From these plantations the Federal Army greatly replenished its supply of food and horses.

The news by "grape vine" was not as slow as this generation might think. The news of Croxton's approach preceded them many hours, and perhaps days, and family silver and jewels were buried in fields, or hidden in wells, and other secure places. Hams, bacon and other provisions were hidden in the many sink holes about the fields of Talladega County. Tracks were covered with fresh plowing. In some cases slabs from graves were removed and treasures placed beneath. In one instance valuables were concealed in the Grecian columns of the portico. In spite of every precaution, treasured articles were taken from homes, some maliciously destroyed.

Sometime around 1916, the Postmaster[9] of Talladega received a letter from some man in one of the Northwestern states, stating that he was among the raiders on Talladega, and like other young boys, wanted a souvenir, and that he had taken a family Bible from a home in Talladega, giving some of the names therein. He was an old man and wanted to return this Bible to the rightful owner. The Postmaster recognized the names, got in touch with the family, and the Bible was returned.

Nearly every family who lived along the route of the raiders had an adventurous story to pass on to future generations, which would make interesting reading.

Talladega County had several permanent conscript, recruiting and recuperative camps located within her bounds, where detachments were occasionally sent. Detachments of Wheeler's Cavalry, Hardie's Batallion, the Second and Ninth Kentucky Cavalry, and many others were at times located at these camps. A detachment was located at Munford when Croxton passed through, and they entered into Battle at Munford.[10]

THE BATTLE OF MUNFORD[11]

There was a small company of soldiers, about 150 in number, known as "Hill's Layouts", augmented by a few regular soldiers, who undertook battle with the Federal soldiers as they passed through Munford.

On the hill where the Academy stood, and still stands, the company had placed two small cannons, which they fired on the enemy several times. This brought about a return fire from the Yankees, and a small skirmish took place. Two men were killed, one a Confederate soldier, another a Federal soldier, whose body was removed and sent elsewhere for burial. The Battle took place on April 23, 1865, 14 days after Lee's surrender, and was no doubt the last battle to take place on Alabama soil.

On November 4th, 1914, the John T. Morgan Chapter of the U. D. C., unveiled a marble monument, (which was donated to them by Mr. Leon G. Jones) where the Confederate soldier fell, and where he was buried. The monument bears' the inscription—

"In Memory of
Andrew Jackson Buttram,
Confederate Soldier,

---

[9] R.M. Jemison was Postmaster at the time.
[10] From an article written by R. G. Roberts, "Talladega in the Days of the Civil War." Found in Scrap Book of R. G. Roberts, Jr.
[11] Ibid

killed here April 23,1865
During Croxton's Raid
Erected by Veterans and their descendants."

The War being over, Confederates, penniless and on foot, wended their way homeward. They knew what the ravage of war was like; they had seen it; had participated in it; and were prepared for the scenes of destruction they would encounter as they journeyed on. Defeat depresses. Absent from home and family, his loneliness was keen, as day and night the defeated soldier, sick at heart, and sore of body, slowly plodded homeward to find that he was to suffer still further under Martial Law.

Under Martial Law

Abraham Lincoln, anticipating victory, made plans for immediate occupation of the conquered country when such a time should come.

On May 4, 1865, General Richard Taylor, occupying territory comprising Alabama, surrendered. In less than three weeks Brevet Brig. General M. H. Chrysler announced through the Talladega papers that he had arrived to take over affairs of a large district, with Talladega as headquarters. The Talladega District consisted of Bibb, Blount, Calhoun, Cherokee, Fayette, Greene, Jefferson, Pickens, Randolph, St. Clair, Shelby, Sumter, Talladega, Tuscaloosa and Walker Counties. General Chrysler and his soldiers were of the Fourth New York Cavalry, and his Staff was in part composed of:

1st Lieut. and Adj. Robert Barber, A. A. A.
Capt. C. W. Becker, Provost Marshall,
Capt. C. Dolan, Outpost Officer
1st Lieut. C. W. Johnson, A. A. Q. M.
1st Lieut. S. F. Taylor, A. C. S.
1st Lieut. H. D. Doty, A. Co.

The local postmaster was replaced by C. M. Hopson, a Yankee.

Buildings and contents on the north and east sides of the Square, previously used for Commissaries of the Confederate Army, were confiscated.

Orders were issued to those who held Confederate property to deliver it to headquarters. They were warned that a list of such persons was on file, and arrest would follow if those in possession of such property failed to comply with orders.

Orders were issued for all Confederate soldiers to report for registration, turn in all arms, and sign an Oath of Amnesty. By June 15th, 6410 officers and enlisted Confederates had presented themselves for parole.

Shipments of grain, flour and other commodities were prohibited.

The purchase of horses and mules from Federal soldiers was prohibited.

Freedmen were notified that they would not be allowed to "straggle about the country"; they were urged to stay on the farms, raise corn and other food products, or seek employment; that no pillaging would be tolerated.

General Chrysler assured both white and freedmen that he was in Talladega to bring order, to protect them, and to see that they had the necessities.

The slave owner was to feed the freedman until some provision could be made. He had helped make the crop and was entitled to his part. To this the farmer concurred. However, there were hundreds of people who had made no crop. It was estimated that there were 250,000 hungry people in the State at the time. Many had depended for some time upon the charity of his neighbor. Their horses and mules long since had been confiscated or stolen.

General Taylor, having surrendered on May 4th, also cancelled automatically the Confederate Government. A Governor was not appointed by the President until June 21st. Therefore, the whole of Alabama was void of Civil Government for seven weeks. During this period there was unrest everywhere. The Negro was free, and had no idea what to do with his freedom. Many had labored under the impression that the master's property was to be equally divided between them when war ended, and that they would never have to work. Some freedmen simply walked out as soon as freed; a few masters, resenting emancipation, ordered the freedmen to move out; some freedmen remained on the farms, but refused to work, were demanding and arrogant, and were asked to leave. But the greater number of ex-masters and freedmen talked matters over, and came to some workable solution until legal action could be taken and a procedure approved. By September many freedmen were reported congregating in town. Thefts, night marauding, and depredations were common. They were moving into town, taking possession of barns, stables and empty sheds. They were tearing down fences for fuel, and stealing food to keep from starving. Notices appeared, listing these atrocities, by the Provost Marshal, warning freedmen that such would not be tolerated, and urging them to seek work or they would be arrested. He warned again that "Idleness will not be tolerated."[1]

When Talladega was first placed under martial law, there was quite a feeling of distrust and resentment among the citizens. Some order was soon restored, however, and there was great respect for the Occupational Army.

When General Chrysler was relieved in November by Brev. Major General A. L. Chetlain, of the U. S. Volunteers, several complimentary tributes were paid to his Staff, especially to "Bob Barber" and "Capt. Dolan". Of the garrison at large it was said "There are those in it, who we are sure cannot be improved upon, and the principal officers all seem determined to do all in their power – to conciliate the people and advance the interest of the country."[2] Other occupied territories were not so fortunate as was Talladega. Many towns

---

[1] Democratic Watchtower, Sept. 6, 1865, on file Tall. Public Library
[2] Democratic Watchtower, Aug. 16, 1865, on file Tall. Public Library

suffered indignities and insults, and pages have been written of atrocities committed during this first post-war period.

When war was declared in 1861, there was only one saloon in Talladega. Immediately after the war ended, six began operations. General Chrysler closed them all. He was thanked through the local papers for his timely act. Evidently they continued operations under cover, for Maj. Gen. Chatlain found it necessary to issue an order a few days after his arrival in Talladega, that "gambling, horse racing, and sale or gift of intoxicating liquors are hereby prohibited to enlisted men in the service of the United States."

Where various headquarters of specific departments were located, I've been unable to determine. Some years ago a dentist and his wife from Missouri came to Talladega for a short vacation. He had a diary of his Grandfather's, kept while stationed in Talladega with the Army of Occupation. He was in the Quartermaster's Corps. From this diary, more humorous than historical, I learned that the Quartermaster's Corps was stationed in the old Southern Inn, which was located just south of the present Southern Railway depot, on the east side of East Street.

I also discovered from the diary, that there was a garrison located at the Willman place, about three miles south of town, with a hospital in connection, which was later used as a Freedman's Hospital.

Talladega was under Martial Law for several years. During this period, there are several subjects which should be treated separately.

Provisional Government

After the War, Talladega was classed among the "Radical" counties of the State. Perhaps because some of her leading citizens had unequivocally adhered to the opinion that a state had no right to secede from the Union. Among these citizens was Lewis E. Parsons.

Abraham Lincoln had proclaimed in 1863 that, under the Constitution of the United States, no state had a right to secede; that the Southern States were still Union States where insurrection had taken place, and that they would be re-instated as such when the war was ended. He again publicly proclaimed this immediately after Lee's surrender. Three days after Lee's surrender, on April 14, 1865, Lincoln was assassinated by John Wilkes Booth. Although Lincoln was hated by some as one who had indirectly brought about war, he was highly respected, and the people of the South realized that the death of Lincoln was a heavy blow to them. President Johnson attempted to carry out the plans of Lincoln, but a hostile Congress refused them. The office of Provisional Governor was created for each state, that some sort of order might be brought about. On June 21, 1865, Lewis E. Parsons, of Talladega, was appointed Provisional Governor of Alabama.

Governor Parsons was a man highly respected by everyone. He was a native of New York State; born April 28, 1817 of an intellectually prominent family, being descended from Dr. Jonathan Edwards. Mr. Parsons studied law in Pennsylvania and New York. He came to Talladega in 1840, and became one of Alabama's most distinguished lawyers. Garrett, in "Reminiscences of Public Men in Alabama" said of him "He has manifestly been a Union man, without disguise, though offering no factious opposition to the majority. All parties believed him honest, and only conservative in his views."

Although Mr. Parsons had expressed his views without compromise, he was elected to the House of Representatives in 1859, and again in 1863, during the War. It can, therefore, be seen that he was highly esteemed by the citizens of Talladega County. Through this public capacity he had gained favor throughout the State.

Although he remained firm in his convictions, the sons of Governor Parsons became Confederate soldiers. Immediately upon his appointment Governor Parsons announced that former officials who had signed the Oath of Amnesty, were re-instated until a new constitution could be made and a new election called.

All previous laws except that "portion which relates to slaves, are hereby declared in full force and operation." Because there was so much want, he immediately appointed Marcus H. Cruikshank, of Talladega, Commissioner of the Destitute for the State of Alabama.

An election was called for selecting members to a Constitutional Convention. Those elected in Talladega County were Joseph D. McCann, Andrew Cunningham and Alexander White. The Convention met in Montgomery September 12, 1865, where they proceeded to change the Confederate State Constitution to conform with the Constitution of the Union. They made ordinances declaring the Constitution and proceedings of the Convention of 1861 null and void; declaring the War debt void; and declaring the abolition of slavery.

A date was set for the election of national, state, county and municipal officers.

The Convention passed resolutions expressing their confidence in "the integrity, patriotism and capacity" of Mr. Parsons, and they acknowledged "the courtesy and kindness which have uniformly distinguished his conduct in his intercourse with us."

The new Legislature assembled on Nov. 20, 1865. Mr. Parsons had not been a candidate for the office of Governor, and Robert M. Patton was elected. His inauguration took place on Dec. 13, 1865, but he did not take office until Dec. 20, 1865.

As evidence of a still higher degree of public favor, the General Assembly, unanimously elected Gov. Parsons as Senator of the United States for a term of six years. However, neither Mr. Parsons, nor any other southern national officer elected, was ever seated. Congress eventually annulled all Provisional Government proceedings, and Alabama was placed under Military control.

Freedmen's Bureau

When the State of Alabama conformed to Union regulations, it was hoped that local affairs would readily be adjusted into the new order of things. They would have, had the citizens been permitted the privilege of governing themselves, but the military rule continued to operate, largely through the Freedmen's Bureau. This Bureau was created by Lincoln over a month before Lee surrendered for the "supervision and management of all abandoned lands, and the control of all subjects relating to refugees and freedmen from the rebel states, under such rules and regulations as may be prescribed by the head of the Bureau, and approved by the President."[1]

The Bureau operated through Dec. 31, 1868. Within their jurisdiction were around 500,000 freedmen in Alabama.

General Wager Swayne was made head of the Bureau in Alabama in July of 1865. His duties involved the issuing of rations to freedmen, making arrests for infractions of the law; of making and of enforcing the carrying out of contracts between employers and freedmen. He was to have full jurisdiction over the freedmen, over and above state or municipal government. In many cases orders were carried out by unqualified subordinates—men who had never been associated with Negroes in any way, and who were absolutely incapacitated and unprepared to cope with fractious situations which naturally occurred. Local men frequently had to plead for the arrested Negro, feeling that certain punishments were too severe.

The Bureau was supported in most part by confiscated property of the Confederacy. Foundries, storehouses and contents, cotton, etc., were sold at auction. Privately owned products were frequently seized illegally, and there was no recourse or protection to the owner.

A great deal of injustice took place. Among the stipulations of the recommended contract between planter and freedman, were "just treatment, wholesome food, comfortable clothing, suitable quarters, fuel and medical attendance." The employer himself, in many cases, had no such comforts. There was no money, and it was impossible for him to carry out his part of the required contract.

The freedmen would desert on any provocation, were insubordinate, and there was constant friction and controversy. The Bureau would usually side with the freedman, and became a great hindrance to discipline and progress.

---

[1] Dr. Owen's History of Alabama, Vol. I, Page 629

Talladega County was to suffer financially a great deal more than other Alabama counties because of activities of the Freedmen's Bureau within her limits.

One of the functions of the Bureau was that of caring for the sick and infirm freedmen. To take care of these over the State, the Bureau located a Freedmen's Hospital "about 2 miles S. E. of Talladega," on property rented from J. W. Riley. A local Board of Trustees was appointed, composed of Dr. Jo H. Johnson, Chairman and Superintendent, G. T. McAfee and Geo. P. Plowman. These men served without compensation. Ample funds were not appropriated to take care of these patients, and it became a burden on the people of Talladega for months before it was closed.

The Bureau also established a school for freedmen in the Baptist High School building, which was later purchased and operated by the American Missionary Association. At this time, the building was named "Swayne Hall", in honor of General Wager Swayne, head of the Freedmen's Bureau, and is still known by this name. Many of our cultured people resided on Battle Street, West, and owned handsome and comfortable homes. The property immediately was depreciated, and a great sacrifice had to be made when they felt forced to move to another neighborhood.

Talladega suffered, along with other counties, through the activities of the "Loyal League." This organization was sponsored by the Freedmen's Bureau, Carpetbaggers and Scalawags, with membership composed almost entirely of freedmen. They were required to sign an oath of loyalty to the Republican party, when not one in a thousand could read the oath. The organizations were usually headed by Negro preachers, with meetings at night in the churches. Many members, after the meetings, would form in groups to pillage, steal, or cause disturbances. The mysterious pass words, the "brass button", ceremonies and emblems, greatly impressed the Negro. Especially were they impressed on certain occasions when they burned the "Fire of Liberty" in a censer filled with chemicals. The Freedmen's Bureau and the Loyal League officers were largely responsible for the increased hostile attitude of the United States Congress toward the South, with the resultant change of Alabama Government, and the corruption that followed. The attitude of Talladega people toward conditions existing at this time was expressed in the Democratic Watchtower[2] under the heading:

---

[2] Democratic Watchtower, July 26, 1865, on file Tall. Public Library

"CIVIL LAW RESTORED"

"The most difficult and delicate business which the convention will have to discharge, will be to devise and adopt suitable laws and regulations to meet the new relations which the Negro now bears towards our political system. There is not a slave now in Alabama. It is not our purpose to discuss the wisdom or the justice of the policy which severed the relations of master and slave, and liberated four millions of Africans in our midst. It is enough for us to know that that relation has been severed by the sword, and that the decree is final. But as wise and true men, who are to become the managers and controllers of the destinies of the Negro, in his new relations, no less than in his former condition, it becomes our duty to legislate for him with wisdom, humanity and forbearance, and thereby promote his moral and physical well-being and our own property.

Laws should be adopted in reference to him, stimulating industry, and severely punishing vagrancy and vice. The Negro is not responsible for the present state of things and no malice should be borne toward him. He is our chief supply of labor at present, and he must look to us as in the past, to guide and direct his labor into productive and profitable channels. He will not always be under the protection and care of the Freedman's Bureau, subsisting on the beneficence of the Federal Government, and the question whether he shall, in his new and changed relation, become a blessing or a curse to us, we, ourselves, must in large measure determine."

Reconstruction
Under
Scalawags and Carpetbaggers

While Alabama had considered herself slowly reconstructing under the 1865 Constitution, there was an undertow of corruption in Congress that completely destroyed every vestige of improvement.

The hostile attitude of Congress toward the South, had increased to such an extent that they refused to seat Representatives from Alabama to both Houses. By Acts of March 3 through the 23rd, 1867, they had annulled the Constitution of 1865, and all other legislative proceedings under it. They disfranchised the Confederate soldiers as disloyal citizens; franchised the Negro freedmen; and placed Alabama under complete Military rule as a dependency, through a Federal Reconstruction Committee. This was created to bring about "internal improvements."

Where chaos had existed bedlam took place.

Alabama was mystified, stunned and resentful. Carpetbaggers and Scalawags took over. These terms were contemptuous epithets.

Webster gives as one definition for CARPETBAGGER, "applied to a political adventurer from the North, seeking profit in the South after the American Civil War." Dr. Owens adds "one with all his belongings in his carpetbag." A carpetbag, in those days, was equivalent to a suit case in these. The Carpetbaggers came from every direction like vultures, to prey on what they thought was a dead South. Many came for political gain, becoming qualified voters at once; but others came for financial gain.

Talladega County, having a Federal post within her bounds, had a large number of Carpetbaggers in action. This was evidenced by an order from the Commander of the post, that no persons were permitted to appear in the uniform of the United States Army unless they were enlisted men. It was the custom of the Carpetbaggers to go into the rural districts, wearing the U. S. Army uniform, representing himself as an authorized agent to confiscate property.

The SCALAWAG was a Southern man who turned against his own party for personal gain, and was held in contempt and with disgust, by his fellow citizens.

Talladega had a number of highly respected "Radicals", to whom the name "Scalawag" was erroneously applied. Many intelligent men of prominence joined forces with the Union officers, sincerely feeling that they could better and more speedily bring about reconstruction. Out of the group called "Radicals" grew the Talladega County Republican party.

At the 1867 Constitutional Convention, under this Reconstruction Committee, Talladega was represented by Geo. P. Plowman and Arthur Bingham.

Among those elected to State offices under this Constitution of 1867 from Talladega County, were:

Green T. McAfee, Senator; H. W. W. Rice and E. T. Childress, Representatives. Arthur Bingham was made State Treasurer. Talladega was fortunate in having neither foreigner nor illiterate Negro to represent her, although those who did accept office were severely criticized for having done so.

The State machinery was set in motion for "Reconstruction" with the following:

Wm. H. Smith, of Randolph Co., Governor
A. J. Applegate, of Ohio, Lieut. Governor
Charles A. Miller, of Maine, Secretary of State
R. M. Reynolds, of Maine, State Auditor
John C. Keller, of Ohio, Commissioner of Industries
Arthur Bingham, of Talladega County, Treasurer.
Judges of the Supreme Court were foreigners.

The House of Representatives was composed of 27 freedmen, Carpetbaggers from 8 states of the Union, and 2 foreign countries, Scalawags and a few loyal Alabamians. "Reconstruction" in Alabama began with this background. There could be no greater misnomer for such a period. It should have been called the "Destruction" period of Alabama, because havoc took place unparalleled in American history.

If Carpetbaggers came South feeling that the South was dead, they soon reversed their opinion.

The people were even more stirred than during secession days. The Reconstructionists had enacted laws to humiliate and crush the South; their organizations among the Negroes, to repudiate all local government and discipline, caused unhappiness among the freedmen, and they were confused.

The Negro was the unhappy victim of circumstances over which he had no control. He was, in many cases, only one generation from savagery, illiterate and ignorant. During the War he had been loyal and dependable. The master had left everything he held dear in his hands - his wife, children, home and estate. The slave had not betrayed his trust. He had shielded and protected his master's property.

The slave had vaguely hoped and longed for freedom, but he had expected it from his master, for what could he do with freedom if the master did not show him what to do with it? He had depended upon a master ever since he was taken into bondage. What could he do with freedom in a strange country? Freedom was an uncharted sea. He had to have a pilot. Now he was confused and afraid. Strangers, who did not love and understand him, were undertaking the task of guiding him. He felt himself being carried on treacherous shoals.

He was more and more confused and afraid, and gradually drifted into a state of indifferent surrender to the new leadership and influences surrounding him.

Such disorder and corruption followed these "Reconstruction" proceedings, which the disfranchised Southerner could not quell legally, that it became advisable to embrace other methods.

Many prominent citizens of Talladega became so depressed over the hopelessness of conditions in Alabama during the Reconstruction period, that hundreds of them emigrated to Texas.

The Census of Talladega County in 1860 and of 1870 are significant:

1860	14,634	White	8,886	Negro	23,520	Total
1870	8,469	White	9,595	Negro	18,064	Total

Drastic measures became necessary. Corrupt politics followed Reconstruction unsurpassed in history. Wm. H. Skaggs candidly and cruelly pictures it in his "Southern Oligarchy."

Voters even boasted that at last they had won a victory by "fighting the Devil with fire". It was possibly a case of "A drowning man grasps a straw."

In 1874 Geo. Smith Houston was elected governor. J. A. J. Sims and A. C. Wood, represented Talladega in the House of Representatives, and Andrew Cunningham was Senator. Levi W. Lawler, of Talladega, was one of three chosen to investigate the state debt, and to recommend adjustments. The debt had jumped from $6,500,000 to $30,000,000 during the Reconstruction period.

With Democrats now in office, there was at last a feeling of peace and relaxation. Relaxation was only mental, for the citizens of Talladega never worked so hard before to bring order out of confusion. They gathered up the pieces and put them back together like a jig saw puzzle. There was poverty everywhere. The Freedmen's Bureau had ceased operations, and the freedmen were left helpless on the hands of the Southerner, for whom he had refused to work during the reconstruction period. Now, that he was on his own resources, there was nothing left for him but to move back to the farm he had deserted, under a completely new relationship. The farmer needed the Negro, as much as the Negro needed the farmer, so they began all over to attempt friendly agreements, which never reached the pre-war cooperative level.

Farm implements were worn out. Horses and mules were scarce. Houses in Quarters for slaves, kept in perfect condition before the War, were in distressing need of repair. Clothes of both farmer and freedmen were old and ragged. There was no money. The Southern man's credit was good. He stood for the freedman, and they slowly pulled along together. The large planter never recovered his former prosperity. It was too late to regain. Too much was at stake. Had he been allowed the privilege of repatriation in 1865, before complete decay had come about, he might have recovered. Now it was too late. Most of the large planters continued to live on their plantations, and most of them died there, but debt and mortgage eventually forced the next generation to sell and move out.

The once beautiful plantation mansions in Talladega County where love and contentment had been dominant forces that bred great leadership, were now burdens. The gentleman farmer could no longer exist off of his land. Other sources must be sought.

The women who lived during Reconstruction Days never surrendered. Though the Confederate outwardly surrendered, and his body eventually buried, his spirit has never died.

Expansion

Talladega experienced a great upheaval of enterprise during "Flush Days". She suffered during the depression that followed; settled into a slow, but steady, building of handsome homes and storehouses, and again experienced great prosperity, which continued ten memorable years. Then came the devastating ravages of war and resultant poverty. The climax came during the horrible days of Reconstruction. Then slow recovery until 1880, when the tide began steadily to change.

The year 1885 marked the beginning of complete recovery, and of Talladega's first really progressive expansion since the town was established.

The growth began when William H. Skaggs was elected Mayor of Talladega at the age of 23. Mr. Skaggs was a native of Talladega, born Sept. 16, 1861. He married first, Ella Earle Yancey, of Selma, in 1885. There were born to them two children, William Yancey Skaggs and Mary Lanier Skaggs. Both children died some years ago. Mrs. Ella Yancey Skaggs died in 1902. Mr. Skaggs was married the second time to Julia Frances Ollis, of Kansas City, Mo. He died several years ago, in New York City. Mrs. Julia Skaggs survives him, and still lives in New York. After leaving Talladega, Mr. Skaggs became a renowned lecturer and writer. He wrote "Public Schools in the South," 1910; "Vice-Regent of God and His Chosen People", 1914; "German Conspiracies in America", 1916; "The Outlaws of Christendom", 1918; "The Southern Oligarchy", 1924. He had another book almost ready for publication when he died.

Mr. Skaggs served three terms, of two years each, as mayor of Talladega. At the time he was elected in 1885, the following aldermen were also elected:

Dr. Jo. H. Johnson and F. E. Wilson, Aldermen First Ward
Dr. B. W. Toole and N. J. Hubbard, Aldermen Second Ward
G. A. Joiner and John R. Barrett, Aldermen Third Ward
John B. Knox and W. N. Boynton, Aldermen Fourth Ward

With this splendid group of co-workers an entirely new municipal system was established during the six years of service. The revenue of the city was increased by reforming the tax and license systems; a public school system was established; water and sewerage systems put in operation; the gas output increased, and many reforms were put into force.

Mr. Skaggs argued that nothing tended more toward promoting material development than education, and that it should be as near free of tuition as finances of the city would justify. Therefore, the building of a Public School was the first real undertaking, after the Charter of the City had been regulated. To erect this building city bonds in the amount of $12,000.00 were issued at 7 percent interest. They were sold at par on the Stock Market of New York.

Many other changes took place about which I will let Mr. Skaggs tell you himself.

By request, Mr. Skaggs wrote me, under date of May 18, 1928, a detailed but incomplete account of transactions during his administration as mayor. The article of 87 pages is too lengthy to quote in full, but this interesting chapter of the history of Talladega is condensed from his "Chronicle":

"MEMORANDUM OF CERTAIN OUTSTANDING EVENTS IN THE HISTORY OF Talladega, Alabama, during the administration of William H. Skaggs as Mayor". By Wm. H. Skaggs:

Col. John W. Bishop was Mayor of Talladega at the time of my first election to that office. He had succeeded Mr. G. K. Miller, who resigned as Mayor when he was appointed Judge of Probate, to fill the vacancy made by the resignation of Judge William H. Thornton . . .

I cannot now recall the various issues that were discussed during the campaign, but after my nomination, I made a speech before the Convention in which I made certain promises. First, and perhaps most important, I promised that, if elected Mayor, I would, without fear or favor, strictly and impartially enforce the laws, especially the penal ordinances.

Reorganization and increase of the police force was absolutely necessary. We needed men of good physique, physical courage, sobriety and good character . . . I knew that Mr. P. S. Williams was a man of cool and unflinching courage, high character and sobriety, and good discretion. He accepted my offer for the place of Chief of Police and the City Council did not hesitate to approve my appointment . . .

During the Reconstruction period, and for some years thereafter, Negroes would gather in large numbers in and around the Baptist church and the schoolhouse on the same lot.

These protracted gatherings were frequently the cause of racial outbreaks and disorderly conduct . . . The chief trouble was not racial; it was between different factions of the Negroes . . .This trouble grew and spread until some definite action became imperative . . . The congregation and membership were so large that they ought to be divided. One faction decided that it was ready to quit the old church and would build a new church if the white people would help them. One leading Negro suggested that they build a "Peace Baptist Church", and the suggestion met with enthusiastic response. I told them that I would write out a form of subscription for the "Peace Baptist Church" . . . Subscriptions for the "Peace Baptist Church" were started as soon as the police court adjourned. . . There was no further trouble at the old Battle Street church.

The city charter was wholly inadequate and out of date. It did not meet the requirements of a growing and progressive community . . . A bill was prepared and introduced which provided for a new and very liberal charter for Talladega. . .

Immediately after the Legislature passed the act granting a new and greatly enlarged charter for the City of Talladega, the community seemed instantly to pass from a political status of a town to that of a city.

In order to carry out the extensive improvements already undertaken and those contemplated, it was necessary to make very great increase in the revenues of the city . . . The privilege taxes were "stretched to the limit." A license was placed on every profession, trade and special line of business not otherwise taxed. Lawyers, physicians, dentists, barbers, bankers, theatres, auctioneers, saloons; in short, there was no profession, except school teachers and preachers, no trade or business in Talladega that escaped the tax gatherer . .

At the time of my election the City had a total funded debt of $750.00 in the form of a short term note with the banking house of Isbell Co., on which it was paying interest at the rate of 18 per cent per annum. This note was endorsed by every member of the City Council because the City had no bank credit and it could not borrow without endorsement. The unfunded debt was very small, perhaps not more than $150.00 for supplies and current expenses.

The public streets of Talladega were in bad condition in 1885. They never had been in good condition, because no durable work had been undertaken. The town had never had in its service a capable engineer or road mender. The only pretense of a paved street in the town was that part of East Street between the public square and the E. T. V. & Ga. (Southern now) railroad station. For many years the major portion of the cotton marketed in Talladega was weighed and delivered for account of the purchaser at the old cotton warehouse on North Street, back of Storey's store, opposite the old Isbell home. From that place of original delivery, it was necessary for the cotton to be hauled to the railroad station for shipment to compress at Rome or Selma. The big wagons used in hauling the cotton from the warehouse to the railroad cut deep holes in East Street and, from time to time, these holes were filled with broken rocks, until that part of East Street was called a paved street. But it was not graded, consequently, it was very uneven and rough, without proper drainage or curbing.

The sidewalks on North, East, Court and Battle Streets, facing the public square, were paved with bricks. In some places the bricks were good and properly placed. There was no curbing and the bricks on the outer line did not stay in place very long. In wet weather a very large area of the public square was a veritable hole of red mud; in the dry season it was a bed of dust and trash. Stepping stones were placed on some of the streets between sidewalks, particularly on North and East Streets at the intersections of those streets, and on North and Court Streets at their intersection. There were no stepping-stones, or other conveniences for the accommodation of pedestrians at any crossings near the public square except those to which reference has been made.

Many citizens thought the stepping-stones were not only a great inconvenience but a real danger. Ankle sprains and other painful injuries, resulting from missteps at these crossings were not uncommon. The stepping-stones were usually several inches above the mean level of the roadway and it required the skill of an expert and sober driver to clear the crossings without bumping over the stones, at the risk of breaking an axle, a wheel or a few spokes. The plain truth about the matter was that the stepping-stones were a nuisance . . .

There were at least three nuisances on or near the public square which I very much desired to abate, and I had resolved that, if I were elected Mayor, I should try to abate these nuisances as quickly as possible. The first of these three nuisances which I had in mind was the stepping-stones; the second was the unsightly market-house situated on or near the south-west corner of the public square; the third was the old custom of feeding stock and cattle on the public square.

The so-called market house was a shapeless building, with latticework of wooden strips, the whole length and width of the building, including the big doors at each end of the building. It was at least well ventilated and daubed with mineral paint. The only heating apparatus was a wood-burning stove provided by each lessee of a stall in the market-house, and the black, unsightly stove- pipe from the stove of each stall extended through the side of the building. The place became notorious, not only because of the unsightly appearance of the exterior and interior of the building, and the unsanitary condition in and around it, but also on account of the brawls and tragedies which had occurred in and near the building.

The only way to abate the nuisance was to close the market stalls and remove the building. At last the stalls were closed and the unsightly building was removed.

From the early settlement of the town, the public square was the principal market place for the products of forest and farm. There were a few small farmers living near town who peddled their pro-ducts in the residential sections of the town; but these products, so essential to the household, were sold in larger quantities on the public square to the men folks, who usually held the purse-strings in those days. As a general rule, women made few purchases except dry goods and millinery; groceries were bought by men in large quantities for the home. Practically every homestead in the town had its own garden, and housekeepers who did not raise their own vegetables usually went without . . .

Wagons loaded with these products would stand on the public square until the products with which they were loaded were sold in bulk or by retail . . .

It was the custom for farmers to stop their wagons loaded with cotton on the public square, where a sample of the cotton was taken and the first price named by the sampler. The farmer would then go with his sample to the different buyers, hoping to get a higher price for his cotton than the price named by the sampler. But, prior to 1885, or thereabouts, practically all cotton-buyers were merchants and, after stating the number of bales he had on the wagon ready for delivery, he was asked how much "trade" there would be in the transaction, i.e., the total amount of purchases which he and his family would make from the merchant to whom the cotton would be sold. If the prospect of liberal purchases of merchandise were attractive, the price offered for the cotton was usually raised above the first bid; if the promise of trade was not liberal there was very little competition in the bidding. In numerous cases where the total purchase price of the cotton would be absorbed in payment on debts, the farmer did not always receive the maximum market price.

After having submitted his sample to all the buyers, the farmer decided to whom he would sell his cotton. The purchaser gave him a Ticket with shipping directions and the farmer with the ticket returned to his wagon and started to the depot to have his cotton weighed and properly marked. During the months of November, December and January, when the bulk of the cotton was usually sold by the farmers, East Street, from the public square to the E. T. V. & Ga. depot was crowded from early morning until late in the afternoon, with wagons of farmers loaded with cotton which had been sold and was being hauled to the depot. They usually drove down East Street to the depot and, after their cotton had been unloaded, they drove back to the public square via Court Street.

In bad weather, East Street from the public square to the railroad was almost impassable, and the approaches to the platform of the depot where the farmers' cotton was delivered and weighed were, if possible, in worse condition than the street. About the time I was elected or a few months thereafter, a new brick, cotton warehouse – the first brick warehouse built in Talladega - was erected by a company organized for that purpose. . . The warehouse was erected in Talladega through the efforts of the recently organized Chamber of Commerce. . . . The new arrangement saved much time, and some petty annoyances which seemed unavoidable under the old system. . .

Wagon yards, enclosed with high board fences, some with crude stalls and troughs for feeding and watering the stock, from well or cistern, with ample supply of water, inside the yard, and rough, frame shelters with bunks which afforded some protection from rain and wind, were usually found at or near market places where farmers, who came from such distance as necessitated their spending a night at the market place, could, for a nominal consideration, secure crude lodging accommodations for themselves and some conveniences and protection for their teams. One of the first, if not the first, wagon yards in Talladega was located at the south east corner of Battle and West Streets. It was just across the street from the big spring branch, only a few hundred feet below the head of the big spring . . . A large and beautiful pool of clear, cool water had been easily formed by proper excavations on the side of the stream near Battle Street. The approach to the pool from the roadway connecting with Battle Street had been car fully prepared. It was broad and pebbly, and there were large sycamore and sweet-gum trees near the pool which afforded ample shade for man and beast. Pebbles covered the bottom of the pool, and on the sides the pebbles were almost covered with beautiful water-mosses. It was the favorite watering-place for horses of the stage coaches, race horses, and horses and elephants from the circus-menageries that came to Talladega were watered at this pool.

The Nance wagon-yard was opened not long after the Civil War, and, in 1885, at the time of my first election as Mayor, it was the most substantial and popular wagon-yard in Talladega. It was located on the west side of East Street, hardly more than the distance of half a block north of the public square.

Almost coincidental with the building of the new fire-proof cotton warehouse, Mr. J. A. Savery established a new wagon-yard on East Street, at the intersection of Coffee Street, with the main entrance on East Street opposite the station of the Anniston & Atlantic (later L. & N.) Railroad. This was the most commodious and convenient wagon-yard which had been established in Talladega, and it was a very valuable addition to the wagon-yard facilities and accommodations of the place.

The construction of the fire-proof cotton warehouse, and the improvement of the wagon-yard accommodations, which have been cited, made possible and practicable the abatement of the third of the three nuisances on the public square which . . . I very much desired to abate as soon as possible after my first election.

The third nuisance of the public square to which I have referred was that of feeding stock and cattle on the public square . . . After their cotton had been unloaded, they drove back to the public square where they left their teams standing until they were ready to start for their homes or to the wagon-yard to spend the night . . . The usual food was corn or oats with fodder, placed on the ground in front of the horse or mule. Occasionally a small box was provided . . . Necessarily much of it was wasted so far as the farmer's stock was concerned. The public square in Talladega was a public feeding-ground that attracted all the strays of the community, including "Aunt Emily's geese", and some of Dan Harnut's old rawbones. The farmer's horse or mule was fed while standing hitched to a wagon, and, in this position with harness on, it could not make a very successful fight for food which the farmer had provided. The predatory strays of Talladega captured and devoured a large portion of the provender which the farmer placed before his stock on the public square, and Aunt Emily's geese were not the most dilatory among the strays that gathered around the feeding stock on the public square. The flock of geese was one of the sights of the town. Their habits were as regular as clock work, and they were as bold as the most voracious beast of prey. Every morning, except Sunday, this flock of geese left their home at seven o'clock, and flew, in regular formation, over Battle Street, about fifty feet above the mean level of the street, and landed at the south-west corner of the public square. They always landed at the same place, unless a wagon or other temporary obstruction occupied their regular landing place when they arrived, in which case, they landed as near as possible to the accustomed landing place.

Immediately following the arrival of the flock of geese on the public square, there was a honking roll call, then a hissing signal of caution, after which the flock divided into squads, each squad moving in a different direction on the usual foraging expedition. The foraging was limited to the area of the public square; they never went beyond . . .

A general but careful survey of the square was made every day and continued until about noon when the farmers began feeding their stock standing on the square, and the different squads of geese immediately turned their attention to the places where the farmers had placed food for their horses and mules. The contest for the food lasted until all the food had been consumed. At four o'clock in the afternoon, the geese reassembled at the place where they had arrived in the morning and, in the same formation, they flew back to their home with Aunt Emily. As before stated, the flock of geese came to the public square every day except Sunday; they seemed to know that no food was distributed on the square on Sunday.

Next to Aunt Emily's geese, the most ravenous foragers that exploited the public square were some of the strays from Dan Hardnut's menagerie . . . Dan was president of the "United Horse-swappers Association of Talladega, Clay and Coosa Counties." This association held semi-annual meetings in Talladega. For many years their meetings were held on a vacant lot on Court Street, near the intersection of Coffee Street. So far as historic association could have any bearing on the policies and practices of horse traders' organizations, whether for pleasure or profit, the place selected for the semi-annual meetings of the horse-swappers of Talladega and some adjoining counties was appropriate. It was the rear end and vacant part of the lot fronting on the public square at the corner of Battle and Court Streets, on which the famous old

Lawson Tavern stood, with the big town pump near by, and beautiful shade-trees in front, at west side, and on the vacant lot back of the Tavern.

Many travelers stopped at the Lawson Tavern, including not only those who traveled by stage-coach, but many who journeyed to that hostelry by private conveyances and horseback. Political and religious questions were the popular topics for discussion in those days, and when not engaged in discussing these questions, or playing games, travelers found other diversions. Inasmuch as horses and mules furnished the only means of travel in that country, at that time, it was not strange that horse trading became a popular pastime at places where travelers met. The Lawson Tavern, with its big, shady, back lot, was no exception to the vogue, and numerous horses changed hands on the old Tavern lot in the early history of Talladega.

The strays that wandered from the horse-swappers' meeting, like other strays of the town, and Aunt Emily's geese, were attracted to the public square because it was the principal feeding place for the farmers who came to market with their teams . . .

Happily, however, new progressive ideas and the growth of the town soon found a solution for this question. Shortly after the building of the fire-proof warehouse and the new wagon-yard, the farmers ceased to feed their stock on the public square, and when the feeding ceased, the strays and Aunt Emily's geese no longer wandered to the old feeding ground.

Before beginning any permanent improvements on the public square, or the streets, it was necessary to find a man who was competent to take charge of the work. . .

The matter of finding a competent man for Street Superintendent was very urgent. Fortunately, my attention was directed to Charles Kern, who, at the time of my first election, was keeping a small eating place on the north side of the square. At the suggestion of Mr. Williams, Chief of Police, Mr. Kern called to see me and my conversation with him impressed me very favorably. I learned that Mr. Kern was a native of Germany, where he had worked on the public roads before he came to America, and he had worked on railroads after he came to this country. He was a very intelligent, sober man with good elementary education, energetic and in fine health . . . I decided at once that Mr. Kern was the man I wanted and the man that Talladega very much needed for Superintendent of Streets . . .

I believe about the first work undertaken after the appointment of Mr. Kern was on the sidewalk and gutters on the public square. I had given this work some investigation and I did not believe any satisfactory and permanent improvements could be made on the sidewalk without stone curbing properly placed. The best curbstone was the granite mined at the famous Stone Mountain near Atlanta, Ga. This stone was being used in all leading Southern cities. It was very expensive but it was the best on the market; in fact, it was the best that nature provided. Our new Superintendent said that he had experience in the line of work required for placing the curbstone and other things incident thereto, but, in this as other improvements, it was necessary to get the approval of the City Council and to find the money with which to pay for the stone.

There was a great deal of outspoken opposition to the proposition for curbstone and other expensive improvements incident thereto. The chief opposition was on account of the expense. Talladega had "gotten along for a long time without such outrageous expenditures for street improvements", and many good citizens thought the town could get along for many more years without such heavy expenditures as sidewalks. It was a hard fight, but I was beginning to learn, soon after my election, that practically every measure I brought forward for change and improvement in any department of city government aroused opposition, and fighting soon became an essential part of the various projects for betterment . . .

For many years, no doubt from the earliest settlement of the place, it had been the custom to hitch horses and mules to posts placed around the Court House. These hitching-posts were stuck around the Court House indiscriminately, and there was no uniformity in the quality or character of timber from which these hitching-posts were hewn or cut, nor any uniformity in height or thickness, or position in which they stood . . . In bad weather, every hitching-post was in the middle of a filthy mud-hole; in dry weather, it was in the middle of a filthy bed of dust. Horses and mules were frequently left standing at these posts for six or seven hours and, as a matter of course, they were restive and champed the posts and pawed the ground around them. The hitching-posts and the ground around them were unsightly . . .

Finally, however, more substantial hitching-posts were erected on several vacant lots near the square and in the wagon-yards, and, as the use of the hitching-posts on private lots increased, those on the public square were gradually removed, and another nuisance passed into history.

The public square was very bare and naked, and it was always untidy. The old Court House that stood in the center of the square was an eyesore. The side fronting north had the appearance of a prison and the grounds were unkept. The only attractive or beautiful objects on the public square were the few remaining shade trees near the Court House. I very much desired to improve and beautify the public square; first, by proper grading and draining; and then, so far as possible, convert it into a park with shade-trees, walks, and a pavilion, with seats where people could assemble. I was afraid to talk too much about turning the public square into a public park, because I was already severely criticized and laughed at for some of my suggestions about public improvement . . .

After the work of placing curbstones along the sidewalks fronting the public square had been completed, a large amount of grading was completed and a large part of the square was properly macadamized. There was very pronounced opposition to my project for shade-trees on the public square, and, as usual, very strong pressure was brought to bear on the City Council by those who opposed the project . . . In spite of the prolonged and rather acrimonious discussion that ensued, I was able to hold a majority of the City Council on my side, and the trees were planted . . . It was a fine beginning for a beautiful park, and, at the close of my third and last term as Mayor, a large majority of the citizens of Talladega often spoke with pride of the wonderful improvement in the appearance of the public square and its environments . . .

The only map of Talladega which I could find was very old, defaced, badly worn, inaccurate and incomplete. The situation would have been less confused had there been a map, because the incorrect and incomplete map was misleading. It was necessary to have a new, complete and correct map, but an authoritative and complete map could not be made without a survey of the city. An accurate and complete survey of the city, showing all existing and projected streets, with large map on proper and durable material, with essential legends; in short, a first-class city map, would represent a considerable outlay, the amount of which could not be estimated in advance. The expense of the work, as a matter of course, was the chief argument of the opposition to this project before the City Council . . .

The fight for a complete survey and a new city map was won, after a brief but hard fight, and the City Council authorized the necessary expenditure. The next important matter in this undertaking was to find a capable engineer and draftsman to do the work. Fortunately, a very efficient and trustworthy engineer was found without great delay. Mr. E. W. Walpole, an Englishman who had located in Florida, was an acquaintance of Mr. J. A. Edwards, of Talladega, and Dr. M. O. Arnold, who had returned from Florida with Mr. Edwards and had made some investments in Talladega. Mr. Edwards was a native of Talladega and served one term as sheriff, and he was one of the most capable and honorable public officials whom the county had ever had. He had gone to Florida for the purpose of establishing a home in the State, but shortly after my first election, when Talladega began to improve, Mr. Edwards returned to his old home and engaged in the real estate business with Dr. M. O. Arnold, of Iowa, whom Mr. Edwards had met in Florida and induced him to locate in Talladega.

Mr. Edwards and Dr. Arnold, learning that I was looking for a capable engineer to make the city map, told me about Mr. Walpole whom they had met in Florida, and of whom they spoke very highly, stating that Mr. Walpole was a man of education, training and experience, and fine character. I wrote to Mr.

Walpole and offered him the position of City Engineer for the special work of making a survey and new map of Talladega. Mr. Walpole came to Talladega with his family and took up the work without delay. I found him to be a very fine gentleman and very efficient in his profession as a civil engineer and draftsman. His work is a matter of record and I have never heard it criticised . . .

At the time of my first election as Mayor, the City Cemetery was in a very bad condition. In plain language it was a disgrace to the community. A large number of family lots were kept in the best possible condition under the circumstances and conditions which obtained in the only public burial place in Talladega, known as Oak Hill Cemetery. This place was a wilderness of live and dead trees, undergrowth, weeds and trash. There were no streets or walks, not any suggestion of order or uniformity in the "old Cemetery" . . . There had never been any survey or map of the cemetery that could be used in locating lots and making improvements.

There was a wide difference of opinion about work which should be done in the cemetery. Quite naturally and properly, every lot owner was very careful and sensitive in discussing the matter, but I tried to meet the issue by appointing a special committee to investigate and report on the matter. This committee was composed of Dr. J. H. Johnson, Dr. B. W. Toole, and Col. W. N. Boynton. This committee was made up of three of the most prominent and highly respected citizens of Talladega and most useful and active members of the City Council. Every member of the committee was my senior by many years and I followed the counsel of the committee in every detail relating to improvements in the City Cemetery. . .

At the time of my first election, in 1885, there was an old, dilapidated gas plant in Talladega. It was out-of-date and in bad condition. The company had the usual form of franchise from the city for use of the streets and rental of street lamps at a stipulated rental, but there was endless complaint from the City about the failure of the company to supply sufficient gas of good quality for the street lamps and private consumption.

I believe that a majority (perhaps all) of the stock of the Talladega gaslight Company was owned in Montgomery and Mr. T. Gardner Foster, of Montgomery, was Secretary and Treasurer of the company. Shortly after my first election, I wrote a very polite but positive letter to Mr. Foster calling his attention to numerous complaints about the unsatisfactory service of his company, and I told him if the service were not greatly improved, without any unnecessary delay, I should advise the City Council to authorize me to take steps to cancel his contract with the city. The immediate response of Mr. Foster was a personal visit to Talladega for the purpose of a full conference concerning the matter . . .

In my conversation with Mr. Foster I stated that I thought Talladega would grow, that I had been elected to make it grow, and, among many improvements which I had in mind, light and water were the most essential of public utilities. I also stated that I was trying to find some feasible plan for financing a waterworks project and if his company was not willing to improve their plant, it would also be necessary for me to finance a gas plant to be built by the city. Mr. Foster seemed to be deeply interested when I told him that I was at work on a project for waterworks for Talladega and he said that he had an acquaintance who was a trained engineer and had successfully constructed several water supply plants, and he thought his acquaintance would be interested in my project for Talladega . . .

In a short time after my first interview with Mr. Foster, perhaps a week or ten days, Mr. Foster telegraphed me that he would be in Talladega on a certain date for the purpose of further conference about the gas plant, and that he would bring with him his friend whom he had referred to in his first interview . . .

When Mr. Foster arrived in Talladega for a second conference with me, he introduced Mr. George P. Anderton, the engineer to whom he had referred in his first conversation with me.

Mr. Anderton told me that he was a Britisher, a native of England, and a civil and mechanical engineer by education and practical training, and that he had constructed several waterworks plants, but that, at that time, he was giving his attention to his sugar plantation, in Plaquemines Parish, where he was then living. . . .

I had long and interesting interviews with Mr. Anderton concerning the project for waterworks in Talladega and the upshot of the matter was that he said he would return to Talladega within a week or so and make a preliminary survey and then submit a tentative proposition.

Mr. Anderton returned to Talladega and made a survey of the area which it was proposed to supply with water for fire protection and domestic uses . . .

After a very exciting and prolonged consideration, the Council authorized the execution of a contract for the construction of waterworks . . . Work began immediately after the contract was entered into.

The work was completed in due time and the project was a great success in every detail. A stand pipe erected on one of the most elevated points in the city, on the north side of North Street, a little more than a block east of the public square, furnished a pressure that was more than was needed for fire protection or other purposes. The citizens of Talladega were very proud of their fine waterworks and it was one of the advertising features of Talladega for many years.

Almost immediately after the city entered into a contract for the construction of waterworks, the water company and the old gas company were consolidated under the name of the Talladega Gaslight and Water Company. A new gas plant was built, new mains put down and extended so as to meet all demands for gas for street lamps and private use. In a short while, the city had an ample supply of good illuminating gas. The original gas plant was located on the south side of North Street, near Spring Street, but the old plant was abandoned when the new plant was erected near the big spring branch on Spring Street.

Anticipating the early construction of the waterworks, immediately after the work of building the plant started, I began an investigation of fire-hose and hose-carriages and hook-and-ladder outfits. In ample time an order was placed for ample supply of the best grade of hose of standard size for fire fighting, two hose carriages of the best make, hook-and-ladder outfit and other equipment needed for volunteer fire companies. Two volunteer fire companies had been organized by young men of Talladega composed of some of the best young men of the city. They began drilling and practice as soon as the hose-carriages, hose and hook-and-ladder outfit was received. They were ready for full practice the first day that the water was turned on the mains. That was a fete-day in Talladega. The two rival volunteer fire companies were out at practice most of the day, finding much pleasure in demonstrating their skill in fighting imaginary fires . . .

Before the waterworks were completed, fire insurance rates were very high in Talladega. There was no protection against fire except the most primitive method of passing buckets with water by hand from pumps and cisterns in the rear of buildings . . . There was a big reduction in rates of fire insurance which resulted in saving several thousands of dollars a year to merchants and owners of buildings in the vicinity of the public square. There was also a big reduction in the rates of insurance on dwellings and household goods.

A system of waterworks in any community made a system of sanitary sewerage absolutely necessary. I had supposed that every citizen of average intelligence would anticipate the necessity of sanitary sewerage as consequent to the building of waterworks. But the necessity had not been foreseen by a number of citizens who bitterly opposed the project of building a system of sanitary sewerage. This was a most important work and I had decided that I would never give my approval to any work in this line except under the personal supervision of a trained sanitary engineer and with the best material that could be used in such work . . .

Mayor Reese, of Montgomery, Mayor Lane, of Birmingham, and several other public officials whom I knew recommended very highly Mr.

Mitchell as a very capable and trustworthy sanitary engineer. His home was in N. J., but he had prepared the plans for several systems of sanitary sewerage in Southern cities, and I finally employed Mr. Mitchell to make a survey and report for a complete system of modern sanitary sewerage in Talladega . . .

My recollection is that his fee was $1,000.00, which I did not think was excessive for a sanitary engineer of high character and national reputation in his profession. But the City Council had not been accustomed to paying for expert services, nor for the work of well-trained specialists in any line of work. Quite a number of citizens, who were not members of the City Council, asserted that the County Surveyor could have made the investigation and report at an expense to the City of not more than $100.00, and that it was an outrage to pay a stranger a fee of $1,000.00 for work which was not worth more than $100.00 at the outside.

But if the City Council and many good citizens were amazed and disgusted at Mr. Mitchell's fee, they were astounded and stood aghast when they heard and read in the town paper estimates of the probable cost of the sanitary sewerage system which it was proposed to construct. My present recollection is that the estimate was $35,000.00; I am quite certain that it was not less than $90,000.00. Of course, the only way to provide the money for the work would be an issue of bonds. At the time I was elected, not a bond had been issued by the City and several issues were already put out and some of our worthy citizens were simply astounded at even the suggestion of another bond issue . . .

The City Council authorized me to enter into contracts for the building of a complete and modern system of sewerage, and, at the same time, a bond issue of $35,000.00 was authorized. An evidence of the growing public confidence, especially in financial circles, in the city administration, was the fact that we received four or five bids on this issue of bonds, whereas it was almost impossible to sell the first issue of bonds for $12,000.00 secured by a mortgage on the public school building.

The first essential step in the work of constructing a system of sanitary sewerage was to secure the services of a supervising sanitary engineer. It was necessary to find not only an efficient, but also an honest and thoroughly trustworthy engineer to place at the head of the work. A very careful investigation of this line of work had taught me that it offered opportunity for almost unlimited rascality and corrupt practices in the purchase of material, especially sewer pipe . . .

Mr. Mitchell, the sanitary engineer who made the survey and report to which I have already referred, in response to my request, recommended an engineer whom he had known for years. Mr. S. M. Neff was the sanitary engineer whom Mr. Mitchell recommended and he was highly endorsed by Mayor Reese, of Montgomery, where he had been engaged in supervising some sewer work . . . I employed him to supervise the construction of the system of sewerage at Talladega, and the whole work, including the purchase of all material, was placed under his control.

For many years, the E. T. V. & Ga. (later the Southern) Railroad had imposed upon, browbeaten and intimidated the people of Talladega. It was the only standard gauge, through line of railroad and the people were wholly dependent upon it for transportation. I was not, therefore, very much surprised, when, after work began on the sanitary sewerage system, to receive an intimation from a representative of this railroad that the City must not attempt to lay any sewer pipe under its right-of-way on East Street or any other street which its line crossed in the City. While I was not surprised at the audacity of the suggestion, it made me furious and my answer was that the City of Talladega was the sole owner and proprietor of its streets and it would occupy them at any time and any place for the public good without regard to the wishes of the railroad company . . .

It now looked very much like a fight between the railroad and the City as represented by the Mayor.

I had conferred very freely with Mr. Neff and he had given me a memorandum showing the depth of the necessary trench and the time it would take to dig the trench, lay the pipe, etc., under the tracks on East Street. I believe his memorandum stated that he could complete the job in five hours, from the south to the north side of the right of way of the railroad. He had already told me that his work would not in any way interfere with traffic on the railroad, that he would not occupy any space on the surface of the right of way and that it would make no difference how many trains passed over or remained standing on the right of way during the progress of his work of laying sewer pipe under the tracks . . .

One day, while we were watching and waiting, I learned that the Chancellor of that division, who could have issued an injunction, would leave Anniston late that afternoon . . . I notified Mr. Neff and he soon had the wagons loaded with pipe and other material moving to the East Street, crossing of the railroad. I had already advised Mr. Williams, Chief of Police, to have an extra force of picked men: and in a little while the whole project, as originally outlined, was moving like clock work. . . . It was dark and big fires were built on each side of the tracks and the men began digging the trenches from each side about eight o'clock. . . . The big fires, presence of extra police and wagons unloading material, all on a dark night. soon attracted a large crowd of curious spectators.

The work was completed and all connections made within twenty minutes of the time estimated by Mr. Neff and it was carried out without a hitch. It was about two o'clock in the morning when the work ceased . . .

I do not believe that I ever carried through any measure that gave the people of Talladega so much joy as the victory over the railroad . . .

After the work on the sanitary sewers had been completed. I retained the services of Mr. Neff to plan and supervise the building of several culverts and rain-water sewers. A large territory east of the public square discharges a large volume of water through two big gullies, one of which crosses East Street at the intersection of Battle Street, and then turns abruptly at right angles along the west side of East Street to Coffee Street, following the line of the latter Street to the Spring branch. For many years, this deep and unsightly gully was covered with an unsightly and dangerous wooden bridge. Mr. Neff built a large sewer across East Street at the intersection of Battle Street which greatly improved the appearance and safety of the streets at that point. The other large gully crosses East Street about two blocks north of the public square. It was very broad and very deep, covered with a wooden bridge that was never in a good state of repair within my memory. A great improvement was made in East Street at this place when the old wooden bridge was replaced by a substantial and sightly brick and stone bridge. A substantial brick and stone bridge was also built over the big gully at the Court Street crossing. Several small bridges and a number of culverts were constructed under Mr. Neff's supervision, and great improvements were made in all repairs which he supervised . . .

There was no public school in Talladega at the time of my election, and there were very few in the State of Alabama at that time. Alabama, and in fact, every one of the Southern States, was very backward in the matter of public schools in 1885. There was a female school, owned by the Synod of North Alabama, in Talladega. It occupied one large brick building located on the same lot as the Presbyterian Church in the rear of that church. For several years, immediately following the Civil War, this building was used by the Peabody School, but that was not a graded school and it was not under the control of the State or City. . . . . There were several small male schools, with very capable instructors . . . but the accommodations at each of these schools were very poor.

(End of Mr. Skaggs' unfinished article)

(Note: Mr. Skaggs never completed his Memorandum. He did put in a Public School system, as related under the head of "Schools.")

As previously stated, there has never been a more progressive period of general expansion in the history of Talladega than during these ten years of the Nineteenth Century. Mr. Skaggs was an ardent and intelligent young man, who dared to venture into new enterprises, to which the general public was frequently opposed. The balance wheel for his youthful enthusiasm was the conservative group which composed his Board of Aldermen. They were loyal and cooperative, but held him in check on many occasions.

In 1889 there appeared a newspaper article headed "WE BOOM", in which many improvements were cited. It stated in part: "We have come to stay and have brought our winter clothes with us. . . . We have completed curbing and paving nearly five miles of the prettiest streets in Alabama. A $25,000.00 Tanning plant is almost done; 17 brick stores are going up, 50 dwelling houses are being erected; new streets are being opened, the public roads are getting a coat of pounded stone, paint abounds everywhere; the saw and hammer make music day and night, and another wide gauge road was completed last Saturday. ...Rah for the Coosadigger and Talleyvalley."[1]

At an early date a Board of Trade was organized to assist the Mayor and Aldermen in the encouragement of new enterprises for Talladega.[2] In August, 1885, with W. J. Rhodes, President and R. Broadstreet, Secretary, this Board was instrumental in organizing a stock company for the purpose of building a "fire proof cotton warehouse 125 x 150 ft., to cost from $2,000 to $3,500.00, according to plans drawn by Geo. O. Wheeler." The building faced S. North Street, opposite the Isbell home. This, as Mr. Skaggs pointed out, was a wonderful accession in simplifying the handling of cotton.

As soon as the water supply was evident, the town felt more secure when the "Rescue Fire Co. No. 1, Inc." appeared with J. G. Savery, Pres.; J. S. Linton, Sec. and E. R. Jacob, Treas.[3] Two years later the company increased its membership to 38, and changed the name to "The Hook & Ladder Company".[4] W. B. Castleberry was president, J. L. McLane, Foreman, W. H. Boynton and H. W. Stamps, Asst. Foremen, and E. C. Cobb, Sec. & Treas. These young men not only experienced civic pride in their achievements, but enjoyed the thrill and adventure of fire fighting. A fire was pretty well advanced by the time the company arrived, because their procedure was necessarily slow. It was the custom for some one to run afoot to the fire house to announce the fire, because there was no telephone service; then proceed to the Court House and ring the court bell. After the members arrived at the fire house, they rolled out the two wheeled reel and ladder which was propelled by hand, and on foot hastened to the location of the fire. Upon arrival, tile hose was unwound, and they proceeded to extinguish the fire. Some years later a wagon and horses were purchased to facilitate this method.

---

[1] Our Mountain Home, Oct. 9, 1889
[2] Reporter & Watchtower, August 12, 1885
[3] General Acts of Ala., Page 317, No. 155, Feb. 26, 1887
[4] Our Mountain Home, Jan 30th, 1889

To further encourage outside interests, The Talladega Land and Improvement Company, Inc., was organized, in the latter part 1886, with a capital stock of $500,000.00[5] which was increased to $750,000.00 several months later. Wm. H. Skaggs was President and Percy R. Smith, of Birmingham, was Secretary. A newspaper article outlined some of their purposes in 1887: "At a Directors meeting of the Talladega Land & Improvement Company, held in the city April 27th, it was decided to begin work at once in the City of Talladega for the erection of a 40 ton charcoal iron furnace, a sash, door and blind factory; an ice factory, and to enlarge the Southern Hotel; also to erect 25 cottages on North end property. Hands are now at work clearing off the grounds preparatory to commencing the building. Spring Lake Park is being graded and beautified on their property purchased from the late Judge Henderson, and a beautiful lake will be formed from the stream that runs through the property. . . . This company owns several thousand acres of land on the north end, and several very handsome dwellings. Streets 60 feet wide are being laid off at right angles on the property, and in a few weeks all of their enterprises will be under full headway. . . . The machinery has been purchased for the ice factory and sash, door and blind factory, and $100,000.00 is in hand for the erection of the furnace."[6]

The Southern Hotel on East Street was enlarged; the sash, door & blind factory was launched as the "Eagle Works"; the ice factory was erected and put into operation; and Spring Lake Park did develop into a lovely civic recreational center with an attractive lake. The Spring Lake Furnace was chartered, but never built. Opening of the streets never took place.

From time to time officers changed in the Loan & Improvement Co. In 1888, J. T. Adams, was President; F. A. Osborne, Vice-Pres.; G. A. Joiner, Secretary, and J. T. Dumas, Treas.; with J. A. Edwards, J. R. Broome, H. M. Langley and W. H. Skaggs, Directors. In the same paper announcing the new officers there was a local item stating that J. T. Adams has purchased a lot from the Company on Speigner Street for $1050.00.

The officers of 1889 were G. A. Joiner, President; S. H. Henderson, Vice Pres.; Cecil Browne, Sec.; J. A. Edwards, Treas. and Sales Agent; Jno. T. Adams, T. S. Plowman, Jno. B. Knox, J. R. Broome and S. P. Bums, directors.[7] It will, therefore, be seen that this company was composed of prominent citizens. Mr. Skaggs had evidently retired to act as President of the Citizens Bank of Talladega, which he established that year.

---

[5] General Acts of Ala., Page 469, No. 212, Feb. 26, 1887
[6] Our Mountain Home, May 4, 1887
[7] Our Mountain Home, Feb. 27, 1889

In the meantime, other loan and real estate associations were actively engaged. In 1888 The Talladega Real Estate & Loan Association was laying off streets and grading. In 1889 a Building & Loan Association appeared with T. S. Plowman, Pres.; J. E. Stone, Sec.; H. L. McElderry, S. J. Bowie, J. T. Adams and J. H. Johnson, directors.[8]

The Talladega Land & Improvement Co. became so overloaded and heavily involved that they either failed or liquidated about 1889, and much of their property had to be salvaged at a great sacrifice.[9] Some of this was purchased by H. L. McElderry, S. J. Bowie and Jno. T. Adams, for $3,000.00. On this land they opened "Our Mountain Home Addition", where 40 lots were sold for about $200.00 each.

Mr. J. E. Stone had already entered the real estate business several years earlier. He purchased land from the Land & Improvement Co.,[10] about which he relates: "Lot 167 of the original survey was willed to Miss Eppie McKenzie by her aunt, Mrs. Jenkins, who lived at the Hunley Place.[11] They sold the frontage on East Street, one acre deep, to F. C. McAlpine, and frontage on Clay County Road[12] to F. E. Wilson, leaving the center corked up. It was a washed hillside, grown up in sassafras and sedge grass; put in my hands, when the Talladega Land & Improvement Company, were buying all the vacant area to sell; but I could not get an offer for it; but made a plat for them, suggesting that they arrange for streets and openings, which they hooted at, but offered it to me at $100.00 per acre. I traded for openings to the property; opened up the streets, made a cash payment of $200.00 borrowed money; took J. B. Terry for my partner, who had $125.00; and we sold out in about two years, clearing about $20,000.00. Many of the large trees that are on the streets were set out by us. We surveyed and planted it ourselves." And thus "Stoneington" was born. Margaret Street was named for Mr. Stone's wife, Margaret Cruikshank Stone; Terry Street was named for J. B. Terry, and Mary Street for his wife.

Stoneington lots were on the market by July, 1888. "Nice broad streets, with a park as a feature" was advertised, and lots were purchased by "some of the nicest people in the County." It was also advertised as being "in the southern portion of the city, well drained, airy and healthy, and on the main

---

[8] Ibid, Jan. 9th, 1889
[9] Letter from J.E. Stone to me, 1928
[10] Ibid
[11] Now owned by J. A. Powers, 610 S. East St
[12] The Clay County Road went South on Cherry Street to McMillan St., turning East, running by the Negro School for Blind.

thoroughfare to Clay County, gold mines, and Chandlers Springs."[13] Two years later 19 new dwellings were under construction in Stoneington.

The Stoneington Heights Co. appeared in 1889 with S. J. Bowie, Pres., J. E. Stone, Sec. & Treas., J. B. Terry and Vanderbilt Slader, associates.[14] They sold only about two blocks before a lull in real estate occurred.

Papers of that period also speak of "The South Highland Development Company", and mention is made in July of 1888, of Mr. M. Jackson and family having moved into their new home in "South Highland." His home was what is now the E. A. McBride residence on East St. S., which would indicate that that portion, and beyond, on East Street, was included in "South Highland."

"The New South Building & Loan Association" was operating in 1890 with John C. Williams, President, J. C. Bowie, Sec. & Treas. and H. L. McElderry, Attorney.[15]

While these various building and improvement companies were busily engaged in expanding the city, private citizens were also active.

Handsome homes were built in 1886 by J. A. Savery, J. A. Thornton, J. O. Adams, M. M. Frazer, J. L. McLane and B. W. Toole, as well as many others. The Arthur Bingham home was so unusually attractive, that a picture of it actually appeared in a local paper in 1889.

During these years of growth, South Street was extended from the present Cherry Street through Moor's Field, which was the plantation of William Moore, whose home was what is now the four room cement building north of Talladega High School, and which at times was known as "The Farm House", "Shelley House" and the "Johnson Home." Most of the homes on South Street, East, were built during the late 80's and 90's

The extension of South Street opened other desirable property in Moor-Field, outside the city limits. An Orphans Home building was erected, and the Presbyterian Children were transferred from Tuskegee to Talladega. The School for the Blind was also erected about the same time.

Not only did the residential part of town expand and develop, but the business section also grew. There were at one time 17 brick stores under construction; others followed. "Trade Palaces" appeared, where semi-annual "Openings" of millinery finery was on display, with fanfare and music, and they were recognized as social events of the season. Music marts, book and stationery stores, stoneware shops, new department stores, and grocery stores opened. A wholesale grocery store, and a Foundry & Machine Shop, a Cotton & Oil Mill, the Talladega Cotton Factory, founded by McMillans & Joiners in

---

[13] Our Mountain Home, July 11, 1888
[14] Letter from J. E. Stone to me, 1928
[15] Our Mountain Home, Apr. 16, 1890

1893; the Highland City Mills founded by J. H. Hicks in 1898. A local telephone system was put into operation by S. C. Oliver, G. A. Mattison and Reno Hawley, and many, many other business concerns found Talladega a desirable place in which to locate as the Twentieth Century was ushered in.

It was during these years that a number of men, who were destined to become the leading business men of the Twentieth Century, came to Talladega.

For many years Isbell & Company were the only bankers in Talladega. They began operations in 1848. Several years later J. G. L. Huey opened a bank on the west side of East Street, N. just north of the Public Square, but he closed it when the War Between the States was declared, and it was never reopened. With the influx of people and money, Mr. Skaggs felt that another bank was needed, and the Citizens Bank of Talladega was established in 1888, with Wm. H. Skaggs, President and J. L. McLane, Cashier.[16] The handsome walnut furniture was made by M. J. Hingle by plans of E. W. Walpole. The bank was still in existence in 1892, with Mr. Skaggs, President, and A. H. Clemie, Cashier, but it proved to be Mr. Skaggs' downfall, for it soon failed, and Mr. Skaggs left town as sort of a fallen hero. But the years have softened memories of money losses, and Talladega people now fully realize and appreciate what Wm. H. Skaggs accomplished in Talladega during his administration. The Bank of Talladega was opened about the same time as the Citizens Bank, with T. S. Plowman, president, but evidently lived only a short while, since there appeared a notice in the paper during the summer of 1888 that the First National Bank had been established with a capital stock of $50,000.00, and that they had purchased the equipment of the Bank of Talladega. The Board of Directors was composed of T. S. Plowman, President, Jere T. Dumas, V. Pres.; James P. Wood, John B. Knox, S. N. Noble, John A. Savery, and J. B. McMillan; with J. C. Bowie, Cashier.[17]   A short time afterwards, J. B. McMillan was made President, and the First National Bank became one of Talladega's most substantial institutions until some time in the early part of the Twentieth Century. Mr. McMillan retired and the stock was absorbed by the present Talladega National Bank, which had been established by John H. Hicks in 1905.

It would be impossible to enumerate all the business activities of Talladega during this period. The building of railroads, furnaces, Chambers Opera House, communities, and Alabama Chautauqua are all handled under separate chapters.

---

[16] Our Mountain Home, June 6, 1888
[17] Ibid, June 20, 1888

There were attempts to locate many other enterprises over the years. For instance, there was an attempt to transfer Howard college from Marion to Talladega, with the backing of J. L. M. Curry and other prominent Baptists, but Birmingham was booming at the time, and out-bid Talladega. The town was also elated over the prospect of a Westinghouse Electric Co. plant being located in Talladega. Surveys were made for this in 1889. Cotton factories and furnaces were chartered which never materialized. A. J. Hinkley and others took an option on the Lyman property on North St. (where the 1st Baptist Church is located) on which to build a $50,000.00 hotel, but it was never built.[18]

Talladega was not only commercially minded during these years, but intellectually and socially minded also. Many historic, civic and social organizations took shape at this time. The Ladies Memorial Association was organized in 1889, which was dear to the hearts of all Confederate Soldiers. Officers in 1893, at which time the Monument to Confederate Soldiers in Oak Hill Cemetery was unveiled, were Mrs. J. Morgan Smith, President; Miss Pauline McAlpine, V. Pres.; Miss Annie Elston, Sec.; and Miss Rosa Knox, Treas.[19]

The Andrew Jackson Chapter of the D. A. R.; the John T. Morgan Chapter of the U. D. C.; the Highland City Book Club; the Talladega Dramatic Club, The Argus Club, Twentieth Century Club, The Literary Coterie, and a dozen other societies appeared.

In fact, there were so many social and civic organizations in Talladega at the time that an article appeared in one of the Birmingham papers listing Talladega as the Club Town of the State.

Not only did Talladega Town "Boom", but the entire county experienced fabulous growth. That of Nottingham, Renfroe, Jenifer, Ironaton, and the various mining communities, are all treated under special headings. The building of Sycamore Mills by Messrs. D. L. and John Lewis in Sycamore in 1893 launched the modern cotton mill industry of the county, and Sycamore became a village.

A great financial crisis swept over the nation during the latter part of the Nineteenth Century. Though Talladega was fortunate enough to pass through to a new century as a substantial and well established town, there were many enterprises, which never developed, but the population in Talladega doubled during these last fifteen years. Dozens of new streets were opened; handsome dwellings were erected, the Square changed from unshapely frame buildings to a modem one of brick buildings; piped water was available; a public school system was in force; gas lights for the home available, and the

---

[18] Ibid, April 3, 1889
[19] Ibid, April 29th, 1893

Nineteenth Century passed out with 5056 well established citizens, many of whom were destined to make Talladega an even greater town in the Twentieth Century.

Early Resorts

CHAMBERS SPRINGS was promoted and operated as a summer resort by Mr. Geo. W. Chambers in the 1890's. The springs were chalybeate and of good quality, located in the Hillabee district, about two miles south-west of Chandlers' Springs. It was quite a popular resort for about ten or fifteen years. However, none of the old cottages, or hotel, remain to remind one of past glory.

CHANDLER'S SPRINGS[1] was founded by James Chandler about 1835. He and his brother, Mordecai, were in the tailoring business in Wetumpka at the time. James was suffering with malarial chills. One day a prominent Indian came into the shop and told him of a spring with wonderful "yellow water" some miles away, that would make him well.

James packed his saddlebags, and set off to find the spring, following the direction pointed out by the Indian. For some days he traveled and searched, and had about despaired of locating the spring, when a deer came out of the forest, at which his horse became frightened and threw him out of the saddle. He followed the path of the frightened deer, and horse, and found them drinking at a spring surrounded by a yellow sediment, which he recognized as his desired destination. An Indian village was located on the hill back of the spring, where they were making syrup from maple sap. From these Indians he acquired the spring and surrounding land. He hired a young Indian to live with him and to help him build a log cabin. James got well. When he went to Mardisville to enter his purchase, his brother joined him and they opened a tailoring shop in Talladega.

The Chandlers gave up their trade in Talladega and built a home at Chandler's Springs on a knoll northeast of the main spring across the branch after the Indians left, and became farmers.

In 1840 the Spring was leased to Sam Watson, who built the hotel in 1844, which served the people for nearly one hundred years.

After Mr. Watson's lease expired, others leased the hotel, some as a summer residence only.

Many physicians all over the State of Alabama sent recuperative and chronic patients to Chandlers throughout the years. It was one of the most popular health resorts in the State, and there has never been found better chalybeate water anywhere.

---

[1] This story of James Chandler was given to me by Mrs. T. M. Nolen, under date of December 22, 1927. She was a relative of the Chandlers.

The building of cottages for rent followed that of the hotel. The grounds were fenced in with an entrance near the south-west corner. The houses were erected on a hill above the spring in a square, with a pavilion in the center. The hotel occupied the center of the south end, flanked by two cottages each on the east and the west of the hotel. On the west side of the square side there were two cottages, with a common center wall and chimney. These cottages had only two rooms with "dog trot" between. Beyond these two cottages a long row of six or eight small rooms were built for use of the hotel proprietor for an overflow of guests. These rooms were, years later, replaced by a large cottage of A. G. Storey of Talladega. On the north side of the square there were four two room cottages, with "dog trots", which had common center walls and chimneys. In later years Mr. Seaborn Johnson of Talladega built a large cottage on the north-west corner, and Mr. T. W. Curry of Mobile, one on the north-east corner, leaving only two old cottages between.

The east side of the square was exactly as the west, but later Mr. J. B. McMillan of Talladega built on the north-east corner and Maj. Joseph Hardie of Birmingham and California on the south-east corner.

Many of the same families spent summers at Chandlers Springs for several generations. Happy and lasting friendships resulted from the fellowship of the group so closely associated about the reading and sewing circles, croquet grounds, spelling bees, mountain climbing, fishing parties and games of all kinds. Nothing was more satisfying than the evening gatherings about the bonfires.

The Chandlers refused to sell lots, but leased the ground on which the cottages were built for a number of years. Therefore, when Jenkins Springs, now Clairmont Springs, on the railroad, opened with a sale of lots, Chandlers began to decline.

There is now only one building left to remind this generation of the glory of old Chandlers Springs.

SHOCCO SPRINGS[2] was originally a portion of a large plantation owned by John Albright, who purchased it from the Indians.

His land extended from the hills north of Shocco, south, to a point near the present Southern Railway.

When John Albright died, his property was divided among his several children. The portion on which the springs were located fell to his daughter, Mandy who had married Vincent Cosby.

Soon after the War Between the States, Jared Thompson purchased that portion on which the springs were located and built a hotel and eight

---

[2] Information given me by Mr. Waddell, grand-son of John Allbright.

cabins. An advertisement in a paper of 1873 indicates that he was doing a thriving business, for he advised that all cabins and the hotel were full, but that ground space was available to those who desired it. Tents were owned by nearly all well-to-do people in those days, especially those who attended Camp Meetings, and patronized "Springs."

In 1888 Mr. E. B. Miller leased the hotel and cottages, and several others followed Mr. Miller[3]

Mr. Thompson died unmarried and the property passed into the hands of his sisters, Miss Mary Thompson and Mrs. Cornelia T. Fleetwood.[4] They eventually sold the springs to Mr. Virgil Adams, who spent quite a lot of money in buildings and opening up new springs. There were originally only three. Mr. Adams was a jovial man, devoted to his family. When the resort opened, the public found a number of springs with concrete bowls 2nd shoulders, bearing the names of various members of his large family circle. One had the choice of drinking from "Rosa", "Rena", "Laura", etc.

Mr. Leon G. Jones purchased the property from Mr. Adams and passed it on to his son, George William Jones. Under the management of the Joneses Shocco reached its zenith as a resort.

Shocco is now in the hands of the Alabama Baptists as assembly grounds.

TALLADEGA SPRINGS has one of the best sulphur springs to be found anywhere, and has been a resort ever since the Creek country opened up; perhaps as far back as 1813, when Andrew Jackson camped at Fort Williams, several miles away.

There was an act passed by the Legislature in 1836 to refund one Cornelius Carmack for having taken care of 8 men of Capt. Boston's Company, who were left sick in Talladega County after the battle.[5] They were no doubt cared for at or near the Sulphur Spring.

A map of 1834, which has names of only five villages in Talladega County, shows the name "Franklin" and below it "Sulphur Spring" in the lower end of the county.[6] It was on the Turnpike Road. The village was called "Franklin" for many years, and was incorporated under that name.

On July 2, 1836, the United States Congress passed a bill authorizing a number of Post Roads in Alabama. Among these roads was one "from Columbiana, in the County of Shelby, via Mineral Springs to Syllacoggy to

[3] Our Mountain Home, June 27, 1888 – Public Library
[4] Information given me by Blanche Fleetwood, daughter of Mrs. C. T. Fleetwood
[5] Acts of Ala., 1831-37, Page 67
[6] Map Dept. of Archives & History, published by Augustine Mitchell

Talladega County."[7] This "Mineral Springs" no doubt referred to the present Talladega Springs.

A map of 1838 shows the name "Sulphur Springs." The spring was known by this name for many years, though old residents[8] state that it was called "Franklin" until the charter of incorporation expired, at which time the name was changed to that of "Talladega Springs."

William McPherson and Benjamine Avereitt purchased large tracts of land in or near Talladega Springs in the early history of the County and lived there, or at Fayetteville, the rest of their lives.

Chief Justice Samuel F. Rice at one time was one of the numerous owners of the springs.[9] The resort was patronized by the elite of the State. The original founders of the resort were foresighted in allowing for a wide main street, down which, in gala days, rock stands were placed at intervals for bonfires in the evenings.

The hotel, and pavilion over the spring, were nearly always full during the summer months.

Masses of people came in the early days in rigs of every description, for picnics and vacations. After the L & N railroad passed through, excursion trains ran to Talladega Springs throughout the summer.

The flow of water is not brisk, and frequently, when crowds were there, people would have to wait for the filling of the marble bowl to be able to dip out a drink.

Around old Talladega Springs hover many sweet memories of the social life of the State.

It began to decline after Mitchell's Dam caused odors of decaying underbrush, inundated by the back water, to be offensive to visitors. Automobiles also came into use about the same time, and people preferred to travel on vacations, rather than to spend their holidays at resorts as was formerly the popular thing to do. A new highway passes within a few feet of the Spring and there is now no sign whatever of the once wide street which passed through the old resort, nor of the hotel, cottages or pavilion.

---

[7] U. S. Statutes at Large. Acts of Congress, Pages 103-5, Dr. T. M. Owen's His. of Ala., Vol. II, Page 1140
[8] Letter from Mrs. M. C. McMillan, Sycamore, dated 11-30-1927
[9] Letter from W. H. Mitchell, Tall. Springs, to me, dated 11-12-1927

Ghost Towns

There were several flourishing villages in Talladega County, which at one time played some significant part in the history of the county but were later abandoned.

MARDISVILLE was the first and largest of this group, but is treated in a separate chapter.

IRONATON. Founded in 1871 by Stephen and Sam Noble, was originally called "Clifton". It was the terminus of the Clifton Railroad, a narrow gauge road used for hauling iron ore, and products of the Clifton Iron Works, which were located at this point. It was incorporated Feb. 17, 1885, under the name of "Ironaton." The census of 1890 shows a population of 562; 1900—735; 1910—982. The town was founded upon the revenue and population incident to the blast furnaces located at this place.[1]

There were two wide main streets, bordered with oak trees, which still stand to bear evidence of a once thriving and prosperous town.

There was a City Hall, a Jail, a Volunteer Fire Department, and four miles of well cherted streets and sidewalks. There was a large commissary to provide for the needs of the community. An ample water system was supplied from a spring on the J. J. McKibbon place, and there were two hotels and a number of cottages to care for the personnel of the furnaces.

The furnaces ceased operations long ago, and only a few dwellings are left within the old limits of Ironaton.

JENIFER dates her beginning back to 1863, when Samuel Clabaugh and James A. Curry built a blast furnace, incorporated under the name of "Salt Creek Iron Works." The town was first called "Salt Creek."[2] The furnace was burned by Federal soldiers in 1865. Horace Ware purchased the property, changed the name to "Alabama Furnace", and under this name the town was first incorporated May 17, 1873.[3] In 1881 Samuel Noble and A. L. Tyler purchased controlling interest, and changed the name to "Jenifer", in honor of Mr. Noble's mother, Mrs. Jenifer Ward Noble. The town was again incorporated Feb. 28, 1889 under this name, with a population of 500. The census of 1890 shows the population as 323; 1900 as 331; and 1910 only 104.[4]

---

[1] Thomas M. Owen's History of Ala., Vol. II, Page 797
[2] Ibid, Vol. II, Page 811
[3] Local Acts of Ala. – 1873, Page 280
[4] Ibid – 1889, Page 973

There is one main residential street, which is canopied by massive water oaks which border the street. A few of the quaint houses remain. The entire property was recently sold to private citizens.

NOTTINGHAM. The building of Nottingham was an entrancing adventure of Boom Days.

During the 1880's capitalists began reopening the mineral industries of Talladega County. The operation of most mines ceased during the Civil War; only those were operated which could serve the Confederacy in the manufacture of supplies.

There arrived in Talladega County one C. D. Morrison, from New York, prospecting for gold.[5] He evidently did not find the gold he expected, since he later decided to promote the building of a "metropolis." He chose a plantation about one mile east of Alpine and named the town "Nottingham," at which time he interested other Eastern Capitalists in the project. The property was surveyed, and the town soon took shape.

The Nottingham Iron & Land Company, with F. H. Wilkins, President; Geo. A. Boynton, Vice-President; and C. D. Morrison, Gen. Mgr.; came into existence, and in December of 1889, they announced that they would erect two iron furnaces of 65 ton capacity each, and that they would immediately erect a hotel 34 x 100 feet, three stories high.[6]

At the same time, a real estate office was opened; a restaurant put into operation; streets were graded; business and residential lots were put on the market, and Nottingham was actually showing evidences of becoming a city. The same paper which gave this news also announced that two storehouses were being erected; that E. C. Blackmon, of Danbury, Conn., was building a two story woodworking establishment; that W. W. Lambert was erecting a handsome residence; that 15 double dwellings were under construction; that E. M. Lewis, of Oxanna, was erecting a two story storehouse; and it also stated that "work on electric light and water works will soon commence."

The town came into being almost overnight, and in the spring of 1890 it was announced that the Bank of Nottingham had been organized with a capital stock of $50,000.00, with J. M. N. B. Nix, of Chattanooga, President and M. W. Howard, of Fort Payne, Vice-President;[7] J. F. Reynolds was cashier. The furnaces were never built, but the hotel was completed, and opened with a flourish. In April, of 1890, a notice appeared in a local paper that the hotel at Nottingham would open for business on April 29th, 1890, and also stated that invitations were being issued to a "Hop" at the hotel on the 17th; that a special

---

[5] Letter from W. A. Cook, Alpine, dated Feb. 23, 1928
[6] Our Mountain Home, Dec. 25, 1889
[7] Ibid, April 1890

train would leave Anniston at 7:00 P. M., stopping at Oxanna, Oxford and Talladega; that it would leave Nottingham at 1:30 A. M., April 30th.[8]

The "Hop" was given by the Nottingham Iron & Land Company, who stated in the invitation that supper would be served at 12:00 midnight. The event was a memorable one for those who attended.

The building of Nottingham was one of the most unprofitable ventures ever undertaken in the County of Talladega. The Bank and a few stores remained open for some years, but the entire town vanished soon after the turn of the Twentieth Century, and the hotel was salvaged for $750.00. This was the most rapidly constructed village, and the most rapidly declining village, ever established in Talladega County.

RENFROE. Although a number of cultured pioneer families settled in the community in pioneer days, the town RENFROE was not founded until 1884, when D. W. Rogers & Co. erected large saw and planing mills there. The original post office was located several miles west of the present site. The town was incorporated Feb. 22, 1887, with about 1,000 inhabitants, most of whom had some connection with the lumber mills. The census of 1880 was 400; 1890—202; 1900—180; 1910—85.[9]

F. A. and W. M. Franks were associated with D. W. Rogers & Co., but in 1889 embarked in the lumber business for themselves nearer Stemley. The Huron Lumber Co. located also at Renfroe.

The Rogers and Franks industries were the direct reasons for the building of the short railroad through Renfroe. From the time the railroad was opened to the public, Renfroe became a rendezvous for pioneers. There was a lake of clear water, with artistic bridges from bank to bank of islets which dotted the lake.

The mills ceased operations in a few years; the lake was drained; and "An Act to repeal an Act to incorporate the Town of Renfroe, in Talladega Co., Ala.," was approved Dec. 8, 1900. Therefore, Renfroe as a manufacturing town, officially died on that date. A post office was operated at Renfroe, until 1956, and the paved highway is now lined with a continuation of new homes.

---

[8] Ibid, April 16, 1890
[9] Thomas M. Owen's History of Ala., Vol. II, Page 1193

Kelly's Springs

The first record in Deed Book "A", page 1, of the County of Talladega was made by James Kelly, "head of a Creek Tribe of Indians" to Elijah C. Walker, in which James Kelly also acknowledges Wm. Vardeman, Justice of the Peace in St. Clair Co., Attorney in power to transact his business. This deed covered his reservation in Sec. 9, Range 6, Township 18, and he received $2,000.00 for the property. It was witnessed by Robert W. Martin, Sylvanus Walker and Wm. Kelly. This price for a half section of land would indicate that there were improvements. The Deed was dated Nov. 31, 1832, nearly a month before Talladega was declared a county.

There are a number of deeds recorded to Elijah C. Walker on Page 2. He paid Cholock-Hadjo "head of a Creek Tribe of Indians" $2,000.00 for his reservation. This in Sec. 4, R. 6, Township 18. It will, therefore, be seen that all the Indians were not swindled in deals for their property, as we are frequently led to believe.

This first mentioned deed is for land called "Kelly's Spring". There are several large springs flowing here from which Kelly Creek rises. It is now known as "Curry Station", and owned by Robert McMillan and others. Col. Wm. Curry purchased this property from Walker & Riddle in 1837 and paid $39.00 per acre for it. He built his home, and in 1838 moved his family from Lincoln County, Ga. to Talladega County.

Kelly's Spring was one of the earliest settlements in Talladega County. It had one of the first United States Post offices in the County, which existed for many years and was one of the early voting Precincts. In writing of Col. Wm. Curry, Mr. Wm. L. Lewis states:

"He purchased the Walker & Riddle farm about five miles out of town, and it was not long before the place began to show unmistakable signs that a master spirit of no common mould presided there. The forest was felled, vast fields were reduced to cultivation, a splendid mansion was reared, flanked with outhouses constructed on a princely scale. Servant houses, barns, cribs, stables, etc., with a large 2nd commodious store house, in which he and Judge Groce who still survives (1876) a noble specimen of men of that day, did business for many years. I must also add an elegant Baptist meeting house stood in the grove nearby, to the erection of which he largely contributed, for the Lebanon Church of which he and his family were members. (Now a negro church). Indeed, the whole situation had the air of a country village, all alive with energy and enterprise."[1]

"What credit is due anymore for the construction of the railroad passing through our valley is due more to Col. Curry and the late Walker Reynolds than to any two men in our county." Mr. Lewis did not mention that there was also a Methodist Church at Kelly Springs. Dr. Anson West, in his History of Methodism in Alabama, states that a Quarterly Conference was held at Kelly Springs Church Aug. 8-9, 1834,[2] and it was in existence as late as 1845.

There was also a large Grist mill at Kelly's Spring, probably on Cheaha Creek, back of the J. J. McKibbon home. This home was built by Jared E. Groce, referred to by Mr. Lewis as a partner of Col. Curry's.

In an issue of the Talladega Watchtower of 1843, there appears an advertisement of the Riddle Brothers at Maria Forge, of implements on sale at the stores of Huey & Co., Talladega, and Curry & Groce, Kelly's Spring.

One especial reason why this spot is of historic interest, is that J. L. M. Curry, a son of Col. Wm. Curry, was reared at Kelly's Spring. J. L. M. Curry was Congressman, U. S. Minister to Spain, Agent for the Peabody and Slater Funds, a great Baptist preacher and an educator. He was once President of Howard College. His statue is one of two allotted to Alabama in Statuary Hall, Washington, D. C.

Another especial reason why Kelly's Spring is of interest, is that the Curry home was the scene of the play, "Alabama", which really put Talladega on the map.

In Our Mountain Home issue of Nov. 11, 1891, the following appears:

"From a private letter received by a Talladega merchant from Mr. T. V. Price, a banker in New York, we take the following:

"The North is very well acquainted with Talladega through the medium of the charming play ALABAMA, and we feel almost as if we knew every citizen of the place."

I shall, therefore, give "ALABAMA" a separate chapter, and consider it one of the most interesting chapters of Talladega County history.

---

[1] Our Mountain Home, 10-18-1876, Talladega Public Library
[2] History of Methodism, by Dr. Anson West, pub. 1893, Page 466

The Play "Alabama"

In 1885 Augustus Thomas, actor and playwright was traveling south with a road show, and passed through Talladega on the way to Birmingham. Travel to Birmingham from the east over the Southern Railway passed through Talladega in the year 1885. In passing through, Mr. Thomas was attracted to the Curry Home at Kelly's Spring. He states regarding this trip:

"On our way from Atlanta, which still bitterly remembered Sherman, we passed through Talladega to the busy little city of Birmingham. A story that Mr. Owens (an actor) had told me of a night in Talladega, the beauty of the town as he saw it, and especially the sight of a razed gateway to the old estate impressed me. I laid there the scenes of the first play that I ever wrote some six years later for Mr. A. M. Palmer. Also I named the play "Talladega", but Mr. Palmer thought that too exclusive for the theme, and we agreed upon the title "Alabama."[1]

On Wednesday, April 1st, 1891, the four-act play "Alabama" first appeared in the Madison Square Theatre. This was done in desperation after failures of three other plays. Mr. Palmer had no faith in "Alabama" nor the author. However, he had a month's use of the theatre, and "'Alabama" was his last straw and an experiment.

On the night the play opened, both Mr. Thomas and Mr. Palmer unknown each to the other, stood behind posts on different sides of the theatre in the gallery, fearfully awaiting the reception of the play. The first act was received with such enthusiasm, that they found each other in the balcony for the second act. The response was so enthusiastic during the second act, with four or five curtain calls, that Mr. Palmer came over to Mr. Thomas, who said "I'm going to see the rest of this performance from the ground floor."[2] They both went down, and the play was declared a wonderful success. However, there were only four weeks for "Alabama" to appear in Madison Square Theatre to capacity audiences. Because of previous failures, Mr. Palmer had rented the theatre to another company.

Arrangements were immediately made for a fall opening in a new Palmer Theatre. In the meantime, "Alabama" was put on road. It appeared in Birmingham on Wednesday night, October 28th, 1891.

---

[1] The Print of my Remembrances, by Augustus Thomas, Published 1922, Page 187
[2] Ibid, Page 293

The Birmingham Age-Herald carried two columns regarding the play on October 29th, 1891, from which the following is quoted:

"ALABAMA" at O'Brien's
The Boards at O'Brien's were occupied last night
by A. M. Palmer's Company, presenting
Augustus Thomas' great southern drama, "ALABAMA."

There follows quite a lengthy description of the play, then – "Notwithstanding the tremendous ovation the members of the "Alabama" company received last night, which was even a bit heartier than any they have received at any point on their triumphant tour through the south, they were a very unhappy lot of mortals—ever since the southern tour began they have been looking forward to visiting Talladega, the spot which gave Mr. Thomas the inspiration for his beautiful play...Mr. George W. Chambers has been endeavoring for weeks to bring about the consummation so devoutly wished by all. Yesterday a meeting of the prominent citizens of Talladega was held, when it was voted to send a befitting floral tribute to the company, which opens at Palmer's Theatre in New York next Monday night...Mr. Chambers sent flowers from Talladega to the Birmingham players."[3]

Mr. Chambers was at the time operating Chambers Opera House in Talladega and he did everything in his power to have the play appear in Talladega, but they were already booked. However, a number of people went over to Birmingham from Talladega to attend the performance there.

During preparations in New York for the opening of the play in November, an artist was sent to Talladega to get a picture of the William Curry home, which both Mr. Owens and Mr. Thomas had seen from the train, but, the home had burned in the meantime with all photographs.[4] It was suggested that the Lawler home at "Orangevale" was a beautiful representative southern home. Therefore, the stage background carried a picture of "Orangevale", but it was surrounded by massive oaks with Spanish moss hanging from the limbs.

The opening scene had a background of a bayou in front of the southern mansion located on a hill, which was owned and occupied by Col. Preston. Mrs. Page, a widow, lived in a cottage on the side, surrounded by a beautiful flower garden. Col. Preston was a bitter Rebel, who resented the fact that a group of Yankees were daring to build a railroad through his plantation.

---

[3] Found in Scrap Book of Mrs. Geo. W. Chambers - clipping
[4] As told me by many old people, and in particular by Miss Ida Curry, born and reared at Kelly's Spring. She was living with her father there when the house was burned.

When War was declared, a son of Col. Preston's had sided with the Union. He was declared a traitor, disinherited by his father, and joined the Union Army. He was instrumental in administering aid and comfort to a dying officer, who asked his name. The officer was told that he had no name, that he had been disinherited because of his attitude toward the Union. The officer told the boy that his name was unstained, and he would be glad to have him take his name of Davenport. The young boy did adopt that name, and eventually became a Captain in the Union Army. Captain Davenport became quite successful after the War, and was eventually made President of the proposed railroad through Talladega.

Captain Davenport, President, decided to come south himself when there appeared such controversy over the right of way through his father's plantation. He had grown a beard, adopted another name, so no one recognized him. A romance followed between Capt. Davenport and Carey, a ward of Col. Preston's. There was a happy reunion, and a pleasing ending. The story is a charming post Civil War drama.

The second opening of the play in New York was on November 2nd, 1891, and was of great moment for Talladega. Wm. H. Skaggs, ex-mayor of Talladega, was sent by the citizens with one thousand cotton bolls tied with white ribbon, arranged by a group of young ladies, and he carried a floral design, which cost the citizens $100.00

The New York Herald, New York Advertiser, New York Mirror, New York World, and other newspapers, gave such glowing reports of the play, and of Mr. Skaggs' presentation, that I would like to quote from all of them, but the following will suffice to give an understanding of the cordial reception given in New York to the play, and to Mr. Skaggs, representing Talladega:

Excerpts from New York papers dated Nov. 3, 1891:

NEW YORK TIMES: "The new order of things began in earnest at Palmer's Theatre last evening. Colonel Preston and Colonel Moberly and the Squire and Mistress Page and Carey, and all the rest with whom we got so well acquainted further down the street 'moved in' and took possession of the home they are hereafter to occupy. Every one of them were applauded with a cordiality and fervor that showed personal regard as well as appreciation for art, and the welcome Agnew Booth received was the heartiest of them all…

"The play went on. Everything has been told about "Alabama." The play does not grow old, but adjectives do, unfortunately, and after a while it is as well to take approval for granted. . . . After the play, something took place which was perhaps, as one of the speakers said 'quite without parallel in the annals of the stage.' At the close of the fourth act the curtain rose again disclosing the players grouped about a handsome piece of floral architecture, bearing the words 'Alabama' and 'Here we Rest'. Then a slender young man,

Mr. W. H. Skaggs, ex-mayor of Talladega, stepped forward and made a speech. He said the people of his town had sent him here to express their admiration of the play; and to say that they accepted it as a picture of the New South and to present these flowers, gathered by Col. Preston's granddaughter on the old Preston plantation. Mr. Palmer spoke a few words on behalf of his company, and Mr. Thomas, the author of "Alabama" said that he had nothing to say except that he was happy and everybody else was happy . . .

"Mme. Bernhardt, who watched it all from one of the lower boxes may not have quite understood what she saw, but she applauded as if she did, and the other people in the house screamed with enthusiasm."[5] Evidently Madam Bernhardt did understand what she saw as reported by the NEW YORK HERALD: "ALABAMA" pleases BERNHARDT" headlines, and article:

"Mme. Bernhardt compliments Mr. Thomas for his play and Mr. Palmer's actors for their playing. . . . During an entr-acte I asked the famous French woman what she thought of it. 'Think of it!' she exclaimed. Why I think it is admirable. I have actually been crying—yes, really crying, and not stage tears. I have seen many American and British plays, and I will confess that as a rule I have been disappointed. I never imagined you wrote such plays. This shows delicacy and genuine instinct for stage effect.' "

Space does not permit further comments. However, Mr. Skaggs' speech was quoted in full by the New York Dramatic Mirror. The New York World stated that "A southern DePew, in the person of ex-Mayor Skaggs, of Talladega, Ala., seems to have been introduced to New Yorkers by the author of "ALABAMA."

Mr. Skaggs was so wined and dined that he stayed two weeks in New York. The climax of his visit was a breakfast given him by Mr. Palmer at the Players' Club on Nov. 18th, 1891. On the back of his menu he acquired autographs of the following guests at the Breakfast: A. M. Palmer, J. H. Stoddard, Augustus Thomas, John Paul Bocock, Frederick C. P. Robinson, Reuben Fox, Gene W. Presbrey, M. Barrymore, Charles L. Harris, Edward M. Bell, Edward S. Abeles, Harrison Grey Fiske, E. M. Holland and Walden Ramsey.

The "M. Barrymore", who took the part of Capt. Davenport, was Maurice Barrymore, the father of Lionel, Ethel and John Barrymore. In fact, the entire cast was composed of prominent actors. J. B. Stoddard was at the time one of America's foremost actors.

---

[5] Photostats of clippings, dated Nov. 3, 1891, sent me by Mr. Wm. H. Skaggs, the ex-Mayor referred to. Photostats in my possession.

There were several citizens from Talladega present at this opening of the Palmer Theatre, among them were Mr. and Mrs. E. S. Jemison and Mrs. Lavinia Groce.

The News Reporter of Dec. 12th, 1891, stated: "Hon. W. H. Skaggs is in receipt of a letter from Mr. Thomas, author of "Alabama", asking another thousand cotton bolls for distribution on the 50th night of the play. The writer says Mr. Palmer designs something especially interesting on this occasion similar to that on the opening appearance and wishes the cotton bolls as a feature. Of course, the public-spirited ex-Mayor went promptly to work to furnish them, which is now being done."

"ALABAMA" made a fortune for Mr. Palmer, and was the beginning of a great career for Augustus Thomas, who later wrote more than sixty plays. The play was popular well into the Twentieth Century. The Business & Professional Women's Club, of Talladega presented the play with local talent about 1923 in the old Elk's Theatre, located on East St., N.

The original play of "ALABAMA" really put Talladega on the map.

Mineral Resources

Talladega County is well watered with bold and sparkling springs, which feed creeks and rivulets flowing into the Coosa River which borders her territory on the north and west. Her beautiful valleys, so well watered, make an ideal agricultural and cattle country. While Talladega County lies within this wonderful agricultural and cattle area, she also lies in the Mineral Belt of Alabama. The Blue Ridge Mountains and hills within her territory abound in valuable minerals of all kinds. These minerals have been mined only on the surface, and future generations should profit by many discoveries of buried treasures yet unknown.

Exciting stories are told of the search for, and the mining of certain metals. Copper, gold, iron and marble, and many other ores were mined profitably over the century.

COAL is mentioned in one instance in the Report of Thomas Pearsall, Commissioner to Survey the Coosa River and Lands adjacent thereto in 1869:

"Near Ft. Williams, on the Coosa River, are presented some indications of coal, but no efforts have been made to prove the fact of its existence . . . Four or five miles above this point within a half mile of the Coosa River, Dr. Lee (now deceased) informed me in April last, that ten years ago, he found coal in the bed of a creek on his farm, and that he had several bushels taken out and sent to Columbiana, where it was used by the smiths and pronounced superior coal."[1]

OIL must have been a subject of interest at one time, since the Talladega Petroleum & Mining Co. was approved as a corporation by the Legislature Feb. 23, 1866.[2]

LEAD works were in force during the Civil War, mined for the purpose of making bullets for the Confederate Government. The expense of extracting the lead from the lime rock made it impracticable, and no further effort seems to have been made after the War.

MICA has been found in the county, and mined with profit. An ancient Mica Quarry was reported in a Smithsonian Report of 1879 by Wm. Gesner, as having been discovered in Talladega County in Sec. 12, T. 20 S., R. 6 E.[3] Mica was quarried during the latter part of the 19th century near Chandler's Springs. It

---

[1] Report of Commissioner of Industrial Resources of 1869-70, Page 1
[2] Acts of Alabama, 1866, No. 259, Page 428
[3] Publications of Ala. His. Society, Misc. Collections, Vol. I, Page 358

was beautifully imbedded in a white porcelain. There were several other mines in that vicinity.

SILVER, although never found in the county, has caused more speculation in its search than any other mineral. Hence, this record.

There is much mystery surrounding SILVER in Talladega County. Pioneers found Indians wearing trinkets, and using utensils made of silver, and the use was continued until their removal to the Indian Territory. It meant death to divulge the secret of location. Neither gifts, coaxing, nor drunkenness brought out the secret of the hidden mine.

Mr. J. E. Stone, a native of Talladega County, gave me a version of a story as told by his father, Isaac Stone, who came to Talladega County in the fall of 1832, and settled in the Plantersville community near Alpine. Mr. Isaac Stone gives a graphic story of his experiences and early life. He states that an Indian by an unpronounceable name, whom he called "George", had two children to die with measles, because, as the Indian custom was, he kept them in water until the fever subsided. Mr. Stone asked permission to treat the third child, who got well, and thereby made a lasting friend of George. From this point I quote Mr. Stone's story:[4]

"My acquaintance with George and proximity to the village gave me the knowledge of the fact that George went into seclusion once or twice during each year, and remained so for some time, and that when the seclusion was ended all the Indians had new silver ornaments—armlets, beads and such other jewelry that their tastes demanded.

I had in the meantime gotten pretty well acquainted with the white settlers, and we had frequently gone ourselves on camp hunts. This was discussed among us as to the source of supply of this silver ore obtained by the Indians, and judging from the amount and the short time which it took to load several pack ponies with this precious metal, it must be easy of access and in great quantity somewhere near; and all began to inquire into the evidence, and make plans to get information on the subject . . .

It was agreed, after much inquiry and deliberation to follow the tracks of the Indian ponies, and a camp hunt was organized. It was agreed that as the Indians passed near my cabin that I would signal the time of their departure on the next excursion, which appeared to be about ready, and which was done timely; all preparations of provisions having been made.

This occurred in the small hours of the night and very quietly, of course. Soon after the signal of the hunter's horn, the whites assembled and at day break began to follow the hoof prints of the Indian cavalcade, which was

---

[4] Letter to me from J. E. Stone, dated Nov. 9, 1927

easily done until we had crossed the River now known as "Coosa", at what was known as Drake's Ferry in the general direction then of Jefferson County across St. Clair County, until Bear, or Wolf Creek was reached in a north-westerly direction.

After reaching this small stream of clear water with graveled bottom no further trace could be found. The hunters divided, part went up the stream, the other down, but not a hoof print or any evidence of the trail which had been clear until then, could be found. After a thorough search without avail, a sentinal was stationed at the ford of this stream and the hunters struck camp, some distance away, and hunted deer until notified by the sentinal of the return of the Indian cavalcade, after which a close scrutiny was made of the direction beyond the stream, still without avail. The only sign found was a piece of rich silver ore in the stream weighing about a pound or more, which seemed to have been freshly mined, and which was taken to be assayed, and proved to be very rich in silver and lead; the Silver predominating—something like 60 percent metal content.

George visited me the Sunday before the Indians left for Arkansas later on and spent the day. After dinner, George sat with me on a bench in the yard, and being fond of fire water, he had gotten more talkative than usual, and then I asked him, as the mine would be of no further use to them to tell me before he left where it was. It seemed to infuriate him and he jumped up, presented his rifle at my breast, and snapped at me, and but for the powder having been jostled from the pan, I would have been shot through. His Squaw on seeing it, ran and took the gun from him and beat him with a board, which, while he seemed to suffer greatly from the chastisement, accepted it with good grace. She told my wife that any Indian who divulged the location of this mine to a white man would be put to death by them, and no persuasion could consequently move them to discuss it further."

Because of this story, prospectors have searched many times over St. Clair, Jefferson and Talladega County, without success.

Other stories are told regarding Silver in the upper part of the county. There were many ornaments of silver among Indians around Ironaton, Munford and Silver Run (which, by the way, was named because of moonlight on a stream of water and not because of silver ore).[5] This fact, caused much search in that neighborhood for silver.

Dr. Eugene A. Smith, famous State Geologist, made a survey of Talladega County in September, 1874, and visited the Stewart silver Mine about

---

[5] Letter from Miss Hallie B. Jenkins, R. F. D. Oxford, to me

two miles from Munford.[6] He states that there was no reason for this mine having been there, other than became of an old legend. He said that a beech tree was found at the mouth of the mine, with Indian cawing, which made those in search of silver feel that it might be the spot where, as the legend went: "It was related that a blind negro living in the community had told of the reason of the marking. . . . The Indians had been wont to blindfold a Negro, bring him to the spot, unbind his eyes, load him up with silver, which the black would carry to the village, after which his eyes were put out so that he could never be able to find the spot where the silver supply was gotten by the Red Man." Dr. Smith indicated that there was no evidence whatever of silver.

Citizens around Ironaton, in pioneer days, felt assured that there was silver in the mountains about them, and made diligent search for many years.

The Silver mystery has never been solved, and perhaps Col. James L. Tait, Commissioner of Industrial Resources in his report of Dec. 21, 1870,[7] is correct in the solution:

"The Indians are said to have had silver in their possession, and to have known its value in the State, but the fact that there is no well authenticated case of discovery since, although diligent search has been made by man); is an evidence in my mind that either it was obtained elsewhere, by these nomadic tribes, or that some other mineral, such as zinc, may have been mistaken by them for the more precious metal, especially in the newly melted state."

COPPER or Pyrites was discovered soon after the settlement of Talladega County. This, however, was found usually in that portion of the county which in 1866 became a part of the present Clay County.

Perhaps the earliest stock company was that of the Alabama Copper Mining Company, incorporated in 1854 by John M. Moore, President, Dr. William Taylor, Secretary, and W. A. Drury, Mining Engineer, and Superintendent. The stockholders were mostly German. Names of Wm. Sulzbacher, Isaac Sulzbacher, H. Heine, Seligman Adler, Bernard Stein, Wm. A. Schulein, Xavier Willman, appear among the stockholders.[8] The mine was located on Copper Mine Creek, and proved unprofitable. The Montgomery Mining Co. purchased the property in 1860. Dr. Wm. Taylor, S. D. Hubbard and a group of Montgomery, Ala. people composed the Company.

Dr. Wm. Gesner, Geologist and Mining Engineer, was Manager and Superintendent. Blue stone and copper salts were sold to the Confederate Government, but after the War, the mine was abandoned.

---

[6] Article from Tuscaloosa News, quoted by Our Mt. Home, Nov. 30, 1927
[7] State Documents, 1869, Page 7, Report of Com. Indus. Resources
[8] Information from Mr. Joe Willman, deceased

The State Geologist stated as late as 1870 that copper was found[9] "in notable quantities in Talladega County."

GOLD was mined in Alabama as early as 1830. Talladega County is listed as being in the "Upper Gold Belt". Among more than a hundred gold mines, some of minor importance, "more than two-thirds were in Talladega slates."[10] The Abacoochee Gold Mine seems to have been among the first, if not the first.

There was a Post Road authorized established by the U. S. Government July 7, 1838, "from Hickory Level by Adrian's Ferry on the Coosa River, Abacoochee Gold Mines to Franklin, Ga."[11] From this we infer that the mine was already in operation prior to July, 1838. Large nuggets were found years later at this mine. The Talladega, or Terrapin Mountain belt, seems to be the region where gold is most prevalent.

The opening of the Abacoochee Mine was followed by many others. Riddle's Mill Hold, or Waldo Mine, of Riddle Bros. in S. 16, T. 19, R. 6,[12] was sold to J. M. Sullivan, who organized the May Virginia Gold Mining Co. He invested $1,000.00 in machinery, rented an office in Talladega and in the spring of 1888, when J. H. Everett was Treas., and Sid W. Lanier was Supt., they were mining 20 tons of ore per day profitably, and there were five distinct veins.[13]

Other mines were operated through the years. The Chincopino; Parson's Kemp Creek; Garrish, Woodward & Co.; Gold Log; Chulafinnee, Long Branch and the Storey mines all opened. The Storey mine was on Talladega Creek, Sec. 17, T. 19, R. 6, and was discovered by Geo. Hunt in the early 50's. He conveyed it to A. G. Storey and Andrew Cunningham.

Mr. Mallory records "April 19th, 1843: "Our country is in a high state of excitement from the gold fever that is now raging, it having been discovered in the hillsides, where it is said to be plentiful. Many of our people have engaged, and fear to their injury and neglect of other pursuits."[14]

Crops had failed for several years. Because of these failures many people turned to mining. Gold has been mined on a small scale continuously, neither extensively nor very profitably, but one wonders what might be done with modern equipment available.

---

[9] Report of Col. James L. Tate, Com. Of Indus. Resources, dated Dec. 26, 1870, Page 4, State Documents, 1871-72

[10] Owen's History of Ala. & Dictionary of Biography, Vol. I, Page 660

[11] Statutes at Large, Vol. 5, Page 280

[12] Geological Survey, E. A. Smith, 1897

[13] Our Mountain Home, March 7, 1888

[14] Journal owned by Mr. E. A. Stewart, Selma, Ala.

SLATE is found "of the Weisner formation in the south-western part of Talladega County." It was quarried to some extent during the War Between the States. The Confederate arsenal in Selma was covered with it.[15] The Slate was of excellent quality, and in large quantity.

SAND-STONE must have been quarried in several localities over the County, but the only place of which I am certain is that on the west side of Kelly Creek on the S. M. Jemison farm. This was quarried prior to, and during the War Between the States. Mr. Landt, a German, and a Mr. Rumley, an Irishman, were Superintendent and stone cutters of the quarry, and the labor was entirely made up of slaves. The stone was mustard colored, and quite pretty when first quarried. Many brick storehouses, and dwellings in Talladega Co. have this stone as foundations, door-sills and window sills. Cemeteries over the county, including Oak Hill in Talladega, have slabs or grave stones of this sand-stone. Although it is said to grow harder with the years, and the lettering is still quite legible after nearly a hundred years of having weathered the storms, it does not make an attractive marker.

The quarry was again opened during the Boom days of 1885-90.

IRON was the prevalent product of the mineral resources discovered in Talladega County. It is believed that blacksmiths employed by the United States Government in this district, prior to the signing of the Treaty of 1832, used native ores to make iron used in their shops. Smiths were sent into the Creek country by Benjamin Hawkins, Indian Agent, as early as 1796. A blacksmith was frequently an intelligent artisan who could forge his own iron into farming implements and kitchen utensils. His trade was one of the essential ones to the frontiersmen. The Smith sometimes became the manufacturer.

Miss Ethel Marie Armes, in her STORY OF COAL & IRON IN ALABAMA, published in 1910, under the auspices of the Birmingham Chamber of Commerce, gives an early history of the manufacture of iron in Talladega County. Miss Armes made intensive and thorough research, and has given to Alabama an invaluable volume. Miss Armes states:

"There were in Talladega County iron works all told eight forges and one blast furnace in operation during antebellum days. Of these, the Maria Forge, erected in 1836, was the first, and Eagle Forge (1846) the second. Then followed in successive order: Cheaha Creek foundry (1846), Robert Jemison and (Samuel) Hunter; Riddles Mill foundry (1848), Edward Spang and Dr. William Summers; Fain's Creek forge, Silas and David Garrigus, A. W. Bowie, Major Walker Reynolds, John T. Ragan; Clairmont Springs forge (1850) Amerine; Rob Roy forge (1852), George M. Riddle, John Moore, Curry (J. A.) and Parks;

---

[15] Owen's His. of Ala. Vol. II, Page 1251

Chinnabee forge (1852), Silas Garrigus; The Knight furnace (1854), J. L. Orr and William Craig Orr."[16]

Taking Miss Armes' findings separately, as she lists these forges, we get a very good history of the antebellum iron activities.

MARIA FORGE was founded in 1836 by John M. Moore, promoter and pioneer iron maker. He started his foundry by gathering up scrap iron over the community for the purpose of recasting. He purchased Section 17, T. 19, R. 6 E, of the Coosa Land District, on Talladega Creek, and proceeded to build a dam, which was only about half completed when he sold his plant to the Riddle Brothers. At the time of purchase, the name was changed to "Maria Forge" in honor of the wife of Samuel Stuart Riddle, Mrs. Maria Bradley Riddle.[17] The Democratic Watchtower carried a notice of this purchase, dated May 17, 1843:

BUY AT HOME

The subscriber begs leave to inform the citizens of Talladega and the surrounding counties, that he has purchased the IRON WORK lately owned by JOHN M. MOORE, situated on Talladega Creek six miles from Talladega, and half a mile below LONG'S MILLS on the Socapatoy Road, and will keep constantly on hand a general assortment of IRON, which he will sell at less than Wetumpka prices, viz: 6½c, and warrant to be equal to any in the United States.

MILL IRONS, etc., made to the shortest notice.

He will also keep a constant supply of assorted Iron at the store of Messrs. T. W. HUEY & CO., Talladega, and at the store of MESSRS. CURRY & GROCE, Kelly's Springs. Orders addressed to the subscriber, at Talladega, or to T. W. Huey & Co., will be promptly attended to.

W. D. RIDDLE,
MARIA FORGE, May 17, 1843."[18]

Samuel Stuart Riddle, Edmund Ross Riddle and Walter D. Riddle, were civil engineers and road contractors from New York. They were employed to survey the first railroads and early dirt roads in Alabama. They were employed in such capacity in Talladega County, when they purchased this plant, and permanently settled.

Iron turned out by the Riddle Forge was stamped with a Boar's head, which was their family crest.

---

[16] Story of Coal & Iron in Ala., by Ethel Armes, Page 82, used by permission from Mr. Edmund C. Armes, Birmingham.
[17] Letter from Laura Riddle, daughter of W. D. Riddle, dated 9-27-1927.
[18] Democratic Watchtower , June 12, 1844, owned by Miss Enfield Joiner

Prior to coming into Alabama, the Riddle Brothers were employed in Hollidaysburg, Pennsylvania, where they were engaged in railroad construction. Associated with them were Silas and David Garrigus, Iron makers, and George D. Wheeler, a civil engineer, who were persuaded to come to Alabama, and they also became pioneer iron makers of Talladega County. Mr. W. D. Riddle, of Birmingham, wrote a concise description of the method of making iron at Maria Forge, as follows:

"Maria Forge, which was located about one mile below Riddle's Mill on Talladega Creek, was run by water power. Wrought iron was made there. The ore was put in a cupelo, heated with charcoal to the right temperature, and let out at the bottom into a puddle. After it stood a while, the hammer man took an iron bar and punched it up, then with a pole axe hammered it into what was called a loop; then with tongs about five feet long laid across a crane, the loop was swung under a five hundred pound hammer, which was lifted by a wooden shaft with lifts on it. The loop was hammered into wagon tires and plow molds. They sold iron at 12½c a pound."[19]

Mr. Mallory mentioned in his Journal under date of October, 1844, that a cannon had been made by a Mr. Moore to be used in a political parade in Montgomery— evidently made at Maria Forge.

Iron was shipped to Wetumpka for river transportation to other points. The Iron of Maria Forge was considered of superior quality, perhaps due to the fact that it was made by experienced iron makers.

EAGLE FORGE, Miss Armes states, was erected in 1846 by Geo. D. Wheeler and Israel Sprayberry. Mr. Riddle writes "The logs to make the lumber used in erecting the Eagle were hauled on a truck wagon, the wheels of which were discs sawed from a large black gum log. I wonder what the machinist of today would think of running an iron furnace or forge, without one foot of iron shafting, without a single iron pully, or a pound of Babbitt metal, with all of the journals being run on wooden bearings?"[20]

Eagle Forge was well off the beaten path, and was abandoned after being operated only a few years, because of overflows. The old chimney still stands.

CHEAHA Foundry is listed as the third, and was erected by Robert Jemison and Samuel Hunter on Cheaha Creek, near Turner's Mill, which was known then, 1846, as Jemison's Mill. The foundry was used for the purpose of making farm implements and cooking utensils for Robert Jemison's and neighboring plantations. It was operated only a few years.

---

[19] Article enclosed in letter from Laura Riddle, dated 9-27-1927.
[20] Ibid

RIDDLE'S MILL FOUNDRY was erected in 1848 by Edward Spang, from Pennsylvania, and William Summers, a practicing physician, who settled at Pond Springs about 1832. This Foundry was located about half a mile from Maria Forge. They made "pots, skillets, stoves, plows and other castings."

FAIN'S CREEK FORGE was erected by David Garrigus and Walker Reynolds from material purchased from Maria Forge. It was erected during the Civil War, and was operated for some time after the War. Mr. Reynolds sold his interest to John T. Ragan, who had worked with Riddle Bros. for some years. Silas Garrigus and A. W. Bowie were connected with this forge at some time.

CLAIRMONT SPRINGS FORGE, operated by one Amerine, must have been operated under another name, since the name "Clairmont" was not applied to the place until early in the 20th Century. An abstract of title to this property reveals that W. P. Chilton owned this mine prior to 1850, and John T. Morgan acquired it from him about 1856. An old hammer from this mine is now on display at Clairmont Springs Hotel.

ROB ROY CATALAN FORGE, located south-east of Eagle Forge on Talladega Creek, and about half way between there and I Chandler's Springs, was erected about 1852 by Geo. M. Riddle and Jno. M. Moore. They sold to James A. Curry and a Mr. Parks. Rob Roy had two fireplaces, remains of which still stand.

CHINNABEE FORGE was erected by Silas Garrigus on Horse Shoe Creek at Seay's in 1852. It was operated successfully for fifteen or twenty years.

THE KNIGHT FURNACE, Miss Armes states was erected in 1854. However, it was built and operated by J. L. & Wm. Craig Orr much earlier. An issue of the Ala. Reporter of August 12, 1847, carried this notice:

"J. L. & W. C. Orr advertise that they are manufacturing cotton gins. Recommended by Thomas Best, James K. Walker, Wm. Montgomery, Wm. A. Morris, Andrew Cunningham and James Montgomery."

Their gins were sold over Talladega County, as well as adjoining counties. The Orrs had well constructed buildings and tenement houses. During the War there was no market for gins and when Jacob B. and Benjamin Knight, refugees from New Orleans, came to Talladega in 1863, with a number of slaves, and ready money, the Orrs sold to them.

Samuel Hunter became interested with the Orrs in 1854; William Craig Orr died in 1860, and the firm name changed to "Orr & Hunter". They sold 800 acres of land, manufacturing plant, and tenement houses to the Knights for a consideration of $20,000.00 on March 11, 1863. This plant was located between Munford and the Old Brick Store, or Simmons Mill, on Choccolocco Creek.

"The Knight Brothers at once converted the plant into a cotton factory for the spinning of yarn, and also erected a blast furnace, having a capacity of about four tons of pig iron per day, the power to operate which, together with the cotton factory, being supplied by the waters of Choccolocco Creek. A foundry was also put in operation, where pots, kettles and many other castings were made. All the different branches of this manufacturing plant were kept in full and successful operation by Knight Brothers until April, 1865, when General Croxton's Brigade, of Federal General Wilson's raiders, applied a torch to everything combustible, and wrought such utter destruction of the entire plant that only a few chimneys and a portion of the furnace stack marked the spot that had been the hive of several industries for so many years. Upon the close of the hostilities between the sections in 1865, the Knight Brothers returned to Louisiana."[21]

The Knight Brothers were bachelors. They had a sister with them, who appeared on several occasions, many of the old Munford residents say, with dresses of cloth made at the cotton mill. They insist that the mill contained looms as well as spindles. The labor for the mill was slave labor entirely.

SALT CREEK IRON WORKS was erected during the winter of 1863-64. James A. Curry, half-brother of J. L. M. Curry, owned a section of land about a mile north-east of Munford on the Alabama & Tenn. Rivers Railroad. He interested Samuel Clabaugh, a brother-in-law of Horace Ware, the Shelby County iron manufacturer, in joining him in erecting an iron furnace. There was a great demand at the time for iron to be used in manufacturing guns, cannons, etc. for the Confederate Army. The furnace operated until Croxton's raiders passed through in April, 1865, and burned the building to the ground, though the stack remained intact.

Horace Ware purchased the property in 1868, and with Stephen S. Glidden, of Ohio, as Manager, rebuilt the furnace, which was put into operation some time in 1872 or 1873. The town was incorporated May 17, 1873 under the name of "Alabama Furnace". A narrow gauge railroad was built between the two, and the Iron Company.

In the meantime, Samuel Noble, A. L. Tyler, and associates incorporated the Clifton Iron Company, with Samuel Noble as President, at Clifton (Ironaton), about 9 miles south of Alabama Furnace, and began operations.

In 1881 the Clifton Iron Company purchased the Alabama Furnace. A narrow gauge railroad was built between the two, and the name of Alabama Furnace was changed to that of "Jenifer", in honor of the mother of Samuel Noble, Mrs. Jenifer Ward Noble.

---

[21] Story of Coal & Iron in Ala., by Ethel Armes, Page 89

The furnace was eventually sold to outside capitalists, who recently sold the entire holdings to local purchasers.

CLIFTON IRON WORKS was established in 1871, under the name of Clifton Iron Company, with Samuel Noble, President, Stephen N. Noble, Superintendent, and John E. Ware, Sec. & Treas. The property remained unimproved and inactive until Dec. 1, 1881, when the Clifton Iron Co. purchased the Alabama Iron Co.'s holdings. In 1884 two fifty ton Charcoal furnaces were built.

In 1888 Mr. Samuel Noble died; Mr. Horace Ware sold his interest, and John E. Ware resigned as Secretary and Treasurer. A Mr. Prime, of Philadelphia became interested, and was made President, and John S. Mooring became Secretary and Treasurer. Stephen N. Noble remained as Superintendent. He doubled the capacity, and was founder of Ironaton. Thomas G. Bush was made President in 1892, and remained as such an officer until 1899. In 1899 the property was absorbed by the Alabama Consolidated Coal & Iron Railway Company, which was organized, with holdings in a number of counties, and headquarters in Birmingham. The name of the village of Clifton must have been changed to that of Ironaton around 1885, since the town was incorporated under the name of Ironaton" at that time.

Ore is still mined on property in and around Ironaton in 1959.

TALLADEGA IRON & STEEL COMPANY was the outcome of Mr. Geo. W. Chambers, who interested English capitalists in erecting furnaces in Talladega.

From a Report of Mr. Ralph Bennett, Galton House, Smethwick, England, dated November 20th 1885,[22] it is interesting to read:

"During the last Summer, Mr. J. N. Lester, of Wolverhampton, introduced me to Mr. Geo. W. Chambers, of Talladega, State of Alabama, North America, who, with his family, was on a visit to his wife's relatives in Birmingham, England, and who had brought before Mr. Lester the matter of his Iron-stone Mines, lying near Talladega, the County Town, Talladega County, State of Alabama.

Previous to this Mr. Chambers and Mr. Lester had conferred together as to the best time and proper way of getting these Ores into the market, and as a preliminary step some samples which he had brought over with him were submitted to Mr. E. Riley, of London, for Analysis, the result of which was as follows:

---

[22] Scrap Book owned by Mrs. Geo. W. Chambers, deceased

Silica	2.80	Magnesia	Trace
Peroxide of Iron	81.47	Phosphoric Acid	.43
Perotoxide of Iron	Trace	Sulphuric Acid	.07
Oxide of Manganese	.52	Carbonic Acid	Nil
Alumina	1.92	Combined Water	11.86
Lime	.31	Moisture	.69
Metallic Iron	57.03		100.07

As analyzed by Mr. Ed. Riley, City Road, London, July 3rd, 1885"

"With the object of verifying Mr. Chambers by an inspection of the Mines myself, I returned with him to America on the 27th of August, in the 'S. S. Germanic', and we arrived at our destination on the 8th of Sept. I lost no time in visiting his various Freehold Mineral Properties, which lay all around the town of Talladega, distances from 3 to 8 or 9 miles, in 12 different lots of 20 to 640 acres each, and comprising in the whole about 2,000 acres . . .

"After inspecting the different lots which I found embraced all the most available Ironstone deposits in the county of Talladega, which occupied me five days, I visited the Blast Furnaces at Ironaton, and the old Alabama Furnace. . . . These were Charcoal Furnaces, and making the very best quality of Pig Iron I ever saw, samples of which I brought back with me. At the time of the war the Confederate Government took possession of these Furnaces and made their guns, etc. here . . .

As regards making Pig Iron at Talladega, I have no hesitation, from information gained on the spot and from my own practical experience, in saying I believe Iron can be produced there at less cost than anywhere else in the world, and I am warranted in making this assertion by the fact of the Ironstone lying so convenient and in such inexhaustible masses."

To verify Mr. Bennett's report, Mr. Joshua Lancaster, Barmouth, England, arrived in Talladega on Dec. 12 1887, to inspect the field. He also made a favorable report upon his return to England, resulting in the founding of "The Alabama Iron Smelting Company, Limited, Talladega, Alabama, United States." £100,000 was fixed as the capital stock, divided into 99,000 ordinary shares of £1 each, and 1,000 Founders Shares at £1 each. Mr. Joshua Lancaster was made manager; H. R. Lewis, Secretary; Solicitors Messrs. Snell & Son, Greenup, George Street, Mansion House, London. Offices were established at Bartholomew House, Bankers, E. C. London. A local paper stated that Mr. Lancaster was a brother to the owner of the yacht which picked up Admiral Semmes and his men of the "Alabama" after their conflict with the "Kearsage" off Cherbourg, France, during the Civil War.

The company purchased approximately 2,000 acres of mineral land. Mr. Geo. W. Chambers, the largest local stockholder, was made a director. Mr. E. E. Shaw was the largest English stockholder, with 2,000 shares.

An article in Our Mountain Home of Nov. 6, 1889 stated in part:

"In casting about for a site, Mr. Lancaster's practiced eye fell upon a tract of thirty acres adjoining the corporate limits, on which was once situated Fort Leslie. This tract intersected by the Anniston & Atlantic and the Talladega & Coosa Valley railways, with a never-failing stream of water running through it, was the property of the Talladega Real Estate and Loan Association, which corporation, without hesitation, came promptly forward and made a donation of the entire tract, which the City of Talladega supplemented by purchasing and donating twenty acres more and adjacent; thus giving the company 50 acres of most valuable property, and a site that cannot be excelled."

The breaking of ground for two blast furnaces almost within the limit of Talladega took place in the summer of 1888. On October 5th, 1889, Miss Rosa Lancaster, daughter of Manager Lancaster, formerly of England, pulled the lever that put the furnace into blast. The next month samples were sent to the State Fair, and Our Mountain Home of Nov. 6th, 1889 boastingly headed an article "TALLADEGA PIGS SET ALL OTHERS SQUEALING FROM ENVY," in which they state "our furnace has not yet been heated to the full capacity, and already the iron-makers of Birmingham, sitting as judges at the State Fair, with the smoke of their own furnaces hovering over them, have awarded to the Talladega Iron and Steel Company the premium for the best pig iron in the State of Alabama.

Another issue of Our Mountain Home, Dec. 4, 1889 states: "Bessemer Pig is what the Talladega furnace is turning out at the rate of 100 tons every 24 hours."

The furnaces were operated successfully for some years, but under date of June 16, 1889, was sold under foreclosure to the Alabama Coal & Iron Railway Company, and July of 1899 began operations under that name.

Eugene Zimmerman, the Iron Magnate of Cincinnati, eventually purchased the property, and his family moved to Talladega for a short period. It was while they were in residence here that the Duke of Manchesterand his attendants made a visit to Miss Zimmerman, which resulted in the marriage later in Cincinnati of Miss Zimmerman and the Duke of Manchester.

Mr. Zimmerman sold to Japanese capitalists, some of whom lived here for a short while. The property eventually passed into the hands of Mr. Watt T. Brown. He sold to Mr. and Mrs. Goldberg, of Sylacauga, who still own the tenement houses on the old furnace property.

Talladega is justly proud of such men as Samuel, John and Stephen Noble; Horace and John E. Ware; T. G. Bush; Eugene Zimmerman; Geo. W.

Chambers; and many other iron makers who had a part in establishing Talladega County as a manufacturing center. Each had a part in the making of Talladega County.

Other blast furnaces were immediately promoted on the town's border after this profitable venture, as indicated by articles appearing in issues of Our Mountain Home and the Talladega Reporters of March 1890. The entire town was excited over the fact that "The Pennsylvania Iron and Steel Company" had just filed deeds and charter in the Probate Office to build three Blast Furnaces, with a capital stock of $1,500,000.00. The company was composed of Messrs. W. D. Solliday and O. C. Camp, of Pennsylvania, and of Geo. W. Chambers and Thomas S. Plowman, of Talladega. One furnace was to be erected "at the East Tennessee, Virginia and Georgia Railroad tank, near the western limits of the city," where "all facilities for the manufacture of cutlery, razors and every manner of steel implement will be at hand without traveling beyond the bounds of Talladega."

The other two furnaces were under the corporation name of "Spring Lake Furnace Company". The site selected was west of the Lake in the north end. This company had secured possession of the vast mineral beds contiguous to the mountain, at the base of which their furnace was to be built.

Talladega was heralded as "The Iron City of the New South", and the "Magical City of Steel and Iron." Mr. George W. Chambers, the promoter of all the furnaces, was lauded as one "great in thought, one great in purpose, he stands pre-eminently as an equal, and alongside of, Alabama's great men, who have laid monuments bright and lasting."

These three furnaces were never erected, and the property was finally placed on the market. Mr. T. S. Plowman and associates eventually erected a cotton spinning mill on the property west of the city, adjoining the Southern Railway Company, known as Chinnabee Cotton Mills.

Perhaps again Talladega will become the Iron City, after the surface ores have been exhausted. Certainly there must be deep veins imbedded in her soils in the valleys, and her mountains surely must be stored with great deposits yet undeveloped.

MARBLE in Alabama, usually means marble in Talladega County, because the largest deposits of the best quality in the state are found in Talladega County. In fact, it is safe to say that there is more marble in this county than in the rest of Alabama put together. Dr. Owen, in his History of Alabama and Dictionary of Biography,[23] says:

---

[23] Owen's History of Ala., Vol. II, Page 934

"The marbles of the State are of two kinds, crystalline or true marble, and noncrystalline. The Crystalline, or statuary marbles, are found mainly in a narrow valley along the western border of the metamorphic rocks, extending from the northwestern part of Coosa through Talladega into Calhoun. The outcrops have a width of about one-fourth mile and in length of 60 miles.

The marble industry in Alabama had its beginning at a very early period of the State's history. A quarry was opened near Sylacauga, in Talladega County, in the late thirties and operated profitably for many years. Four brothers—Scotchmen—George, David, Alexander and Thomas Herd, developed the enterprise. Their finished product consisted chiefly of tombstones, urns, statues, etc."

Dr. Owen continues: "The main deposits of true marbles in the State are found in the southeastern portion of the Coosa Valley region, in the more or less metamorphosed strata, although some are found in all the limestone and dolomite formations. The best, or most crystalline, are along the great Talladega thrust fault that divides the Coosa Valley from the crystalline strata. Marble of fair quality and considerable quantity exists in Bibb, Calhoun, Cherokee, Chilton, Coosa, Jefferson and Shelby Counties, but the best and largest deposits are in Talladega County, most of them of white, bluish, and dark colors, which take a superior polish. The prevailing color is white, or of a creamy tint, particularly desirable for interior finishing and decoration. The product of the Talladega County quarries is said to have the fine crystallization of statuary marble and to be unsurpassed in carving qualities. Alabama marble is well adapted to exterior use, being a very pure carbonate of lime, exceedingly strong and durable, but much of it is almost too fine for such use. Its texture, its lustre, its tinting, make it eminently suitable for interior and decorative work."

A State Geologist said of the marble deposits of Talladega County:

"I think it is fairly safe to say that on the whole the marble from this quarry (Gantt's) and immediate vicinity is of the highest grade of commercial white marble now on the market and obtainable in large quantity. There are small quantities of marble produced in both Italy and Vermont that are somewhat freer from coloring than the best grades that can be produced in Alabama in any quantity. But on the other hand, the poorest grades in Alabama greatly surpass the poorest grades produced elsewhere, so that the average of the Alabama deposit is probably somewhat higher than that of any other so far developed, not excluding even the marble from the Carara district of Italy. The marble from this State has now a well established reputation and has been used in more than 200 important buildings throughout the United States."[24]

---

[24] Ibid.

The Herds were undoubtedly the pioneer quarriers of marble, and their product was widely known throughout the State. Having placed their insignia on tombstones,[25] they can be easily traced in nearly every old cemetery in the county, as well as over the state. George Herd, it seems, was the sculptor of the group.

The Herd quarry eventually fell into the hands of Dr. Edward Gantt. Dr. Gantt was with Andrew Jackson during the Battle of Talladega, and returned to Alabama some years later, having lived in other parts of Alabama before he moved to Talladega County some time prior to 1846. His quarry plant was burned in 1865. Dr. Gantt died Nov. 24, 1867 before rebuilding, and the plant has passed through the hands of several companies since that time.

Another company which dealt in marble products of their own quarry, was that of H. P. Oden & Company. The Odens had an insignia of their own and their grave stones can be located over the county and state also.[26]

In 1858 the firm of H. P. Oden & Company consisted of Henry P. Oden, Andrew W. Bowie, James G. L. Huey and others. Dave Murphy is spoken of as a sculptor, or prominent monument cutter, in some way connected with this company. He built Alabama's first penitentiary, and was also a quarrier. Prior to 1846 other quarries were opened over the county. It is known that John K. Taylor was operating one at Cragdale, and Henry McKenzie was operating one about a mile east of Cragdale prior to this time.

An article entitled "The Gold Mining and the Marble Industry of Talladega County", by W. Taylor, of Cragdale, is included in the report of State Geologist Eugene Allen Smith in 1897. In this article Mr. Taylor, one of the Cragdale Taylors, states that a company was formed in 1846 of John K. Taylor, Edward Gantt and Henry McKenzie, for the purpose of quarrying marble in their various plants, which certainly indicates that these quarries were already in existence before 1846. The Alabama Reporter of July 20, 1848, carries an advertisement of "White and Blue Marble" products of Messrs. Taylor, Gantt & McKenzie. Other papers at the time spoke of trips of prominent citizens out to Cragdale to see the new saw which had been purchased by Mr. Taylor for use at his quarry.

Mr. Taylor stated that "John Leak & Sons, of St. Louis, bought the Taylor property in 1878. Mr. Leak sold to Geo. W. Chambers, and Mrs. L. McKenzie Taylor owned other marble property."

There were many dealers, and cutters, in marble products in the early days, among them were John Allen and Joseph N. Savery, who advertised in

---

[25] Mrs. Caroline Lane Peace Luttrell, Sylacauga, Ala.
[26] Ibid.

1850 that they were cutters for "Mantel pieces; bureau, sideboard and center table tops; tomb stones and slabs." These people continued in this business for many years. In 1869 John A. Bergin is listed as a manufacturer of marble products.

The Watchtower of Jan 1, 1877 stated that Messrs. E. W. Linn, Enoch Ensley, T. T. Hillman, George L. Morris, and Michael Muldron had organized a company at Sylacauga for the purpose of quarrying marble.

When the Washington Monument Society sent out letters to each of the United States requesting them to send a representative native stone to be placed in a proposed monument to George Washington, in the Capital, the Grand Lodge of Masons of Alabama, adopted a resolution Dec. 6, 1849, to send a block of marble from Gantt's Quarry of Talladega County. The block was four feet long, 2 feet high, and 12 inches thick. The block was sent with the inscription -

"Alabama Marble

Presented by the M. W. Grand Lodge of Free

and accepted

Masons of the State of Alabama

to the

Washington Monument Society."[27]

This stone is near the base of the monument and has frequently been seen by various county visitors to Washington.

There were many quarries, about which I have been unable to locate anything of especial interest. Aside from those already mentioned, there were Nix's Quarry, near Sycamore, and Bowie's near Rendalia, which were in operation some time about, or prior to, the Civil War. Most of the quarries were forced to cease operations during the War, and for several years afterwards, when there was little market for marble products. Interest revived during the Boom days of 1885-95.

Some time during this period Signor G. Moretti, a sculptor from the famous Carara District of Italy, moved to Talladega County. He became familiar with the quality of Alabama marble at his studio while living in New York, having used it in his work. He acquired a quarry in the lower part of Talladega County and had his first public exhibit at the Atlanta Exposition in 1895.

Some years later he was instrumental in forming a company which purchased the McKenzie quarry, which he operated for some time. The Talladega Marble Company was incorporated with a capital stock of

---

[27] Owen's His. of Ala., Vol. II, Page 934-935

$366,000.00 by H. M. Atkinson. P. S. Arkwright was President; G. Moretti, Vice-President; R. E. Cullinane, Secretary and Treasurer. Messrs. Arkwright, Atkinson and Cullinane were from Atlanta.[28] Work began on six cottages to house workmen, and a peculiar looking, castlelike, Italian residence was erected for Signor Moretti and his wife in February of 1906.

When Alabama planned an exhibit for the St. Louis World's Fair, Signor Moretti was employed to choose and make this display. The outcome was the Iron Vulcan now standing guard over Birmingham, on Red Mountain.

Source of material is too limited to attempt a full list of those quarriers who have played a minor part in contributing their time, money and labor toward the development of marble in Talladega County.

Sylacauga has always been the center of the marble industry in the State of Alabama, and is correctly called "The Marble City." In her vicinity marble is extensively and profitably quarried at this time, and the supply appears to be inexhaustible.

---

[28] Our Mountain Home, Feb. 21, 1906, at Public Library, Talladega

The Early Church

First settlers of Talladega County arranged at once for places of worship. In some communities there were no ministers of the Gospel, but people met for song and prayer, and as soon as possible, ministers were contacted for services at least once a month; frequently they served without remuneration. Many descendants of pioneer families might find it interesting to read minutes of the early churches, and it is possible that they might find incorporated therein charges of profanity, drunkenness or other bad conduct against their forebears. None of the churches in those days would permit such misdemeanors among members. Especially was drunkenness the charge around Christmas time. The sin of a church member was the concern of the entire membership, and a member was frequently "turned out", or excommunicated for a period, during which time he was given the opportunity to repent. He had to appear before the Board for examination, before he could be reinstated.

There were many common customs of the early church. For instance, few churches owned hymn books. Some individuals possessed them, and brought them to services, but the songs were "lined" by the preacher, or leader. He would read two lines, raise the tune, the congregation would join in, and this procedure continued until the hymn was completed. In this way many of the old hymns were memorized.

There were no musical instruments in the church for years. Another common custom was that of the men sitting on one side of the church and the women on the other. This was practiced that the men might have their boxes of sawdust placed at intervals for the surplus tobacco juice, which was offensive to the women. Be it remembered that a sermon in those days frequently lasted from one to two hours, and, no doubt, the men needed tobacco for stimulation. Perhaps the women partook of a pinch of snuff every now and then for the same reason.

Kerosene was not in common use until after the Civil War, and evening services were rare, or in winter by candle light. In summer, at the camp grounds, where they pitched tents for several weeks at the time, and had services day and night, bonfires were built in the evenings. After kerosene came into use, large pegs were placed between windows in churches, and members brought lanterns and placed them on these pegs as they arrived. One's missing lantern was an event to be noted.

It has always been the custom of Baptists to immerse for baptism, and for Presbyterians and Episcopalians to sprinkle, but either was done by the Methodists. A candidate for membership in the early Methodist Church was asked which mode he preferred. It was not unusual for half of the candidates for membership to be sprinkled in the building, and the other half taken to the creek for immersion.

There was no Catholic organized church in the country until the Twentieth century.

Centuries ago church bells were most carefully chosen. Stories have passed on to us of silver and gold coins, and jewelry, being cast into the smelting pots to insure Divine blessings, and to give bells clearer and sweeter tones. While this was not true a century ago, church bells were carefully chosen, and a bell in the church tower was an essential part of the equipment; certainly in villages, towns and cities, and frequently in the country. The early church bell was not only used for a call to services; but great events, or approaching danger, were announced by the ringing of the church bell. Frequently, as late as the early part of the Twentieth century, a village was awakened in the deep of night by the tolling of some church bell in the community, because Negroes were still following the custom of tolling the number of years of the deceased immediately following death at any time of day or night. If the departed was nine years old, the bell tolled nine times; if ninety years of age, the bell tolled ninety times. The bell tolled after a funeral, from the time the body left the home, or church, until it arrived at the grave.

Another custom at church funerals was that of leaving the casket open during the preaching of a lengthy sermon from some Biblical text. At the conclusion of the service, during the singing of a hymn, the congregation was given the opportunity to have a last look at the deceased before closing the casket. This is still practiced among Negroes and some whites in remote rural districts. It was not unusual for a funeral sermon to be preached weeks, months and at times a year, after the person was buried. In winter, when many churches had no heat; in bad weather when roads were impassable, and when a minister was not available; this postponement became necessary. But a sermon was always preached.

Nearly all of the ante-bellum churches were built with galleries for colored members. Negroes withdrew immediately after the War of their own volition, and the whites aided them in building churches of their own. The early church was the social as well as religious center of every community. In rural districts members arose early on church Sundays, and arrived at the church as early as possible. Quilt patterns, settings of eggs and receipts were exchanged by the women, and maybe a bit of gossip. Hard times, politics and business matters were discussed by the men, and perhaps also a bit of gossip. The various groups would then reverently and solemnly assemble in the sanctuary for a spiritual uplift in prayerful worship, after which they would dissolve until the minister passed that way again.

The more devout would sit in the "Amen" corner. Two or three benches were always placed on either side of the pulpit perpendicular to those of the regular benches for the general congregation. All during the sermon pious men emphasized the statements of the preacher by loudly acclaiming "AMEN!" which was echoed by others. These outbreaks brought the worldly thinker back to the sermon, and frequently awakened the slumbering child, who joined his voice to that of the pious. Next to the old Home, the old Church is a home-comers most sacred spot, where common sins were once confessed, and Divine forgiveness was received; where sweet and lasting friendships were formed and never forgotten.

CHURCHES

THE TALLADEGA BAPTIST CHURCH

The first known church organized in the County was "Talladega Baptist Church". Therefore, it seems proper to give it first place in the history of churches in our county. This church is situated in Talladega County on the waters of the Talladega Creek, between that and Weokee. It was constituted the 29th of April, 1832, at the house of brother John Lawler, by Elder J. M. Scott of Shelby County.[1] This house was situated on a road that runs through Mardisville, west, converging with the Alpine road west of the P. A. Duncan home. It seems reasonable to believe that this group expected the county to bear the name "Talladega" but had no idea that the Battle Ground would be chosen County Seat, nor that they would choose "Talladega" as the name of this seat. The first minutes are concise, and give a full record of the meeting:

"On the Twenty-ninth day of April, A. D., 1832, the following named persons (viz.) John Lawler, Jesse Millinder, Margaret Lawler, Abner Lawler and Sarah Lawler, met at the house of John Lawler (Talladega Co., Ala.), when and where they were by James M. Scott and Joab Lawler, a Presbytery of ministers called for that purpose, regularly constituted a church by the name of the "Talladega Baptist Church", as also appears by the following certificate:

We do hereby certify that we have been called upon by several brethren in this vicinity, to attend as a presbytery for the purpose of constituting them into a church; we have attended agreeably to their request, and after inquiry as to their wishes and order, proceed to constitute them a Gospel Church by the

---

[1] A History of the Rise and Progress of the Baptists in Ala.," 1840, by Hosea Holcombe, p. 249.

name of Talladega according to the following Constitution of Abstract of Principles.

(S) James M. Scott,
Joab Lawler.

"Done the 29th day of April, 1832."[2]

The Abstract or Principles and Rules of Decorum followed.

The church doors were opened and Elizabeth Barny joined by experience.

Because members of this early church were residents of this district before the county was created, it is interesting to record the membership for the year 1832:

April, 1832	John Lawler	By Letter
	Jesse Millinder	Do
	Margaret Lawler	Do
	Abner Lawler	Do
	Sarah Lawler	Do
	Elizabeth Barney	Experience
June, 1832	Joseph Ray	Letter
	Thomas J. Foster	Do
August, 1832	John McDaniel	Do
Sept., 1832	Jacob Eldridge	Do
	Elizabeth Eldridge	Do
Oct., 1832	Henry Hinkle	Do
	Martha Hinkle	Do
	Nancy Sawyer	Experience
	Elizabeth I. Lawler	Do
	Elizabeth Lawler	Do
Nov., 1832	James Barney	Letter
	Mary Millinder	Experience
	James Drennon	Letter
	Thomas S. Drennon	Do
	Amelia Drennon	Do
	Susan Drennon	Do
	Grizzle Drennon	Do

---

[2] Minutes of the Talladega Baptist Church , in private collection at Talladega Public Library

	Amelia E. Drennon	Do
	Benjamin Hubbert	Experience
	Edward D. Cross	Do
	Rebecca Hubbert	Do
Dec., 1832	Robert Hubbard	Letter
	Peggy Hubbard	Experience
	Shadrach Drennon	Do
	Anna Drennon	Do
	Isaac Hudgins	Do

The Church had 32 members before Talladega was declared a county.

At the November, 1832, meeting a committee of John Lawler, B. Mattison, James Barney, S. McGahey and Jacob Eldridge was chosen to select a site for a meeting house, and at the December meeting the committee reported that they had chosen the site. However, nothing more is said of a meeting house until May, 1836, when the minutes carry the statement: "The subject of building a meeting house was again brought before the Church. Bro. John Lawler, one of the Trustees, made known that the Trustees had made some alterations in the plan of the house, and had partially let out the building at $750.00, and had agreed to give their bonds for the payment of $230." They further stated that the building was to be 36 x 44 feet with a 12 ft. pitch. This building was erected about three-fourths of a mile west of the present P. A. Duncan home, near the Alpine highway.

The minutes show that they began having camp meetings at "Weowoka Camp Ground" in 1835, and they were still meeting there annually for some years after the War. The March, 1833, minutes state "A portion of the members petitioned for leave to be constituted into a separate church on Tallasehatchee, which was granted."

There were 47 members at the time, and 24 withdrew to organize a new church.

The Talladega Church was greatly strengthened in 1839, when 20 members were added at a camp meeting at Weowoka:

Nathaniel W. Mallory	Edna Cross
Adam W. Smith	Julia C. Mallory
Tryon Fuller	Ann Welch
John Kendall	Jno. W. Mallory
Lucy J. Mallory	Nathaniel Welch
Wm. S. Jenkins	Nathan Spiller
Albert G. Sims	LaFayette Wilson
Isabel McAdams	Isaac Hudson

Geo. W. Allen   Jno. B. Phurrow
Allen T. Fenn   Pleasant King

In 1867 a part of the colored membership withdrew and organized a church of their own. "The use of the Church was granted them until the end of the year."

In September, 1868, the following appears: "300 members in fellowship on the Church Book up to September, 1868, but scattered like sheep among the mountains."

After the War there was restlessness that follows all war, many members moved away, and the membership decreased. Most of the remaining members were centered around Alpine. It was, therefore, deemed advisable to build a new church at that place. In January, 1872, the minutes show that they worshipped first in this new building at Alpine.

"Before the Civil War, this was the strongest Baptist Church, financially, in the State, St. Francis Street Church, Mobile, not excepted. Two members, Mr. Jenkins and Maj. Walker Reynolds, if living now, would be rated as millionaires."

"Rev. Oliver Welch was pastor from 1836 until 1868. He declined accepting a salary, and told the church they could add his salary to their contribution for missions, which they did, and in that remote period, would send $1,000.00 a year to the state convention for missions."[3] On the premises of the Alpine Baptist Church, there is a marble boulder, placed there in 1933, in commemoration of the one hundredth Anniversary of the organization of the Coosa River Baptist Association "on Nov. 8, 1833, near this spot."

The group which withdrew from the Talladega Baptist Church, and organized the TALLASEHATCHEE Church, built near Sylacauga, and the church was recognized as one of the strongest congregations of the county for many years. The old cemetery registers the names of many pioneers who reverently worshipped at old Tallasehatchee. The church was organized in March, 1833, by Elder Phillip Archer and other members of the Talladega Baptist Church (now Alpine). [4]

MT. ZION was also a strong church in that part of the county for more than fifty years. They appear to have had some sort of service weekly, on

---

[3] Letter from Miss Ran Welch, Alpine, to me, dated 11-25-1927
[4] Hosea Holcombe's "A History of the Rise and Progress of the Baptists in Ala." 1840, p. 249.

each Sabbath, and when other congregations were frequently without services, they worshipped with Mt. Zion.

FORT WILLIAMS CHURCH was organized some months before they became an authorized church. They worshipped as a Baptist group near old Fort Williams, in the extreme lower end of the county, until they were duly authorized and constituted a church on July 25th, 1833, and they immediately took steps to join the Mulberry Baptist Association, of Shelby County. After four attempts to become a constituted church, Elders James Scott and Phillip Archer finally did come and pronounce them a church, as stated, on July 25, 1833, with 9 members:

Thomas Robertson	Obediah Radford
Matilda Moony	Thomas Calvert
Ruthey Lee	Margaret Calvert
Rebecca Robertson	Martha Calvert
Simeon Chapman	

At this time they named their church "Fort Williams".[5]

Later during the year 1833 they added to the church roll: Abijah Lewis and wife, Betsy W. Lewis, Charity Lewis, Mary Lewis, Joshua Monk and Rachel Robertson, by letter.

By experience they added George Lewis and Joseph Mooney.

A new church building was erected in 1852 nearer Fayetteville, on property donated to them by Wm. McPherson.

Fort Williams Church merged with Cedar Spring Church, which was still in existence in 1834, in the present Fayetteville Baptist Church, which church building is on the same land where the second Fort Williams church building stood.

COOSA RIVER ASSOCIATION
OF UNITED BAPTIST CHURCHES

True to the systematic custom of the Talladega County Baptists, they have bound the minutes of their Association, and have a complete record of the affiliated churches. The Coosa River Association was organized at Talladega meeting house in Talladega County on the 8th of November 1833, of only five churches, all of them in Talladega County. Four ministers were present, who

---

[5] Information furnished me by Ruth Burks, Church Clerk, Fayetteville, from "Old Church Book" on file Jan. 1952

were included in the churches forming the Association; namely, Sion Blythe, Joseph Hill, Phillip Archer, and Wm. McCain.

The minutes begin when they were assembled at Providence meeting house "Begun and held on Chock-o-lock-o from the 11th to the 13th of October, 1834."[6]

"A sermon introductory to business delivered by Brother Philip Archer from Isiah 62 Chapter, and 1st and 2nd verses."

Jordan Williams was clerk, and Leon Blythe was Moderator; 229 members were represented by the following delegates:

Church	Delegates	Members
Talladega	Joab Lawler, John Lawler, B. Madison	47
Providence	Wm. McCain, T. Neal, J. Ray	57
Pond Spring	T. Hill, L. Murphey, C. McGhee	31
Tallassehatchee	P. Archer, G. Hill, J. Drennon	61
Cedar Spring	G. Blythe, J. Williams	10
New Hope	W. G. Foster, J. Madden	23

Churches in St. Clair and Benton (Calhoun) Counties also belonged to the Association. The following table is only that of Talladega Co., listed as they entered the Association:

Church	1834	1835	1836	1838	1839
Talladega (Alpine)	47	64	88	88	121
Providence	57	44	21		
Pond Springs	31	23	29		
Tallassehatchee	61	27		37	33
Cedar Spring (Fayetteville)	10	8			
Good Hope (Talladega First)		20	38	62	74
Mt. Zion		38	39	63	90
Chearhaw			30	23	
Smyrna			17	27	32
Salem			18	72	84
Clear Creek				14	
Lebanon (Kelly Springs)					57
Blue Eye					61
Kymulga					15

---

[6] Minutes of the Coosa River Baptist Association, in private collection at Talladega Public Library

There are many rural Baptist churches of the 19ᵗʰ century worthy of recognition, but one of exceptional note is that of ANTIOCH Baptist Church. It was constituted a church in the summer of 1840 by Rev. S. G. Jenkins, with the help of Rev. Phillip Archer in the north-east part of Talladega County. There were twelve charter members:

Rev. S. G. Jenkins and wife	William Mashborn
Rev. Phillip Archer and wife	Lewis Manning
Col. Y. B. Jenkins and wife	James Bittle
Mr. Hance Hendrick and wife	John Rowe

In 1841 the church had 20 members, and joined the Coosa River Association.

"At the time S. G. Jenkins proposed to organize and construct Antioch Church, he was criticized by his neighbors for wanting to build a church so near a Stillhouse, as Ben Ball was running a still near by; but he answered "Fear not good friends, by the help of the Almighty we will capture both Ben Ball and his still." And he did that very thing, as Ben Ball joined the church, and went home and chopped up his still."

A log house was erected for worship temporarily, but in 1855 Lewis Manning deeded a lot on the south side of Road, where an appropriate building was erected. The present building was erected in 1886.

Rev. S. G. Jenkins served the church for 39 years. He baptized more than 500 people. Many other consecrated ministers have served the old church since Rev. Jenkins died in 1880.

In 1940 the church had on roll 169 members, when they celebrated their anniversary. Few rural churches can boast of such a record as can Antioch church, which entitles it to record in this volume.

Grandchildren of the Rev. Sterling G. Jenkins, T. B. and Miss Hallie B. Jenkins, who gave me information regarding this church, still live in the neighborhood, at Mt. Airy, the ancestral home, and still worship at Antioch.

GOOD HOPE BAPTIST CHURCH

This heading should probably be "First Baptist Talladega", since the church has borne that name longer than it bore the name of "Good Hope". However, we are dealing more with "beginnings", and the First Baptist Church in Talladega was originally called "Good Hope". Mrs. Lou Taylor, as previously stated, gave us our earliest record of old Talladega. She stated that "Dr. Sam Henderson says in his Pen Sketches of the Churches, that he arrived in Talladega in 1835, and that the Baptist Church had been organized only a month; that they met in a little school house which was kept by a Mr. Rukes, whose wife was a Baptist, he allowed us the use of his school house."[7]

Judge J. W. Vandiver stated: "Baptists organized May 31, 1835, in a log school house on the north side of South St., opposite the M. E. Church with 10 members, 3 being Negroes.[8] It was organized by Rev. Joab Lawler and Rev. Oliver Welch. A lot was purchased for a building on the N. W. corner of Spring and North Sts. A frame building was erected, and was used until the brick building on East Street was ready for occupancy.

The Good Hope Baptist Church was not as strong in numbers as many of the churches. It was not affiliated with the Coosa River Association until 1835, when there were seven churches in Talladega County represented, and Good Hope was sixth in line of membership.

In 1850 there were three rural churches larger: Talladega (Alpine) had 220 members: Mt. Zion 138, Salem 107 and Good Hope only 103. While the membership was smaller in number several of the rural churches, it was a great spiritual force in the early life of Talladega.

Services were held in the basement of the building on the West side of East Street under the name of "First Baptist Church of Talladega," the building was dedicated on July 1878. A portion of an editorial in a local paper follows:[9]

"The new Baptist Church building in this city was, on last Sabbath morning, formally consecrated to the worship of God, the dedicatory sermon being preached by Rev. I. T. Tichenor, D. D., President of the Agricultural College at Auburn. 'According to the glorious Gospel of the blessed God which was committed to my trust,' was the text used, and it is found in the verse, 1st chapter, of 1st Timothy."

"The cost of the house aggregates $11,000. The main room measures 70 x 40 feet and will seat comfortably 600 people, not including the gallery which has the capacity of accommodating about 150. The basement, used for Sunday School purposes, will seat 500. The church is neatly furnished, the aisles and pulpit are carpeted, and benches are comfortable and nicely painted, the pulpit furniture, consisting of six pieces purchased in the North, is neat, tasty, enduring. The large reflector in the center of the ceiling gives a brilliant light and is ornamental in itself."

The First Baptist Church grew rapidly and it became advisable to seek more spacious quarters. They acquired one of the most beautiful lots in Talladega, on North Street, when they purchased the old Wadsworth, or Lyman,

---

[7] Mrs. L. M. Taylor's History of Talladega , in private collection at Talladega Public Library
[8] J. W. Vandiver's History of Tall., in private collection at Talladega Public Library, Chapter 4
[9] Editorial in Our Mt. Home of 7-17-1878; Editor Jno. E. Ware. In Scrap Book of Mrs. Graham Perdue, daughter of Jno. E. Ware, living in Birmingham.

home. The dwelling was razed, and the present Church School plant erected in 1932-33. They had first service Feb. 25, 1933, in the Sunday School auditorium where they worshipped until the church building was erected in The first service was held Jan. 19, 1948 in the present sanctuary. The following ministers have served this church during the years:

Joab Lawler	1835-36	M. D. Early	1889
Thomas W. Cox	1836-38	Thomas Henderson	No Record
H. E. Taliaferro	1838-40	J. A. French	1890-96
Thomas Chilton	1840-41	T. M. Callaway	1896-1906
Samuel Henderson	1843-46	Jas. D. Gwaltney	1906-10
P. E. Collins	1853	J. M. Thomas	1911-42
Richard Pace	1856	Perry Claxton	1942-51
J. J. D. Renfroe	1858-60	J. B. Marlow	1952-55
J. F. B. Mayes	1860-64	T. M. Hamby	1956
J. J. D. Renfroe	1864-88		

A number of new Baptist churches have been established in the Twentieth Century, which are actively growing in every way. This volume, however, is confined principally to those known churches which existed in the nineteenth century.

THE METHODIST CHURCH

The Methodist Episcopal Church, in America, was only 47 years old when Methodism was introduced into Talladega County. There had been scattered Methodist Societies of the Episcopal Church throughout the States, and in England, for years, but not until Christmas week of 1784, one year after the close of the American Revolution, was there a Methodist Episcopal Church organization.

The Methodist Conference of Alabama was in session Christmas week of 1832, one week after the Creek country was divided into counties, and Rev. Jesse Ellis was immediately appointed minister of the newly created Talladega Mission, within the Coosa District, and Rev. R. G. Christopher was made Presiding Elder.

Minutes show that "The Quarterly Conference, the first ever held on this side of the Coosa River, in the State of Alabama, was held at Bethel Meeting House May 25, 1833, and was presided over by the Rev. R. G.

Christopher.[10] Local preachers present were Leonard Harris Taylor, John Gilliland and J. Hutchinson. Exhorters: James T. Whitehead and John Box. Class Leaders: Adam A. Lackey; Stewards: Harris Taylor, James M. Hutchinson, Wm. Garrett (who later wrote "Reminiscences of Public Men in Alabama"), Robert C. Wilson and R. Jones.

At the end of the year 1833 there were reported 266 white members and 20 colored in the district, which at that time included Talladega, Shelby and Counties.

We do not know where the Rev. Jesse Ellis resided when he arrived in January, 1833, but it must have been in Mardisville, since Talladega Battle Ground was not voted county seat until March, 1833.

BETHEL was the first county Methodist church, and it is regretted that we haven't the names of those who founded that church. They had some sort of "Meeting House" in May, 1833, but they did not have a Deed to the property until 1839, when N. Gannaway, and Thomas H. P. Scales, Trustees, recorded a Deed.[11]

In 1838, Bethel Church was one of two churches within the Jacksonville Circuit, which had a Sunday School. The Jacksonville Circuit at that time comprised north Talladega County and County. The Talladega Circuit was comprised of the South Talladega County and Shelby County.[12] Bethel Church is still a strong church, and is now worshipping in the third church building erected through the years.

KELLY'S SPRING CAMP GROUND was the third meeting place mentioned in the records, and was located back of the Tom Curry place at Curry Station. It was still in existence in 1945, but there is no record available of membership or activities, other than "as one of the paying Societies."[13]

OWEN SPRING was born at a Quarterly Conference held at Kelly's Springs August, 1834, when Trustees for a Meeting House to be built on Creek" were appointed. This location was on property owned by the and later by the Lanes, and given to the church as long as it was used for the purpose of worship, at the conclusion of which time the property was to revert back to the Montgomery estate. This was about mile North of Choccolocco Creek on the Eastaboga Highway. "Owens Spring was a noted place, financially one of the

---

[10] History of Methodism in Ala., by Dr. Anson West, Page 463
[11] Ibid, Page 465-66
[12] Ibid, Page 480
[13] Ibid, Page 465

strongest appointments on the Circuit, at which a Quarterly Conference was held nearly, or quite every year."[14]

The community thinned and the membership was eventually transferred to Eastaboga, where a new church was erected and the name changed to "Craig Memorial," in honor of the minister serving the church at the time.

CEDAR CREEK became a preaching place about as early as any. A Quarterly Conference was held there Sept. 27, 1834. It was at, or near the place known as FAYETTEVILLE, in the lower end of Talladega County. It bore the name of Cedar Creek until 1838, when it gave place to the name of Fayetteville."[15]

JONES CAMP GROUND located near Nottingham,[16] was in existence in 1834, and for some years later.

MARDISVILLE church was on a Circuit at first, then with Talladega Church as a Station, but the membership finally moved to Talladega some time about 1845. It was never a very strong church.[17]

SYLACAUGA appears on the records first when a Quarterly Conference was held there on June 16, 1838, and "for long years Methodism was quite weak at this place." However, it is perhaps the strongest Methodist church in the county at this time.[18]

RISER'S CHAPEL. On March 24, 1838, Trustees Martin Wm. Kelly, Wm. H. Hudson, M. E. Charr, George Riser and John Ashley, were appointed to choose a lot "near to Brother Ashley's", on which to built a church. John Ashley deeded 3¾ acres of land on March 17, 1840 to the Trustees, and for many years this was one of the strongest Methodist churches in the county.[19]

ANTIOCH Society went on record Sept. 28, 1839, and was organized at Carter's School House four miles N. E. of Talladega on the Road by Leonard Tarrant in September, 1843, a committee was appointed to build a church.[20]

CHINNABEE was on record in 1839, by Leonard but lived only a short while, since Bethlehem was established, and the membership moved to this church.[21]

BETHLEHEM appears for the first time in June, 1843. However in September of that year they reported the existence of a thriving Sunday School

---

[14] Ibid, Page 467
[15] Ibid, Page 467
[16] Ibid, Page 467
[17] Ibid, Page 469
[18] Ibid
[19] Ibid
[20] Ibid, Page 470
[21] Ibid

under its auspicies, with a Superintendent, Secretary and a Librarian, Teachers, and 30 pupils. Since its organization Bethlehem has been an outstanding church. Judge Tarrant organized this church.[22]

DRY VALLEY came into existence in November, 1843, when a committee was appointed to build a meeting house. Judge also organized this church.

In 1838 much interest centered around the building of a parsonage for the Circuit. Where it was finally placed we do not know, but Dr. West states "The Parsonage for the Jacksonville Circuit, which was secured and made ready for the preacher and his family at the beginning of 1844, was near the Academy at Marble Spring on Chockolocko Creek, near Owens Spring Campground."[23]

It is interesting to read the following report of "The Committee on Church Property as recorded in Quarterly Conference Minutes of August 28, 1868 for Talladega District:

We have been unable to get material for a correct report; at best, we can approximate the truth.

There is in the bounds of the District, Church property secured by Deeds according to law valued at $26,850.00.

The property of

Harpersville Circuit	$6,525.00
Talladega Station	6,000.00
White Plains Circuit	2,385.00
Jacksonville Circuit	1,000.00
Coosa River Circuit	340.00
Alexandria Circuit	3,100.00
Talladega Circuit	3,500.00

"All this property consists in lots and houses of worship, there being not a single Parsonage on the District; on some of the there are a churches which are not secured by law, but we are unable to find the exact number, nor the value. Most of the church property is in good condition, but the larger number of church buildings are of a poor class, unfinished frame buildings and log cabins. But few of them are with stoves, which causes them to be uncomfortable in the winter. There are a number of preaching places, where no church buildings exist. On most of the circuits, however, there are some

---

[22] Ibid, Page 488
[23] Ibid, Page 488

finished houses of worship, which are provided with lamps and stoves. At Talladega Station there is a good brick building; at Columbiana, Fayetteville, Sylacauga and Jacksonville, there are good frame buildings."[24]

Many of the rural churches have been abandoned since the advent of the automobile, and memberships moved to villages and towns.

This report of 1868 does not mention the Munford Church, though it was probably on the Talladega Circuit, nor does Dr. West mention this church as having been one of the early churches. However, old residents of Munford recall that one has existed continuously for over 100 years. It is possible that it was served by local ministers, as many other rural communities were, and that no reports were made to the state conferences.

FIRST METHODIST EPISCOPAL CHURCH, SOUTH

"At the Talladega Battle Ground, the Spring branch, and not far from where the United States Soldiers, who fell there in the Battle (of Talladega) in 1813 are buried, in some sort of a Meeting House, the Rev. Jesse Ellis preached in 1833, and there a Quarterly Conference was held for Talladega Circuit March 8, 1834. At that Quarterly Conference a Committee was appointed to secure a lot for a Meeting House and parsonage. On Sept. 20, 1836, Commissioners of the County of Talladega, having due authority in the premises, in consideration of to them in hand paid, did execute a Deed to the Trustees of the Methodist Episcopal Church to Lot 113, in the plan of the Town of Talladega. A small wooden church was erected on that lot, and there the Methodists worshipped perhaps 20 years or more."[25] Thus Dr. West gives us the only history we have of this early Methodist Church.

The building was evidently erected prior to date of recording the deed, for in the spring of 1835 Court records state: "The sum of was paid to the Trustees of the Methodist church for the use of the building in holding Circuit Court."[26] On account of the pressure of business, deeds were not issued on dates of purchases.

The Trustees who purchased the lot were Jacob Shelley and John Moore. The lot was located about half between Court and Spring Streets, on the north side of South St., and extending back to Coffee St. The building faced east.

The property was later purchased by Andrew who deeded it to his daughter Sophia and it is now in possession of Mrs. Thornton's daughter,

---

[24] Minutes of the Quarterly Conference in the hands of Mrs. Emma Thornton Calhoun, Talladega
[25] History of Methodism in Ala., by Dr. Anson West, Page 466
[26] County Commissioner's Court Records, Page 88, Book "A"

Eugenia Thornton. The church was in Talladega Circuit for some years, with only once a month. It then joined Methodist Church as a Station. Services were held twice a month in each church but Mardisville was too weak to support her part, and Talladega went back into the Circuit in 1845, and remained there for twelve years.

In the year 1854 James G. L. Huey, Superintendent of the Sunday School, and John T. Morgan, a young lawyer, out of the frame building and began a conversation regarding the need of a larger and better place of worship, which resulted in a decision to see about the vacant lot on the S. E. corner of South and Court Sts.

Alabama Conference was convening in Talladega at the time. The next day John T. Morgan purchased the lot, and the deed was made to him until the matter could be brought before the congregation.

The idea of a new building was accepted, and building plans went forward immediately with James G. L. Huey, Alexander J. Cotton and Wm. H. Trustees. In the meantime John T. Morgan moved to Selma, and it was not discovered that the deed was in his name until the building was completed. Mr. Morgan made deed to the trustees Oct. 10, 1857. This building was the first brick church erected in Talladega County. At the close of the year 1858, Talladega was made a Station. The membership at the time was 208, composed of 143 and 65 colored members. Soon after the new church was completed, many of the members felt that they should have a musical instrument. This brought about much ado among members, many of whom considered musical instruments worldly objects. However, after much dissention, the objections were over-ruled, and an organ was purchased and placed in the center of the sanctuary so that everyone could be near the instrument.

During the Civil War, many members died, and at the close of the war there were listed 106 white members and 105 colored members. The Negro members withdrew of their accord, and the white members contributed liberally toward the building of a church for them.

Among the prominent members of the church at the time of entering the new building were:

Rev. James S. Lane, a local preacher "and man of worth", James G. L. Huey, Sunday School Superintendent and Class Leader; A. J. Cotton, First Probate Judge of the County; George Miller; James S. Chambers and J. W. Martin, Class Leaders. John B. Huey, H. H. John L. Harris, Thomas J. Cross, John A. Winbourn, Charles Carter, Dr. Joseph H. Johnson, C. M. Shelley, W. J.

Rhodes, J. B. M. Landers, Abner Jones, Dr. J. H. Vandiver, Stewards. Wm. H. Thornton, Steward and Class Leader.[27]

Among the other prominent members of the church at the time were: General Jacob D. Shelley and Col. J. J. Woodward, among the men. James G. L. Huey became Superintendent of the Sunday School in 1842 and served in that capacity until 1867. Among those who were prominently associated with the Sunday School, and also members of the Church were:

Miss Susan Dixon, "a tower of strength"; Mrs. S. F. Rice, Mrs. Rebecca Moody, Miss Mary Jane Douglas, Miss Charlotte Walker, Miss Sarah J. Shelley, Miss Mary C. Shelley, Miss Alabama Stephenson and Miss Martha Stephenson.

Dr. West lists as other active workers of the church:

Mrs. Mary Ann Harris	Mrs. Dr. Whitson
Mrs. Savery	Miss Lizzie Frazier
Mrs. Hogan	Miss Mariah Whittaker
Mrs. A. T. Plowman	Mrs. Margaret Kennedy
George McLane	J. T. Adams
Mrs. Carroll	Mrs. Chambers
Mrs. Donahoo	Mrs. John B. Huey
Mrs. Harvey Joiner	Mrs. Martin
Mrs. Scott	Mrs. Stephens
Mrs. Thompson	Mrs. Dr. Vandiver

Mrs. Jane C. Parsons wife of Gov. L. E. Parsons
Mrs. Emily A. Johnson, wife of Dr. Jo. H. Johnson[28]

Among the features of the new church, were many colorful memorial windows, placed in honor of devout and ardent pioneer members. The windows have long since disappeared from this old edifice, which is now used as a county educational and medical center.

In 1888 members of the Missionary Society solicited funds from members of the church to renovate the sanctuary, and with the help of Vandiver and Son, who let them have materials at cost, made many improvements. A choir loft was made on the west side of the pulpit, and opposite to the Amen corner, carpet strips were placed in the aisles, new pews were purchased, and the entire cost amounted to less than $400.00.

During the early part of the 20th Century other changes took place. A wing was built in 1904 across the back to take care of the increased numbers

---

[27] History of Methodism in Ala., by Dr. Anson West, Page 693
[28] Ibid, Page 698

attending Sunday School. The sanctuary was fully carpeted, a choir loft was built back of the pulpit, and the first pipe organ ever installed in Talladega purchased. This organ was pumped by hand, and proved quite embarrassing on many occasions. The organist for 35 years was Mr. Allious Williams, a blind man, and one of the best organists in the state. The "pumper" was either the janitor or some school boy who pumped back of a screen on the side of the organ. There were times when he would doze and would not recognize Mr. Williams signal to pump. It would then become necessary for someone in the audience to come forward and awaken the "pumper" before the meeting could proceed.

The membership soon outgrew the sanctuary. In 1913 about 125 members, who resided on the north end of decided to withdraw and organize a new church. Therefore, at the annual Conference in November, 1913, W. R. Battle was assigned to this new church and plans went to erect a church building. Therefore, on May 1914, Trinity Methodist Church was formally organized, and has become one of the strongest churches in the district. However, the history of this church belongs in the 20th Century. The membership of First Methodist Church continued to increase and it became evident that the lot was not large enough for further expansion. In 1919 it was decided to start a fund for a new church. The recommendation was made by John H. Hicks, immediately started the subscription with a liberal contribution. The outcome was the erection of the fourth and present building.

John Hicks Dumas, young grand-son of Mr. John H. Hicks, turned the first shovel of dirt for this building on October 1921, with an appropriate ceremony. Dr. L. C. Branscomb delivered the address, and Rev. Clare Purcell, pastor at the time, presided. In May, 1922, Mr. Z. H. Clardy laid the first brick, and the Corner Stone was laid October 1st, 1922. Mr. Purcell was given the privilege of placing the last brick in the building. The first service was held in the new church on April 1924. The sermon was preached by the pastor, Rev. Clare Purcell, who later became one of the most beloved Bishops in all Methodism. Bishop A. N. Ainsworth worth dedicated the church October 1924.

An unusual thing about the building of this church is the fact that it was fully paid for when completed, and could be dedicated without delay.

Among the members transferred from the third building to the fourth were three who had been members when the membership was transferred in 1857: Mrs. E. A. Stephens, Mrs. J. H. Lawson and Miss Mary V. Thompson.

For years the Woman's Missionary Society had looked forward to the time when this new church should be built, and under the leadership of Mrs. E. G. Stringer, started an organ fund. The money was on hand when the building was completed and the organ was installed in time for the first meeting. On either side of the organ there is a bronze plate. On one is inscribed:

In reverent memory of
Mrs. Fannie Carroll Stringer,
to whose interest, efforts and zeal
we are largely indebted for this
instrument of praise
1924

On the other side is inscribed:

This tablet in memory of
Allious Wellington Williams
for 35 years organist of this church
is lovingly placed by the Baraca Class
of which for many years he was a
faithful member
1925

Soon after this last building was completed, Mr. J. E. Montgomery, of Montgomery, Ala., who was once a resident of Talladega, placed a pulpit Bible in the sanctuary with the following inscription:

J. E. Montgomery
In memory of his Sister
Mrs. John R. Barrett

Mr. and Mrs. Barrett were faithful members of the old church, and were instrumental in organizing a mission Sunday School in the old City Hall on Battle Street the latter part of the 19th Century. Church services were conducted at 2 p. m. each Sunday by various ministers. This mission Sunday School eventually developed into the Spring Street Baptist Church. There were more Baptists in the Sunday School than Methodists, so when they organized the church, it became a Baptist Church. It is now one of the strongest and largest in the county and bears the name of Central Baptist Church.

Seven Annual Conferences have been held in Talladega through the years, as follows:

December 13th, 1854	Presiding Bishop	J. O. Andrews
October 17th-20th,1864	Do	D.W. Clark
November 19th, 1873	Do	E. M. Marvin
November 19th, 1884	Do	J. C. Keener

November 15th, 1893	Do	W. W. Duncan
November 23rd, 1904	Do	A.W. Wilson
October 28th, 1924	Do	W. A. Candler

The following ministers have served as pastors of the First Methodist Church:

1833	Jesse Ellis	1874-75	Jno. H. Anderson
1834	Wm. C. Crawford	1876-78	J.M. Boland
1835	Daniel B. Barlow	1879-81	C.C. Ellis
1836	Edward H. Moore	1882	W.C. Hearn
1837-38	Wiley Thomas	1883	Jno. B. Gregory
1839-40	Theophilas Moody	1884-85	W.C. Hearn
1841	Jesse Ellis	1886	Z.A. Parker
1842	Edward J. Hammill	1886-88	W.E. Mabry
1843	Theophilas Moody	1889-92	W.T. Andrews
1844	Varnum L. Hopkins	1893-95	J.F. Sturdivant
1845	Lewis G. Hicks	1896	A.B. Jones
1846	O.R. Blue	1897-99	V.O. Hawkins
1847-48	T.H.P. Scales	1900-3	J.W. Newman
1849-51	Edward J. Hammill	1904-7	L.C. Branscomb
1852	Joseph Hamill	1908-09	G.W. Read
1853	Jno. Wesley Starr	1910-11	H.C. Howard
1854	D. Carmichael	1912	J.A. Duncan
1855-56	J.C. McDaniel	1913-16	K.N. Mathews
1857	J.S. Moore	1917-20	E.B. Norton
1858	B.B. Ross	1921-24	Clare Purcell
1859	Thomas P. Crymes	1925-27	A.M. Freeman
1860	James S. Lane	1928	L.F. Stansell
1861	T.F. Mangum	1929-32	L.D. Patterson
1862	J.W. Miller	1933-34	R.T. Tyler
1863	T.J. Couch	1935	D.C. McNutt
1864-66	R.B. Crawford	1936-39	O.K. Lamb
1867	W.R. Kirk	1940-43	J.E. Morris
1868	F.T.J. Brandon	1944-46	J.F. Dunn
1869	Charles A. King	1947-49	Foster K. Gamble
1870	Anson West	1950-53	Paul Clem
1871	Daniel Duncan	1954-57	Allen Montgomery
1872-73	C.D. Oliver	1958	Charles L. Frederick

The Church School was in operation as early as 1838 almost entirely by the women of the church without having an authorized superintendent. After much pressure was brought to bear, J. G. L. Huey was persuaded to act as Superintendent in 1842. Others followed:

J.G.L. Huey	1842-68	N.J. Hubbard	1897-07
Wm. H. Thornton	1868-79	M.N. Manning	1907-11
Myles J. Greene	1879-88	L.J. McConnell	1911-19
W.J. Rhodes	1888	G.M. Clark	1919-20
J. Melville Thornton	1889-97	Alonzo Abrams	1920-24

There followed N. J. Hubbard, A. B. Baxley, P. L. Howard, H. T. Vance, Oliver Coker, E. Hussey, Mrs. E. A. and Oliver Coker.

THE PRESBYTERIAN CHURCH

First Presbyterian Church

On October 1893, the First Presbyterian Church of Talladega celebrated the 25th anniversary of the dedication of their church building located on North St. On this occasion Dr. B. W. Toole read a history of the church which was later printed in pamphlet form. From this "Historical Sketch of the First Presbyterian Church of Talladega, Alabama",[29] I have culled the following:

"The organization occurred on Saturday, November 28, 1834, in a log house situated near our large town spring, the building then being used as a court house and the place for public meetings. This section of the country was then in the bounds of South Alabama Presbytery. Rev. Robert Holman and Rev. Field Bradshaw were the authorized commissioners to do this. There were fourteen members in the organization, and their names should be preserved, Charles Miller and wife, George Miller and wife, Patrick Johnson and wife, William Caruthers and wife, Harper Johnson and wife, Robert Hett Chapman, Dr. Henry McKenzie, Miss Amanda Talmage, George Watkins.

"One day after the organization, which was Sunday, November 30, 1834, the sacrament of the Lord's supper was celebrated. As a fact of incidental interest it may be stated, in the absence of any written record of the date of the organization, the certain and exact is known because of its association with a

---

[29] Historical Sketch of the First Presbyterian Church of Tall. Alabama, by Dr. B. W. Toole, copy of which is in my possession, presented by Miss Nannie B. Golden

most noted solar eclipse which occurred on Sunday, November 30, 1834. It was a total eclipse, and occurring as it did at midday, was well calculated to make a deep impression on the minds and memories of those who witnessed it, both civilized and semi-civilized, as was the case the tribe of Creek Indians, who had at that time not been removed from the State. The eclipse commenced at fifty minutes after eleven o'clock, while the religious services were in progress, and ended at forty minutes after two o'clock, lasting for a period of nearly three hours. There just after one o'clock total darkness for about two minutes. This fact is referred to, as stated before, because by it the exact date of the church organization is established through the testimony of one of the original fourteen members, and present that day.

"Messrs. Wm. Caruthers, Patrick Johnson, Charles Miller and Robert H. Chapman were then elected and ordained ruling elders and Wm. Caruthers was made Clerk of the session. Rev. Robert Holman acted as stated supply for the church until the fall of 1835. Rev. Richard Cater at that time moved to Talladega and took charge of the church as stated supply, and continued as such till the latter part of the year 1838, or early 1839, when Robert Chapman succeeded him.

"In the latter part of 1834 Rev. Robert Holman bought public auction a lot for church purposes; a part of that lot is the ground on which this church now stands. A portion of the original purchased lot was sold in order to procure funds with to build a church. In 1835 a frame building, about 30 x 40 feet, was erected by Messrs. George and Charles Miller, contractors. The front of the building occupied the ground about the pulpit now stands.

"In 1859 the question was raised and discussed whether the Presbyterian congregation would erect a new church. It is to be regretted that no written and authentic records can be found showing the various stages of this movement with the subscription list and names of the persons who contributed.

"In 1859 and 1860 the congregation, having decided to build, raised by subscription between ten and eleven thousand dollars. About the time this was accomplished the signs of the approaching civil war were plainly manifested. A council of the chief and wise men of the congregation was held to consider what ought to be done as to building since the dark and foreboding clouds of civil war were surely forming. It was argued that part of the money was already secured and paid in and the subscribers were then able to pay the amounts subscribed. If the war should come, then when it should be over, whatever would be the result, victory or defeat, the people would be impoverished and could not give; that it was better to use the money now when they had it and could spare it, put up the building, place it in such condition as to preserve what was done if not able to finish it, and trust to the future to complete it. This conclusion proved to be an eminently wise one. They determined to go forward.

"About the first of June, 1861, after the most tragic drama the 19th century had commenced at Fort Sumter in April, the work of building this church was begun, and we who for twenty-five years have been permitted to worship here have reason to be grateful to the men of that generation for the wisdom displayed in acting as they did. The architect, whose name I am unable to give, lived in Philadelphia and was a man prominent in his profession. The plans and designs as made by him embraced a basement. When it was finally determined to commence to build it was believed to be necessary, because of the cost and amount of money which could be relied on, to omit the basement and carry out the plans in other respects. This was done. It is a matter of regret that this course seemed to be necessary. Some of the subscribers proposed to have the basement and omit the tower and spire, so as to keep within the amount of money at their command, claiming that the tower and spire could be built in the future if they were able, but the basement could not. But this view of the case was not adopted. Some years later our Baptist brethren, when about to erect a new church, got our plans, drawings and specifications and modeled their church from them with the exception of the tower and spire, which they omitted. They profited by the experience of their neighbors and have a comfortable and useful basement and have reasons to congratulate themselves in this particular. The plans, drawings, etc. were then sent to some church in South Alabama and have never been returned, hence my inability to give the name of the architect.

"About twelve months after the work of erecting the church had commenced the very substantial framework for the roof was put up and covered with the best quality of shingles that could be procured; the windows, doors and openings were closed with plank to protect the work already done from injury by the weather. It stood there uncompleted, none of the inside work having been done, for at least six years.

"Just prior to the erection of the new brick building the old wooden building, which had been used for worship for twenty-six years, was removed to make room for its successor. During the period from the early part of 1861 to the third week of October, 1868, the congregation worshipped in the chapel of the Synodical Female Institute, now Isbell College."

"The dedication services were at 11 a.m. October 18th 1868. There was a large congregation present, all of the available space being occupied. There were no morning services in the Baptist and Methodist churches. Rev. G. W. H. Petrie, D. D., of Montgomery, preached the dedicatory sermon from the following text: Luke 21st chapter, 5th and 6th verses, "And as some spake of the temple, how it was adorned with goodly stones and he said, As for these things which ye behold, the days will come in the which there shall not be left one stone upon another, that shall not be thrown down."

"Fifty-nine years ago it was a little band of fourteen, five years ago there were one hundred and thirty-three, today (1893) the number is three hundred and thirty."

"From the best information obtainable the Sabbath School was established in the year 1857. Since it has been kept up with considerable regularity."

Repairs and enlargements of buildings connected with the church have been made throughout the years, but the main auditorium remains the same as when dedicated in 1868.

The following ministers have served the First Presbyterian church throughout the years:

Rev. Robert Holman	1834-35
Rev. Richard Cater	1835-39
Rev. Robert Hett Chapman	1839-44
Rev. A.B. McCorkle	1845-71
Rev. F.A. Ewing	1872-84
Rev. J. M. P. Otts, D. D.	1884-89
Rev. Wm. W. Houston, D. D.	1889-91
Rev. Joseph H. Skinner	1892-94
Rev. Lynn R. Walker	1895-1902
Rev. F.B. Webb, D. D.	1902-20
Rev. A.C. Ormond	1920-29
Rev. Wm. Crow, III	1929-37
Rev. Lewis Lancaster, D. D.	1937-38
Rev. Wm. Crow, D. D.	1938

One of the beautiful and sacred features of the Presbyterian Church building is that of the memorial windows, which are worthy of record:

1—Dr. James Croll Knox
  Born Mar. 28, 1812
  Died Mar.27, 1877
  A Ruling Elder and One of
  the Founders of this church
2—Rev. Alexander B. McCorkle
  1806-1886
  Lucilla A. McCorkle
  1822-1907

6—William Nathan Boyton
7—Mary Meade Hardie
  Who Labored More for Others
  Than for Self
8—George Stovall Walden
  Emily Patton Walden
9—William Hughston Burr
  Sarah Borden Burr

3—Elizabeth Armstrong Turner
1799-1860
4—Barckley Wallace Toole
1834-1898
5—In Memory of
Venable Holt Walker
By the
Vennie Walker Society

10—Pauline McAlpine DuBose
1872-1914
Missionary to China from
1872-1914
11—Annie Hardie Lewis
By Her Sons

MARDISVILLE Church must have been organized about the same time as that of the Talladega church, if not some earlier, and it was perhaps the stronger church for a few years. At least it was progressive enough to possess a church bell, which was transferred to the First Presbyterian Church in Talladega when the brick building was completed in 1868. At this time, no doubt, the membership was moved to the Talladega Church. It is regretted that we have no records of this church.

MARBLE SPRINGS Presbyterian Church has frequently been called the "Mother" Presbyterian Church of Talladega County, because tradition has placed it as the first authorized Presbyterian church in the county. If this be true, it was not an organized church, because the minutes are still in existence,[30] from which information contained in this sketch is derived.

"Marble Springs Church was organized in March 1837, about 8 miles east of Talladega, on the road leading from Talladega to Jemison's (Turner's) Mill, by Rev. Robert Holman assisted by Samuel Leeper an Elder from Mardisville Church. The original members were Alexander English and his wife, Mary English, his daughter Elizabeth English, his daughter Jane Walker, Wm. Caruthers and wife, Robert McElhaney and wife, Nancy Margaret Lewis, afterward English.

"Robert McElhaney and Wm. Caruthers were ruling Elders, Robert McElhaney was Clerk of the Session."

During 1838 James Montgomery and his brother, William Montgomery were chosen Elders, they having been "Elders of Church, Jackson Co.,

Until the church was non-existent, Montgomerys and their descendants were ruling Elders.

Rev. Holman preached there until 1839. Rev. Robert McApine of Talladega preached as Stated Supply until 1844, when he resigned because of the distance, and suggested that Marble Springs join with First Church,

[30] Minute Book in possession of Mrs. Margaret Montgomery (A. S.) Callaway, Hogansville, Ga. Loaned me by her.

Talladega, in employing a minister, which suggestion they accepted. Rev. A. B. McCorkle was then Stated Supply until 1867. Rev. J. Newman a refugee from East Tennessee served until he died in 1868. Then followed Revs. R. Houston, James M. McClean, J. K. Spence, R. H. Boteler, W. N. Warren, Lynn R. Walker and Geo. Dunglinson.

Marble Springs was one of the most prominent Presbyterian Churches of the county for many years and may have been called "Mother Church" because it had the largest membership. During the year 1840-48, there were added to the roll some of Talladega County's most prominent citizens.

1840 Susan Bowie, Jane Jack and Wm. L. Lewis, Samantha Lewis, Sarah S. Lewis; In 1841, Alexander Bowie; In 1843, Mrs. Reutelia H. Isbell. In 1845, Joseph T. Cunningham, three servants, Agnes Cunningham and Amanda Cunningham; In 1846, there was a revival and the names of James A. Walker Mary Daniel H. Jackson, Julia A. Jackson, Andrew Cunningham, Wm. B. McClelland, Martha McClelland, Amanda McClelland, Mary McClelland, Samuel F. McClelland, Ann A. Bowie, Martha S. Elhaney, Samuel People, Andrew J. Siddell, Mary Creswell, Mary Wilson, Margaret Hendrick, Craig Orr, and Cynthia Orr, Bowie Cunninghams, were added to the church roll. In 1847 Thomas Best and 17 others were added to the roll.

At the end of 1848 there were 68 white and 4 colored members. 37 families were represented with 84 members in 1851. There was a flourishing Sunday School in 1856, and in 1857 the record shows that there were 75 members and 7 officers and teachers. The Sunday School disappeared in 1880, because of distance and newly organized nondenominational Sunday schools in communities. Many of the old members were buried south of the church, where imposing monuments were erected to their memories. The first wife of J. L. M. Curry was buried there, Chancellor Bowie and his wife, Montgomerys, Cunninghams and many prominent citizens, were buried at Marble Springs. The church was sold many years ago, a cotton gin was unsuccessfully operated in the building for a short while, and the building finally dropped to pieces. There is now no evidence of either a church building or a cemetery. What became of the monuments no one knows, but the cemetery is now a cotton field as well as the spot where the church stood, about 300 feet from Choccolocco bridge, S. E. of the Creek and on the east side of the Eastaboga Highway.

There are now only a few people who have so much as a memory of the once sacred spot.

FOREST HILL CHAPEL is referred to by Dr. B. W. Toole: "August, 1873, the pastor, assisted by Rev. James M. McLean had a protracted meeting at

Forest Hill Chapel, six miles north of the town.[31] The Chapel was located on the James Huston plantation, and the membership was composed almost entirely of that family."

Another interesting old Presbyterian Church is that of NEW LEBANON, in the north-eastern part of the county, above Silver Run. Services are still held at this sacred old church. It was constituted a church on Dec. 17, 1848, with the following 15 members:

Col. Samuel Jack	John Hendrick
Mrs. Ann Jack	Hance Hendrick
Mrs. Lucinda Orr	Mrs. Rachel Hendrick
John Orr	Mrs. Ann McClurkin
Mrs. Abigail Bradford	John McClurkin
Dr. H. G. Hendrick	Mrs. Margaret Forgy
Wm. Y. Hendrick	Mrs. Elizabeth McCulley
Mrs. Julia Hendrick	

The Rev. C. R. Smith was the first pastor.

A deed was made by Wiley W. Mattison and wife for a building site. The building was erected and John McClurkin made a sacrament table, which was put together with pegs, and which is still in use by the church. Another gift that is still in use, is the pulpit Bible presented by John W. McKibbon in 1860.

New Lebanon Church had one of the most active congregations in the county until the latter part of the century. At one time, in 1861, 40 young men united with the church.[32] They are proud of the fact that it has produced several Presbyterian ministers.

Many on the rolls through the years have been familiar figures in the social, business, political and religious life of, not only Talladega County, but of many other parts of the State. People have left the rural communities for broader fields, and New Lebanon Church, like many other churches in rural districts, has suffered in membership. In spite of this fact, the church has demonstrated fortitude and determination in continuing the worship of the Lord as a group.

There was at one time a Presbyterian Church near Riser's Chapel, as evidenced by an old cemetery, but records are unavailable. In whatever place a

---

[31] Historical Sketch of the First Pres. Church, by Dr. B. W. Toole
[32] From a History of New Lebanon Church, by Mrs. Nora (Merlin R. O'Rear), at the 100th Anniversary of the Church.

Presbyterian church is planted, there is a natural spiritual growth, and a cultural atmosphere that is felt throughout the community.

THE PROTESTANT EPISCOPAL CHURCH

Rev. T. A. Cook, an Episcopal minister, came to Talladega in 1844. He established and built the "White Chapel Female Seminary" the same year, and was one of Talladega County's first and best teachers, having taught in various county institutions during his life. He was also the first Episcopal Missionary in Alabama. He had organized a mission in Florence and built a church there at the cost of $1500.00 in 1837. He had also founded a church in LaFayette in 1838.[33]

As recorded in the Diocesan Journal of the Convention of 1846, Bishop Nicholas Hamner Cobbs stated in his annual address: "Feb. Visited Talladega and preached twice. In this town the Rev. Mr. Cook resides, having charge of a large Female School. Being in feeble health, he does not now attend to the duties of the ministry, but I trust it will not be long before he will again be able to go forth and proclaim the message of salvation. It is melancholy to reflect that, in all that beautiful country lying East of the Coosa River, there is not an officiating minister of the church. May the Lord, in his good Providence, soon send forth faithful clergymen to labor in that neglected field."[34]

It is in order to state here that Bishop Nicholas Hamner Cobbs was one of the greatest Episcopal Bishops of all time, and perhaps the most evangelically inclined, and the most beloved.

The next year no mention was made of Talladega, but the Bishop records that on March 27, 1848 he spent another two days in Talladega. The report showed 4 Communicants and "the Rev. Cook has determined to labor in this Missionary field."[35] In the Bishop's address of 1850 he stated that on the Sunday after Easter he preached twice in Talladega. "Here a Parish has been organized and the prospects of the church are improving." 12 Communicants were reported with a congregation of 50.

We are indebted to the Rev. Mr. Cook for information regarding this early church, as he recalled it in 1887, at which time he wrote a "Sketch of St. Peters Church", from which I quote: "Some time during the year 1850, the Rt. Rev. Nicholas H. Cobbs, D. D. prevailed on the Rev. Thomas A. Cook, who was then teaching a large female school, to add to his labors, the task of gathering the 'Scattered Sheep' of the Church."

---

[33] Thomas M. Owen's History of Ala., Vol. I, Page 536
[34] Diocesean Journals, Vol. II, Page 13. Information from Rev. Randolph F. Blackford
[35] Ibid, Page 17

The Rev. Cook "gathered two scattered Sheep". "Services were held in an upper room of an old brick store on the south-west corner of the Public Square, long since burned down." It is regretted that Mr. Cook failed to record the names of these two pioneer "Sheep."

In spite of the fact that there were only two communicants, the room was frequently full, and the congregation orderly and attentive.

The communicants increased to 14, "mostly new settlers and a few confirmations." A church building evidently was planned for Mr. Cook reported in 1852 "Owing to the scarcity of money, our church building has been postponed for the present at least." It is strange that Mr. Cook failed to mention in his "Sketch" that the church was called "GRACE CHURCH" in its infancy. All reports of the early church were headed "Grace Church, of Talladega."

A report of 1853 showed 10 communicants, but there were no reports for the years 1854-59.

The Bishop records a visit to Talladega in 1861, but nothing further is reported.

The year 1862 brought to Talladega, the Rev. Joseph J. Nicholson, which changed the course of the church.

Mr. Cook, in the meantime, had purchased a small pipe organ for $150.00, and "soon the services assumed a churchly form, with chants and hymns according to ancient regulations." The communicants decided to build a church, and the news brought liberal subscriptions from other denominations. $1500.00 was soon realized. Mr. Cook donated a large convenient lot on which to erect a church, and ground was broken for the building. However, clouds of war were gathering, and this was no doubt the reason for their not having built it. There was still another reason, for about this time the small group was forced to move from the upper room "to an old store house, by the town spring," which was unfit for the purpose, and the "Sheep", so few in number, scattered again.

Mr. Cook, being overworked with teaching and preaching, felt impelled to withdraw again from the ministry, and the Bishop sent "The Rt. Rev. Mr. Sturdemeyer, who held services in the old Baptist Church one Sunday." "Mr. Sturdemeyer preached one sermon and no more." There is no reason given for the quick retreat.

"After him came the Rev. Wm. D. Christian, who remained one or two years and went to Louisiana."

During the Civil War a conscript camp was located near Talladega. The Rev. Joseph J. Nicholson, an Episcopal Minister, from Mobile, was chaplain of the camp. "He held services in an upper room opposite the spot where ground was first broken several years before." The church flourished during this period, one reason being the fact that the Rev. Nicholson brought his congregation with him, and another that several zealous church families from Mobile were refugees to Talladega during the War, and participated in the service.

The Rev. Nicholson preached each Sunday in Talladega and through the courtesy of the Commander preached once a month in Jacksonville. In his report to the Convention of 1863, Rev. Nicholson stated "At Talladega there have been through the winter about 40 communicants, 10 or 12 of whom are citizens, the rest being proximately or remotely connected with the Army. I have also established here a Sunday School, which numbers about 20 pupils and 5 teachers."[36]

His report further shows that $8.00 rent was paid for a room in which to worship.

Reports were vague for the next few years. Rev. J. D. Easter made the report of 1868, showing 14 communicants.[37]

The faithful group was again without a shepherd until the Rev. James Franklin Smith, an evangelist, came in December 1869 and served intermittently, as rector, for many years. It was during his ministry that the first chapel was built. The church name appears to have been changed from Grace Church to St. Peter's at the time of dedication to this building. In the address of the Bishop at the Convention of 1872 he states that he had visited Talladega during the year and "The congregation is steadily growing at that point under the pastoral care of the Rev. J. F. Smith, Evangelist, and measures are being taken for the speedy erection of a church at this place." Our Mt. Home of April 25, 1872 states: the material is on the ground. Mr. Wm. Stockdale has taken the contract for erecting it (the Episcopal Church) and work will soon be commenced."

The report of Rev. Smith dated May 7, 1872, shows:

Communicants	45
Baptized, not Communicants	55
Total Parishioners	100

His report also shows a Sunday School with 15 pupils and 2 teachers, and that the Rector received a salary of $50.00 per annum, and "rent for service room $125.00." He adds 'We have in course of erection a Chapel 22 feet wide by 30 feet long, which will be finished, we hope, in a few weeks."[38]

Bishop Wilmer stated in his annual address to the Convention of 1873 "April 2: (30th day of Lent) Preached at the new Chapel at Talladega. April 3

---

[36] Ibid, Vol. III, Page 19
[37] Ibid
[38] Ibid, Vol. IV, Page 29

(31st day of Lent) Preached at the same place morning and evening, confirming 5 persons . . . The temporary house of worship was built at a very small cost, but is, in all its interior arrangements, most churchly in appearance. . . . Church and lot cost $1500.00.

I would call the attention of our church people to this unpretending building, as an example of how much substantial good can be realized from a very small expenditure of money."

The report of 1873 shows the Communicants as 50, and that the Rector's salary was raised to $75.00 per annum. It also records that the church had received a severe blow in the death of Col. John D. Hoke, Senior Warden.

Rev. Smith, Alabama evangelist, and rector of St. Peters' Church, set up permanent records in a Parish Register.

"Firsts" are always interesting. Therefore, the following communicants as of September 1st, 1869, are worthy of note:

Mrs. Cook	Miss Jennie Parsons
Mrs. Mariah Gorman	Mrs. Arthur Bingham
Mrs. Julia McKibbon	Mrs. Nancy Welch
Mrs. Josephine Willman	Dr. C. H. Gorman
Mr. Richmond Nickles	Mrs. Sarah Nickles

There were only two men among them.

The first baptism registered is that of "Malotte Bartleson, September 7th, 1870."

The first marriage record is that of Allen Deas, Enterprise, Miss., to Mary Rumph, March 25, 1871.

There is another interesting item listed among the communicants throughout the years—that of Eugene Zimmerman, the steel magnate, who once owned the furnace located southwest of city limits of Talladega, and his daughter, who married the Duke of Manchester.

St. Peters was admitted into Union with the Diocese in 1874.[39] After the Rev. Smith retired he was made Rector Emeritus of St. Peter's until he died February 4th, 1899.

In 1893 a two story frame rectory was built on the east of the Chapel. This was moved and eventually razed to make room for the new and present church building.

The present St. Peter's Church School was organized Sept. 18, 1893, and taught by Miss A. Hawley, of Fayetteville, N. C.

---

[39] Thomas M. Owen's History of Ala., Vol. I, Page 427

Mrs. Kate Finnegan began a Kindergarten in 1894.

The Guild was first organized on August 15th, 1898

In June, 1910, Miss Louise C. Willman presented a beautiful circular memorial window to the church, inscribed: "Christ the Great Teacher, To the Glory of God, and in loving memory of Xavier and Josephine Haas Willman, by their sons and daughters."

St. Peters was undoubtedly the first Episcopal Church in Alabama, East of the Coosa River, and was tireless in organizing missions throughout the district. St. Peter's was fortunate in having both great evangelists and missionaries of Alabama as communicants, who, during their period of service in Talladega, were also instrumental in organizing many churches throughout Alabama. Among the most important were the Elyton Church, which mothered all the Birmingham Episcopal Churches; and Grace Church at Anniston: "Grace Church, Anniston was founded in 1881, no organization having been attempted before, but the Rev. J. F. Smith had been ministering to the congregation since 1875."[40] St. Peter's has sponsored the following Missions:

THE CHAPEL OF THE CROSS was formally established when the cornerstone was laid Sept. 20, 1895 by the Rev. J. F. Smith.[41] This chapel was located on the North side of Talladega Creek near the old Dr. Stockdale home. The membership consisted almost entirely of Riddles and Stockdales. The first service was held in the Mission Chapel on the "19th Sunday after Trinity, 1896." It eventually was abandoned and fell a victim of decay.

TRINITY EPISCOPAL CHURCH was first built at Nottingham, the cornerstone having been laid November 28, 1895, by Rev. Thomas A. Cook. The first service was held on "Whitsunday, 1896." The membership consisted almost entirely of Cooks and Gormans. In 1910, a new chapel was erected at Alpine, and the membership moved to this place. The mission still exists.

ST. ANDREWS EPISCOPAL CHURCH was served by Rev. J. F. Smith some years before it became a permanent mission in December, 1896. This church is located at Sylacauga, and still exists, with a comfortable chapel, it being the second erected.

ST. JAMES MISSION in Alexander City was organized by Rev. R. F. Blackford in 1947.

ST. MARY'S MISSION at Childersburg, was organized by Rev. R. F. Blackford, in 1948.

All of these missions are served by the rector of St. Peters' Church, in Talladega.

---

[40] Ibid, Page 538

[41] St. Peter's Parish Register, of Talladega, Ala.

The following rectors have served St. Peter's during the years:

Rev. Thomas A. Cook	1850-?
Rev. Sturdemeyer	few days
Rev. Wm. D. Christian	2 yrs
Rev. Joseph J.D. Easter	1868
Rev. J.F. Smith	1869-87
Rev. G.H. Hunt	1872
Rev. Joseph Jameson	1888-89
Rev. W.T. Allen	1891-92
Rev. W.L. Mellochampe	1893-95
Rev. J. Coleman Horton	1889-1901
Rev. E.G. Hunter	1901-15
Rev. Charles K. Weller	1916-1919
Rev. Joseph H. Harvey	1924-36
Rev. R.C. Klingman	1938-40
Rev. Marhsall Seifert	1941-43
Rev. Wm. Stoney	1943-45
Rev. Randolph F. Blackford	1945-1958

Some of these dates may be inaccurate since there was no definite record.

The new church, erected in 1928, is artistic in every respect, and there is ever an atmosphere of reverence within the building, and, while there may have been a struggle to keep the "sheep" from scattering in the early days, they are certainly well established in 1959.

Schools

One of the stipulations of the act admitting Alabama as a State of the Union, was that the Sixteenth Section of every Township should be set aside for the use of schools. Where these sections had already been legally purchased, equally valuable provision should be made in each Township. 36 Sections, in the state, or the equivalent of an entire Township of six miles square, was reserved for a "Seminary of Learning". Therefore, the original University of Alabama was built with a portion of the funds derived from the sale of sections of land. The early local schools were also supported in part by the Sixteenth Section fund.

A Township constituted a School District, and three trustees, under the general supervision of the County Judge acted as a Board in each district. In many instances the entire Township was composed of illiterate people. This condition existed for some years.

On Feb. 15, 1854, a bill was passed by the legislature of Alabama providing for a State Superintendent of Education, and in 1856 County Superintendents replaced the old system. This bill was sponsored by A. B. Meek, of Mobile, and endorsed by J. L. M. Curry of Talladega, and Robt. M. Patton of Lauderdale.[1] W. F. Perry, of Talladega, was made first State Superintendent of Education.

This undertaking was an uncharted sea and it took some time to regulate and to put into action the system. Several years during the War Between the States, there were no funds available, and most of the rural schools ceased operations, but the village schools continued under private teachers.

In 1868 J. G. Chadraun, a grandson of a member of the Vine and Olive Co. which settled in Marengo County, was Superintendent of Education in Talladega County. He reported schools taught in the county as follows:

1st Qtr.	2nd Qtr.	3rd Qtr.	4th Qtr.	Total
11 White	34 White	42 White	4 White	91
6 Colored	13 Colored	22 Colored		41

Average days taught 168½

---

[1] Memorial Records of Ala., Vol. 1, Page 189

The report for the first and fourth quarters, being the winter months, indicate the condition of the schools. There were only a few which had heating facilities.[2] Mr. Wm. L. Lewis was Supt. of Education in Talladega County in 1871. He stated in his report that schools ceased after the public fund was exhausted, which lasted from 3 to 5 months, and that most of the school buildings were without chimneys, and had large cracks in the floors and walls, rendering them uninhabitable in winter, and he added:

"You will see from my annual report that there have been 48 different white schools taught, and a large majority by young ladies; which I believe is injurious to the cause of education, for in a majority of cases there are students who do not wish to attend the schools taught by young ladies; nor do the ladies desire such students in their schools."

His report carried the following figures:

Schools taught: Primary, 22; Intermediate 19; Grammar 6, High 1; making a total of 48. There were 680 Females and 630 Males registered, making a total of 1310. The branches taught and the number of pupils:

Orthography 1144	Arithmetic 633
Geography 319	Writing 707
Reading 936	Grammar 321

The number of teachers—17 Male and 34 Female. The average salary was $31.00, and the average days taught 77.[3]

He bemoaned the fact that there were no requirements as to the character of school, nor qualification of teacher. The early school buildings were poorly equipped. Benches had no backs and books were passed from generation to generation. To keep them from wearing out where they were held for study, Thumb Cards had to be used. These cards were found in packages of soda, tobacco, etc., and were highly prized. There were no tablets. Slates were a necessary part of a pupils equipment. Pupils studied aloud during the entire day, where classes from the first to the seventh grades were taught in the same class room by the same teacher.

Friday afternoons were set aside for exhibitions, when speeches were made, and Spelling Bees took place. The annual examinations were oral, with the school board acting as examiners. This public examination lasted for several days, and was the greatest event of the school year.

The history of our town schools begins with the term of 1834-35.

The large planters with children brought instructors with them. These instructors lived and taught in the homes of the planters. As the county

---

[2] State Documents, 169-70, Report of N. B. Cloud, Supt. Of Pub. Ins.
[3] State Documents, 1871-72, Page 79 of the Report of Joseph Hodgson, Supt. Of Public Instruction of Ala.

increased in population, academies were erected in many Townships, with money derived from the Sixteenth Section fund, supplemented by local contributions. The private teachers naturally drifted to these community academies.

Miss Susan S. Speer, daughter of a Methodist minister, from Tennessee, claimed to be the first teacher in Talladega Town. She taught "on the west side, about 20 yards from the spring branch, in a simple log cabin in 1834 which was later called the Presbyterian church."[4]

In 1834 she (Miss Speer) moved to Talladega County for the purpose of teaching school, and it seems in order to pause for a brief sketch of Talladega's first teacher who valiantly answered the call for teachers in the Creek Country.

Susan S. Speer was born April 12, 1815 in Nashville, Tenn. She was educated in Virginia. Her father, Moses Speer, was a Methodist "Circuit Rider", who went to Texas, no doubt as a Missionary, long before Texas became a part of the Union. A letter written from Texas to Susan in 1837 states that he was possessed of 1280 acres of land. Her mother, Amelia Ewing Speer, was the daughter of one of the founders of Nashville, Tenn., and she was in deep accord with her husband's calling. She joined him in Texas about the time Susan came to Talladega. The young daughter evidently inherited her parents zealous and adventurous spirit, for she felt impelled to come to the Creek country when there was an urgent call for teachers.[5]

It would be interesting to know of Susan's trip from Nashville to Talladega by stage coach, and to know where she stayed when she arrived. However, it seems reasonable to believe that she stayed at one of the several taverns. She was only about 20 years old, and full of interest in the new country.

Susan told her grand-children many interesting stories of her early life in Talladega. There were hundreds of Indians walking about in the new town: and the squaws carried their babies in blankets tied on their backs. She had a day school for the neighborhood, but she also had a select school for young ladies. Her school house was located on S. Spring Street. It was of log construction with puncheon floor and benches. Susan told of the Indians sticking their heads in the windows all during the day; especially during the lunch period. She and her pupils always shared their lunches with the Indians, because it was well to keep on their good side. Susan's ardor was unlimited, and her efforts untiring, in helping any one who wanted an education. She even taught poor girls, free of charge, until many became teachers themselves. On

---

[4] History of Talladega by Mrs. L. M. Taylor, Chapter 8. Also Memorial Records of Ala., Vol. II, Page 973

[5] Letter from Mrs. D. H. Smith, Houston, Texas, Gr. Gr. Daughter of Susan Speer McPherson

Sept. 21, 1837, Susan Speer married William McPherson, an attractive young widower, who had settled as a merchant and planter in and around Fayetteville. William McPherson proved to be one of the most colorful and useful characters of the county. He was a native of New York, and while living there he had seen the first steamboat launched—the "Clermont." Among his other interesting experiences was that of hearing the funeral sermon of Alexander Hamilton.

After Susan married and moved to the plantation of William McPherson, who at one time owned around 10,000 acres of land and 100 slaves, she continued her interest in civic, religious and educational movements. She organized what she thought to be the first Sunday School in the County in 1840, and rode horseback about the community organizing new ones. She and William conducted a Sunday School for their slaves. William lived to be 106 years of age. They reared a large and useful family of 9 children, many of whose descendants are now living in Talladega County. Thus Talladega County had a wonderful beginning in the educational field, and was considered, throughout the Nineteenth Century, one of the best educational centers in the State of Alabama. For some years Talladega had four boarding schools, when the town had less than one thousand inhabitants.

In 1835 two academies were built. One of these schools was for girls and the other for boys.

The school built for girls was on the lot back of the Presbyterian Church, and was later enlarged by the Presbyterians for a college building. Mr. and Mrs. J. Clark were first teachers in this girls academy. A Mrs. Rhoam (Rhome, Rome, or Rowe), and her daughters, who had once been missionaries to India, followed the Clarks. The Rhoams brought the first piano to Talladega.

The Male Academy was situated "on the hill South-west of the spring."[6] This is now part of Oak Hill Cemetery. The building was later used for a pest house during an epidemic of small pox, and eventually burned. Mr. Richard Cater, once pastor of the Presbyterian Church, was first teacher. Following him were: 1839—Geo. S. Walden, 1841—Rev. A. W. Chamblies and Wm. Johns, 1844. J. M. Thatcher, Prof. Wm. F. Perry taught there from 1848 to 1853.[7] He left Talladega to accept the position as first Supt. of Education in Alabama. He later became a Brig. General in the Confederate Army.

This school was evidently called "Talladega Institute", since an advertisement in the Alabama Reporter of Sept. 12, 1850, stated that "the Talladega Institute will open Sept. 30th" and signed by Wm. F. Perry and L. M. Sparrow.[8] It was later taught by R. P. Latham, John Wilmer and P. E. Collins.

---

[6] History of Talladega by Mrs. L. M. Taylor, Chapter 8
[7] Publications of the Ala. Historical Society, Vol. II, Page 148
[8] Paper found in J. A. Bingham's Scrap Book collection

WHITE CHAPEL FEMALE SEMINARY

The first boarding school was unquestionably erected near the J. A. Bingham home, north of Talladega. This was erected by Mr. T. A. Cook in 1844. Mr. Cook was an Episcopal missionary to Alabama, and was destined to become one of Talladega's greatest educators. The school was called the White Chapel Female Seminary" and had as many as ninety students at the time.[9]

Talladega in those days was quite denominationally conscious, which the following advertisement, appearing in the Sept. 4, 1850 issue of the Democratic Watchtower,[10] better explains:

"White Chapel Female Seminary
The exercises of this school will be resumed on Monday, 8th of July, next.

The Proprietor takes this opportunity to thank his friends, who have so liberally patronized him during the past session, and to solicit a continuance of favors.

To all such as have daughters who need an education, he can safely say that he has the OLDEST, the CHEAPEST, and the BEST school in the county. It is the oldest, because it has been in the county near six years. It is the cheapest, because board and tuition cost no more than $10.00 per month. It is the best, because it has been sustained in a flourishing condition, notwithstanding the most unmanly opposition that ever was exerted against our devoted Institution.

The fact that the White Chapel Female Seminary is one mile and a half from the town of Talladega, is an advantage to its students, and no disadvantage to the town.

Many of the best citizens of this county, and others from a distance have expressed a preference for the present location of the school. A sufficient recommendation exists in the fact that the Seminary was crowded at an early part of the season.

We wish those who hear any tales about religious influences, proselytizing, etc., to see patrons and pupils of the school before they believe such and many other rumors, which are set afloat for a CERTAIN purpose.

Mr. Norman has purchased a splendid Piano Forte, and Bass Viol, and will teach as usual at $25.00 per session. It is unnecessary to add, that the Seminary is supplied with Apparatus. We have not published this before, as it

---

[9] Memorial Records of Ala., Vol. II, Page 950
[10] Paper found in J. A. Bingham's Scrap Book collection

was not common for workmen to advertise their tools. Prices for Ornamental branches, and day schools, the same as here-to-fore. Teachers, Thomas A. Cook, Principal, Proprietor and Trustee; Mrs. Eliza Cook, Associate, Mr. John B. Norman, Professor of Music.

Mr. Norman advertised that he would "continue to give lessons at the White Chapel Female Seminary and in town. Pupils who prefer to receive instruction privately will be waited on at their residences."

Mr. Cook taught in several other schools during the War Between the States, but retired to his farm in, or near, Alpine, about 1874, where he remained the rest of his life.

As stated, Talladega was quite denominationally conscious in 1850. There was a movement launched in 1849 by the Presbyterians to erect a college for women, in which the citizens entered enthusiastically at first, but later some of the Baptists and Methodists withdrew, with some controversy and started a movement sponsored by the Masons, to erect a non-sectarian school for women. Out of this grew the Masonic Institute.

THE MASONIC INSTITUTE

In 1850 nearly all of the Male population of Talladega belonged to the Masonic Order, and they readily subscribed toward the building of a Masonic School. A large lot was purchased on South Street and the corner stone was laid on April 12, 1850, with great ceremony.[11] Chancellor Stiggins made the address, in which he denounced denominational schools.

The school building was, and still is, a stately structure of Grecian architecture. It originally had two winding stairways on the outside front of the building, to the second story. There was a balcony across the third story front. The school opened in 1851. Evidently it was not successful, for the Masons disposed of it, with an indebtedness, in 1855 to the Alabama Methodist Episcopal Church, South.

TALLADEGA CONFERENCE INSTITUTE

The following culled from the History of Methodism in Ala. by Dr. Anson West gives a concise history of the Talladega Conference Institute:

"At a session at Talladega, Ala., beginning Dec. 13, 1854, the Alabama Conference adopted measures for the establishment of a Female High School at the town of Talladega to be called the 'Talladega Conference Institute'. A board

---

[11] Diary of James Isbell, owned by W. N. Boynton, his gr. Gr. son

of Trustees, consisting of four preachers: J. Hamilton, James S. Lane, D. Carmichael and O. R. Blue; and five Laymen: J. G. Huey, John M. Moore, J. E. Groce, John T. Morgan, and A. J. Cotton (all of Talladega) was appointed, with powers and restrictions usually conferred upon Trustees, subject to the supervision and control of the Ala. Conference of the M. E. Church, South."[12]

"The Masons of Talladega built a fine edifice for school purposes at Talladega, and a school was opened under the auspices of the Masonic Fraternity. The School became financially embarrassed, and it was turned over, as herein stated, to the Alabama Conference. The effort was made by the Conference to liquidate debts and make the School, under the management of the Church, selfsustaining, but the effort failed. First the Rev. James S. Lane, and then the Rev. Joseph T. Abernathy was appointed Agent for the School. The Rev. B. B. Ross, and the Rev. F. M. Grace were put in charge of the school as officers and teachers, but success was not achieved, and in 1858 the property was turned over to the State of Alabama, since which time it has been used as a school for the Deaf- Mutes and Blind."[13] (See School for the Deaf.)

PRESBYTERIAN COLLEGIATE FEMALE INSTITUTE

The Presbyterians are usually advocates of education, and pioneers in that field wherever they go. The first Talladega ministers History of Methodism in Ala., by Dr. Anson West, pub. 1893, Page 730 of this faith, taught school in addition to their regular ministerial duties.

During the summer months of 1849 subscriptions were taken for the purchase of the Academy back of the Presbyterian Church, for the purpose of opening a Presbyterian School for girls. There was a great deal of local opposition to a denominational school, but school did open in the fall of 1849. The Board advertises in the Alabama Reporter, issue of Sept. 12, 1850, that the "Presbyterian Collegiate Female Institute will open Nov. 4," (1850). "The new building now in course of erection will be ready for use at or near the opening of the approaching season. The Institution will then contain a chapel 70 x 35 ft., three spacious school rooms, 2 music rooms, a Library, and a large lecture room for experimental purposes.

During the last session, the institution has been furnished with two elegant pianos, a serephina and a guitar."[14] Rev. James Hoyt, A. M. Principal, Mrs. Sarah White and Miss Elizabeth Riddle, Assistants, Mrs. Frances Hoyt, Teacher of Music.

---

[12] History of Methodism in Ala., by Dr. Anson West, pub. 1893, Page 730
[13] Ibid.
[14] Paper found in J. A. Bingham's Scrap Book collection.

Rates and Tuition, per season of five months:

Preparatory Course	$10.00
First year of Regular Course	15.00
Remainder of Course (Except Languages)	25.00
Remainder of Course with Languages	25.00
(French, Italian, Latin and Greek)	
Music on the Piano or Guitar	20.00
Use of Piano for practice	5.00
Use of Guitar for practice	2.00

Signed by A. G. Storey, Treas.

Directors: L. E. Parsons, A. Cunningham, Alexander White, H. A. Rutledge, Wm. B. McClellan and James Isbell.

The "Board of Instruction" for 1852 was made up of John Wilson, A. M., Principal; Mrs. Sarah White, Miss Sarah Elizabeth Riddle, and Mrs. Wilson was listed as head of the "Ornamental Department", with Miss Florida Taul as Asst. in Music. The teacher of music was to be elected later.

For the year 1855 Prof. Frederick R. Lord, was made Principal; Mrs. Sarah White, Miss Mary Shepperson, Assts.; Prof. Thomas R. Watts was Principal of the Music Dept., and Miss Juliet White was his assistant. The graduates listed for the first four years were:

1851—Miss Darthula M. Bradford, Talladega and Miss Lucy Ann Dufries, Talladega.

1852—Miss Clara J. Crutchfield, Talladega; Miss Mary E. M. Gamble, Chattooga Co., Georgia; Miss Frances H. Woodward, Benton County.

1853—Miss Margaret E. Cobb, Benton County; Miss Mary Isbella Hardie, Talladega County; Miss Eliza D. Hall, Coosa County and Miss Sarah A. E. McAlpine, Coosa County.

1854—Miss Francina R. Bradford, Talladega; Miss Esther A. Hemphill, Choctaw Mission; Miss Louisa McKenzie, Talladega; Miss Mary V. Spiva, Wilcox County; Miss Margaret A. Walker, Dallas County; Miss Juliet White, Talladega; and Miss Mary Ann Leonard, Coosa County.

The Institute of 1850 not only had a Board of Directors, but also a Board of Visitors, which usually was composed of prominent men of the community in which the school was located, and out of town patrons of the school. The special duty of this Board was to attend the commencement exercises, which usually lasted from three to four days, during which oral examinations took place in their presence. It was their privilege to personally ask questions, and examine the pupils, if they deemed it necessary, or proper. A written report of their findings usually followed, addressed to the Board of Directors, who also exercised the right and privilege to examine each pupil.

For years, a 30 to 32 page catalogue was published and distributed, and these old catalogues are most revealing, as to the nature of the early Academy or Institute.

A catalogue issued August 22nd, 1851, lists 93 pupils, 49 of whom were from the town of Talladega, 11 from Talladega County, and the remaining 33 from 13 Alabama Counties, and several from Georgia and Tennessee.[15] Among the interesting items included in the catalogue were:

BOARD: "Pupils from a distance can obtain board, with washing, fuel, lights, etc., in families for $10 per month. Talladega being surrounded by a grain producing country, provisions and board are considerably cheaper than in the lower section of the State."

SESSIONS AND VACATIONS: "The scholastic year is divided into Winter and Summer Sessions. The next Winter Session will commence on Monday, the 6th of October, and close on Friday, the 27th of February. The Summer Session will commence on Monday, the 8th of March, and close on Friday, the 30th of July. This arrangement gives a vacation of one week in the spring, and one of two months in August and September. A short respite from study is also given during the Christmas holidays.

The last four days of each Session will be employed in a public examination, which will be accompanied, at the end of the Summer Session, with a Concert of vocal and instrumental music, and an Anniversary Address."

"N.B.—The Public Examination, at the close of the present year, will commence on Tuesday, the 19th of August, and terminate on Friday, the 22nd. An Anniversary Address is expected from Rev. S. K. Talmadge, President of Oglethorpe University."

"During the Winter Session, the exercises of the Institution will commence at 8 o'clock A. M., and close at 4 P. M. During the Summer Session, they will commence at 8 A. M., and close at 4 P. M. A recess will be taken in the winter from 12 to 1, and in the summer from 12 to 2 o'clock."

Under rules of ORDER, No. 12—"No pupil will be allowed to encumber her desk with articles foreign to the business of the school room. NO. 13 - The use of all articles of food, fruit, confectionary, snuff, etc., during study hours, is strictly prohibited."

HOURS OF STUDY "Except in the Preparatory Course: all pupils are required to devote two hours daily to study at their homes, or boarding places.

---

[15] Catalogue owned by Miss Alice McMillan

Parents, and those who have pupils boarding with them, are earnestly solicited to see that this regulation is complied with."

CHURCH ATTENDANCE "All the pupils of the Institution are expected to attend public worship, when practicable, at least once on the Sabbath, following their preferences as to the place of attendance; also, to be connected with a Sabbath-school in some one of the churches."

"REMARK: Public worship is held in the Presbyterian church only two Sabbaths in the month, and on those Sabbaths there is also preaching in some one of the other churches of the village. Hence, the above regulation, while it never operates so as to require the pupils to attend the Presbyterian church, it does require them to attend other churches two Sabbaths in each month.

"The Directors feel justified in thus calling attention to this regulation, as their enterprise has from the first encountered a strong prejudice on account of its denominational character. They also feel justified in stating further, that themselves, their families, and the teachers of the Institute, are in the habit of attending worship regularly at other churches when there is no preaching at their own. They esteem it a duty as well as a privilege thus to honor the sanctuary. And without intending to claim for themselves an undue measure of Christian charity, they cannot refrain from asking, whether the respect which they and the pupils of their Institution have thus uniformly shown to other churches, has been reciprocated? The inquiry is not prompted by any censorious feeling. All they desire is, that their friends in other religious connections will have the candor to do them justice."

During the War Between the States the school was evidently used as a private school. Miss Annie Chapman taught there in 1863. In 1868 it appears as The Talladega Institute School with J. H. Logan, Principal. In 1869 as "Talladega Collegiate Institute", for male and female, opening Sept. 6, 1869 for a season of five months with charges: Collegiate Dept. $25.00; Intermediate Dept. $20.00; Primary Dept. $15.00; Music on Piano $20.00, and contingent fee of $1.00. This contingent fee was to take care of heat in the school room. Children of clergymen were invited at half the usual rate.

Rev. A. D. McAdory, was listed as Principal,
J. H. Logan, A. M., Asst. Principal,
Miss Mollie Henderson, Principal of the Intermediate Female Dept.
Miss Mary Clisby, Asst. Do
Miss Emma Ornberg, Principal of the Music Dept.
Mrs. Mary Venable, Principal of the Primary Dept.

Signed by J. C. Knox, Pres. of the Board and M. H. Cruikshank, Sec.[16]

In 1873 the name appears as the "Synodical Female Institute", with A. H. Todd, Principal; Miss Lydia Borden, Asst. Principal; and Miss Elizabeth J. Seeley, Music and French.[17]

Miss Lake Sullivan was Principal of "Isbell Female College" in 1889. In 1891 the name appears as "Isbell College for Young Ladies". "New buildings with all modem improvements, Calisthenics, Music, Art Studies, High Standard, Thorough Christian Training. The Bible a Text Book", was advertised, with Board and Tuition $190.00 per annum. Rev. P. P. Winn, A. M. President; Dr. B. W. Toole, Pres. of the Board of Control.[18]

The Synod of Alabama eventually purchased the property and operated it under the name of "Alabama Synodical College for Women." A new building was erected in the Highlands, and was operated for some years unsuccessfully, and finally abandoned. After being vacant for several years, the building was sold to citizens of Talladega in 1925 for a hospital, and it is at present used for this purpose. The Presbyterians operated for nearly 75 years, outliving the other denominational schools by 70 years.

THE BAPTIST MALE HIGH SCHOOL

At a meeting of the Coosa River Baptist Association, in session at Mt. Zion Church, located in Alexandria, Benton (Calhoun) County, Sept. 20, 1851, the Committee of Education, with J. L. M. Curry, Chairman, made the following recommendation:

"This portion of East Alabama has facilities for female education, not surpassed probably, by any in the State. Your Committee believe, that as a fit accompaniment there should be an institution of a high order for the proper education of males. They, therefore, unanimously recommend to the Association the adoption of the following Resolutions:

Resolved that this Association recommend the erection of a Baptist Male High School to be located at Talladega.

. . . That Brethren Walker Reynolds, Wm. Curry, Oliver Welch, S. G. Jenkins, Rufus M. Mynatt, J. M. Crook, George Hill, James Headen, W. W. Mattison, H. E. Taliaferro and J. L. M. Curry, be requested to act as a Board of

---

[16] Paper found in J. A. Bingham's Scrap Book collection – Our Mt. Home, Sept. 14, 1860
[17] Paper found in J. A. Bingham's Scrap Book collection – The Talladega Watchtower, Nov. 5, 1872
[18] Paper found in J. A. Bingham's Scrap Book collection – The Advance, June 29, 1886

Directors for the ensuing year."[19] The Association approved the project, and appropriated $3,000.00 toward it.

Public subscriptions were solicited, and the building begun in 1853. The minutes show in 1854 that Prof. John Wilmer was Superintendent, Assisted by W. S. Jeffries, a graduate of the University of Alabama.

The minutes of 1856 include the Fourth Annual Report, which opened Sept. 7, 1855, in the new building with Prof. John Wilmer, Prin., assisted by D. C. Williams. In 1857 R. P. Latham, "a graduate of the University of Va.," was Principal, and in 1860 A. S. Worrell, Principal, with T. W. Davis, Asst.

Rev. Oliver Welch, who was born in Virginia in 1791, and died in Talladega County in 1874, came to Talladega in 1834. He was pastor of the first organized Baptist church established in Talladega County for 32 years. It was originally called "Talladega Baptist Church", but was moved to Alpine soon after the War Between the States and the name changed to that of "Alpine Baptist Church". Mr. Welch served without remuneration, and was instrumental in aiding in establishing several other Baptist churches over the county. He also served as one of the trustees of the Baptist High School during the years of its operation.

Mr. Welch, like so many other planters of that day, kept a journal. From his journal we have a fuller description of the preliminaries toward the erection of the Baptist Male High School, as follows:[20]

Oct. 6, 1851—We had a meeting of the managers of the High School adopted by the Association. Elected Bro. Headen President of the Board, and Bro. J. A. Curry, Secretary, besides talking a great deal on the best method of carrying out this great object.

Jan. 10, 1852 —Went to Talladega meeting - pretty day. Bro. Jabe Curry was with us. He presented the Baptist High School for our consideration. I subscribed $1,000.00, Mr. Walker Reynolds - $2,000.00

Sept. 18, 1852—Early put off for Talladega. The Association then organized by electing Bro. Collins Moderator. The most important business during the meeting was a new impulse given to our High School. There was $3,500.00 subscribed, which, added to the former subscription, make $14,000.00. We thanked God and took fresh courage. Met at night at Mr. Reynolds' and organized a new Board, though the old one was continued. Appointed four agents. Hope to succeed.

---

[19] Coosa River Baptist Association Minutes, found in the Tall. Public Library
[20] From Gordon T. Welch, grandson of Nathaniel Welch

Dec. 6, 1852—Today our School Board met, and counting up we find we have $21,000.00 subscribed. We feel much encouraged. Today we are comparing books.

Dec. 30, 1852—Went to Talladega to meet the Board of Trustees on our High School. We closed the subscription of $25,000.00.

May 9, 1853—Went today to Talladega. School Board met. Let out the brick work at $8.00 per thousand. Engaged the lumber at $8.40 per thousand feet delivered in good order.

June 20, 1854—Went to Talladega to School meeting. Bro. Wilmer was elected Principal of the Baptist Male High School.

In 1861 A. W. Poindexter was Principal, and G. A. Woodward, Assistant.[21] In 1864 W. D. Lovett was Principal.

War was declared. No funds were available. The building was mortgaged, and eventually sold to the American Missionary Association, which founded Talladega College for Negroes in 1867.

This building stands on a hill at the extreme west end of North Street, and is one of the most imposing buildings ever erected in Talladega. During the latter part of the Civil War it was used as a prison for federal soldiers. In 1865 Federal General Wager Swayne was placed at the head of the Alabama Freedman's Bureau, and he used the building for about a year as a school for freed Negroes, until he aroused the interest of the American Missionary Association. In Gen. Swayne's honor the building was named Swayne Hall, and for years was used as the Administration building of Talladega College.

It is interesting to note here under the heading of Baptist Schools, that Howard State College was born in November, 1841, in Talladega, at a Baptist State Convention.[22] A charter was granted by the State on Dec. 29, 1841.

FOREST HILL SEMINARY
For Girls only

This school was established in 1846 and was located "on the branch at the West end of South St." with Prof. C. P. Samuel, (A northern man) Principal. Miss Annie Chapman, Asst. Principal; Miss Minnie C. Lornard, Instructor of Music; Miss Bettie Samuel, Asst. Instructor of Music; Miss Martha Lawson, Principal of the Ornamental Dept.[23] It was not incorporated until Feb. 5, 1858.

---

[21] Alabama Reporter, November 17, 1865
[22] J. L. M. Curry, Reminiscences, published in Ala. Historical Quarterly. Also found in Scrap Book of J. A. Bingham
[23] Alabama Reporter Spt. 3, 1863. Tall. Public Library

SOUTHWOOD SELECT SCHOOL
For Boys

This was located on the west side of East St. S., on the hill which is still known as Southwood. It is now a residential portion of Talladega.

It was taught by W. W. Wilson, Principal, in 1863, whose pupils were said to be the best behaved boys in town.[24] It was taught in the 1880's by William and Sumter Bethea.

During the War Between the States everything was demoralized; many of the male teachers had to go to war, money was scarce, and many regular schools ceased operations. Private schools were the order of the day, and we find many of them advertised. Miss M. C. McAlpine advertised a school in the "Presbyterian Chapel" and again in the "Talladega Presbyterian Institute.[25]

Sallie McGhee advertised a school in the "Presbyterian Female Institute" in 1864.

Miss Mattie Stephenson advertised a school "in the Methodist Church Basement" during the years 1864 and 1865.

F. R. Lord taught a "Select School for Boys" sometime during the war which was probably the old Southwood Select School for Boys.

SPECIAL SCHOOLS.

"INFANT SCHOOL" — "Mrs. Mitchell respectfully informs the citizens of Talladega and its vicinity, that she will open a school for Infants and Children, both Male and Female. Boys under eight years.

She flatters herself that, although among strangers, yet having had considerable experience in the arduous."[26] This advertisement appeared in 1847. She does not limit the age of the females.

MUSIC SCHOOL — Advertisements appear in papers during 1842 and 1843 of this school operated by "Walker & Glazener."

After the War Between the States, many other private schools appeared. It would be impossible to record an accurate list at this late date. However, the Parish School, located where the present First Baptist Church plant now stands, was an outstanding male school in the 1870's. The Parishes boarded the out of town pupils in their own home, and in a four room dormitory, which stood west of the ante-bellum home on McConnell St. This

---

[24] History of Talladega by J. W. Vandiver, Chapter 23
[25] Alabama Reporter, Sept. 8, 1864. Tall. Public Library
[26] Alabama Reporter, Aug. 12, 1847 – Dept. of Archives & History, Montgomery

school was also taught by Messrs. Lyman and A. H. Todd, and later by the Wrights, who called it the "Talladega Military Academy", and the boys were required to wear uniforms and to drill.

The Fourth District Agricultural School & Experiment Station, established about 1895, and operated in Sylacauga for many years, was one of the County's Progressive educational acquisitions.

NORTH SIDE PUBLIC SCHOOL

The greatest movement toward educational progress in Talladega, was that of embracing the Public School System in 1886.

Until a school building could be erected, the girls and boys were taught separately. The Trustees of the Isbell College for Women offered space for teaching the girls; and the boys were taught in an old building located in the block between East and Percy St., Broom St. and Brignoli Sts. Geo. E. Brewer was the first Public School Superintendent.

The following is a list of the young women who were teachers the first year under the public school system:

Miss Ida Wallis (Mrs. I. W. Elliott)
Miss Eppie Stamps (Mrs. Pittinger)
Miss Emma Thornton (Mrs. A. T. Calhoun)
Miss Ida Houston (Mrs. J. W. Rogers)
Miss Miriam West (Daughter of Dr. Anson
West, Methodist Minister)
Miss Clara Cruikshank
Miss Rosa Miller (Mrs. Sam Earl Green)
Miss Nellie Toole (Mrs. A. G. Storey),Music Teacher.

Superintendents who have served the public schools of the City of Talladega are in order as follows:

George E. Brewer
Joseph B. Graham
W. W. Seales
J. E. Strickland
————— Bross
Howard Griggs
John D. McNeel
Daniel A. McNeill
Omar Carmichael

J. A. Baxley
Judson Sneed
J. A. Copeland
F. L. Harwell

The North Side Public School building was erected in 1856, when Wm. H. Skaggs was mayor. C. Wallis was contractor. When the building was completed, the property was valued at $16,000.00. The issuing of bonds amounting to $12,000.00 for the purpose of paying for this building probably brought forth more controversy and opposition by the citizens than any other movement ever launched in the town.

Our Mountain Home of Sept. 18, 1889, stated that school opened on Sept. 16th with 180 pupils under the following teachers:

First Grade	Miss Clara Cruikshank
Second Grade	Miss Emma Thomton
Third Grade	Miss Sallie McCorkle
Fourth Grade	Miss Fronie Oliver
Fifth Grade	Miss Vivian May
Sixth Grade and Asst. High Teacher	J.C. Levengood, from Indiana
Supt. and High School	J.B. Graham

In September, 1892, the Superintendent proudly announced that school opened with 190 pupils, 50 of whom were in the High School. At that time the High School was composed of the Seventh, Eighth and Ninth Grades. This was the only public school building in Talladega until the Twentieth Century.

Around the North Side School are centered many pleasant memories of those who attended in the Nineteenth Century. The planting and naming of the trees on Arbor Day in 1894 was a great event

The Skaggs Literary Society, composed of High School pupils, met at 1:00 on Friday afternoons, when all books were laid aside for the week. Pupils learned the art of "declaiming", and debated the weighty subjects of the ages, such as "Resolved that Hamlet was Insane," "Resolved that a House Burns Down," and other timeless subjects. Talents were developed during those days of feeble effort.

GRAHAM SCHOOL No. 1, named in honor of Joseph B. Graham, for many years Superintendent of the City School, was erected in 1904 for small children. The school overflowed, and in 1939 GRAHAM SCHOOL NO. 2 was erected.

TALLADEGA HIGH SCHOOL was built in 1924-25 on the old Shelley-Moore-Johnson homestead property, which was donated to the city for this purpose by Mrs. Lou McElderry Jemison. Additions have been made over the years as needs presented themselves.

CENTRAL SCHOOL building was erected in 1925 on property purchased from the McMillan estate. The lot had served as the McMillan garden and orchard since the building of the home about 1845. The school building was erected by the city for the purpose of taking care of the great volume of grammar school children.

JEMISON DOMESTIC SCIENCE COTTAGE, named in honor of Mrs. Lou McElderry Jemison, who gave the cottage to the city, was erected in 1930.

DIXON JUNIOR HIGH SCHOOL building, named in honor of Mr. J. Kelly Dixon, prominent lawyer, and for many years chairman of the City Board of Education, was erected in 1942-43. The auditorium in this building has proven a great asset to Talladega.

MARY HICKS DUMAS STADIUM, erected in 1928-29, was named in honor of Mrs. W. L. Dumas, who was a prominent and beloved member of the City Board of Education for many years.

NEGRO SCHOOLS

Prior to the War Between the States, Negroes were taught privately by owners of slaves, when taught at all. There was a free primary school for Negroes immediately following the war, located on the same lot with Mt. Zion Baptist Church. Mrs. C. M. Hopson was principal. She was a respected white woman from one of the New England States. She had several white assistants. Her husband was "Reconstruction" Postmaster at the time.

THE PEABODY SCHOOL FOR NEGROES existed for some years following the war, with Dr. J. M. Brown as instructor. This school was a teacher training school.

TALLADEGA COLLEGE has been one of the outstanding Negro colleges in Alabama since it came into being. It was established in 1867, though Swayne Hall had been used for the purpose of teaching Freedmen prior to the purchase of it by the American Missionary Association. Talladega College has operated throughout the years since, and has produced many graduates, many having entered Yale and Harvard Universities. A number of the students enter the business world, and are a credit to the institution.

The old Baptist High School, now called Swayne Hall in honor a of General Wager Swayne, Chairman of the Freedman's Bureau of Alabama after the war, was the only building for several years, but the plant has grown steadily as the student body increased.

Savery Library would be a credit to any university system. De Forest Chapel, for years, had the finest pipe organ in the county. This chapel was named in honor of Dr. Henry S. de Forest, one of the beloved presidents, and the father of Dr. Lee de Forest, Inventor.

In 1939 the General Education Board of the American Missionary Association and 800 other donors replaced the first library with an imposing structure known as the Savery Library. In the main lobby of this building are two tablets, in memory of the faith and far-sightedness of the man for whom the library is named and of the founders of Talladega College.

These tablets bear the following inscriptions:
This building named in honor of
WILLIAM SAVERY

1852 – A carpenter, in bondage, he labored to build old Swayne Hall.
1865 – A Freedman, with others, he organized the first school for negroes in this county.
1867 – A man of faith, he led the Freedmen's Bureau and the American Missionary Association in the purchase of old Swayne and the founding of Talladega College.
1869 – An incorporator and original trustee of the college he builded well for the generations to come. "His Book of Toil is Read."

IN MEMORY OF THE FOUNDERS
in 1865,

THOMAS TARRANT AND WILLIAM SAVERY,
returning from a Freedmen's Convention
at Mobile, organized a school, in the
home of David White, supported by a
Society of Freedmen headed by
HARRY KNOX. the school was soon
located in a building erected near the
Isbell Branch not far from the this present
site. Two years later it was merged in
the college founded by the American
Missionary Society to provide
Education, "From which no one shall be
debarred on account of race or color."

"Their Works Do Follow Them."

Talladega College is a great instrument in elevating the Negro race to a higher cultural level.

The first teachers at Swayne Hall were:[27]
Rev. Henry E. Brown, Oberlin, Ohio
W. M. P. Gilbert, New England
Mrs. H. E. Brown, Oberlin, Ohio
Miss Phebe Beebe, Tipton, Michigan
Miss Sophia Tyler, Chagrin Falls, Ohio
Miss Josephine Pierce, Tallmadge, Ohio

Executives:
Rev. H. E. Brown 1867-70
Albert A. Safford 1870-76
Rev. Edward P. Lord 1876-78
Dr. Henry S. DeForest 1879-96
Rev. Geo. W. Andrews 1896-1904
Rev. Benjamin Nyce 1904-1908
Rev. John Metcalf 1908-1916
Rev. Frederick B. Sumner 1916-1933
Dr. B. G. Gallagher 1933-43
Dean J. T. Cater 1943-45
Dr. A. D. Beittel 1945-52
Dr. A. D. Gray 1953-

WESTSIDE JUNIOR HIGH SCHOOL building was erected in 1930.
EASTSIDE ELEMENTARY HIGH SCHOOL building was erected in 1947-48.
WESTSIDE SENIOR HIGH SCHOOL building was erected in 1947-48.
There are many interesting facts revolving around the progress of the City and County Schools, which should inspire some person to write an entire volume regarding them.

---

[27] Information from Miss Margaret L. Montgomery, Teacher at the Talladega College

RURAL SCHOOLS

MARBLE SPRINGS ACADEMY [28] was the first to be authorized by the State. It probably existed before the date of authorization, which was Jan. 30, 1839. It was taught by Wm. L. Lewis, and later by D. W. Finn, and others, and was located on the Eastaboga Road, between bridges spanning Cheaha and Choccolocco Creeks, near the old Marble Springs Presbyterian Church. It was attended by children of the Bowie, Montgomery, Best, McClellan, Jemison, Curry, Carter, Groce, English, McElheny, Kirksey, Cunningham, Jackson, and other families of that neighborhood.

MARDISVILLE MALE ACADEMY was one of the earliest schools in the county, and was no doubt established in 1834. In 1840 R. C. Smith was Principal, and in 1848 Wm. A. Stewart was Principal. D. W. Finn and his brother both taught there at some time.

MARDISVILLE FEMALE ACADEMY FOR YOUNG LADIES was probably founded at the same time as that of the Male Academy. In an Alabama Reporter or July 20, 1848, it is advertised with Mrs. S. White, as Principal, and Mr. Norman as Teacher of Music.

WEOWOKAVILLE MALE AND FEMALE ACADEMY was in existence as early as 1843. In 1848 D. W. Finn was Principal and Simon Morris, James Mallory and George Riser, were Trustees.

EASTABOGA ACADEMY[29] was in existence as early as 1848, and in 1852 an advertisement lists Lemuel M. Sparrow, Principal, and Thomas E. Sparrow, Assistant. The Academy was incorporated for business reasons in 1858, from which time minutes were kept of the meetings of the Trustees. Because these are the only minutes of an early academy to which I have had access, it is well to note some of the Articles of incorporation, since these stipulations were the usual ones of that period.

"AN ACT INCORPORATING EASTABOGA ACADEMY IN TALLADEGA COUNTY: "Be it enacted by the Senate and House of Representatives in General Assembly convened That

"James Montgomery, D. H. Jackson, C. G. Cunningham, Isaac Kirksey, William Montgomery and J. E. Groce, of the County, and their successors in office are hereby constituted and declared a body corporate, by the name and style of the Trustees of Eastaboga Academy," etc.

They were authorized to "receive donations, purchase, possess and hold property."

---

[28] Ala. Acts., Page 52, No. 56

[29] Ala. Acts, Page 192, No. 132, Minute Book in possession of Mrs. Margaret Montgomery Callaway (A. S.), Hogansville, Ga., youngest daughter of A. Montgomery, Eastaboga.

Sec. 2 "Be it further enacted, that it shall not be lawful for any person to sell spirituous or vinous liquors within a mile in any direction of said Academy, and if any person shall sell spirituous or vinous liquors contrary to the provisions of this Act, such person shall be subject to indictment and on conviction, may be fined not less than one hundred and not more than five hundred dollars for each offence." In 1861 payments were made to the following teachers: Samuel Hall, Miss M. Londie, Miss M. Weatherly, Miss Ann McCain and F. R. Lord. James E. Hogan, Mr. Gooch and Miss Stewart are listed as teachers in 1865. For some years after the war, Alonza Montgomery was Principal.

J. E. Groce served as President of the Board of Trustees, and Wm. Montgomery, as Secretary for 25 years.

FAYETTEVILLE MALE & FEMALE ACADEMY was perhaps one of the early rural schools, since "Cedar Creek" was settled earlier than the county seat by a cultured group of people. The Academy was incorporated Feb. 8, 1859. In 1863 they advertised that the Rev. James McLean was Principal.[30]

THE MIDWAY HIGH SCHOOL OF MUNFORD was one of the outstanding schools of the county. Boarding pupils came from Elyton, Talladega, Jacksonville, and from many other towns for a "classical education." Mr. Dobson and Mr. McDonald, famous educators of that period, taught there. Rev. T. J. Gooch was Principal during the war. He advertised that it was "one of the most healthy localities in Alabama." This school was one of a few in the county which continued to operate during the war.

PLANTERS INSTITUTE[31] was established around 1850 by Isaac Stone, J. S. Swain and Sandy Morris, and was supported by many wealthy planters of the surrounding neighborhood. It was incorporated Feb. 9, 1860. It was both an Elementary and High School. Many older children boarded in the village to attend the High School. Noted educators taught there, among them, Messrs. James Barber, of Connecticut in 1872, A. H. Todd, Lyman and Rev. T. A. Cook.

LINCOLN MALE & FEMALE ACADEMY was in full swing in 1860, with Rev. L. Law, Principal, Mrs. M. A. Law, Assistant, and Miss M. A. Christian, Teacher of Music.

BLUE EYE SCHOOL advertised in 1863 "with all Departments open for pupils" with Thomas J. Elrod, Principal.[32]

---

[30] Alabama Reporter, Nov. 5, 1863. Tall. Public Library. Ala. Acts, Page 83, No. 93.
[31] Article by Miss Edna Todd, daughter of A. H. Todd, in my possession. Ala. Acts, Page 337, No. 245. Talladega News, July 2, 1872
[32] Alabama Reporter, Nov. 5, 1863. Tall. Public Library

SILVER RUN SCHOOL was advertised in 1865 with Thomas Elrod, Principal.[33]

LINEVILLE MALE & FEMALE ACADEMY was authorized by the State Feb. 9, 1860. Where this was located, I do not know, since Clay County did not exist until 1866. The school was evidently located on the County line in some direction.

UNION SEMINARY was advertised in 1865, with Rufus Albright, Principal, with Rev. W. Horton and John Usery, Assistants.[34]

There were, of course, many other excellent schools in various localities, about which I have no information. Certainly there were early schools and academies located at Sylacauga, Childersburg, and in the Hillabee district, which was in Talladega County until 1866. Newspaper advertisements and state records are my sources of information for the group listed.

It would be interesting to follow the rural school system up to the present, since Talladega County has made wonderful progress but the modem school advancement would easily fill a complete volume.

ALABAMA INSTITUTIONS
SCHOOL FOR THE DEAF

An appropriation was made in 1852 by the General Assembly of Alabama, to provide for the education of the "indigent deaf mutes of the State." A school was started at Robinson Springs, Autauga County, but was an unsuccessful effort, and soon closed.[35]

"Each succeeding Legislature re-enacted the appropriation, but without practical result until the year 1858."[36] Dr. Jo. H. Johnson, of Georgia, was employed to open the school at Auburn in the spring of 1858, but the building selected was found unadaptable for this purpose, and the school was opened in October, 1858, in Talladega. Dr. Johnson was a Methodist, and was, no doubt, familiar with the financial condition of the M. E. Conference School located in Talladega, and was probably fully responsible for having acquired the Talladega Conference Institute building for the State, to be used for the purpose of teaching the "deaf, dumb and blind." The building was turned over to the State and "twenty two were admitted the first year, fourteen of whom were beneficiaries of the State."[37] Later the State purchased the building.

[33] Alabama Reporter, Sept. 8, 1864. Tall. Public Library
[34] Alabama Reporter, Nov. 17, 1865. Tall. Public Library
[35] Information from Miss Margaret L. Montgomery, Teacher at the Talladega College
[36] Memorial Records of Alabama, Vol. I, Page 178
[37] Ibid

The Institution was hardly established when war was declared, and Dr. Johnson, as Captain, left temporarily, in 1861, to organize Company G of the First Alabama Infantry. In a short while he received an injury which brought him back to Talladega, and he resumed his institutional work.[38]

In the Tenth Annual report to the Governor, for the year 1868-69, Dr. Johnson stated that there were 13 acres in the lot and that they owned 80 acres of woodland four miles out. He further stated "The main building is one of the best in the State, built of dark colored pressed brick. It is one hundred and two feet long by fifty-four wide, containing 21 large rooms, all of them well plastered, lighted and ventilated except two on the 4th floor."[39] The expenditures for the school year 1868-69, including salaries, provisions, etc., were $9,941.19. The Board of Commissioners were:

"Hon. M. H. Cruikshank, President,
Dr. Wm. Taylor,
Geo. S. Walden, Esq.,
A. G. Storey,
N. B. Cloud, M. D.
Jo. H. Johnson, Sec."
Faculty of the Institution:
"Jo. H. Johnson, Principal,
Mr. Reuben A. Asbury, Instructor of the Blind,
Mrs. E. A. Johnson, Teacher of the Deaf and Dumb,
Mr. John A. Hoge, Teacher of the Deaf and Dumb,
Mrs. C. B. Asbury, Matron,
Mrs. Frances Simmons, Housekeeper."

The pupils were listed by name and residence, showing 25 Deaf and 10 Blind.

Dr. Johnson was a splendid physician, and practiced his profession, but his heart was in this institution, and he and his family gave their lives to the work. Dr. Johnson; his wife; his brother, Seaborn, a mute; his son J. H. Johnson, Jr.; his son Seaborn, and his daughter Miss Annie, all were teachers in the school at some time. The Deaf and Blind were taught together until the year 1866, when they were separated in classes. However, not until 1887 was adequate provision made for complete separation of the pupils. At this time a building was erected for the Blind.

---

[38] Memorial Records of Alabama, Vol. II, Page 968
[39] State Documents, Report of the Board of Commissioners and Officers of the Ala. Institution for the Education of the Deaf, Dumb and Blind, 1869-70

SCHOOL FOR THE BLIND

A separate department for the Blind, as stated, was established in 1866, when Mr. Reuben A. Asbury, from Cave Spring, Ga., was employed to teach them.

In 1887 several acres of land were purchased in Moor's Field at the extreme end of South Street, and a building was erected to house and teach the blind, with J. H. Johnson, Jr., as Principal. This building stands in the center of a large group of buildings erected later. The school for the Blind has always been operated under the same superintendent as that of the School for the Deaf.

NEGRO SCHOOL FOR DEAF AND BLIND

The opening of a school for negro deaf and blind children was an experiment, and the appropriation was small. Hence, the deaf and blind pupils lived and were taught in the same plant.

Property was acquired about a mile out of town on the old Chandlers Springs Road and a building was erected in 1891. J. S. Graves was made Principal, and held the position until he died in 1923.

Several years ago a completely new plant, with several buildings, was erected on the Sylacauga Highway, for the purpose of teaching the Negro deaf. The old buildings were renovated, and used exclusively for the Blind. The new school for the Negro deaf is modern in every respect.

DOWLING HOSPITAL

The hospital was erected in 1938 on the campus of School for the Deaf and takes care of all patients among the pupils under the care of two registered nurses. It is called "Dowling Hospital," in honor of Dr. H. G. Dowling. Dr. J. S. Ganey has written a full history of buildings, superintendents, and complete list of teachers, in his "Historical Sketch of the Alabama Institute for Deaf and Blind," published in 1942,[40] which is accessible in Talladega Public Library to those interested in a more detailed history of the State institutions for the Deaf and Blind.

Superintendents of the Institutions follow in order:

---

[40] Sketch printed, 1942, Tall. Public Library

Dr. Jo. H. Johnson	1858-93
J. H. Johnson, Jr	1893-1913
F. H. Manning	1913-1929
Dr. Dan A. McNeill	1929-33
Judge S. C. Oliver	1933
Judge D. H. Riddle	1933-38
Dr. J. S. Ganey	1938-1946
Dr. H. G. Dowling	1946-1948
Dr. J. H. Bryant	1948-1955
E. A. McBride	1956-

Early Lawyers([1])

It is almost impossible to believe that another small group of people, in any part of America, ever included so many distinguished lawyers as were among the early settlers of Talladega. It is true that a majority were quite young and became prominent after leaving Talladega, and it is also true that some had attained prominence prior to their residence in Talladega. But the fact remains that this intellectual personnel was at one time a part of Talladega.

Talladega was the focal point around which revolved the business transactions of the Coosa Land District. Hence, lawyers drifted with the crowds where fees could be easily earned.

Prior to 1832, before the signing of the Creek Treaty, this portion of the state was under the jurisdiction of the Autauga County Civil and Criminal Courts. It was later placed in the Third Circuit and Judge Horatio Perry held the first Circuit Court on Talladega Battle Ground" in March of 1833.[2]

Pioneer attorneys did not have an easy time defending clients. Because of the shortage of jail facilities, and the expense of transporting and boarding offenders of the law, punishment was quickly meted, rather than confinement in jail. In December, 1833, in the case of one Ruffin Curtis, the expense of guarding and transporting to Montgomery, where criminals were kept until trial, amounted to $146.12½ in a few days.[3] Be it recalled that Talladega County had no reserve fund at the time. Therefore, a speedy punishment was in order. A murderer in the first degree had little chance of repeal. He was hung at once. Sti-a-se-gee, alias Pow-as-see E-mer-the-ler, better known as "Indian Davy", killed Henry Bell in 1834, and became the first to receive capital punishment in Talladega County. He was hung on the edge of town, on North Street between the Baptist Church and the A. G. Storey home on Friday, Dec. 4th, 1834. The exact spot is debated. He was buried near the L. & N. Railroad tank, between that and North Street. For many years children and colored people were afraid to venture near the spot after dark.[4]

---

[1] Where references are not specifically noted, biography can be found in either Memorial Records of Alabama, Vols. I and II; Thomas M. Owens History of Ala. and Dic. Of Biography, Vol. III and IV; Notable Men of Alabama, edited by Hon. Joel C. DuBose; Reminiscences of Public Men of Alabama, by Wm. Garrett; History of Alabama, by Brewer; or in Reminiscences of J. L. M. Curry, at the Talladega Public Library.

[2] Thomas M. Owens His. of Ala. and Dic. of Biography, Vol. I, Page 429. Also Acts of Ala. 1826-29

[3] County Commissioners Court Record, Page 10

[4] Sketch of Talladega, by Frank Willis Barnett, without date, in my Scrap Book

One of the first interesting cases to come before the Court was that of Fanny Chinnabee, wife of the famous General Chinnabee, in the fall of 1333. She asked the Court to allow her dower in her husband's lands. The Judge held that Chinnabee never owned the lands, and she lost her case. The Commissioners Court of Reviews and Roads, and the Orphans Court, were presided over by the Judge of the County Court, and all major business matters and problems of the County were transacted through these Courts. The Probate Court was not created until 1850. A. J. Cotton became the first Probate Judge.

There were no law schools in Alabama until 1872, although unsuccessful efforts had been made to establish one at the University of Alabama as early as 1845.[5] Law was "read" in the offices of lawyers who had already been admitted to the Bar. Talladega had, as previously stated, a great number of eminent lawyers. Among the early students were Alexander White, John T. Morgan, Charles Pelham, James Benson Martin, Samuel King McSpadden, J. L. M. Curry and many others.

The first general assembly of the Talladega Bar seems to have been on Tuesday, Nov. 15th, 1836, when it met to pay tribute and to pass resolutions on the death of Samuel W. Mardis.

It is regretted that we have no accurate list of the earliest group who practiced their profession in Talladega. Perhaps the best method of arriving at the important part some of them played in county, state and national affairs, is through a short sketch of those who shared in this professional field.

GREEN TALIAFERRO MCAFEE, Teacher, merchant and lawyer was legislator from St. Clair County in 1832, and drew up the bill establishing the nine counties from the Creek Country. He became first Talladega County Judge. He served in many other official capacities.

JOHN WHITE came to Talladega County in 1832. He was the father of Alexander White, and of the wife of Joseph G. Baldwin, author of "Flush Times of Alabama and Mississippi". Before coming to Talladega John White served as Judge of the Circuit Court in North Alabama. He practiced law ten years in Talladega. He settled at Berney's (Alex Autrey home), where he died in 1842 and is buried there in a secluded spot. Judge White's tombstone was found in another location inside the city limits of Talladega. It was moved to Oak Hill Cemetery in the lot of the Talladega County Historical Association for perpetual care.

MICAH TAUL SR., Lawyer and planter, born May 14, 1785 in Montgomery County, Maryland; settled in Mardisville, Alabama in 1846; died May 27, 1850, age 65. He Served as a Colonel in the War of 1812. Grave was

---

[5] Thomas M. Owen's History of Ala., etc., Vol. II, Page 1359

marked in 1930 by his great-granddaughter, Marianne McClellan, with official grave marker of the National Society of the United States Daughters of 1812.

MICAH TAUL JR., Lawyer and planter; born November 25, 1832, in Winchester, Tennessee, son of Mary Hayter and Micah Taul Sr. Settled in Mardisville, Alabama in 1846; served as Secretary of State Senate 1856-1857; a Lieutenant in the Civil War; Secretary of State 1865-1868; State Railroad Commissioner. He died February 13, 1873, in Tampa, Florida.

JOAB LAWLER was born June 12, 1796, in Monroe Co., N.C. He was a Circuit Clerk and County Judge of Shelby County before coming to Talladega County in 1834 as Receiver of Public Moneys for the Coosa Land District. He was a member of the United States House of Representatives from 1835 to 1838. He acted as Treasurer of the University of Alabama from 1833 to 1836. He was a lawyer and Baptist minister. He died while in Washington on May 8th, 1838.

G. R. RICE was sworn in at the Commissioners Court Nov. 13, 1833, as a practicing attorney.

J. B. MARTIN was also sworn in on November 13th, 1833. He was made Judge of the 10th Judicial Circuit in 1860. He was killed during the Civil War.

LEONARD TARRANT, Lawyer, Judge of the County Court of Shelby, Indian Agent, Methodist minister and legislator, moved to Mardisville in 1834 to act as Indian Agent, which office he first held in Montevallo. He was so trusted by the Indians that they requested his appointment as Agent. "President Andrew Jackson remarked that every (Indian) Agent he had commissioned had dissappointed him, except one, and he was a Methodist preacher. That preacher was Leonard Tarrant."[6] Judge Tarrant lived on a hill west of Mardisville where he died and is buried in an old family cemetery, which has become a Negro cemetery, Harmon Family. He was one of the county's most respected citizens. "The duties that devolved upon him were responsible and delicate, in standing between the land buyers, with their cunning, and the ignorant Indians, and fully tested his character for unswerving integrity in the difficult path both by temptations and bribes on the one hand, and threats on the other."[7]

WILLIAM H. CALDWELL came to Talladega in 1833, and lived about a mile out on the "Jackson Trace Road". He was a wise and sympathetic counselor of the young, and occupied a small log office on the east side of the square.[8] He died unmarried about 1843.

---

[6] Garrett's Reminiscences of Public Men in Alabama, Page 532
[7] Ibid
[8] Article by "Memorabilia", 1876, found in Public Library

FELIX GRUNDY MCCONNELL was born on April 1st, 1809 in Nashville, Tenn., and came to Talladega in 1834. He possessed a magnetic personality and a fiery disposition, and was always in demand for political rallies. He served in the State House of Representatives in 1838 and as a senator from this district in 1839. He served as a Member of the U. S. House of Representatives from 1843 until he died in office on September 10th, 1846.

GEORGE W. STONE was born on October 24th, 1811, in Bedford Co., Va., and came to Talladega in May, 1834. He entered into partnership with Wm. P. Chilton and was made Circuit Judge in 1843. He moved to Lowndes County in 1849, and became Associate Justice of the Supreme Court of Alabama in 1856, later becoming Chief Justice. "Chief Justice Stone will doubtless live in history as the most impressive figure in our judicial annals."[9] He died in Montgomery on Nov. 11th, 1894.

WILLIAM PARISH CHILTON was born on August 10th, 1810 in Adair Co., Kentucky, and came to Mardisville in 1834, later moving to Talladega, where he practiced law for some years. He represented Talladega County in the House of Representatives, having been elected in 1839. He became Associate Justice of the Ala. Supreme Court in 1847, and later Chief Justice. He died on January 21st, 1871, in Montgomery.

ELI SHORTRIDGE was born in Paris, Ky., in 1794. He represented Tuscaloosa Co. in the Ala. House of Representatives in 1828 and served a short term on the Supreme Court bench. In 1835 he was elected Judge of the Circuit Court, and moved to Talladega. He held this office until he died in Talladega July 20th, 1843.

SAMUEL W. MARDIS was born June 12th, 1800, in Tennessee. He served Shelby County in the State Legislature in 1823; was elected to the U. S. House of Representatives in 1831, and re-elected in 1833. While serving in this capacity he acted as one of the witnesses to the Creek Treaty of 1832. Because of his part in bringing about the treaty, the name Jumper's Springs was changed to that of Mardisville in his honor. He moved to Talladega in 1835, where he died Nov. 15th, 1836.

THOMAS D. CLARKE was born in North Carolina, and settled in Talladega in 1835. He was a direct descendant of Daniel Boone. He was elected to the Ala. House of Representatives in 1843, and later made Attorney General. He eventually moved to Tuscaloosa, where he died in 1847.

GEORGE P. BROWN settled in Talladega in 1839 as partner to Wm. P. Chilton. He married the daughter of Rev. Thomas Chilton, and was one of

---

[9] Memorial Records of Alabama, Vol. II, Page 151

Alabama's most brilliant, intelligent and promising lawyers.[10] He died soon after moving to Talladega.

ALVIS Q. NICKS was born in Lincoln Co., Tenn., and came to Talladega in 1833. His honest and pleasing manner attracted the Creeks and they chose him as Creek Indian Adviser, and he became one of the locating agents of Indian reservation lands. He served the county in the House of Representatives in 1851-52 and became a candidate for Governor in 1853, at which time he was defeated by Gov. Winston. He moved to Texas soon afterwards.

ROBERT EMMETT BLEDSOE BAYLOR was born on May 10th, 1793, in Lincoln Co., Ky. He died at Gay Hill, Texas, Jan. 6th, 1874. He appears to have been living in Talladega in 1839, where he was converted and joined the Baptist Church, and soon became an ordained minister. He had represented Tuscaloosa Co. in the House of Representatives before coming to Talladega, and moved to Texas where he became quite prominently associated in civic and religious affairs. He served as Representative in the U. S. House of Representatives at one time. Baylor Co., Texas, and Baylor University of Waco are named in his honor.

All of these lawyers were living and practicing law in Talladega prior to 1845. A list of registered lawyers in Alabama, as of 1845, is recorded in Garrett's Reminiscences of Public Men of Alabama, with localities from which they registered. Included is this list are 24 lawyers practicing in Talladega, some of whom have been mentioned previously in this sketch. The list follows:

1—ALEXANDER BOWIE was born Dec. 14, 1789, in Abbeville, S. C., and located in Talladega in 1835. He settled on Choccolocco Creek at "Loch Lomond", his plantation home, about eight or nine miles north-east of Talladega. He was a scholarly and cultured gentleman, who was associated with educational and political affairs of the county and state. He was for years a Trustee of the University of Alabama; was one of the founders, and first president, of the State Historical Society in 1850. He was made Chancellor of the Northern Division of Alabama in 1839, which position he held until 1845. He died on Dec. 30th, 1866, and is buried in the old Marble Springs Presbyterian Church cemetery, which cemetery has been turned into a cultivated field, with no trace of the once imposing monuments.

2—FRANKLIN WELCH BOWDEN was born on Feb. 17th, 1817, in Chester District, S. C., and came to Talladega in 1838. He became associated with Thomas and W. P. Chilton and Tignell W. Jones. In 1844 he was elected to the House of Representatives in Alabama, and during the years 1846-49 served

---

[10] Our Mountain Home, July 12, 1876. In Talladega Public Library

as a member of the United States House of Representatives. He was declared at one time "the most gifted orator that State has ever produced."[11] Bowden College, Carroll Co., Ga., was named in his honor. He moved to Henderson, Rush Co., Texas, later, where he died June 15th, 1857.

3—E. E. BRYSON

4—WM. P. CHILTON, listed prior to 1845.

5—THOMAS GRAY GARRETT was a brother of Wm. Garrett who wrote "Reminiscences of Public Men in Alabama". He married a Rice, sister of Mrs. Joseph A. Woodward. He practiced law in Talladega and served as Solicitor of the Ninth District from 1841 to 1845.

6—TIGNAL W. JONES was a partner at various times of Wm. P. Chilton, F. W. Bowden, J. L. M. Curry and A. W. Bowie. He moved to Texas after having resided in Talladega several years.

7 — W. W. KNOX was one of a large family of prominent citizens of early Talladega. He served as Clerk of the Circuit Court for many years.

8 — W. J. McLIN

9 — G. T. McAFEE is listed prior to 1845.

10 — GEORGE FLEMING MOORE was one of a large pioneer family of Moores who were prominently associated with the early life of Talladega County. He moved to Montgomery, where he was associated with the fraternity of Masons.

11 — JOHN TYLER MORGAN was born June 20th, 1824 in Athens, Tenn. He studied law in the office of Wm. P. Chilton and was admitted to the Bar in Talladega in 1845. His childhood was spent near Clairmont Springs, then in Talladega County. He moved to Selma, Ala. about 1856, from which point he joined the Confederate Army. He was made a Brig. General of the C. S. Army in 1863, in which capacity he served during the rest of the War. He became nationally renowned as United States Senator, which office he held from 1876 until he died on June 11th, 1907 in Washington, and was buried in Selma. Being a distinguished national figure, his record can be found in every well known history of Alabama.

12 — LEWIS ELEPHALET PARSONS was born in Boone Co., N.Y., April 28th, 1817. He came to Talladega about 1840 and was a law partner at one time of Alexander White. He served Talladega County in the House of Representatives 1859-60, and became Provisional Governor June 21st, 1865, which office he held until December 20th, 1865. He was made U. S. Senator in 1868, but, like other Southern men, elected at that time, was never seated. He died in Talladega in June 8th, 1895.

---

[11] Brewer's History of Alabama, Page 540

13 — PHILIP E. PEARSON was born in Winnsboro, S. C., and was the father of Mrs. John J. Woodward. He lived in Talladega only a short while, having moved to Matagorda, Texas, where he became a famous lawyer.

14 — SAMUEL FARROW RICE — was born June 2nd, 1816, in Union District, S. C. and came to Talladega in 1838. He was a partner at various times of Philip E. Pearson, John T. Morgan and Thomas D. Clarke. He edited the "Talladega Watchtower" for six years, and was elected to the Ala. House of Representatives in 1840. In 1852 he was elected an Associate member of the Supreme Court of Alabama, and moved to Montgomery. In 1853 he became Chief Justice. He was one of Alabama's most picturesque figures. He ran four times unsuccessfully for a seat in the U. S. House of Representatives.

15 — H. W. RICE was at one time Judge of the County Court, and represented Talladega County in the House of Representatives in 1868.

16 — DANIEL SAYRE was born on Jan. 13th, 1800 in Franklin, Ohio. He married a sister of John T. Morgan and practiced law in Talladega for a short while. He was better known as the founder and editor of the "Alabama Reporter" in 1844. He later moved to Montgomery, where he died on April 7th, 1888.

17— B. H. SPYKER was associated with Daniel Sayre as a lawyer and in connection with the "Alabama Reporter". He later became associated with L. E. Parsons, as editor of the "Southerner".

18 — CHARLES STONE

19 — GEORGE S. WALDEN — was a partner at one time of S. K. McSpadden and of Col. Martin at another. He served Talladega County in the House of Representatives in 1861 and Talladega town as Mayor in 1862. He was prominently connected and a highly respected lawyer of Talladega. He was listed on the faculty of the University of Alabama during 1841-1844.

20 — H. P. WATSON was at one time Register in Chancery, and listed as Second Lieutenant in the Mexican War.

21 — ALEXANDER WHITE was born October 16th, 1816, in Franklin, Tenn. and was son of Judge John White, pioneer settler. He read law in Talladega and was admitted to the Bar in 1838. In 1851 he was elected to the U. S. House of Representatives and in 1865 represented Talladega County at the Constitutional Convention. After having made the famous "Bonnie Blue Flag" speech at a Democratic Convention, he became a member of the United States House of Representatives on the Republican ticket in 1873. He moved to Texas in 1876.

22 — JOHN JEFFERSON WOODWARD was born on October 8th, 1808 in Winnsboro, S. C., and moved to Talladega in 1837. He first lived on a plantation, but later moved to town. He edited the "Talladega Watchtower" at one time. In 1847 he represented Talladega County in the House of

Representatives; in 1849 he became Circuit Judge; and from 1853 until 1861 he served as Solicitor of the Ninth District.

23 — T. B. WOODWARD

24 — HUBBARD HOBBS WYCHE came to Talladega in 1833, and was one of Talladega's first Commissioners. He played a prominent part in the administration of early affairs of the town and county. He was unmarried, brilliant and handsome, but indulged too often in strong drink and finally died in the insane asylum.

There were many young lawyers in the making in 1845, who were still reading law, among whom, and perhaps the most prominent were:

JABEZ LAMAR MONROE CURRY, who was born June 5th, 1825, in Lincoln Co., Ga. He came to Talladega in 1838 and read law in Talladega, after which he graduated from the Dane Law School of Harvard University, and was admitted to the Bar in Talladega in 1846. He practiced law in Talladega for some time, and later played prominently in affairs of the State of Alabama. He served two terms as a member of the United States House of Representatives, but resigned in 1861 to enter the C. S. Army, where he became a Colonel. He was Agent for both the Peabody and Slater Funds. He was Minister to Spain in 1885, and was sent to Spain as Ambassador Extraordinary to witness the coronation of Alfonso XIII, by whom he was very much beloved, and while there was decorated with the Royal Order of Charles III. His statue is one of two from Alabama in Statuary Hall at the capital in Washington.

SAMUEL KING MCSPADDEN was born on Nov. 12th, 1823 in Warren Co., Tenn., and died in Center, Ala. May 3rd, 1896, where he had resided for many years. He came to Talladega about 1845; read law under Samuel F. Rice, and was admitted to the Bar in 1848. He was made Brigadier General of Militia in 1856, and later Colonel in the C. S. Army. He was elected Chancellor of the Northern Division in 1865; was a state senator 1882-85; and again made Chancellor in 1885.

CHARLES MILLER SHELLEY was born on Dec. 28th, 1833 in Sullivan Co., Tenn. He moved to Talladega with his father and mother in 1836 and lived on North St. E., where Chilton St. enters North St. He served as a lieutenant of the Talladega Artillery in 1861. In January 1862, he recruited the 30th Alabama and was commissioned colonel. He was captured at Vicksburg in 1864 and later appointed brigadier general. He moved to Selma after the Civil War, where he became Sheriff of Dallas Co. at one time and served as a member of the U. S. House of Representatives, having been elected in 1877 and again in 1881. He married twice, both daughters of Felix G. McConnell. He eventually moved to Birmingham, where he died on Jan. 20th, 1907.

NATHAN G. SHELLEY represented Talladega County in the House of Representatives in 1851, but moved to Texas in 1853, where he later became a Brig. General in the C. S. Army.

TAUL BRADFORD was born on Jan. 20th, 1835, in Mardisville. He was the son of Jacob T. Bradford, Register of the Coosa Land District. He read law in Talladega and was admitted to the Bar in 1855. He served as Lt. Col. in the C. S. Army; as Representative from the county in 1870-2, and was elected to the United House of Representatives in 1874. He died in Talladega October 28th, 1883.

WILLIAM CALVERT HILL, son of George Hill who fought in the Battle of Talladega under Andrew Jackson, was born in Bibb Co. in 1822. He graduated from the University of Alabama in 1844, and from the Law School of Harvard University in 1846. At one time he was a partner of Judge J. Woodward, later becoming Solicitor of the Circuit. He died in 1852.

ASHLEY C. WOOD was born in Bibb Co. July 10th, 1832, and came the same year with his parents to Talladega County. He attended school in Talladega and graduated from the University of Alabama. He was admitted to the Bar in 1857, and practiced law in Fayetteville. He was legal adviser under Gen. Johnston during the Civil War.

JOSEPH A. WOODWARD, SR. was born April 11th, 1806, in Fairfield District, S. C., and came to Talladega in 1860. He was graduated from the University of South Carolina, and was elected to the United States House of Representatives from the Winnsboro District, S. C., in 1843. He served five terms as such a representative before coming to Talladega. He was closely associated with John C. Calhoun and Horace Greeley. He died in Talladega in 1885.

JOHN WEBSTER BISHOP was born on Dec. 19th, 1831, and came with his parents to Talladega, while quite young. He graduated from the University of Alabama in 1854, and studied law in Talladega. He was made Judge of the City Court in 1893 and was later made Mayor of Talladega. He died in Talladega October 10th, 1900.

GEORGE KNOX MILLER[12] was born on December 30th, 1836, and was the first male child born in the town of Talladega. He was born in a log cabin which is now part of the Carson Whitson family home, "Whitwood", on South Street. He was editor of "Our Mountain Home" 1881-1884, and was in demand as an editorial writer all of his life. He served as City Court Judge, Mayor 1875-1884; Probate Judge 1884-1898. He died in Talladega on November 12, 1916 and is buried in Oak Hill Cemetery.

---

[12] History of the Talladega County Courthouse, 1982, by Bettye R. Lessley of Sylacauga, Alabama.

GENERAL PETER PARSONS is listed among the earliest lawyers, though his name does not appear on the list of Alabama lawyers of 1845. He was a brother of Enoch Parsons of Montgomery Co., and of Silas Parsons of Madison Co.

JOSEPH HEPBURN PARSONS, LEWIS ELEPHALET PARSONS, JR., and GEORGE W. PARSONS were three sons of Prov. Gov. Parsons who practiced law in Talladega.

ANDREW WILLIAM BOWIE was born Feb. 5, 1822, Abbeville, S. C. and came to Talladega in 1835. He graduated from the University of S. C. in 1842, and was admitted to the Bar in Talladega the same year. He served in the Mexican War with honor, as Captain; also, the Civil War as Captain of the Mountain Rangers. He died in Talladega and is buried in Oak Hill.

SYDNEY JOHNSTON BOWIE was born in Talladega on July 26th, 1865. He graduated from the School of Law at the University of Alabama in 1885 and was admitted to the Bar the same year. He was associated with Mr. John B. Knox and Mr. J. K. Dixon in the practice of law for some years. He served several terms as a member of the U. S. House of Representatives. He moved to Calhoun County in 1901, and eventually to Birmingham, where he resided the rest of his life.

JOHN HENDERSON, JR., was born in Monroe Co., Tenn., in 1824. He was the son of John Henderson, pioneer, who came to Talladega in 1835. He read law in the office of Wm. P. Chilton and was admitted to the Bar in 1848. He was a law partner of Wm. S. McGhee in 1855, and Circuit Judge in 1866.

JOHN T. HEFLIN was born on August 13th, 1820 in Walton Co., Ga. He was admitted to the Bar in 1841, at which time he came to Talladega, where he resided for some years as lawyer, and as Circuit Judge during the years of 1860-65. He moved to Birmingham in 1882, and died there.

ABRAM JOSEPH WALKER was born on Nov. 24th, 1819, in Madison, Tenn. He graduated at the University of Tennessee in 1851 and came to Talladega in 1852. He entered the practice of law with John T. Morgan and was at one time Chancellor of the Northern District of Alabama. He was elected Judge of the Supreme Court in 1856, and Chief Justice in 1859.

GEORGE EDWARD BREWER was born in Tuskegee on Sept. 12, 1862, and died in Talladega on July 24th, 1899. He graduated at the University of Alabama in 1884, and came to Talladega as Superintendent of the first public school in 1886. He was admitted to the Bar in 1889 and was made Judge of the Circuit Court in 1895.

MARCUS HENDERSON CRUIKSHANK was born in Autauga County in 1826. He read law in Talladega under Alexander White and L. E. Parsons, and became a member of the firm in 1847. He was Register in

Chancery at one time, mayor of Talladega at another, and editor of the Talladega Reporter. He represented the district as a member of the House of Representatives of the Confederate States during 1863-65. He was Commissioner for the relief of the destitute in Alabama after the war.

GEORGE PARIS PLOWMAN was born on July 8th, 1808, in Brunscombe Co., N. C., and moved to Talladega in 1833, where he served as Judge of Probate two terms. He had two sons who became prominently connected with civic affairs of Talladega. GEORGE H. PLOWMAN, served as mayor, at some time during the war, but later moved to Texas. THOMAS S. PLOWMAN lived in Talladega all his life and served the district one term in the United States House of Representatives.

CHARLES PELHAM was born on March 12, 1835, in North Carolina. He was a brother of "the gallant John Pelham" of Jacksonville, but came to Talladega in 1858, where he began the practice of law, and resided on Battle St. E. He was elected Judge of the Tenth Judicial Circuit in 1868, and to the U. S. House of Representatives on the Republican ticket in 1873. He later moved to Worth, Ga., where he died Jan. 18, 1908.

JOSEPH FORNEY JOHNSTON, lawyer, Governor of Alabama and U. S. Senator, was born March 23, 1843, in Lincoln Co., N. C., and died Aug. 8th, 1913 in Washington, D. C. He is listed in several instances in Our Mountain Home as one of Talladega's most prominent citizens. He attended school at the Talladega Baptist High School, and entered the Confederate Eleventh Alabama Regiment in Talladega.

JOHN WASHINGTON INZER, was born Jan. 9th, 1834, in Gwinnett Co., Ga. He studied law in the offices of John T. Morgan and Judge A. J. Walker in Talladega. He was admitted to the Bar in 1855, and left Talladega to locate in St. Clair County, where he became Judge of Probate and Judge of the Sixteenth Judicial Circuit in 1907.

JOSEPH BROWN GRAHAM was born on March 18th, 1864 in Spring Garden, Cherokee Co., Ala. He died July 6th, 1903 in Talladega. He was made superintendent of the city schools after North Side Public School was built, which position he held from 1887 to 1893. He served in nearly every capacity as educator in the state and south. Graham School was named in his honor. He entered the practice of law with C. C. Whitson the latter part of the Nineteenth century.

C. C. WHITSON was a native of Talladega. He was admitted to the Bar in 1885, and was considered one of Talladega's ablest lawyers from the time he entered the practice until he died. He was born on Nov. 5th, 1862, and died Feb. 9, 1912. He was a member of the Alabama Legislature in 1900-01.

BORDEN H. BURR was born in Talladega Nov. 2, 1876. He attended the Webb School at Belbuckle, Tenn., graduated from the University of

Alabama in 1896 and from Washington & Lee University in 1898. He entered the practice of Law in 1898 with Whitson & Graham and later became a member of the firm of Knox, Dixon, Bowie and Burr. He eventually moved to Birmingham.

E. H. DRYER was a native of Tuskegee, born 1863. He came to Talladega when quite a young man, and followed Wm. H. Skaggs as Mayor of Talladega, and it was during his administration as Mayor that the first City Hall, on Battle Street, was erected. He practiced Law in Talladega until 1909 when he became Referee in Bankruptcy and moved to Birmingham. He died in 1946 and is buried in Oak Hill Cemetery, Talladega.

CECIL BROWNE was born on Jan. 27, 1855 at Montevallo. He attended the University of the South at Sewanee, Tenn., and read law in the office of Judge John T. Heflin at Talladega. He was admitted to the Bar Feb. 13, 1878 in Talladega. He served two terms as state senator and as a member of the legislature one term. He was prominently associated with almost every phase of the judicial courts during his life.

E. S. JEMISON, a native of Talladega, attended LaGrange College, read law in the office of L. E. Parsons, and was admitted to the bar in Talladega at an early age. He left for Texas soon afterwards where he remained most of his life. He was a Colonel in the Confederate Army of Texas. After the war, he entered the Cotton Brokerage business and wholesale grocery business in Houston. He later purchased a seat on the New York Cotton Exchange, and was controlling stockholder and President of the Houston, East Texas Railway Company, which railroad is now a part of the Southern Pacific system.

E. D. ACKER was born Feb. 14, 1861, at Lincoln, Talladega Co. He graduated at the University of Alabama in 1884. He taught in various schools for many years, and was well known as an able lawyer.

H. L. MCELDERRY practiced law for some years, and was connected with the firm of Knox, Dixon & Bowie. However, he is better remembered as President of the Talladega National Bank for some years, and as one of Talladega's beloved philanthropists.

JOHN KELLY DIXON was born April 8, 1870, at Fayetteville. He graduated at the University of Alabama and entered the practice of law in Talladega in 1892. He was connected with John B. Knox, W. P. Acker, S. J. Bowie, B. H. Burr, and other lawyers during his life. He was chairman of the City Board of Education for many years, and the Dixon Junior High School is named in his honor.

JAMES BRAXTON SANFORD was born in Talladega County Nov. 12, 1870. He was admitted to the Bar in 1896 and practiced law in Sylacauga and Talladega all his life. He represented Talladega County in the State Legislature in 1907 and 1908, and later became Judge of the Circuit Court.

JEHU WELLINGTON VANDIVER was born Sept. 17th 1850 in Calhoun Co. He studied law in the office of Judge John T. Heflin, and was admitted to the Bar in 1872. He served at various times as solicitor of the Tenth District, Register in Chancery, President of Alabama Chautauqua, Mayor of Talladega and Judge of the City Court. He was also author, editor and lecturer.

JOHN B. KNOX was born in Talladega on Feb. 16th, 1857. He studied law in the office of Judge John T. Heflin, and was admitted to the Bar in Talladega in 1878. He first practiced law in partnership with Frank W. Bowden, but moved to Anniston in December, 1888. However he continued his legal connection in Talladega until he died.

ALEXANDER MICHAEL GARBER, lawyer and Attorney General of the State of Alabama, was born at "Chessland" near Livingston, Ala., May 15, 1867. He graduated from the University of Alabama in 1886, and came to Talladega in 1891 to enter the practice of law, but about 15 years later located in Birmingham.

GRAVES EMBRY read law in Birmingham and was admitted to the Bar there January 31st, 1888. After practicing there several years, he returned to Talladega County, where he was born. He practiced in Talladega until he died in 1955.

A. R. BARCLAY is listed as a member of the Constitutional Committee in 1861, from Talladega County.

FRANCIS BUGBEE is listed as an early lawyer of Talladega. He was a graduate of Yale University and a relative of the Woodwards. His name appears for only a short while.

W. B. CASTLEBERRY was born June 16, 1869, at Columbiana. He entered the practice of law in Talladega in 1890. He served one term as State Senator, and for years as Judge of the City Court.

BENJAMIN MACLIN HUEY, was born in Talladega June 15, 1840, and died May 26, 1906 at Marion, Ala. He was the son of J. G. L. Huey, who built the home which is now known as the educational building of Trinity Methodist Church. He studied law in the office of A. J. Walker, was admitted to the Bar in 1866, and moved to Marion for the practice of his profession.

R. H. ISBELL was the son of James Isbell, and co-partner with him in the banking business. Though he was a lawyer, he was better known as a banker and real estate dealer.

SAMUEL MCCLELEN began the practice of law in Talladega in 1834, though we have no record of further activities. He died here in 1846.

LEE M. OTTS was the son of John M. P. Otts, a beloved Presbyterian minister. He was admitted to the Bar in 1887 in Talladega, but later moved to Greensboro.

J. MORGAN SMITH was better known in Talladega as the husband of Miss Kate Duncan, of Talladega, whom he married in 1863. He practiced law in Talladega for some years after the Civil War, but moved to Birmingham in 1888, where he became prominently associated with the legal and civic life of that city.

A. A. STERRETT is listed as a member of the Constitutional Committee of Alabama, from Talladega in 1875.

MARCUS MARTIN SMITH was born May 6, 1852, in Talladega County, and read law in the office of D. K. Castleberry. Ad- mitted to the Bar in 1880, and practiced his profession in Ashland and Pell City later.

Having involved myself in the endless task of a sketch of the legal profession of the Nineteenth Century, it becomes necessary to list many, who are worthy of more careful regard, with the hope that someday a more thorough historian will give each lawyer his rightful place in the history of Talladega. This list, I am sure, is incomplete, because it is compiled from old newspaper records, and hearsay, but the following does represent a number of lawyers who practiced law in Talladega prior to 1900:

William Barclay	Jno. D. McNeel
D. K. Castleberry	J. T. May
D. T. Castleberry	J. T. Moore
Wm. H. Chapman	V. S. Murphey
Robert Hett Chapman	B. F. Mullendore
George Connelly	James B. Newman
Edward Dameron	William Newman
John C. Duncan	Otis Nichols
B. Eason	Wm. P. Oden
W. T. Edwards	J.C. Oakes
H.H. Freeman	A.A. Patterson
——— Foster	J.J. Pierce
Wm. C. Griffin	H.M. Rutledge
A.Hall	Thomas Scott
Thomas Hayden	J.T. Shanklin
Tom Henderson	C.O. Samuel
——— Humphries	John Rather Taylor
William Ivey	David Trice
M.D. Ivey	John D. Townsend
J. Lawerence Jones	Oscar Watkins
J.T. Leftwich	Jno. E. Ware
C.O. Lowery	John Winbourne
Wm. McGregor	B.F. Wilson
N.S. McAfee	J.F. Webb

Some prominent public men of Alabama, who, at one time, lived in Talladega:

Governor of Alabama   Joseph Forney Johnston
Prov. Governor of Alabama   Lewis Elephalet Parsons

United States Senators:

Lewis Elephalet Parsons, 1866 (Not seated)
John Tyler Morgan, 1877-1907
Joseph Forney Johnston, 1907-1913

Members of the United States House of Representatives:

Robert E. B. Baylor	1829-31--also later from Texas
Samuel W. Mardis	1831-35
Joab Lawler	1835-38
Felix G. McConnell	1845-46
Franklin W. Bowden	1846-51
Alexander White	1851-53, also 1873-75
J. L. M. Curry	1857-61
Charles Pelham	1873-75
Taul Bradford	1874-77
Charles M. Shelley	1877-83
Thomas S. Plowman	1897-99
Sydney J. Bowie	1903-05
Joseph A. Woodward	1843-53
Thomas Chilton	
James S. Jones	
Kenneth Roberts	1950

Associate and Chief Justices of the Supreme Court of Alabama:

George W. Stone   Wm. P. Chilton
Eli Shortridge   Abram Joseph Walker
Samuel F. Rice   John White

Chancellors of the Northern District:

Alexander Bowie   Abram Joseph Walker

Samuel King McSpadden

George Fleming Moore was made Justice of the Supreme Court of Texas.

The Medical Profession([1])

Territory surrounding Talladega was sparsely populated in the early days, and compensation for medical services small; therefore, of necessity, pioneer physicians entered into other fields as well as that of practicing medicine. There was a scarcity of drugs and other medical supplies, and the practice of medicine must have been an art rather than a science. A great many of the doctors were planters, and others entered into the mercantile business.

Some years ago Dr. J. L. Stockdale wrote an article entitled "The Early Days of the Medical Profession in Talladega County,"[2] from which I have derived names of a number of doctors prior to 1850.

Short sketches of these follow:

DR. WILLIAM EDWARDS married the daughter of Thomas Rowland, tavern keeper. He appears to have been practicing when the county site was chosen in 1834, and it is possible that he was living here prior to 1832. He later erected a two story building on the north side of Battle St., E., about where the Talladega Supply business is located. Across the street from his home he later operated a livery stable, where the stage coach and horses were kept during the years of that mode of travel. He later moved to a farm on Choccolocco Creek, then back to town, and eventually to Texas.

DR. WILLIAM SOMMERS (Summers) settled at Pond Springs, now known as Elliott Lake, about 1832. He had a large practice until he died in 1852. He was also a planter, and was widely known for his genial manner and the number of pranks he frequently played on his friends. His name also appears among those interested in mining.

DR. HENRY MCKENZIE appears first as one of the commissioners chosen to select a county seat in 1833, and as a property owner of a part of the Talladega Battle Ground. He built in the first block on North St., W. He had a brother DR. BENJAMIN MCKENZIE who also practiced medicine at the same time.

DR. ELISHA DODSON settled at Fife, near Eastaboga, as early as 1833. Fife, it will be remembered, was one of the county's first post offices, and a well settled area.

---

[1] Where references are not specifically noted, biography can be found in either Memorial Records of Alabama, Vols. I and II; Thomas M. Owens History of Ala. and Dic. of Biography, Vols. III and IV; or Notable Men of Alabama. Edited by Hon. Joel C. DuBose, Vols. I and II
[2] Article from local paper, found in Scrap Book of J. A. Bingham

DR. JOSEPH D. HEACOCK, a native of Pennsylvania, settled in late 1833 or early 1834 near Sylacauga, in the Tallasehatchie neighborhood, where he practiced medicine and farmed all his life. He had two sons who became physicians. One son, Dr. Robert Price Heacock was killed during the Civil War. Another son, Dr. John W. Heacock, was not only prominently associated with the medical profession, but with the political and farming interests of the county. He moved to the town of Talladega later and was instrumental in opening Brignoli Street. Dr. John W. Heacock's oldest son, Joseph D. Heacock, has been a distinguished physician in Birmingham for many years.

DR. JAMES C. KNOX, a native of Georgia, came to Talladega in 1835, where he practiced medicine all his life. He was a leading surgeon, known and beloved by the entire county. He was the father of fourteen children, many of whom became prominently connected with nearly every phase of the civic life of Talladega.

Mrs. Taylor mentions several others who came to Talladega prior to 1835. Among them were Dr. Ruble, whose wife was a sister of Capt. J. D. Shelley. Dr. Peter L. Penn, of Virginia, died in Talladega in 1835, and was among the first to be buried in Oak Hill Cemetery.

Dr. Stockdale mentioned as having located in the county in 1836, Drs. Wheeler and Osborn L. Echols, at Mardisville, and Dr. Milton McGuire in Talladega. He lists Dr. Elias Brock as having settled at Plum Branch in 1837 and Dr. James Townsend as having arrived the same year in Talladega, though Mrs. Taylor mentions him as having settled at Pond Spring.

Between 1837 and 1844, Dr. Stockdale mentions Drs. Thomas Riser, Harrison and Rippatoe as having settled near Sylacauga.

DR. ED GANTT is also mentioned in this group. He first came to Talladega in 1813 with Andrew Jackson, and took part in the Battle of Talladega. He later settled below Sylacauga. Dr. Gantt became more widely known for his activities in the marble industry of the county, than as a physician. He opened and operated marble quarries at what is now known as "Gantt's Quarry."

During this period of 1837-44, a Dr. Poe was located at Mardisville; Dr. Albert S. Acker at Blue Eye (Lincoln); Dr. James Simmons at Brownville; Dr. Benton W. Groce at Kelley's Springs; and Drs. Hunt, Pearson and Mason at Talladega. Most of this group were permanent settlers and widely known. Dr. Pearson was highly educated in the medical institutions of Paris, France. He was a brother-in-law of Chief Justice S. F. Rice.

Dr. Stockdale states that the Talladega Medical Association was organized in 1844, which is no doubt true, because an Act was approved by the

Legislature on Jan. 27th, 1845, establishing a "Board of Physicians in Talladega."[3] The State Medical Association was not organized until Dec. 1, 1847. Hence, it will be seen that the medical association of Talladega County was established several years prior to that of the State of Alabama.

Doctors of the county did not appear to be actively connected with the state organization for some years. Dr. Barclay W. Toole, of Talladega, appears as President of the state association in 1897, and Dr. Groce Harrison then of Talladega was the featured speaker in 1901 in Mobile. The State Association first met in Talladega in April 21-24, 1903. Dr. Samuel W. Welch was state president in 1908 and Dr. B. B. Simms in 1915.

At the time the Talladega Medical Association was organized in 1844, a medical board was appointed for the purpose of examining applicants for licenses to practice in the county, for exemptions from road duty and military duty, and for persons charged with lunacy, etc. This board was composed of Drs. James C. Knox, Henry McKenzie and William Sommers. Between 1844 and 1850, Dr. Stockdale lists Dr. Thomas Chilton, Walter W. Wylie, John Harrington Vandiver, (whose biography states 1857), at Talladega, and Dr. Balus Abercrombie at Blue Eye; Dr. R. Pinckney Lawson at Howell's Cove; Dr. Jacob King at Bluff Springs; Dr. Martin G. Slaughter at Pinckneyville, and a Dr. Jones at Chinnabee.

Dr. Stockdale, having written from memory, and not from record, naturally left out a number of doctors, some of whom had probably retired before Dr. Stockdale came to Talladega. Dr. Stockdale does not mention himself among early doctors, nor have we an accurate biography, but we do know that he settled near "Stockdale Station" in pioneer days, and lived in a quaint two story log house, which was razed about thirty-five years ago. Among doctors not mentioned were —

DR. MATTHEW LYLE DIXON, who was a surgeon in Andrew Jackson's army, and who settled in Talladega later, and died here in 1836.

DR. WILLIAM TAYLOR, whose home was at "Cragdale"; was one of the promoters of the medical college in Mobile, and of the School for the Deaf in Talladega. He was editor of the "Democratic Watchtower" at one time. He was the son of John K. Taylor, who operated a Cotton & Wool Warp Mill and Grist Mill at "Cragdale", better known as "Taylor's Mill", and "Water Works". John K. Taylor and Dr. Taylor were among the first who quarried marble in the county.

DR. WILLIAM AMERICUS WELCH began the practice of medicine about 1843 at Alpine. He was the father of DR. SAMUEL WALLACE

---

[3] Alabama Acts, 1843-, Page 95

WELCH, who practiced in Talladega, and who was for many years head of the State Department of Health, in which capacity he became widely known for his progressive methods. Dr. S. W. Welch was also associated with Dr. B. B. Simms in operating the Talladega Infirmary.

Dr. —— Dixon, who lived at the A. G. Storey place, was one of the Presbyterians who were instrumental in building the Synodical College in 1850.

Dr. —— Sims, was mentioned by J. L. M. Curry, as one of the early doctors, and he stated that he lived at the extreme end of North St. E. in what was later known as the "Mark McElderry Place".

It was customary for professional cards of doctors and lawyers to appear in local newspapers in the early days. From these old newspapers the following cards were found:

Among those of 1850 were Drs. Wm. H. Moore and M. G. Moore, located at "Messrs. M. G. & F. B. Moor's Drug Store, No. 2 North Street." A continuation of this store is still operated as a drug store under the name of "Henderson Drug Store," and is perhaps the only one in Talladega which has been continuously operated in the same business.

Others having cards were Drs. Knox (J.C.) and Wyley (W.W.), Drs. H. McKenzie and C. G. Cunningham. Dr. R. A. Moseley at "Moseley's Drug Store" and Drs. William Harrison and William Harrison, Jr.

DR. H. G. HENDRICK was born in South Carolina, but was brought to Talladega as a child in 1833 by his parents. He studied medicine in Charleston and Philadelphia, and began the practice of medicine in Talladega in 1852. He retired to his farm in 1873, which is located about one mile from Court Square on East Street, S. The home has been owned continuously by his heirs and is now occupied by George W. Jones.

DR. JOHN N. SLAUGHTER was listed as a teacher at one time, and as a practitioner at Talladega Springs at another.

DR. JOSEPH H. JOHNSON came to Talladega in 1858 in connection with the School for the Deaf and Blind. He also practiced his profession, and was one of Talladega's most valued citizens.

DRS. T. J. CHILTON and R. P. LAWSON appear as "practicing physicians, west side of the Square" in 1855.[4]

Professional cards of DR. ROBERT BURTON and of DR. JOHN W. DOWSING appear in papers of 1855.

DR. R. A. MOSELEY, Jr., graduated in Medicine in 1861, and located in Talladega. His father, Dr. R. A. Moseley, Sr., was a physician, but more widely known as a druggist, who came to Talladega some time before the Civil

---

[4] Alabama Reporter, March 8th, 1855. In Talladega Public Library

War. In 1868, R. A. Moseley established "Our Mountain Home", and was one time mayor of Talladega. He was a personal friend of Frances E. Willard, and was instrumental in interesting Talladega citizens in prohibition.

DR. JOHN DIXON, who was brought to Talladega by his parents the year he was born, 1832, began the practice of medicine at Fayetteville. He was widely known in the lower part of the county as an excellent and beloved physician. He was the father of DR. DUNCAN P. DIXON, who practiced medicine in Talladega fifty years in the Twentieth century.

DRS. JOEL W. WATKINS and JOHN WATKINS settled at Mardisville about 1850.

DR. AUGUSTINE IRVINE MCALPINE also settled at Mardisville about the same time, and became a permanent citizen. His family has been one of the outstanding families of Talladega ever since. The old home of Dr. McAlpine still stands south-west of Mardisville.

DR. J. V. HUFF appeared on record also about the same time.

DR. —— MAYS was a pioneer doctor who settled at Chandlers Springs. He was a half brother to the Chandler brothers.

DR. C. H. GORMAN began the practice of medicine at Plantersville before the Civil War, and continued there all his life.

After the Civil War the medical professional group began to change. Many of the older doctors retired; some were restless and moved west, and new doctors appeared in every part of the county.

DR. BARCKLEY WALLACE TOOLE, native of Tennessee, and a noted surgeon, came to Talladega in 1865. He immediately became widely known over the county for his skill and interest in civic affairs. His son, Arthur Toole, became a doctor, and Dr. Arthur F. Toole, his grandson is now practicing in Talladega. Another son, Dr. F. M. Toole is practicing Dentistry in Talladega.

DR. GEORGE PAUL HARRISON practiced in Talladega some time during Reconstruction days.

DR. PAUL GIST came to Talladega in 1868.

DR. JOSEPH C. BLAKE was practicing as early as 1868. He lived in Mardisville for some years before moving to Talladega.

DR. HARRY RIVES BOSWELL, a native of Talladega County, graduated from the Louisville Medical College in 1870, and immediately entered into the practice of medicine at Talladega, and continued until his death in 1896.

DR. T. J. POWELL was practicing in Childersburg for some years after the Civil War.

DR. THOMAS J. LEE appears as a partner of Dr. Powell in Childersburg in 1887.

DR. D. C. KELLER, a graduate of the University of New York and of the Philadelphia Medical School, was mustered out of the Union Army in Talladega, and immediately settled here.

DR. E. D. RHODES came to the county in October of 1865, and settled near Alpine. He was the father of Mr. Ira W. Rhodes.

DR. A. G. SIMS, a native of Mardisville, began the practice of medicine about 1869. He attended the University of Alabama and graduated from the medical department of the University of Nashville. Two of his sons, Albert G. and J. Anthony and a grandson, J. A. Jr., are practicing physicians at this time.

DR. J. T. HARRISON settled near Munford in 1869. He graduated at the Nashville Medical College. Dr. Harrison practiced in a wide area of the upper part of the county, and was frequently called into consultation by other doctors over the county. He and his son, Dr. W. Groce Harrison opened the first sanitorium in Talladega.

DR. W. GROCE HARRISON graduated in medicine at the University of Maryland Medical College, in Baltimore, in 1892, and immediately began the practice of his profession in Talladega. In 1901 he moved to Birmingham, and was known as an authority on Eyes, Ears, Nose and Throat ailments. His son, Dr. Tinsley Harrison is prominently associated with the School of Medicine of the University of Alabama, located in Birmingham.

DR. LEWIS ARCHER BOSWELL, a native of Virginia and inventor of an airplane, settled near Eastaboga in 1869. He is listed under the chapter entitled "Inventors."[5]

DR. J. T. DONALDSON, cultured and beloved physician, settled at Eastaboga in 1870.

DR. WILLIAM F. THEDFORD, and later his son DR. KENNON THEDFORD, were early practitioners of Talladega.

DR. GEORGE ARMSTRONG HILL began the practice of medicine in Fayetteville about 1870. He lived on a plantation and also practiced in Sylacauga.

DR. E. B. FREEMAN opened a drug store sometime in the 1860's and also practiced medicine.

DR. MYLES JEFFERSON GREENE was born October 30th 1827 in Baldwin County, Ga. He studied medicine at the South Carolina Medical College in Charleston, where he graduated in 1851. He came to Talladega several years later, where he practiced until 1888, when he moved to Montgomery.

---

[5] Full details of Dr. Boswell's Invention can be found in the "The Old Free State, A contribution to the History of Lunenburg County and Southdale Virginia" by Landon C. Bell, Ph. D., M. A., LL. B., Chapter 11.

Obituaries of SAMUEL H. DICKSON, M. D., and of JOHN H. PARRISH, M. D., appear in the January 14th, 1872 issue of the Talladega News, as having been practitioners in Talladega.

Among license payers listed in 1870 were GRAY & HALL, DRUGS; J. C. McDERMIT, M. D.; JOHN DIXON, M. D.; B. W. GROCE, M. D.; W. A. WELCH, M. D., and M. T. W. CHRISTIAN, M. D.

Vandiver's Drug Store appeared soon after the Civil War, and ROBERT BARBER, who was mustered out of the Union Army in Talladega as Asst. Adj. General, opened a drug store in 1865. It burned in 1866, and he moved to Montgomery.

The "Boom" of 1885 brought another marked change among the doctors, and new ones arrived every few years for some time.

DR. J. S. McCANTS arrived in 1886.

DR. B. B. SIMMS arrived in 1886.

DR. E. B. WREN came about 1887.

DR. O. R. EARLY, Physician, surgeon and obstetrician, appeared on record in 1888.

During the 1890's DR. E. P. CASON, THOMAS R. NEWMAN, WALLACE REVERDY BISHOP and DR. W. GROCE HARRISON, were practicing in Talladega.

DR. JOHN WALTER GRIMES was practicing at Talladega Springs in 1899.

DR. JAMES PICKETT COLVIN settled in Lincoln in 1897. He was the father of GUS COLVIN, who is now practicing at Lincoln.

DR. H. L. CASTLEMAN settled at Sylacauga during this period.

DR. PITCHFORD settled at Eastaboga and DR. D.B. HARRIS settled at Munford about this time.

Among others listed, without dates of practice, were W. G. Conway, W. D. Caldwell, Sycamore, L. E. Ray, Coker, S. M. McAlpine, J. C. Powell, LaFayette Taylor, and W. T. Castleberry.

This sketch is a feeble effort toward recording a history of the medical profession of Talladega County, and I regret that it is not within my power to give a fuller and more accurate account, but ethics of this group of professional men are self-effacing, and records do not give credit that is due them.

VETERINARY SURGERY

Though we have no early records regarding the profession of Veterinary Surgery in Talladega County, no doubt Dr. Robert Spence, a native of Scotland, was the first to practice the profession. He settled here in 1848.

There is no other profession that has grown more rapidly. Especially has this become more popular in the county during the 20th century, and more particularly in the past twenty years since the county has developed a profitable cattle business.

DENTAL SURGERY

The earliest local dentists prior to 1850 were perhaps Drs. C. L. and J. W. Simmons, whose professional card stated that they were located next door to the "Indian Queen Hotel", and a Dr. C. C. Porter, of Jacksonville, who came "one week every two months" to Talladega for dental practice.

Dr. J. McD Whitson announced in 1855 that he had a "Dental Chair" and was located at Moore & Taylor's, Druggists.[6] His professional card later stated that Dr. B. J. Burgin was a partner. Dr. Hampton was associated with him in 1868.

Dr. H. C. Bartleson began practice soon after the Civil War. He moved to Paris, France, and resided there some time, where he had several "Crown Heads" as patients. He returned to Talladega, remained several years, then moved to New Smyrna, Florida.

Dr. J. E. Berkstresser opened an office in Sylacauga soon after the Civil War. The State Dental Association was organized in 1869, but there is no record of early Talladega Dentists having been associated with the organization. Dr. S. H. Baird entered the practice in 1886. Dr. Corley came about the same time. Dr. W. F. Slaughter is listed in 1888, and Dr. Dutton Steel Lightcap in 1890.

Dr. William Marion Sorrel opened an office in Sylacauga in 1888, and became quite prominently associated with the civic affairs of the town.

Dr. Charles W. Lokey opened an office in Talladega in 1897, but soon moved to Birmingham, where he is still practicing.

Certainly there were many other practitioners prior to 1900, but no record is available.

---

[6] Alabama Reporter, March 8th, 1855. In Talladega Library.

Talladega Hospitals

The beginning of any public enterprise is usually in the minds of some individuals long before the project is launched. Therefore, it is impossible to give credit to those who were the inspiration of hospital progress in Talladega.

CONFEDERATE HOSPITAL

The first hospital, about which we have definite information, is the improvised hospital for Confederate soldiers in the Exchange Hotel during the Civil War. This building was owned by a group of citizens of Talladega, and was located on the N. W. corner of North and Court Sts., where the United States Post office building now stands. Most of the wounded soldiers were sent to Talladega via the old Alabama & Tenn. Rivers Railroad (now the Southern Railway). Talladega rallied to the great need for nurses and materials. Bandages were made from prized sheets of individuals, and food was shared from poorly stocked pantries. The wounded had the best Talladega could furnish in loving care and provisions.

However, there lies in Oak Hill Cemetery mute evidence that this was not sufficient to save many of the seriously wounded, for there are 64 graves marked "Unknown Confederate Soldier." Although a Confederate corps of Surgeons and attendants were in charge of the hospital, it will be seen that many of the wounded died. At one time wooden markers carried the names and dates of births and deaths of most of the now "Unknown Soldiers", but Time and Weather obliterated this information years ago, and the United Daughters of the Confederacy and the Memorial Association thought it advisable to place the present markers.

FREEDMAN'S HOSPITAL

The Freedman's Hospital was supported by the State, and was founded soon after the Civil War, for the purpose of caring for the aged and sick freed Negroes sent here from all parts of the State of Alabama. The Trustees were Talladega men, who served as such, free of charge. Some of the reports carried complaints that the hospital was too great a tax on the town. Since only bare necessities were furnished by the State, it is reasonable to infer that Talladega residents supplemented where needful. The following is quoted from one of the reports:

"Report of the Secretary of the Board of Trustees, Freedman's Hospital near Talladega, Alabama."[1]

to His

Excellency, Wm. H. Smith, Governor of Alabama, November 5th, 1869."

Signed by Jos. H. Johnson, Secretary of the Board of Trustees, and approved by G. T. McAfee, President; and Geo. P. Plowman, all Talladega Citizens.

"I rented from the owner, Mr. J. W. Riley, the buildings and grounds occupied by the remainder of the patients, for $30.00 per month. The premises embraced several acres of cultivatable land, with good, comfortable new cabins, amply large and well suited for the accommodation of the inmates. The hospital is about two miles Southwest of the Town of Talladega. A bountiful clear stream of water runs through the grounds. An abundance of good fuel was included in the rental. The Board procured the service of Dr. E. B. Freeman, as medical attendant, and employed Mr. G. P. McAfee as Steward, with commissary powers and duties. The salary paid each of these gentlemen is $50.00 per month. The other employees of the hospital are, a cook, nurse, teamster, and laundress. They are paid from $6.00 to $10.00 per month. There were 73 patients on the roll on the 1st of January, 1869, of whom 23 have been discharged and six died, as will appear from the report of the attending physician . . .

The property of the Hospital consists of a pair of good mules, a wagon and harness, plows, and other garden implements; also 100 iron bedsteads and bedding, together with stoves, cook stoves, kitchen furniture, etc."

In another report dated January, 1871, signed by W. H. Thornton, Secretary.[2] The number of patients were reported, and Mr. Thornton adds: "The houses, yards, etc., are at all times kept thoroughly cleaned of all dirt and rubbish by the attending nurse." Appropriations included all expenditures for food, clothing, attendants, etc., and were, for 1869 $4,019.98; 1870 $5,767.03; 1871 $4,098.01; 1872 $3,383.63.

The hospital was discontinued in January of 1876.

HARRISON SANITORIUM

In 1900 Dr. W. Groce Harrison, a graduate of the University of Maryland Medical School, and his father, Dr. J. T. Harrison, rented the J. M.

---

[1] State Documents, 1869-70
[2] State Documents, 1871-72

Lewis home in the Highlands—which later became known as the Nurses Home of Citizens Hospital and opened a private hospital. This was the first hospital for Citizens of Talladega. Other doctors were permitted to send patients to this hospital, but were not otherwise associated with it.

In 1901, the Manning home on South St., was purchased by the Drs. Harrison. They enlarged the residence and converted it into a more modem hospital. There was no provision made for charity patients; and the hospital had an average of only 4 patients per day, with one trained nurse in charge. The population of Talladega at the time was 5,056. The Harrison Sanitorium closed March 1st, 1905, and Dr. W. G. Harrison entered the special practice of treating eyes, ears, nose and throat in Birmingham. Dr. J. T. Harrison returned to private practice.

TALLADEGA INFIRMARY

In the early part of 1912 Dr. B. B. Simms and Dr. S. W. Welch purchased the Lanier Home on the West side of S. Court St., just back of the McAlpine House. They remodeled the house and converted it into a 14 room hospital. Dr. Lawson Thornton, graduate of Johns Hopkins, in Baltimore, was associated with them, but in 1913 Dr. Thornton moved to Birmingham, and later to Atlanta, where he became one of the nation's noted Orthopedic Surgeons.

Miss Bertha McElderry, graduate of Johns Hopkins School of nursing, was Superintendent of the hospital. During the First World War, when the hospitals at Fort McClellan were overflowing, 25 patients were brought to Talladega Infirmary from the Fort, under the auspices of the Red Cross, with Miss Bertha McElderry, a Red Cross Registered Nurse, as supervisor Talladega Infirmary at the time was operated by a Board of Directors, with Dr. S. W. Welch acting Chairman. At another period Mr. A. G. Storey was Chairman. All Talladega doctors were affiliated with the hospital during this period.

In 1920 the building and equipment were sold to Dr. C. W. C. Moore.

MARY ELIZABETH HOSPITAL

Dr. C. W. C. Moore purchased from Drs. Simms and Welch, the Talladega Infirmary in 1920. Dr. Moore and his family resided in the building, which gave the added attraction of a Resident Physician. In honor of his two daughters, Dr. Moore called the Hospital "Mary Elizabeth. He added twelve beds and opened a small training school of six nurses.

There was no provision made for public charity patients, and there were no other doctors associated financially with the hospital. However, there was an open staff, and all doctors were permitted to bring patients to the hospital. Dr. Moore employed from two to five registered nurses, as the need demanded.

Mary Elizabeth was operated until 1925, when a group of citizens purchased the Alabama Synodical College and converted it into a General Hospital. Dr. Moore transferred 4 patients to Citizens Hospital the day it was opened.

CITIZENS HOSPITAL

The Chamber of Commerce sponsored a movement in 1924 to purchase a building suitable for a General Hospital. The result was that in the early part of 1925 a building on the Highlands, erected by the Synod of Alabama for a College for Girls, was purchased by local stockholders and contributions. This building had been used for a college only a few years, was well built, in excellent repair, and well suited to conversion into a hospital.

A new Corner Stone was placed on the building, as follows:
On one side —
"Citizens Hospital
fostered by Chamber of Commerce,
T. D. Boynton, Pres.
W. A. Crites, Sec.
H. L. McElderry, C'man Hospital Com.
W. L. Dumas, C'man Board of Directors."
On another side —
"Citizens Hospital
erected 1925
Building Committee,
L. W. Clardy, Chairman
Dr. C. W. C. Moore
Dr. C. L. Salter
J. W. Cowen
S. H. Henderson."

GOODNOW HOSPITAL

Near the turn of the 20th Century, Talladega College erected a hospital building for Negro pupils on Battle St., W. The hospital had a small training school for nurses, some of whom are still practicing in Talladega. Goodnow Hospital is still in operation for college pupils.

Dr. French Craddock and associates opened a hospital, in the 20th Century, in Sylacauga, from which a number of well trained nurses have graduated. The new Sylacauga Hospital is one of the most modern in the state, and has a nurses training school in connection with the general hospital

Inventors

Dr. Lewis Archer Boswell[1] — Dr. Lee de Forest.[2]

DR. LEWIS ARCHER BOSWELL was born May 9, 1834, at "Aspen Hill", Wattsboro, Lunenburg Co., Virginia. He was highly educated as a surgeon, having attended school at the University of Virginia, the Jefferson Medical College at Philadelphia, and at Johns Hopkins University. He served as surgeon in the Confederate Army at a Hospital in Richmond, Va.

After the War he located at Greenwood, Miss., where he married Miss Bettie Liddell.

In the early part of 1868 Dr. Boswell read an article entitled "Bird Flight" in the Edinburgh Review, by the Duke of Argyle, which impressed him to such an extent, that he embarked on an experiment for the construction of an air plane "embodying his ideas of the principles which should control the flight of a heavier than air mechanism."

His friends teased him to such an extent that he finally junked his model in the Yazoo River.

In 1869 his wife inherited "Red Hill" plantation, near Eastaboga, in Talladega County, and they moved to that home, where Dr. Boswell died on November 26th, 1909.

After removing to Alabama, Dr. Boswell resumed his activities in aeronautics, and received several patents in 1874:

No. 155,218, Sept. 22, 1874, on a "New and Useful Improvement in Aerial Propeller Wheels."

No. 34,416, Feb. 7, 1874, on an "Improvement in Wind-Wheels."

He "had actually demonstrated that a craft heavier than air, propelled by his Aerial Propeller Wheels would fly through the air. The model submitted with his application (for patent) was built according to plans and under his directions by a jeweler in Talladega by the name of Lowry . . . The model was about 12" long, and its power was furnished by a clock spring mechanism."

Although Dr. Boswell's friends continued to jest about his air plane enthusiasm, he never relinquished his efforts toward completing his model with

---

[1] Dr. Boswell – Material found in "The Old Free State", Chapter II, A Contribution to the History of Lunenburg County and Southside, Virginia. By Landon C. Bell, Ph. D., M.A., L.L.B. "Dr. Boswell Invents an Airplane."
[2] Dr. Lee de Forest – Material found in "Father of Radio, the Autobiography of Lee de Forest." Published 1950 by Wilcox & Follett Co. Chicago.

the necessary motor with which to propel the engine. He eventually found such a motor with gasoline engine, which he felt sure could be used with perfect results, but Dr. Boswell had given so much time to his air plane activities, to the neglect of his practice as a physician, that he did not have the $1,000.00 with which to purchase the equipment. He appealed to the banks, and took the matter up with the Government, but received no encouragement.

Under date of May 26, 1903, he was issued another patent, No. 728,844, for a "New and Useful Improvement in Steering Mechanism of Dirigible Air Ships."

With this new invention, Dr. Boswell completed another model. The drawings and specifications were prepared by his nephew, Garland Boswell, of Wattsboro, Virginia. Dr. Boswell sent these to Glenn Curtiss, who had also been working on airplanes, and who later became the maker of the Curtiss Airplane, of Hammondsport, N. Y.

Dr. Boswell, like many pioneer inventors, has never received his due recognition, because he was financially handicapped, and the result of his years of labor fell into the hands of those who could use his ideas, for a successful model. But credit is due Dr. Boswell for having first invented certain mechanism which is used today in the manufacture of airplanes.

LEE de FOREST was born in Council Bluffs, Iowa, August 26th, 1873, in the parsonage of a Congregational Church. His father, Dr. Henry Swift de Forest, a devout minister, of French Huguenot ancestry, was still pastor in Council Bluffs in the fall of 1879, when he was called by the American Missionary Association, to serve as President of Talladega College. The college had been established in 1867 for the education of Negro Freedmen. Dr. Henry de Forest had a keen feeling of his responsibility toward Negro Freedmen, and he devoted the remaining 17 years of his life in an attempt to elevate them, physically, mentally, morally and spiritually. He died in Talladega Jan. 26, 1896.

He never fully realized the sacrifice to which he subjected his family in accepting and serving in this position. His children were reared in Negro surroundings, with illiterate associates, and at a time when the South had not yet adjusted itself to the outcome of the Civil War. His family suffered from the resultant feeling which existed at that time in the South.

Because of this ostracism, it is possible that Lee de Forest withdrew himself unconsciously from companions who were not his intellectual equal, and developed the scientific talent, which, under other circumstances might have remained dormant.

After Lee de Forest graduated from Yale in 1896, he was connected with several electric companies where he had opportunities to do research. He became a tireless worker in developing and utilizing wireless energy, which he discovered had endless possibilities. There are 208 inventions listed in his

"Father of Radio, the Autobiography of Lee de Forest", published in 1950 by Wilcox & Folletts & Co., Chicago.

Perhaps his most important invention was that of the "Audion", which made Radio possible. His inventions are being used in nearly every apparatus of modern military equipment, and they have made radio, television, wireless telegraphy, and the wireless telephone possible.

Because of these great inventions, Dr. Lee de Forest has found a place among the world's greatest inventors of all time.

Dr. de Forest still lived in Los Angeles, California where he died on June 30th, 1961.

Writers and Pamphleteers
of Talladega County

In compiling a roster of the writers and pamphleteers of Talladega County, we are tempted to claim several prominent authors because of their association with Talladega. William Garrett, who wrote "Reminiscences of Public Men of Alabama", one of the most valued histories of Alabama, possibly lived in Talladega County a short while before settling in Benton (Calhoun) County in 1833. His name appears among the Methodist laymen who attended the first Quarterly Conference at Bethel Church in Talladega County. His brother, Thomas Gray Garrett settled in Talladega and married a Rice, sister of Mrs. Joseph A. Woodward, of Talladega. William Garrett frequently visited here, and was quite well known in Talladega.

Joseph Glover Baldwin, who wrote "Flush Times in Alabama and Mississippi", married Miss Sidney White, daughter of Judge John White, and sister of Alexander White, pioneers of Talladega County, and was a frequent visitor to Talladega before moving to California. Though he possibly never lived here, his connection is at least interesting.

Another distinguished author and lawyer we would like to include on our list is Dr. Hannis Taylor. He was minister to Spain in 1893-1897; he received honorary degrees of LL.D from seven Universities, including Dublin and Edinburgh; and was internationally known as an authority on legal questions. He wrote "The Origin and Growth of the English Constitution"; "International Public Law"; "The Process of Law"; "Jurisdiction and Procedure of the Supreme Court of the United States"; and many other volumes. The nearest we can come to claiming Dr. Taylor, is that he was the son of Robert Nixon Taylor, and a step-son of Mrs. Lou McKenzie Taylor. His step-mother, Mrs. Lou McKenzie Taylor, was Talladega's first-born white child, and wrote the first History of Talladega.

Though we have no direct claim on these three noted writers of Alabama, we do feel justified in boasting of our connection with them.

While those listed here were not all natives by any means, and some lived in Talladega only a short while, the fact that they did live here at some time, gives us license for including them among the writers of Talladega County.

Newspaper editors, many of whom wrote fluently and ably, are included in the chapter on "Newspapers", and are not listed here.

ELISHA DAVID ACKER, native of Lincoln, Talladega County, Teacher and Lawyer, compiled and privately printed a volume of several hundred pages, on the "History and Genealogy of the Acker Family."

MELANE GORDON BARBER, g. g. grand-daughter of Hugh G. Barclay, one of the founders of Talladega, wrote "A Christmas Poem, PEACE", published in 1938 by the Geo. Peabody Press, New York.

REV. RANDOLPH F. BLACKFORD, Episcopal Rector, wrote "Under Seven Flags", privately printed in 1950, and in 1957, "Fascinating Talladega County."

PETER ALEXANDER BRANNON lived in Talladega at one time as a pharmacist. He is one of Alabama's best known authorities on historical subjects, and has written numerous articles; compiled and edited many more. He is now Director of the Department of Archives and History in Montgomery, Ala.

CLARENCE CASON, son of Dr. and Mrs. E. P. Cason, was reared in Talladega. He was head of the Dept. of Journalism at the University of Alabama when he died some years ago. He wrote "Ninety Degrees in the Shade", 1935; "A Composite Book for Journalists", 1927; "History of the Vickers and Browning Department", 1919. He also wrote numerous articles for magazines.

DELL MULLEN-CRAVEN, a native of Talladega, daughter of Robert and Emmie Davis Mullen, edited the Journal of her grandmother, Mrs. Mary E. M. Davis, under the title of "'The Neglected Thread."

GEORGE W. CRAWFORD, of Talladega College, wrote "Talladega Manuel of Vocational Guidance". Privately printed by the Talladega College Press, 1937.

DR. WILLIAM CROWE, Presbyterian Minister, wrote "Those Fifty Days", published by the Frederick Publishing Co., St. Louis. He has also written numerous articles for newspapers and magazines, and a syndicated series "Under the Study Lamp."

DR. JABEZ LAMAR MONROE CURRY, Congressman, Baptist Minister, Diplomat and Statesman, wrote a number of books, among them: "Constitutional Government in Spain," 1889; "Establishment and Disestablishment in America," 1889; "William Ewart Gladstone", 1891; "The Southern States of the American Union", 1895; "The Civil History of the Government of the Confederate States, with Some Personal Reminiscences," 1901.

MRS. MARY EVELYN MOORE DAVIS, a native of Talladega, daughter of John and Marion Lucy Crutchfield Moore, was educated at the old Presbyterian College in Talladega. She "acquired a just celebrity as a poet. Some of her verses are among the rarest gems of Southern Literature."[1] She moved to Houston Texas while quite young. Among her published books were: "Minding

---

[1] Brewer's History of Alabama, Page 545

the Gap and Other Poems," 1870; "In War Times at LaRosa Blanche Plantation"; "Under the Man-fig, An Elephant's Track and Other Stories," 1897; "Under Six Flags", 1898; "The Little Chavalier," 1905; "The Price of Silence", 1907.[2]

MRS. MARY E. MORAGNE DAVIS, Mother of Mr. Bob Davis, and the Misses Kate, Ellen and Mamie Davis, printed privately a small volume of fascinatingly written poems of memory under the title of "Lays from the Sunny Lands," 1888.

DR. LEE de FOREST, Inventor, who is classed with Edison and Marconi, was the son of Dr. Henry Swift de Forest, President of Talladega College during the years 1879-1896. He spent his childhood in Talladega. In 1950 he wrote "Father of Radio, the Autobiography of Lee de Forest.", which gives a full account of his numerous inventions.

MRS. IDA WALLIS ELLIOTT, widely known as conductor, and owner, of "Elliott Tours", collected and edited a book of Jokes and Anecdotes, entitled "Laugh and Let Laugh".

MRS. SCOTTIE McKENZIE FRAZIER is a native of Talladega, grand-daughter of Dr. Henry McKenzie, one of the founders of Talladega, and niece of Mrs. Lou McKenzie Taylor. She is well known as a columnist of Dothan, Ala. She wrote "Fagots of Fancy" in 1920, of which she says – "These little verses are not according to the laws of rhyme and meter; they are not the product of labor, but a spontaneous outburst." "Things that are Mine", 1922, are poems similarly written.

DR. BUELL GORDON GALLAGHER, one time President of Talladega College, 1933-38 wrote "American Caste and the Negro College" Columbia University Press, 1938. He has also written many articles for religious and educational journals.

DR. J. S. GANEY, Legislator and one time Supt. of the Alabama Schools for the Deaf and Blind, wrote "Historical Sketch of the Alabama Institute for the Deaf and Blind," 1942.

MRS. EVELYN KING GILMORE, wrote poems for various journals, as well as magazine articles. Mrs. Gilmore lived in Talladega several years, but now resides in Selma.

EDDIE GILMORE, son of Mrs. Evelyn Gilmore, is internationally known as a news commentator and journalist with the Associated Press. He spent several boyhood years in Talladega, where he attended High School.

DR. LEON HOWARD, a native of Talladega, prominent educator, son of Percy Leonidas and Georgia Heacock Howard, has published two books.

---

[2] "Story of Alabama" by Mrs. Marie Bankhead Owen, Vol. III, Page 206

"Herman Meville, a Biography", and "Connecticut Wits." He is preparing another book for early publication. At present he is Professor of American Literature at U. C. L. A. in Los Angeles, California.

MRS. L. A. JEMISON, a native of Talladega County, daughter of Col. Thomas and Frances Turner McElderry, is known in Talladega better as a philanthropist than as a writer. She was founder of the Talladega Public Library; a liberal contributor to the Talladega High School, having donated the property on which the school was erected, and presented the Domestic Science Building to the City; she contributed toward equipping the Citizens Hospital, and presented the Nurses Home to them. She gave Jemison Park to the city, and contributed to the various churches, and to many other civic institutions. Mrs. Jemison wrote a number of books, which have never been widely read because they were never put on the market. Only a limited number of each book was privately printed. These were distributed, as gifts, among her friends and relatives. She wrote a number of stories for magazines. A number of these, and her first books were written under the pseudonym of "Ellery Sinclair". Among her books are: "Victor", "Christie's Choice", 1886, "Mavounit", "Nauche Micco", "Linked Hands", "Theo", "A Texas Vendetta", and "Old and New".

MARY JULIA JEMISON, Native of Talladega County, has written numerous poems of a religious nature, which have been published in religious magazines.

MRS. MARGARET A. JENNINGS, lived at the home of William Curry, at "Willow Glen", during the War Between the States. She contributed a poem almost every week to the local papers, as well as those of Marion and Selma during this period. The Democratic Watchtower of Jan. 31, 1866, paid tribute to her as both a writer and "sweet singer", and stated that she wrote for the "Metropolitan Record, perhaps the ablest paper in New York." Among her most praiseworthy poems was "Another Star Shines on High", which was a tribute to the noble Gen. Stonewall Jackson.[3]

ROSA BELL KNOX, a native of Talladega, daughter of Wm. A. and Belle Wadsworth Knox, is a well known and gifted writer of juvenile stories. She has also written a number of magazine articles and book reviews. Among her many books are: "School Activities and Equipment," 1927; "The Boys and Sally, Down on a Plantation", 1930; "Miss Jimmy Deane", 1931; "Gray Caps", 1932; "Marty and Company 7", 1933; "Patsy's Prayers", 1935.

DR. HERMAN KRANOLD, of Talladega College, wrote "The International Distribution of Raw Materials," Published by Routledge, London, 1938.

---

[3] Democratic Watchtower of Jan. 31, 1866, found in Talladega Public Library

B. PALMER LEWIS, son of J. M. and Annie Eliza (Hardie) Lewis, a native of Talladega, wrote "John Hardie of Thornhill, His Life, Letters and Times", privately printed by the Avondale Press of New York City, 1928.

MRS. CAROLINE LANE PEACE LUTTRELL of Sylacauga, past State Regent of the Daughters of the American Revolution, compiled a volume of ancestral records of the Ala. Members of the D. A. R.

MRS. IDORA McCLELLAN PLOWMAN-MOORE, a native of Talladega, daughter of Gen. Wm. McClellan, of "Idlewild", was better known as "Betsy Hamilton", under which name she wrote for years. Mrs. Moore was a Chautauqua entertainer, and wrote a column of character sketches for the Atlanta Constitution under the heading "The Backwoods Familiar Letters, Betsy Hamilton to her Cousin Saleny." Because of her assumed name, she was affectionately known all her life, by young and old, as "Betsy". Her "Southern Character Sketches" was published in 1921. A later edition was privately printed by one of her step-daughters, Mrs. Julia Moore Smith. "Betsy" was beloved throughout the South.

DR. JOHN MARTIN PHILLIPS OTTS, Presbyterian Minister, wrote "Nicodemus with Jesus"; "At Mother's Knee", "The Fifth Gospel", and several other books.

TERRELL PAULINE PARKER privately printed a delightful little booklet of poems entitled "Singing and Sewing", in 1951.

JOSEPH HEPBURN PARSONS, Lawyer, native of Talladega, son of Prov. Gov. L. E. Parsons, wrote "Historical Papers upon the Events of Rare Interest in the Napoleonic Era", printed and beautifully bound in two volumes. He spent some years in France while writing these volumes. He was writing a History of the Confederacy when he died.

MRS. ALICE V. DUNCAN-PIERPONT, wrote a biography of her grandfather, who was an early settler of Talladega County, privately printed the volume in 1947, entitled "Reuben Vaughan Kidd, Soldier of the Confederacy." Mrs. Pierpont, once a resident of Talladega, now lives in Virginia.

MRS. E. B. PUREFOY, founder of the nationally known "Purefoy Hotel", of Talladega, edited two books: "The Purefoy Cook Book" and "Just Ask Me – Handy Household Hints." The latter compiled jointly with Louise P. McClung.

MRS. CELIA BOSWELL SIMMONS, Native of Talladega, daughter of Dr. Harry R. and Celia Parsons Boswell, and granddaughter of Prov. Gov. L. E. Parsons, wrote a child's book when she was nine years of age, entitled "My Book."

WM. H. SKAGGS, Lawyer, writer and lecturer, a native of Talladega, and one time Mayor of Talladega wrote a number of books, among which were: "Public Schools in the South," 1910; "Vice–Regent of God and His Chosen

People," 1914; "German Conspiracies in America," 1916; "The Outlaws of Christendom," 1918; "The Southern Oligarchy", 1924. Mr. Skaggs had another book almost ready for publication when he died. He wrote numerous newspaper and journal articles.

MRS. ANNE SOUTHERNE TARDY resided in Talladega for several years at the Purefoy Hotel. Her book of poems, privately printed in 1935, entitled "Sun Through Window Shutters", is made up of delightful little poems. She also wrote a "History of the National Society of the Colonial Dames of America, in the State of Alabama, 1898-1937"; printed by the Commercial Printing Company, Birmingham, 1938.

ALICIA JOEL TOWERS, a native of Talladega, wrote a book of poems entitled "Piney Woods Poetry."

JUDGE JEHU WELLINGTON VANDIVER was a native of Calhoun Co., grandson of Judge G. T. McAfee and first County Judge of Talladega. He was a lawyer, editor and lecturer. He wrote many articles for the Montgomery Advertiser, Birmingham Age-Herald, Puck, Life, Judge, Black Cat Magazine, and others. Notable among his articles were "Yarns of the Court House Gang" and "Sunshine in Alabama." He wrote a "History of Talladega County", published serially many years ago in Our Mountain Home.

E. L. C. WARD, lawyer, editor and writer, once editor of the Talladega News Reporter, wrote "Heart Shots", "You", and "The Scrap Book." He was President of the Alabama Press Association for two terms.

A. J. WALKER, lawyer and Chief Justice of the Supreme Court of Alabama, perhaps should not be classed as a writer, but he did compile the "Present Code of Alabama" soon after the War Between the States. He practiced Law at one time in partnership with John T. Morgan.

DR. ANSON WEST, a devout Methodist Minister, who lived at one time in Talladega, and who is buried in Oak Hill Cemetery, in Talladega, wrote a "History of Methodism in Alabama", "Printed for the Author, Publishing House, Methodist Episcopal Church, South, Barbee & Smith, Agents, Nashville, Tenn., 1893".[4]

REV. WASHINGTON WILKES, Baptist Minister of Fayetteville, Talladega County, Ala., was one of the County's most gifted poets, of his day. Among the many poems which deserve special mention were "Our Times", "The Aged Pilgrim Waiting to Die", "Looking Through my Window Glass", "Women of the South", "The Broken Cup."

ALEXANDER WHITE, Lawyer and Congressman, should be properly classed as an orator, rather than writer, but his famous speech made at

---

[4] Front Page of the "History of Methodism in Alabama."

a post-war convention held in Selma, is a literary gem, and easily places him among the literary men of the age. Because he was a citizen of Talladega for many years, having built, and resided in, the old home now owned by Bemis Brother Bag Company, it seems appropriate to record that speech which made him famous:

The Bonnie Blue Flag

"THE BONNIE BLUE FLAG no longer reflects the light of the morning sunbeam, or kisses with its silken folds the genial breezes of our Southern clime. The hands that waved it along the crest of a hundred battlefields, and the hearts that, for the love they bore for it, so often defied danger and death, no longer rally around it. Another banner waves in triumph over its closed and prostrate folds, but proud memories and glorious recollections cluster around it. Sir, I will refrain. The South needs no eulogy. The faithful record of her achievements will encircle her brow with glory bright and enduring as the diadem that crowns the night of her cloudless skies. The scenes of Marathon and Platae have been reenacted in the new world without the beneficent results which flow from those battlefields of freedom, and our country lies prostrate at the feet of the conqueror. But dearer to me is she in this hour of her humiliation than she was in the day and hour of her pride and power. Each bloodstained field, each track of devastation, each new-made grave of her sons, fallen in defense, each mutilated form of the Confederate soldier — her widow's tear, her orphan's cry—are but so many chords that bind me to her in the midst of her desolation, and draw my affections closer around my stricken country.

When I raise my voice or lift my hand against her, may the thunders rive me where I stand! Though I be false in all else, I will be true to her. Though all others may prove faithless, I will be faithful still. And when, in obedience to the great command, 'Dust to dust', my heart shall return to that earth from whence it sprang, it shall sink into her bosom with the proud consciousness that it never knew one beat not in unison with the honor, the interests, the glory of my country."[1]

This speech was made at a Convention held in Selma, when Mr. White represented Talladega County at the Convention, in 1865.[2]

---

[1] Garrett's "Public Men of Alabama," Page 564
[2] Ibid, Page 563

Entertainment

1540 civilization was heralded by Coosa Indians on Talladega soil, with fyfe, drum and song; prophetic, perhaps, of influences which would endue the permanent settlers with a longing for cultural entertainment.

The early settlers made provision for such entertainment, when a Town Hall was included in their plans. The Town Hall was situated on the East side of the Square, over stores located where Raff's and Wright's Drug Store are now operating. Before the Civil War, road shows performed to appreciative audiences, first by flickering candle light, and later by sputtering gas lights, in this old Town Hall. It was in the old hall that Blind Tom performed to a packed house. The whole country turned out to hear him. Blind Tom, a small Negro man, was the greatest musical genius, not only of his day, but perhaps of all time. He never had a music lesson, but could repeat perfectly the most difficult selection played in his hearing. His coming to Talladega was a great event.

Piano and guitar lessons were "musts" in the education of every young woman. Since young ladies were taught such an art of entertainment, there was a constant flow of local talent displayed in the auditoriums of the girls schools. Especially was this true of the old Presbyterian College, because the auditorium was larger, and the stage more appropriately arranged for concerts.

Mr. Geo. W. Chambers, a progressive business man, recognizing the need for a permanent hall of entertainment, included such an auditorium when he erected the storehouse on the southwest corner of Court and Battle Sts., where the Talladega Furniture Co. is now located.

Chambers Opera House was on the second floor of this building, and was a great addition to the cultural life of Talladega. The auditorium proper was 75 x 43 feet, with a seating capacity of 1100 people.[1] Be it remembered that at the time Talladega Town had a population of less than 3,000 white people. However, people of the entire county patronized the theatre, and the house was usually full. The vestibule was resplendent with full length mirrors. Handsome paintings of noted writers, actors and actresses were hung in the main auditorium. The boxes and stage were appropriately decorated, and the entire house presented an artistic appearance. The stage was 43 x 36 feet, and equipped to take care of any performance of the day. It was one of Alabama's most up-to-date play houses and Talladega people enjoyed the privilege of witnessing many of the popular plays and operas of the 1880's and 1890's.

---

[1] From article found in Scrap Book of Mrs. Geo. W. Chambers from "The South"

Naturally, entertainment shifted from the Town Hall and school auditoriums to Chambers Opera House. For years it was used for graduating exercises, political rallies, and local entertainments of all kinds, in addition to the road shows.

In 1894 a group of the intelligentsia of Alabama organized "The Alabama Chautauqua Association". They raised a large tent at Shelby Springs, employed the best talent available in the United States, and ran excursion trains from various points for the convenience of patrons. The adventure proved quite successful, but Shelby Springs was situated on one railroad only, and there were not sufficient boarding facilities for the crowd. There was so much complaint about this inconvenience, that it was deemed advisable to change the location.

The Chautauqua Board of Trustees met in Birmingham that fall to accept bids for a permanent location.

Talladega citizens, in the meantime, had organized a local association of 65 men, for the purpose of bidding for the location. The bid was readily accepted, and Alabama Chautauqua was moved to Talladega permanently.

It was necessary for the Association to bestir themselves to be ready for the 1895 summer assembly. An unpainted frame building, with many windows without shutters or window panes of any kind, was erected on the present Public Library lot. The building had steps across the entire front leading into a vestibule opening into an auditorium which seated 2,000 people.

Talent was brought from time to time from many parts of the world. The Swiss Bell Ringers, from Switzerland, a Marimba Band from Central America, great orators, singers, humorists, magicians, and all types of entertainment attracted visitors from every conceivable direction.

The greatest annual occasion was that of the College Oratorical Contest—Auburn, Tuscaloosa, Howard and Southern Universities presented their prize orators in the annual contest.

Students from all parts of the state arrived to take part in the great celebration. Young women, and even children, dressed in colors of the college they boosted. Great streamers floated from carriage and horse; parasols carried large bows of college colors. The stage groaned under the enormous emblems, colors and designs of the four groups. Talladega annually experienced the most colorful and gayest event ever to occur in Alabama, during that period.

Summer excursion rates were established from Maine to California, and Talladega became the cultural center of the South; nationally classed as a resort town.

Friends and relatives, not heard from in years, turned up from every direction. Every available space was utilized to provide comforts for the guests.

School buildings were opened for boarders, and every provision was made to take care of the flow of people who came to Chautauqua.

The luxury of Alabama Chautauqua proved too expensive. Talladega's taste was for the best only, and the "best" was more than was financially profitable. Therefore, Chautauqua sessions were closed after about ten years of luxurious enjoyment. One thing is worthy of note, however. During this period Talladega more than doubled in population. In 1890 there were 2063 inhabitants; in 1900 there were 5056. Whether Chautauqua had anything to do with this increase is purely conjecture. The Chautauqua building was torn down in 1906 to make room for the Talladega Public Library.

Tent Lyceum and Chautauqua courses followed, but Talladega people never fully rallied to these, and they eventually stopped entirely.

While this sketch deals primarily with Nineteenth Century activities, the Talladega Music Club deserves mention, since that organization followed on the heels of Chautauqua, and became the outstanding source of musical inspiration for years. Their aim was to encourage the development of music appreciation and education. They not only rendered many classical and difficult arrangements themselves, but annually brought outside talent to Talladega for twenty years.

Since Elks Theatre was the focal point for such local activities as rendered by the Music Club the first part of the 20th Century, mention should also be made of this place of entertainment. Elk's Theatre was situated on the East side of East Street, N., about half a block from the Square. It was erected in the early part of the 20th Century, and was modern in every respect. When it was opened, the society folk instituted the dignified custom of wearing evening dress for dress circle and box seats. Al. G. Fields Minstrels was the opening performance, and the building was ablaze with modem electric lights. "Faust", "The Fortune Teller", Isben's plays, and many popular plays and operas were brought to Talladega. Local assemblies took place at Elk's Theatre from the time it was erected until it burned in 1928.

Of course, it would be ridiculous to say that these few sources of mentioned entertainment were all in which our ancestors indulged, but it would be impossible to bring out all sources. However, others will be outlined in another chapter as "Amusements".

Amusements and Celebrations

In February, 1836 a special tax was ordered by the Court, from which funds were to be obtained for building a court house. Among the taxed items were "a race horse 50c", "Race track kept for use $10.00", and "every pack of playing cards sold loaned, given away or otherwise disposed of, $1.00", etc. We assume, therefore, that horse racing and card playing were among the amusements of the pioneer.

Certainly we know there was one privately owned race track at "Thornhill", and there were probably others.

A public race track was maintained the last half of the Nineteenth Century on the north side of the present Southern Railway, near what is known as Hyena. This track was a part of grounds where a County Fair was held for years. These fairs were annual events, and the principal attraction, aside from the races, was the ascension of a balloon. For days before the ascension people stood in silent wonder, as the great black object was slowly inflated, while being held to the ground by staked ropes, and finally by lookers-on themselves. There was a feeling almost of reverence as a man attached himself to the ropes, and the balloon was released to soar into the heavens. The impossible was taking place. No modern airplane was ever so awe inspiring.

The high diver usually followed the balloon ascension. A County Fair was more than a display of products; it was a spectacular event to be remembered.

As previously stated, in 1837 we find citizens assembled at the Indian Queen Hotel for a Christmas Ball at 2:00 P. M. There were many such occasions. Entire families of adults participated in the dance. No young lady would ride unchaperoned with a young gentleman at any time; certainly not to a Ball. These Balls of the pioneer sometimes began in the morning and lasted all day. Dinner was served when the dance took place at private homes. Day time dances were necessary because some Indians were still in the country, and it was not safe to travel at night. Then, too, the only mode of lighting was that of fire light or candle light. Of course, in time, as roads were opened and all Indians were removed, or were in subjection, dances took place in the evenings.

A great many social activities took place on the plantations. Our earliest and most spacious mansions were in the rural districts.

"Dancing was really, in those days, a merry-making business. Except the minuet, which was introduced only to teach us the graces, and the congo, which was only to chase away the solemnities of the minuet; it was all jovial, heart-stirring, foot stirring amusement. We had none of your mathematical cotillions; none of your immodest waltzes; none of your detestable disgusting gallopades. The waltz would have crimsoned the cheek of every young lady who attended a ball in my day; and had the gallopade been commenced in the ball-room, it would have ended in the street."[1]

"Round Dances" were not permitted. The Virginia Reel was the popular dance of the pioneer, and the Square Dance was to liven up the evening.

Among rural amusements were the Corn Shuckings and Quilting Parties. The slave owning planters usually had their corn shucked by slaves, and frequently a great deal of the quilting was done by trained servants. However, others turned these affairs into social events. Corn Shuckings were indulged in by both sexes. The finding of a red ear of corn brought forth a great deal of excitement, for it meant a kiss for the partner. Quilting Parties were spend-the-day affairs, and women looked forward to the social feature. Instead of "Showers" of today for a prospective bride, there was often a Quilting Party in celebration of the announcement and the quilt was presented to the bride.

The gentleman planter indulged in the hunt. Every large planter had his pack of hounds. There were bird, deer, rabbit, coon, "possum and fox hunts. The most thrilling was that of the Fox Chase. Before dawn the sound of the host's ram's horn would break the silence of the night. It was answered from hill and dale, as each neighbor thrust his horn out of the window and blew an answering blast. After the chase the party repaired to the host's home for a hearty breakfast.

Another rural amusement among gentlemen was that of the Shooting contest. A small charge was often made for the privilege of entering the contest. The prize was usually a beef, quartered; first prize being choice of quarter, etc.[2]

Come May Day, every one, young and old, in town and country, indulged in a picnic. All during the spring and summer, churches, fraternal organizations, day schools and groups of young people, properly chaperoned, of course, enjoyed picnics from sun up to sun down. Baseball was the favorite amusement on such occasions, and a score of 49 to 62 was much more entertaining than one of 2 to 1 of our day.

After railroads came into use, there were excursions to summer resorts, or other play grounds. Talladega Springs and Shelby Springs were especially popular excursion points. When the B. & A. Railroad came into existence, Island Park and Renfroe became the popular places for picnics. Island Park was a secluded spot on Talladega Creek, where several springs furnished a sparkling

---

[1] From Georgia Scenes, by Baldwin, Page 161
[2] From Georgia Scenes, by Baldwin Page 274

beverage, and the creek was convenient for wading and swimming. Renfroe had a large landscaped lake, and was a beauty spot of the county.

While a wedding reception could not be classed under "Amusements", it certainly was a popular celebration and a great social event. Baking took place for days before. According to old letters, receptions of 1850 and 1880 were very much the same. There was no cup of tea, a cookie and a small sandwich. A reception in those days was a capital letter event, and was very much like a magnified banquet of our day. There was usually a large turkey at one end of the table and a roasted pig at the other. Between turkey and pig the table was ladened with all sorts of jellies, preserves, pickles, salads, pies, cakes and breads. There was always the home cured ham and enormous platters of fried chicken for every eating occasion. Refreshments, in fact, consisted of meats and sweets mostly.

Talladega was an important circus town, and the only town near the counties of Clay, Shelby, St. Clair, Coosa, Calhoun and Randolph where big shows, such as Robinson Brothers, pitched their tents. Every sort of side show and wild animal was in evidence. Great parades took place. People began arriving the day before the circus, and the square was a mass of people trying to talk above the clamor of vendors of balloons, cheap jewelry, walking sticks, and every sort of useless ware imaginable. It was a day of horse-swapping and trading of every sort; one looked forward to by merchants as a day when people spent their money recklessly. Circus day was a great day in every respect.

One of the most thrilling events of the latter part of the Nineteenth and early part of the Twentieth Centuries was the annual Firemen's Tournament. The fire departments of Selma, Rome, Dalton, Newnan, Gadsden, Anniston and Talladega, composed the Association, as I recall it. When it met in Talladega, Battle Street was closed from Court Street on the Square to the side tracks west of the factories. A grand stand was erected in front of Talladega Cotton Factory, and a temporary fire house was built in the middle of Battle Street, just in front of the grand stand, which was without walls, occupied on the ground floor by the fire truck and horses, and on the second floor presumably by men asleep. A fire of some sort was started near Court Street, the alarm was given and then the fun began. The firemen slid down a pole from the second floor, hitched their horses and raced to the fire. Of course, there were all sorts of contests; the swiftest horses, the quickest work in putting out the fire, etc. The Tournament lasted several days, and nothing was ever more thrilling than these races. Maybe Talladega was reliving her early love for horse racing.

Although Circus Days and Tournaments were the most thrilling days of early Talladega, the citizens turned their attention after the Civil War to the sacred celebration of Memorial Day.

Prior to the Civil War, Independence Day was sacredly celebrated in every part of the county on July 4th. There were barbecues, and great addresses, and always the Declaration of Independence was solemnly read. Then came war, and for 60 years afterwards the most sacred annual occasion was the sad one of April 26th, when Memorial Day was celebrated as a Decoration Day. All farm work ceased, the horses and mules were hitched to carriage and wagon, and people headed for Talladega for the solemn celebration. They began to arrive toward sun up, to get a good spot for horse and wagon, and to arrange for a place where children could see the parade. The court house lawn was a veritable dinner table, as the county people spread their cloths for dinner.

There were no school bands in those days but there was always some sort of local brass band that played a funeral dirge as the parade moved to the cemetery.

The parade began at the opera house where some notable orator had spoken in reverent tones of our beloved South and of those who gave their lives for a "Lost Cause". This speech was sandwiched between appropriate songs and recitations; all planned by the Memorial Association and the United Daughters of the Confederacy.

The mounted marshal of the day led the parade. The Talladega Rifles, the great pride and joy of Talladega, with shouldered rifles, followed the Confederate veterans. Some veterans were mounted, and all in uniform. School children dressed in white, carrying bouquets of flowers, marched in the procession. The Memorial Association and Daughters of the Confederacy, with disabled veterans rode in decorated carriages. Upon the arrival at the cemetery, a salute was fired over the Confederates' graves by the Talladega Rifles, and the children marched around the graves and placed the flowers.

Memorial Day was the one day in the year in which every citizen in the county took part. Every home had been touched in some way by sorrow and the ravages of war. It was the one day when every adult heart beat as one. There was always the renewal of old friendships, and the celebration was a bond that held the community together for at least two generations.

Every home had a sacred bush of "snow ball" hydrangea, which never failed to bloom in April. These shrubs have become almost unknown, and it has now been many years since wreaths of flowers were placed on the graves of the Unknown Confederate Soldiers. These graves are cared for by the Cemetery Association, in silent and affectionate memory of those who gave their lives for "A Cause."

After one of the local livery stables acquired a Tallyho, a summer luxury became that of Tallyho rides and moon-light picnics. Mixed swimming parties were unheard of in the early days, but became popular during the last twenty years of the century. The indulgence was in modest bathing suits with hose and shoes. When it was whispered that a certain college girl had returned with an "Annette Kellerman" bathing suit, and that she would appear at the Lake in it, people flocked to witness the immodest procedure. It was not long before most swimmers were donning the new type of suit, and the high neck, long sleeve, shin length bathing suit went out of existence, and shoes and stockings were dropped from the bathing outfit.

The Twentieth century dawned with new amusements, new apparel and new ideas, as the sedate Nineteenth century passed out of existence.

A History
of the
Andrew Jackson Chapter
of the Daughters of the
American Revolution ([1])

On October 11th, 1890, the National Society of the Daughters of the American Revolution was formally organized.

Mrs. Kate Duncan Smith, once a resident of Talladega, but at the time living in Birmingham, became one of the first, if not the first member from Alabama.

Mrs. Smith interested her good friend, Mrs. Sofia Lawson Thornton, of Talladega, in becoming a member. Mrs. Thornton was admitted into the National Society Dec. 3, 1896. She was appointed Organizing Regent of a D. A. R. Chapter for Talladega in 1897. With this idea in view, Mrs. Thornton called together a few of her friends on Mar 22, 1897, for the purpose of organizing such a chapter. Minutes of this meeting were recorded. However, the national charter was not received until January of 1898, and the first official meeting was held at the home of Mrs. Thornton on January 25th, 1898. The following authorized charter members answered to the first roll call:

21,375 Mrs. Mary Lawson Blake
21,837 Mrs. Sarah Borden Burr
21,374 Miss Caroline R. Elston
21,838 Mrs. Tennie Venable Edmundson
12,023 Mrs. Lula Bondurant Harrison
21,839 Mrs. Nellie Hall Johnson
21,373 Mrs. Annie Elston McAfee
21,840 Miss Mittie McElderry
21,841 Mrs. Margaret C. Stone
21,783 Mrs. Nellie Toole Storey
15,990 Mrs. Sofia L. Thornton
20,784 Mrs. Annie C. Thornton
20,782 Miss Jessie Miller (Mrs. T. L. Welch)

---

[1] Prepared for Andrew Jackson Chapter from chapter minutes

At this meeting the following were elected officers:

Mrs. Sofia L. Thornton, Regent
Mrs. Sarah B. Burr, V. Regent
Mrs. Tennie V. Edmundson, Rec. Sec.
Miss Mittie McElderry, Cor. Sec.
Mrs. Nellie H. Johnson, Treasurer
Miss Carrie Elston, Registrar
Mrs. Lula B. Harrison, Historian

A Board of Management was composed of Mrs. McAfee, Chairman, Mrs. Blake, Mrs. Storey, Mrs. Annie C. Thornton and Mrs. Stone.

The following names were proposed for the chapter: "Dolly Madison", "Old Hickory", and "Andrew Jackson". The vote resulted in the choice of the name "Andrew Jackson".

At the May meeting in 1898, it was voted to purchase a hickory gavel at a cost of $2.50, from a tree felled on the premises of the Hermitage. It is interesting to note that this gavel is still in use by the Regent. That first year, 1898, chapter colors of Yellow and White were chosen. However, the chapter motto, "What we do, we do forever," and the chapter flower, the "Violet", were not chosen until June, 1908.

The minutes of the chapter from October, 1898, through 1904, were filled with records of the activities of the chapter in connection with the removal of the soldiers killed in the Battle of Talladega; and with lists of contributions and expenses incident to this removal to Oak Hill Cemetery. Not until May 16, 1900, were they enabled to have a memorial program when the three lots were formally presented by the city, and Mr. Leak had completed the monument.

Benefits of all types were given, public subscriptions were solicited, Congress was appealed to through John T. Morgan, and finally an announcement was made at the Nov. 18th, 1904 meeting that the monument was fully paid for. The monument is a pyramid just inside the east entrance to Oak Hill Cemetery.

These women fought manfully for this monument, and it is a credit to the entire town of Talladega.

During the next few years the chapter met at the Public Library, to which they contributed annually to a book fund. They also purchased, annually, lineage books and placed them in the Library.

In 1910, Andrew Jackson Chapter joined chapters from Sylacauga and Anniston in placing markers along the Jackson Trace.

1911 was a memorable year, in that the Alabama State D.A.R. convened in Talladega from Dec. 5th through the 8th. Formal meetings were held in the auditorium in the basement of the Public Library. Many social functions were given in honor of the visitors. The Highland City Book Club entertained at a luncheon at the home of Mrs. H. L. McElderry; Capt. and Mrs. T. S. Plowman offered their lovely and spacious home for a reception one evening, which was a delightful affair; Mrs. A. G. Storey had the visitors for tea one evening; and the pupils from the School for the Blind gave a recital one afternoon.

On Nov. 9, 1913, the Andrew Jackson Chapter celebrated the Hundredth Anniversary of the Battle of Talladega. It was one of the most perfectly planned historical events ever to occur in Talladega. The subjects of the floats were carefully chosen, depicting chronologically the early history of Talladega; the historic themes were checked in every detail, and the entire county entered into the celebration. Papers over the state entered into the spirit of the occasion, and for weeks prior to the celebration historical articles appeared in newspapers over the state.

Automobiles were scarce at that time, but visitors poured into Talladega on every one of her sixteen passenger trains from every direction. After a Tea in honor of visiting D.A.R. and celebrities, the Daughters repaired to the Post office and unveiled a bronze tablet they placed there in memory of the seventeen soldiers who lost their lives in the Battle of Talladega.

In 1918 the Chapter staged a Patriotic Rally on the Square. The program began when Sunday School pupils from the four leading churches entered the Square from the four corners, singing "Onward Christian Soldiers," lead by a great choir stationed on the east porch of the Court House. W. B. Harrison was the orator of the day.

That same year, the 40 members decided to build gates and a fence around Oak Hill Cemetery. Contributions were solicited through the papers, and more money was readily subscribed than was needful. The actual expense, or cost, was $407.56.

In 1929 trees were planted in Jemison Park, one in memory of Mrs. Sofia Lawson Thornton, and the other in memory of Mrs. Nellie Toole Storey. The two past members were without question the most ardent and loyal members the Andrew Jackson Chapter has ever had the honor to enroll.

That same year, 1929, the Chapter voted to purchase an acre of land on the Coosa River, fifteen miles below Sylacauga, at Old Fort Williams, where 80 of Andrew Jackson's soldiers were buried.

In 1932 there were only 22 members registered, and they decided to celebrate the One Hundredth Anniversary of the Creek Treaty, ceding this Territory, by studying the History of Talladega County.

In 1938 the Daughters entered heartily into the celebration of the One Hundred and Twenty-Fifth Anniversary of the Battle of Talladega, which was staged by all local civic organizations. Andrew Jackson Chapter had a Luncheon at the Presbyterian Church for out of town visitors. 136 guests were served.

In 1939 an acre of land was purchased at the Kate Duncan Smith D.A.R. School for $50.00, in honor of Miss Mittie McElderry, who was at the time, the only charter member belonging to the Andrew Jackson Chapter.

In 1940 the chapter had dwindled to 12 members, the minimum number allowable for a chapter. War was declared, and most of the members became so absorbed in Red Cross and other war activities, that they let the chapter charter lapse, in 1943.

Again feeling the need for such a patriotic organization, the Andrew Jackson Chapter was re-organized on November 1st, 1947, by Miss Grace Jemison, as Organizing Regent, at her home. Fifteen members composed the group who re-organized, and a number of other members were added within a year.

Kymulga Cave
Lun Hamga

The existence and location of Kymulga Cave was widely known for years before the white man came to live in Talladega County. Long before 1725, the caverns were known as "Lun-Hamga", which was a Muscogee name. In 1775 the name seems to have changed to "Nanne-Hamgah", which is a combination name of the Chickasaw and Muscogee. Both names meant practically the same, and something like "Ancestors Issued Out of the Hill."

In the report of Benjamin Hawkins, Indian Agent, to the United States Government, regarding his visit to the Upper Creek Country, he states under the head of "AUBECOOCHEE" —

"There is, north of the town, a very large cave on the side of a high hill; the entrance small; it is much divided, and some of the rooms appear as the work of art; the doors regular. There is saltpeter in crystals."[1]

He does not speak of the cave by any specific name. The cave to which Hawkins refers, however, is what is now known as Kymulga Cave, located about 15 or 16 miles south-west of Talladega on the highway between Winterboro and Childersburg.

Miss Emma M. Mathis, of Ashville, Alabama,[2] one of the present owners of the cave, has spent a great deal of time in research for authentic information regarding the history of this cave. From her findings much of the information contained in this sketch is derived.

As stated, the cave was well known throughout the country long before the white man arrived to settle. As far back as 1710 and 1715 it is referred to in the Journal of the Commissioners of the Indian Trade of South Carolina.[3]

At one time the opening of the cave was much higher and smaller. The present entrance was made later by owners of the property. The opening is into a chamber 378 feet long, 165 feet wide and 127 feet high. Onyx and marble, made colorful by Natures' forces, have formed figures and markings that, as Hawkins says "appear as the work of art."

Geologists state that the original small opening must have existed for centuries.

---

[1] Letters of Benjamin Hawkins, 1796-1806. Georgia Historical Society, Volume IX, Page 170
[2] Letter and Sketch from Miss Emma M. Mathis, Ashville, Ala., furnished me under date of Oct. 19, 1940
[3] Sept. 20, 1710 and April 12, 1717, Journal of Commissioners of the Indian Trade of South Carolina

There are many legends in connection with Kymulga Cave. One legend alleges that when the Indians first came to this country they discovered a well beaten path to the opening of the cavern, which was made by animals. Upon investigation, it was discovered that an "isti Papa", or person eater, dwelt within the cave. This animal was presumably a Jaguar, which animal was a symbol of bravery among the Indians. The Jaguar was eventually killed and the bones were reverently kept and used throughout the years for medicinal purposes. A small amount of powder ground from the bones was used particularly in case of illness to insure the recovery of Indian Chiefs, and a small amount, in some sort of concoction drunk by warriors before entering war, insured strength and bravery to the warrior. This was practiced as late as 1796, when Hawkins visited the community.

In an attempt to ascertain the origin of the Creeks, another legend was told to Gallatin:

"There is some diversity in the accounts given by the Muscogees of their origin. The chiefs of the delegation, who attended at Washington, in the year 1826, agreed, that the prevailing tradition among them was, that the nation had issued out of a cave near the Alabama River."[4]

This cave was no doubt Kymulga Cave, near the Coosa River, and not the Alabama River as translated, which helped to verify the legend of "Lun Hamga" as told by James Adair in his "A History of the American Indians." He states that -

"It is worthy of notice that the Muskohgeeh cavern out of which one of their politicians persuaded them their ancestors formerly ascended to their present terrestrial abode, lies in the Nanne-Hamgar old town inhabited by the Mississippi-Natchee Indians, which is one of the most western parts of the old inhabited country."[5]

Be it remembered that a group of Natchez Indians from Mississippi, settled in the vicinity of Kymulga Cave.

Mr. Adair speaks of the village as "Nanne-Hamgar". The Natchez spoke both the Muscogee and the Chickasaw languages. Hence the combination word, which means "the issuing out of the hill." Lun Hamga means "ancestors issued out." Mr. Adair in describing the cave speaks of it as —

"Above 600 miles to the westward of Charles-town in South Carolina, adjoining to the old Chikkasah trading path."

---

[4] Found in "The Creek Country", by Benjamin Hawkins et als, Page 13
[5] "A History of the American Indians" by James Adair, published in London in 1775, reprinted in 1930 by the Colonial Dames of America, in Tenn., Page 204

It should be recalled that South Carolina extended to the Mississippi River through this district at the time. The cave is also referred to in the Forty-Second Annual Report of the Bureau of Ethnology.

In the year 1723, traders were warned to take the Upper Path. One who traveled in that year was Joseph Wright, a land owner in the Province of South Carolina, and well known as a Trader by the Indians. Finding that he had reached the end of life's journey, he experienced the natural desire for a monument, so he carved on a stone in the caverns of Lun Hamga, the following:

'J. W. WRIGHT, 1723'
After which he expired.[6]

Another story is told in the Journal of Captain Tobias Fitch, a representative of the South Carolina Government, who visited the cave in 1725.

"In the olden times the title Hobayi indicated 'one who understood all the strategic arts of war.' Very few Indians received that title. In Lun Hamga lived Hobayi-Hadjo (Far-away-furious in battle). In the year 1720 Hobayi-Hadjo was a guest of the South Caroline Assembly Meeting in Charleston. In company with Chekilli of the Lower Creeks, two other Creeks, and four Cherokees, he sat beside President Arthur Middleton before the assembly and heard all the guns of the Fort fired in their honor."[7]

When Tobias Fitch returned their visit in 1725, the Creeks made great preparations, and greeted him in part as follows:

"We are glad to see you here and, though we not such entertainment to give you as when we come to you, yet such as we have we give you freely, and we are glad to see that you can eat such as we live on. When you are at home your diet is kept more under command. Your cattle and ducks are at your doors. Now, with us it is not so. We are forced to hunt and take a great deal of pains to get our provisions before we eat them; but we shall not think any trouble too much to get entertainment for you while you stay with us be it as long as it will, you being the first beloved white man that ever we saw in our town."

There are many other stories in connection with Kymulga Cave. One of the modem stories is of Indians resorting to the cave, and hiding while troops of Andrew Jackson were here in 1813.

---

[6] Page 6 of the sketch furnished me in 1940 by Miss Emma M. Mathis.
[7] Mereness Travels in the American Colonies, Page 189 – Spelling reversed (Journal of Capt. Tobias Fitch). Found in the sketch furnished me in 1940 by Miss Emma M. Mathis

Mr. James Mallory records in his Diary under date of Dec. 28, 1845 "Visited the cave with a large party this morning."[8] Mr. Mallory lived in that vicinity, and there must have been many such excursions to the spot throughout the years.

Some say that saltpeter was used from the cave during the Civil War. The cave is believed to extend many miles east, but has never been explored. Some years ago a large city water storage tank was constructed in a sink hole on the hill where the present water plant is now located. One day soon after the tank was filled with several millions of gallons of water, the bottom dropped out of the tank, and with one gulp the earth swallowed the water. No trace or direction of the water was found, but many believe that it flowed through a passage in this cave. "As the crow flies" the water works must be 12 to 15 miles east from the western opening of Kymulga Cave. Hence, if this surmise be true, the cave must be at least 15 miles long.

If properly explored, Kymulga Cave may prove more interesting and extensive than Mammoth Cave.

---

[8] Diary of Mr. James Mallory, in possession of Mr. E. A. Stewart, Selma, Alabama

Altitudes

Dr. Thomas M. Owen gives a list of altitudes in Alabama, Vol. I, pages 40 through 45, in his History of Alabama and Dictionary of Alabama Biography. He states that "the highest point is Pulpit Rock in Jackson County, with an elevation of 2,018 feet. Other striking elevations are: Horn Mountain 1919 feet, etc." Dr. Owen is probably confused here with "Pulpit Rock" on Cheaha Mountain in Talladega County.

Dr. Owen does not list among the altitudes that of Cheaha Mountain, but he states in Vol. 1, page 11 that the "highest altitude is 2407 feet, at Cheaha, Talladega County." It will be seen therefore that two of the highest points in Alabama are located in Talladega County.

Altitudes, as culled from Dr. Owen's record, follow:

Alpine	460	Ladiga Mt.	659
Alpine Mt. (Sleeping Giant)	1,551	Lincoln	503
Andaluvia Mt. (Pope)	1,134	McFall (Eastaboga)	594
Barclay	514	Munford	613
Cheaha Mt.	2,407	Nottingham	453
Childersburg	412	Silver Run	622
Horn Mt.	1,919	Sycamore	546
Jenifer	577	Sylacauga	547
Kahatchee Mt.	1,301	Talladega	553
Kymulga	427	Weogufka	600

Index

H

K

L

T